Beyond Pearl Harbor

Beyond Pearl Harbor

The Untold Stories of Japan's Naval Airmen

Ron Werneth

Schiffer Military History
Atglen, PA

Dedication

This book is dedicated to the late Jerry Larsen, who taught me that anything is possible, if you dream, never give up, and work hard. Thank you Jerry.

I also dedicate this work to my late father, Fred Werneth. Early in my life he taught me the importance of studying history, and more importantly, remembering those who lived it. Thanks Dad.

This work is also dedicated to all of the World War II veterans in Japan, the United States, and England who trusted me with their stories and opened their hearts to me over the past eight years. You will always be a part of me and my family.

Book Design by Ian Robertson.

Library of Congress Control Number: 2008926864

Printed in China.
ISBN: 978-0-7643-2932-6

We are interested in hearing from authors with book ideas on related topics.

Published by Schiffer Publishing Ltd.
4880 Lower Valley Road
Atglen, PA 19310
Phone: (610) 593-1777
FAX: (610) 593-2002
E-mail: Info@schifferbooks.com.
Visit our web site at: www.schifferbooks.com
Please write for a free catalog.
This book may be purchased from the publisher.
Please include $5.00 postage.
Try your bookstore first.

In Europe, Schiffer books are distributed by:
Bushwood Books
6 Marksbury Avenue
Kew Gardens
Surrey TW9 4JF, England
Phone: 44 (0) 20 8392-8585
FAX: 44 (0) 20 8392-9876
E-mail: Info@bushwoodbooks.co.uk.
Visit our website at: www.bushwoodbooks.co.uk
Free postage in the UK. Europe: air mail at cost.
Try your bookstore first.

Contents

Acknowledgments

I am truly indebted to so many people who have supported my research for this book over the past eight years. *Beyond Pearl Harbor* really was a "group" effort that could not have been completed without the help of numerous people who believed in the value of this project. There are so many individuals and organizations that assisted me throughout this endeavor that I apologize if I forgot to list your name in this section.

First, I would like to say a big thank you to historians Henry Sakaida and Gary Nila for helping me get the ball "rolling" back in 1999. Both of these fine gentlemen believed in me since day one and understood exactly why I wanted to meet these forgotten Japanese World War II Navy airmen. Eight years ago, they graciously offered their help with my initial introductions to the veterans in Japan. Furthermore, Henry and Gary have constantly shared their expertise and words of support that helped keep me working on this intense project over the years.

Two other individuals—noted historian Mick Prodger and Graham Orphan, editor of *ClassicWings* magazine—also played important roles in my research overseas. When I was so nervous about "taking the plunge" and moving to Japan, they both said the same thing, "If you don't go, you will always regret it." They were so right about this decision. If I would have listened to my family and stayed in Chicago, undoubtedly this book would never have been completed, and I would have missed a once in a lifetime chance to meet the men who changed history forever. I would never have met my wife, many good friends, and had the experience of living in another country, which really shaped my whole outlook on life. Mick was a constant source of help with his thoughtful feedback and assistance on a variety of issues that are too numerous to mention here. His firm DesignPanache (San Antonio, Texas) designed the dust jacket for this book. I appreciate the help of my friend Mike Flanigan, who took the beautiful cover photo and several other pictures in this work.

In Japan there were so many people who helped me with my research and trusted me with preserving the stories of the last surviving WW II Japanese Navy airmen. A "core" group of retired Japanese WW II Navy veterans, including Jirō Yoshida, Ensign Takeshi Maeda, Ensign Haruo Yoshino, Lieutenant Commander Zenji Abe (deceased), and Lieutenant Kunio Iwashita helped make my research possible in Japan. I feel the biggest thing they did for me was simply trusting a foreigner (who couldn't even speak Japanese!) with their precious stories and introducing me to their comrades. Words can't express how much I value what these men did for me during my time overseas.

I want to thank all of the other distinguished veterans who shared their stories and photos to make this book possible. They include the following aviators and mechanics of the wartime Imperial Japanese Navy: Ensign Yuji Akamatsu (deceased), Lieutenant Commander Keiichi Arima, Lieutenant Commander Iyozō Fujita (deceased), Lieutenant (junior grade) Kiyoto Furuta, Lieutenant (junior grade) Kaname Harada, Ensign Hideo Honma (deceased), Ensign Kenji Hori, Ensign Taisuke Maruyama, Lieutenant Commander Hirata Matsumura (deceased), Lieutenant Takayoshi Morinaga (deceased), Maintenance Warrant Officer Hachirō Miyashita, Lieutenant Commander Yoshio Shiga (deceased), Maintenance PO1c Kaname Shimoyama, and Maintenance Lieutenant Hiroshi Suzuki.

Another person who played a very important role in the research and translation of the majority of the interviews and documents used in this work was Keigo "Hammer" Nakahama. He did his best to make sure the material was translated properly, and constantly assisted me with Japanese cultural issues and travel throughout the country while conducting our interviews together. I am sure that without his help this book would have never been written.

Early on in my research I was assisted by my friends Dr. Hiromi Ozaki and Yukihirō Yamamoto, who kindly offered their support with my research. Yamamato-san traveled all the way to Kyūshū with me to translate my interview with the late Yuji Akamatsu. Another person who helped me back in 1999 was Hiroyuki Takeuchi, and I appreciate all the help he gave me with my initial research and interviews in Japan. Last but not least, during the last few years of research, Hiroko Morii, a wonderful woman, offered her help in translating several of the veterans' documents used in the research for *Beyond Pearl Harbor*. I feel very fortunate to have a good friend like Morii-san in Japan.

Acknowledgments

I can't forget the friendship, support, and kindness of my Japanese friends Akinori Itoh, Dr.Yasuho Izawa, Koji Kutsuzawa, and Yoji Kutsuzawa. Itoh-san, who lost his father in World War II, has been a great friend and a constant source of advice since we met over six years ago. Dr. Izawa, a noted Japanese aviation historian, helped me with my research and shared some of his expertise in this field. The Kutsuzawa brothers are both great "international" friends, who did so many things to help me during my stay in Japan that they can't even be mentioned here.

The beautiful Japanese aircraft profiles in this book were painted by my good friend, the multi-talented yet very humble George Zielinski. He worked tirelessly to try to make his illustrations as accurate as possible, and even painted additional pictures that became family heirlooms to the veterans they were presented to. Thank you George.

Several other researchers who are friends, historians, and veterans played special roles in the research and support necessary in order to complete this project. Each of these individuals have their areas of "expertise," and took the time to support my work throughout the years. I would like to offer my warmest regards and thanks to the following people: Derek Brown, Charles Darby, John DiVirgilio, Second Lieutenant William B. Freeman (WW II USMC fighter pilot, deceased), Bruce Gamble, Christopher Girsch, Mark E. Horan, Dan Kell, James Lansdale, Jean-François Masson, Helen McDonald, Bobby McElroy, Jr., Osamu Miyata, Tomoko Nishizaki, Marcus Perkins, Naomi Shin (daughter of Zenji Abe), Christopher Shores, Commander John Sykes (WW II Royal Navy Fleet Air Arm pilot), Captain "Jack" Thompson (WW II AAF fighter pilot), Robert Mikesh, Barrett Tillman, Andrew Weiss, and Captain Ernest J. Zellmer (WW II USN submarine veteran). I appreciate the help given to me by Helen McDonald and the superb National Museum of the Pacific War (Fredericksburg, Texas). This museum allowed me to use several of their documents in this book. I would like to acknowledge the Battle of Midway Roundtable and appreciate the help of several members and Midway veterans who supported my research.

Three other noted Japanese Navy "specialists" and authors, Jonathan Parshall, Osamu Tagaya, and Anthony Tully helped me on numerous occasions during the research of this book. They freely shared their wealth of researched information about the Japanese side of several engagements and have helped me for several years. Osamu was a constant source of support, especially with providing the appropriate Japanese military terms to help make my text authentic and as accurate as possible. Jon also allowed me to use several of his illustrations for this work. Tony is one of the most knowledgeable Japanese Navy historians in the world, and was a constant source of support and friendship over the years. Thank you gentlemen.

In the United States, I had the assistance of three more historians: John B. Lundstrom, James Sawruk, and Justin Taylan. Over the years John has helped me numerous times with my research and writing. I fondly remember his private "tour" of the Milwaukee Public Museum prior to his retirement from his position at that facility. Jim was incredibly helpful, and shared his vast knowledge and official records of the Pacific War. Justin tried bravely to locate two wartime Japanese aircraft wrecks that were lost on 17 October 1942 during a mission to attack American ships off Guadalcanal Island. You can read more about his exploits in Kaname Harada's story featured in this book.

J. Michael Wenger was another historian who played a crucial role in the completion of this project. Mike basically "took me under his wing" and did everything he could do to help me complete this book properly. For example, he shared invaluable original wartime Japanese documents that became the "backbone" of several of the veteran stories in this work. Mike provided numerous rare photographs, and freely shared some vital Pearl Harbor research that took many years to gather. I feel so lucky to have such a good man and friend who shares the same passion as I do.

I appreciate that my editor Ian Robertson and Schiffer Publishing agreed to publish this book, and understood the historical importance of saving the stories of these WW II airmen for future generations. I believe readers of this book will appreciate their efforts in preserving the veterans' accounts and pictures featured in this work.

I also would like to take this time to say thank you to two special individuals who helped me with my writing since the very beginning: the late Gerald Larson and Fred Wilkens. I will never forget how Jerry encouraged me to continue writing and taught me how special life really is. Likewise, Fred is also another fine gentleman who is a close family friend and retired English teacher. He worked hard to edit and proofread the entire manuscript over the last few years. Undoubtedly, without their attention to detail and encouragement this project probably would never have been completed.

In all, even with the help of so many good people around the world, the people who really were my biggest supporters were my family, both in the United States and Japan. I would like to say thanks to everyone in the Werneth and Okabe families who understood my purpose for writing this book. I appreciate the help of my uncle, Myron Lyskanycz, and the great support of my mom while finishing this book. Special thanks has to be given to my wife Kaori, who is the most patient, loving, and beautiful woman any man could have. She understood why I needed to research and preserve the stories of Japan's forgotten veterans. Thanks again to all of you!

Special Note

All of the times listed in the veterans' accounts are local times. The author chose to use some Japanese military terms and words to make the text as authentic as possible. Please see the glossary towards the end of the book for translations of the Japanese terms used in the text. Also located in this part of the book is a helpful map of the Japanese Navy air bases listed in the text and a "strike" chart of the Pearl Harbor attack.

Japanese Naval Air Force Ranks[1]

Commissioned Ranks
Taishō Admiral
Chūjō Vice Admiral
Shōshō Rear Admiral
Taisa Captain
Chūsa Commander
Shōsa Lieutenant Commander
Tai-i Lieutenant
Chū-i Lieutenant (junior grade)
Shō-i Ensign

Enlisted Ranks *(Before June 1941)*
Kōkū Heisōchō Aviation Warrant Officer (WO)
Ittō Kōkū Heisō Aviation Petty Officer, First Class (PO1c)
Nitō Kōkū Heisō Aviation Petty Officer, Second Class (PO2c)
Santō Kōkū Heisō Aviation Petty Officer, Third Class (PO3c)
Ittō Kōkūhei Aviation Seaman, First Class (Sea1c)

Enlisted Ranks *(After June 1941)*
Hikō Heisōchō Flight Warrant Officer (WO)
Jōtō Hikō Heisō Flight Chief Petty Officer (CPO)
Ittō Hikō Heisō Flight Petty Officer, First Class (PO1c)
Nitō Hikō Heisō Flight Petty Officer, Second Class (PO2c)
Santō Hikō Heisō Flight Petty Officer, Third Class (PO3c)
Hikō Heichō Flight Leading Seaman (LdgSea)
Jōtō Hikōhei Flight Superior Seaman (SupSea)
Ittō Hikōhei Flight Seaman, First Class (Sea1c)

Introduction

Looking back on the multi-year journey that led to this book, I have difficulty in comprehending it. If someone told me ten years ago that I would one day live in Japan and interview the country's last surviving World War II Navy aviators and mechanics, I would have never believed him! When I was a boy, my father took me to air shows and tried to teach me about World War II. As a result, my passion for WWII history blossomed, and I became fascinated by the aircraft of that time, and more importantly the personal stories of the men who fought during the conflict. As I became more and more interested, I wanted to learn about what happened on the "other side." However, as I searched for books and other materials to read, I found countless works about Germany and its military men, but very few English language publications existed about WWII Japanese Navy airmen. Furthermore, I realized that most books, and even postwar movies, invariably focused on the European Theatre. I kept on saying to myself, "Why do these historians and popular media focus only on the European Theatre?"

As my interest in the war grew, I became very engrossed in the Japanese side of the conflict and its fascinating culture. While my passion about the war grew, I read all the books that I could find about Japanese aviators. During my "quest," I found a handful of good books by historians such as Henry Sakaida and Osamu Tagaya that had some quotes from the veterans and had valuable information. However, I still wanted to know more. How did the Japanese pilots feel when they attacked Pearl Harbor? Did they really "hate" America and her people? Were they really ordered to conduct suicide attacks? Did they really think that it was an honor to die for the Emperor? However, I could never find any answers to my questions in books or documentaries on television.

In early 1999, I decided to meet and interview some of these Japanese Navy veterans before their stories were lost, due to the passage of time. However, how would a foreigner with no Japanese language skills go about doing this? First, I wrote and called several museums and Japanese militaria collectors for assistance. I had limited success with this method, and was able to get contact information for just one veterán, legendary Zero fighter pilot Saburō Sakai. Hence, I decided to visit a college friend in Japan and interview this well-known veteran at the same time. However, after arriving in Tokyo, I was saddened to hear that my friend would not call Sakai-san "out of the blue" because it was impolite to do this. During this first trip to Japan I had a good time, visited several important cultural spots, and tried lots of interesting new foods, but was very disappointed about missing my big chance to interview Sakai-san.

When I returned home, I was not ready to give up on the project. I was very fortunate to become friends with historians Gary Nila and Henry Sakaida, who both understood my passion and offered to help. Henry Sakaida, one of the few westerners ever to interview WWII Japanese veterans, wanted to help me. He introduced me to one of the few bilingual veterans in Japan, Jirō Yoshida, who also offered his assistance. They made me an offer, "As long as you respect Japanese culture and history, you are welcome to come to Japan and interview several veterans." This really changed my life in many ways. At the same time, I became friends with Jerry Larson, a wonderful man who helped me by encouraging me to write and to interview these forgotten airmen. Sadly, he passed away just before I embarked on my journey to interview some of these veterans.

With the support of these individuals, I interviewed a core group of distinguished WWII Navy veterans who participated in operations such as Pearl Harbor and the Battle of Midway. This even included Sakai-san, the Zero pilot mentioned above. In summary, this second visit to Japan was so successful that a new idea came to my mind—why not try to record the stories of these forgotten veterans for future generations? Though not setting out to write a book, I wanted to learn more about the war and the men who experienced it over half a century ago. However, I was so moved by these ex-navy airmen and their untold stories that it became my "mission" to ultimately research and publish this work.

After my short trip to Japan, I returned home and began my research in earnest. However, it was very difficult to do so while living in Chicago with limited Japanese language resources. I also realized there was a lot more still to learn in Japan while these men were still healthy and able to tell their stories. Hence, I concluded that the only way to really learn about what happened during the war from the Japanese side was to move to Japan. With the encouragement of several friends, primarily historian Mick Prodger and magazine editor Graham Orphan, I decided to take the plunge and moved there in November 2000.

Life in Japan wasn't easy, but it was very rewarding, and I learned something new every day. To help pay my bills I worked as an English teacher during the week, and then spent almost every holiday conducting research and interviewing the veterans in Japan. I was very fortunate to meet Keigo "Hammer" Nakahama, who also worked with me at my school. "Hammer" was simply incredible, because he was a native Japanese person who spoke English perfectly. He spent countless hours researching and translating Japanese materials to prepare properly for each interview. "Hammer" was instrumental in teaching me about Japanese culture so I could conduct my meetings with the veterans while observing proper etiquette.

Prior to going to Japan, I tried to go there without any preconceived ideas or stereotypes of the Japanese veterans. Because I neither served in WWII nor had a father that fought in the war, I thought that this would be feasible. After interviewing a few veterans and establishing a good rapport with them they wanted to help me. However, I could never approach a potential new contact directly without the introduction of a mutual veteran friend. Most Japanese people, especially WWII veterans, would be reluctant to open their hearts to a complete stranger, and even more so if the person were a foreigner. If I wanted to find a particular veteran (for example, an aviation mechanic who served on board an aircraft carrier), I would ask some of my veteran friends for some potential people to interview, and they would introduce me.

I believe, for the most part, the veterans understood why I wanted to interview them, and they really enjoyed talking with me about their war experiences. Because of this I interviewed veterans accessed by very few people, and attended several reunions which are not usually accessible to foreigners or the general public. I feel so fortunate and honored to have met these fine gentlemen and attend some once in a lifetime events.

In general, I think the WWII Japanese Navy veterans are very private people, but once I gained their trust, they opened up and talked frankly about their war experiences. They also seemed very happy that a younger person (especially from the West) wanted to talk with them. Remarkably, out of the fifty plus veterans that I wanted to meet, only a small handful turned down my interview requests.

Because of spending over seven years of my life doing research and traveling to many parts of Japan to meet these long-forgotten men, I eventually befriended several of these veterans, all of whom left an indelible mark on my life. I feel blessed to have met Japan's last surviving elite WWII Navy airmen and learn their stories firsthand. I also am very lucky to have become acquainted with so many good people in the United States, Europe, New Zealand, and Japan while conducting research for this work, including several historians, friends, and my wife.

The goal of this work is not to tell the entire story of every big battle that occurred in the Pacific Theatre during WWII; there are plenty of good books that cover this material. Instead, I focus on the lives of the Japanese Navy airmen and what they experienced over sixty years ago. While I directed my questions about what the men felt and saw during WWII, I also made an effort to find out what happened in their postwar days and how they feel today. I believe readers of this book will discover these WWII Japanese Navy veterans offer moving and introspective reflections about the conflict that changed their lives forever. Wherever possible, and with the help of several other seasoned historians, I was able to locate and incorporate the original American, British, and Japanese war records to support and clarify the veterans' stories in this work.

My other goal for this book was to tell the stories of many different WWII Japanese Navy airmen, not only the fighter pilots. However, there were countless more men who flew multi-place aircraft such as the Type 97 carrier attack plane, and others who served as aviation mechanics to keep the aircraft flying. I strongly feel that these brave men were largely forgotten, and they all served important roles during the war. Hence, this work tells the stories of those veterans as well.

Let's travel together back to the Japan of over half a century ago, with war clouds looming on the horizon and its navy training hard to prepare for a possible future conflict...

Part 1

Carrier bomber (*kanbaku*) veterans' accounts

The first section of this book covers all the veterans involved with flying or maintaining the *kanbaku*, or carrier bombers. The full Japanese name is *kanjō bakugekiki*. To help make my text user-friendly and still utilize some original Japanese terminology, I chose to use either *kanbaku*, dive-bomber, or carrier bomber. During the war, members of the Japanese Navy didn't use western code names like "Val" to describe the Aichi D3A1 Type 99 *kanbaku*, so I chose not to use them in this work as well. This particular type of aircraft was manned by two men, a pilot and an observer/radioman.

In the beginning of the second Sino-Japanese War (1937), the primary dive-bomber utilized by the Japanese Navy was the Aichi D1A1 Type 94, but it was quickly replaced by the Aichi D1A2 Type 96. This particular aircraft was used frequently during this conflict, including the notorious attack on the American gunboat *Panay*. The Type 96 was a biplane (*kanbaku*), and powered by a Nakajima Hikari nine-cylinder, air-cooled, radial engine rated at 730 horsepower for take off. The Type 96's armament consisted of two fixed forward-firing 7.7 mm Type 92 machine guns (in the cowling) and one flexible 7.7 mm machine gun in the rear. The aircraft could carry a bomb load of either one 250 kilogram (551 pound) bomb under the fuselage and two 30 kilogram (66 pound) bombs underneath the wings. It was still in service in 1941-42, but was not used much for combat missions.

Beginning in late 1939, in China, the next carrier bomber used by the navy was the Aichi D3A1 Type 99. It was extensively used for operations in 1940, and joined the fleet in the spring of 1941. This particular aircraft was the dive-bomber utilized heavily during the beginning of the war, and had a lot of success during operations at Pearl Harbor and in the Indian Ocean. In late 1941, Japan's Navy dive-bomber aviators were well-seasoned and highly-trained, so they were able to have a lot of success with this aircraft.

Early examples (Model 11) of this *kanbaku* were powered by a Mitsubishi Kinsei 43, air-cooled, radial engine rated at 1,000 horsepower for take off. Later versions of the Type 99 (Model 11) were fitted with the Mitsubishi Kinsei 44, air-cooled, radial engine, which was a little more powerful than the Kinsei 43.

Just like its predecessor (the Type 96), this carrier bomber had just two fixed forward firing 7.7 mm machine guns and one flexible 7.7 mm machine gun in the rear. Bomb load also was the same as the Type 96 *kanbaku*. Later versions of the Aichi D3A2 Type 99 carrier bomber (now designated Model 22) were fitted with one Mitsubishi Kinsei 54, air-cooled, radial engine rated at 1,300 horsepower for take off. It also had an increased fuel capacity compared to earlier models. The Type 99 saw combat through 1944, but suffered heavy losses later in the conflict because it couldn't keep up with the Allied aircraft of that era, so the aircraft was used for training units and (*tokkō*) suicide missions.

One of the sleekest *kanbaku* utilized by the Japanese Navy during the war was the Yokosuka D4Y *Suisei* (Allied code name "Judy"). This particular aircraft first entered combat during the Battle of Midway (to serve as a reconnaissance plane), but technical problems plagued the *Suisei* carrier bomber, so it couldn't be used as a dive-bomber for some time. The first unit to use the *Suisei* as a dive-bomber was the Rabaul-based 501 *Kōkūtai* in October 1943. This sharp looking *kanbaku* really didn't join the fleet until the first half of 1944. However, by this time in the war many of Japan's seasoned aviators had already perished in previous combat, so a lot of the new pilots were "rookies." Because of this young pilots who manned this aircraft during the Battle of the Philippine Sea (June 1944) were essentially slaughtered, so this engagement is often referred to as the Marianas "Turkey Shoot." Towards the end of the war *Suisei* carrier bombers served as *tokkō* attack aircraft and as night fighters.

Early models (D4Y1-D4Y2) of the *Suisei kanbaku* were powered by two different, liquid-cooled, radial engines: an Aichi AE1A Atsuta 12 (twelve-cylinder) rated at 1,200 horsepower for take off; and the Aichi AE1P Atsuta 32 twelve-cylinder, which had about two hundred horsepower more that the previous powerplant mentioned. The later D4Y4 *Suisei* (Model 43) lost their streamlined design when the aircraft was fitted with an air-cooled Mitsubishi MK8P Kinsei 62, fourteen-cylinder engine rated at 1,560 horsepower for take off.

All of the various models of the *Suisei* had two fuselage mounted 7.7 mm machine guns, but the armament varied for the rear portion of the fuselage depending on the version of the aircraft. Some models had one flexible rear-firing 7.92 mm machine gun, while others utilized a 13 mm machine gun (in the rear). Also, some variants of the breed were fitted with one oblique firing 20 mm cannon (mounted inside the fuselage).

Normal bomb load for this dive-bomber was 310 kilograms (683 pounds) and maximum was 560 kilograms (1,234 pounds). However, *Suisei* used for one-way *tokkō* missions were fitted with a bomb load of 800 kilograms (1,764 pounds).[2]

Lieutenant (junior grade) Kiyoto Furuta

"Everyone thought about how to beat the enemy."

During my interview with veteran Hachirō Miyashita he talked glowingly about a navy dive-bomber pilot friend named Kiyoto Furuta. Miyashita-san said that his friend Furuta-san was one of the few men left who experienced World War II from China until the end and saw heavy action in many battles, such as Pearl Harbor, Midway, and the Solomon Islands. His fellow Akagi *pilot Zenji Abe had this to say about him, "During the war, Kiyoto Furuta was a senior petty officer of the* Akagi kanbaku *group in 1941, because he was a very experienced aviator. He was muscular and tall in appearance. Furuta-san was easygoing and well-respected by both senior and junior comrades." So, I asked for an introduction and was able to hear some great wartime stories from a healthy and fit ninety-one year old veteran. He currently lives quietly in a rural area of the Yamaguchi Prefecture.*

Early Days in the Navy

I was born on 12 October 1914, in Tokuyama City, which is now called Shunan City, in Yamaguchi Prefecture. There were six children in my family, including three boys and three girls. I was the eldest son. I joined the navy at Kure on 1 June 1931 because I wanted to do something for my country. While I was there, I did my basic training, and then on 15 November 1934 I joined the battleship *Shinshu*. On 21 January 1936 I began my flight training as a member of the 32nd pilot training class, and it lasted for seven months. After graduation in July I did a special training class for dive-bombing, and we used the Type 94 carrier bomber (Allied code name "Susie").

Five members from my class, including myself, transferred to the Saeki *Kōkūtai*. The *buntaichō* was Lieutenant Ichirō Komaki, who would become, several years later, senior air staff officer of Combined Fleet. Lieutenant (junior grade) Takashige Egusa, a member of our group, was promoted to the rank of lieutenant and succeeded Lieutenant Ichirō Komaki as the *buntaichō* in November.[3] I flew with Egusa's group for one year, and I felt he was a very fearless leader. His personality was easygoing, and all of us thought that Lieutenant (junior grade) Egusa was an excellent pilot.

Flying in China

During the 1930s there was a tense situation between Japan and China. Japan wanted to expand and become stronger economically. Thus, it eyed nearby China and took over Manchuria, which became a puppet state. Then, on 18 January 1932 there was rioting in Shanghai, so Japan landed some forces near the city. For several years tensions continued to deteriorate, and on 7 July 1937 a small battle occurred between Chinese and Japanese forces near the Marco Polo Bridge, which is located southwest of Beijing. After this incident war broke out between the two nations.[4]

We continued doing flight training, such as dive-bombing technique, gunnery, and communications until July 1937. Then, on 7 July 1937, war broke out with China, and all of our armed forces were placed on war footing. My air group was reorganized as the 12th *Kōkūtai*, and I joined the group just five days after the war started. We prepared our planes and left for Shanghai, China, sometime in August. In Shanghai, there was a newly built airfield called Kunda, which Japanese engineers built on the Shanghai University grounds. There was a golf course nearby, and we used those two places for our airplanes to operate from.

Japanese Navy *kōkūtais* formed one after another to go to China after war broke out, and my group was one of them. In China, Japanese ground forces were almost beaten by the Chinese, and the conflict was going badly for our nation. In order to support them, numerous Japanese airplanes flew combat sorties and tried to annihilate them from the air. Initially, Nanking was the Chinese capitol, and we went there often to attack the enemy's airfields. We tried to destroy the Chinese aircraft on the ground so it would be easier for Japan to establish air supremacy over China.

In Ōmura, Japan, the 13th *Kōkūtai* also was formed. Both our group and the 13th *Kōkūtai* used dive-bombers for our missions. At first we attacked the Nanking area. Then a large contingent of Japanese Army soldiers landed in the Shanghai region, and they

An early wartime picture of the young Kiyoto Furuta in his flight gear. Note he is wearing the early-style goggles. (Furuta Collection)

Lieutenant Commander Takeshige Egusa, who was a well-known *kanbaku* aviator in the Imperial Japanese Navy. Furuta-san flew with him in flight training and combat missions in China. During the Pearl Harbor attack, Egusa was the overall leader of the dive-bombers during the second wave. (Egusa family via Wenger)

occupied Shanghai. Our job was to bomb the places prior to the advance of our ground forces. However, the combat area spread wider and wider. Every day we took off from Shanghai, flew our missions, and came back. Our first airfield at Kunda was temporary, and later we moved to a better equipped airbase with more airplanes. After changing airfields a few times, we finally moved to Nanking after the city was occupied. Our forces occupied several airfields in that area, and our aviators flew numerous combat missions in support of the Japanese Army's operations. Nevertheless, we couldn't destroy all the Chinese forces on the Chinese mainland. I flew Lieutenant (junior grade) Takashige Egusa during the Nanking attack missions. I actually flew with him on a daily basis. In December of that year we were separated after I left the group. Egusa-san was a dive-bombing authority in the navy, and later led a group of Type 99 *kanbaku* during the second wave of the Pearl Harbor attack.

In December 1937 I came back to Japan, and was transferred to the carrier *Sōryū*. We practiced very hard every day by doing landings on the carrier. After completing our training, we loaded our planes on the carrier and embarked for the East China Sea. Our carrier was based in the East China Sea, and we attacked targets on the Chinese mainland. I did this hundreds of times, and attacked the enemy's important bases one by one. For example, we attacked Hong Kong and many cities in the area. While I was on board *Sōryū* I was chosen, for the first time, to be the pilot for the *buntaichō* Abe-san. For one year we flew over the Pacific to many places. I flew as the lead pilot in our formation and honed my flying skills a great deal.

Beginning on 15 December 1939, I did training to familiarize myself with the Type 99 *kanbaku* at Saeki Air Base. Then, my next assignment was being a flight instructor at Suzuka Air Base, and I did this assignment until the fall of 1941. During this time I

Lieutenant Takehiko Chihaya, Furuta's flying partner during Pearl Harbor and a leader of a group of *Akagi* Type 99s during the second wave attack. (Prange Collection via Wenger)

also got married. One day, a navy messenger visited me and said that I was ordered to go to the carrier *Akagi* and become the flying partner for Lieutenant Takehiko Chihaya. On 8 October 1941 I was officially assigned to the carrier. At that time Chihaya-san was at Tomitaka Air Base, located in Miyazaki Prefecture, Kyūshū. He was the leader of the dive-bomber pilots who were practicing there. Chihaya-san was a very sincere, intelligent, and a warm-hearted person. We actually met for the first time when we served together on the carrier *Sōryū* in 1938, but we didn't meet again until three years later on the *Akagi*. He also was my partner for the Pearl Harbor attack.

Fellow Akagi *shipmate Zenji Abe shared his memories of Lieutenant Chihaya. "He was in the 62nd Class of the Naval Academy and was two years senior to me, but was the closest person to me from that class. We were both* buntaichōs *on the* Akagi *for almost one year. Lieutenant Chihaya was a medium-sized man with a round face, and his eyes were very clear. Chihaya-san also was a goodnatured gentleman, but wasn't too talkative. Furthermore, he was one of the people I most respected among the men in the 62nd Class. Lieutenant Chihaya died on 11 June 1944 in the Marianas. After he died Chihaya-san was posthumously promoted two ranks to the rank of captain."*

My position as the flying partner and pilot for Chihaya's aircraft took a lot of responsibility, and I had to always be ready to do whatever would be required for us to complete our assignment. At the end of the training period we—all the prospective participants for the Pearl Harbor attack—flew with Lieutenant Commander Takashige Egusa, overall commander of the *kanbaku* group, in the lead. We did simulated dive-bombing attacks over Saeki Bay, which was set as the hypothetical target. This marked the completion of transition to "war footing" for our group. I was in the leading airplane, which landed on the carrier first. *Akagi* then became my new home, and we left the Japanese mainland.

Pearl Harbor

Although the Pearl Harbor attack occurred over sixty years ago, I still remember it well. I was a member of the Type 99 *kanbaku* from the carrier *Akagi*. Prior to flying my mission, I thought that it was really important to fulfill my responsibility as a pilot for my commander's airplane. I tried my best to do my duty and paid attention to doing that. As I mentioned before, Egusa-san was the overall Type 99 carrier bomber group leader with his partner WO Tatsuki Ishii.[5] My observer, Lieutenant Takehiko Chihaya, and I flew in the second position of the formation (behind the fighters), and led the two *Akagi chūtais* with the other carrier's Type 99s. Our group consisted of seventy-eight Type 99s during the second wave attack. As for the other *kanbaku*, seventeen came from *Sōryū*, another seventeen from *Hiryū*, and twenty-six from *Kaga*.

We gathered over our mother ships, and all seventy-eight Type 99 carrier bombers flew in a large formation towards Hawaii. During my mission it was a clear day with good visibility, and a great day for flying. Our group of Type 99s passed over Honolulu and flew towards Pearl Harbor. As I approached Ford Island, there

The young PO1c Furuta was assigned to the aircraft carrier *Akagi* until it was sunk during the Battle of Midway. (NHC via Wenger)

was intense enemy anti-aircraft fire coming from the American ships below. At a descending altitude of fifty degrees, I aimed at the enemy battleship's mast using my scope. At the same time, Lieutenant Chihaya reported the altitude of our aircraft through a voice tube by watching the altimeter's hand. The hand rotated rapidly at 12 meters (about 39 feet) per second; 800 meters (2,624 feet), and then when it reached 600 meters (1,968 feet) my radioman said "*Yōi*." After this, when the hand pointed at 400 meters (1,312 feet), he said "*Tei*." Then I released the bomb and pulled back the control stick and tried to get back to level flight (about 150 meters, or 492 feet). After completing our attack, I identified the ship as *Maryland* from its position in the battleship formation. I am pretty sure we scored a hit on the enemy ship, but I wasn't able to confirm it because we were flying at such a low altitude.[6]

While we were flying at low altitude, our airplane was hit countless times by machinegun fire from below; it was extraordinary. We were flying in the second wave, one hour after the first wave, so they knew we were coming. They were ready and just waiting for us to come. Everyone started to shoot at us. Because of this, my Type 99 was hit in the fuel tank (located in the right wing) and fuselage. Unfortunately, one of our three fuel tanks became empty in no time. Prior to taking off, we were ordered to attack Ewa Marine Air Corps Station near Barbers Point after completing our attack on the battleships. Therefore, after attacking the battleship, I headed to Barbers Point. I identified the airfield (Ewa) at an altitude of 1,000 meters (3,280 feet) and dove down to strafe the target with machinegun fire. The *Sōryū* and *Hiryū* Type 99 *kanbaku* pilots were rookies, so it was better that they attacked the airfields instead of small ships. Zero fighters also strafed airplanes on the airfields as well.

Both my right wing and left wing had a fuel tank that held 500 liters of gasoline. In my Type 99, there was another fuel tank under the seat. As I flew towards the ocean, I smelled gas and saw a trail of smoke coming from my aircraft. I then saw gas leaking from my wing, and it looked like water being poured out of a bucket! Because of this, I thought that adjusting the engine would cause a

PO1c Furuta and Lieutenant Chihaya attacked the *Neosho* during the Pearl Harbor attack. It is depicted here passing the *California* heading to the Navy Yard during the second wave. (NA via Wenger)

The attacking Japanese aircraft during the second wave encountered intense anti-aircraft fire. (NA via Wenger)

fire, so I never touched it again during my mission. While flying towards our rendezvous point, I told my commander, Lieutenant Chihaya, about the damage.

Before departing for our mission, Lieutenant Commander Egusa ordered us to guide all the Zero fighters to their mother ships by dropping several lumps of silver powder on an imaginary line drawn between the mother ships and Cape Kahuku at a point approximately 37 km (23 miles) from the ships. The dispersed powder formed a white line on the sea, which would act as a beacon for Zeros to gather together. Chihaya-san dropped ten bags of silver powder into the ocean. By doing this, you could create white lines in the water (for navigation purposes) because the powder floats. Zero fighters normally had difficulty navigating back to the carrier. However, multi-place airplanes like my Type 99 had a specialist aboard who could navigate well. So, Lieutenant Chihaya dropped this powder to help the Zero fighters get back to the carrier and sent a message to the other airplanes saying that we would leave soon because of the damage to our carrier bomber. Luckily, the Zero fighters were able to return safely to the carrier. As for our aircraft, we were able to get back to the carrier with just five minutes of fuel left.

According to veteran Lieutenant Commander Keiichi Arima, Furuta's flying partner later in the war, this is how the powder (for navigation purposes) worked, "You dropped a piece of solid cone-shaped material with your hand through a hole in the floor of the aircraft. This was done to show the direction of the carrier to other pilots. The powder was initially silver in color, but it became white when dropped into water. Each lump of solid material melted in the water and spread outward, creating the shape of a circle. For example, when you dropped it six times in succession, you had six circles. In other words, they formed a line in the water when you looked from an aircraft flying above."

After we landed on board *Akagi* our mechanic, Maintenance PO1c Yoshimura, checked out the damage to our airplane and found dozens of bullet holes which came from below. Fortunately, there was no lethal damage to our plane. Another bullet hit the area below my seat. If the bullet penetrated a little harder, it would have hit the fuel tank. The most important thing was the engine, but it was not damaged, so we were lucky.

Pilots' relationships with mechanics

On board the carrier *Akagi*, Maintenance PO1c Yoshimura and two other young men serviced Type 99. On the aircraft carrier *Shōkaku*, Maintenance WO Hachirō Miyashita, who now helps organize the annual reunion of *Mizumi-kai*, our veterans' group, serviced my bomber.[7] During the war he worked around the clock to make sure my aircraft was mechanically sound before each of my missions. So, I couldn't thank him enough for his service, and always felt that the mechanics took excellent care of my Type 99 *kanbaku*. When we had time, we gathered together and chatted. On other occasions, we even drank together. In short, I got to know my mechanics very well.

Skills to be a good pilot

In order to be a good pilot in the Japanese Imperial Navy, there were certain skills that were important. You had to be able to take off and land on a carrier as many times as necessary. In order to do that, it took great skill. You also had to be good at doing dive-bombing attack technique and accurate at dropping your bombs. I felt, if you were able to do this, you could fly combat missions from just about anywhere. The most difficult thing to do for a pilot is to take off and land on a carrier. If it is just landing and taking off from the land, anyone could do that. In the case of a carrier, the deck was only 35 meters (115 feet) wide and 300 meters (982 feet) long, so it was very challenging. If you couldn't do this, you were useless in the Pacific War.

As a naval aviator, you had to think about several things during a mission. If today's assignment was attacking a particular city, you had to be familiar with the terrain. If it's the case of an engagement over water, you had to know which type of ship that you were going to attack: a carrier, battleship, or cruiser. You also had to know your target before taking off. However, in an ocean battle, it was usually carrier versus carrier, so unless you attacked an enemy carrier at least once, you really weren't completing your assignment. Finally, you had to think about how to go to the enemy's location and the best way to complete your mission successfully.

An exhausted *Akagi* aviator after completing his Pearl Harbor mission. (Makiel Collection via Wenger)

A *shōtaichō's Akagi* Type 99 takes off to attack the British cruisers on 5 April 1942. (Wenger Collection)

Action after Pearl Harbor

After the Pearl Harbor attack I participated in lots of missions, such as the Port Darwin attack on 19 February 1942, and also in the Indian Ocean during April of that year. During the Indian Ocean missions we sank the British cruisers *Cornwall* and *Dorsetshire*, and the carrier *Hermes*. Next was the ill-fated Midway Operation, which occurred during the first week of June.

The Battle of Midway

I took off from the carrier *Akagi*, which was probably 300-350 kilometers (186-217 miles) northwest of Midway Atoll. There were seventeen airplanes behind me, and we headed towards Midway. On our way to Eastern Island (part of Midway Atoll) I saw a vague formation of aircraft, which were to the left and in front of us. They looked a little bit bigger than crows and actually were our Japanese airplanes. This occurred about midpoint in our flight to Eastern Island. Suddenly, one of our airplanes was on fire after being attacked by an enemy Grumman F4F Wildcat fighter. Several other Japanese airplanes were hit and spiraling down with black smoke. After this, our Zero fighters began to engage the Wildcats. I avoided the air battles by going a little bit to the right; then I bombed Eastern Island. Anti-aircraft fire over the target area didn't seem that heavy to me. I thought it was a waste bombing an empty enemy airfield with no aircraft, though. We just bombed the airfield and returned without suffering any losses to our *Akagi* carrier bomber group.

The Japanese attackers did some damage to the facilities on both Eastern Island and Sand Island (Midway Atoll). On Eastern Island, bombs destroyed the power plant, command post, mess hall, and post office. The gasoline lines also were severed, so the refueling on the airstrip had to be done by hand. Another bomb struck one of the rearming pits near the airfield and killed four men. The runway itself was hit, which caused some craters, but damage was minor.

As for Sand Island, once the attackers finished their business, the facility was releasing a large column of black smoke. Japanese bombs destroyed the laundry, dispensary, Navy mess hall and galley, brig, and contractor's building, which were located on the eastern side of the island near the seaplane facilities. The water lines and three of the oil storage tanks also were burning heavily.

Akagi's Type 99s "in action" during early spring 1942. (Both photos from the Wenger Collection)

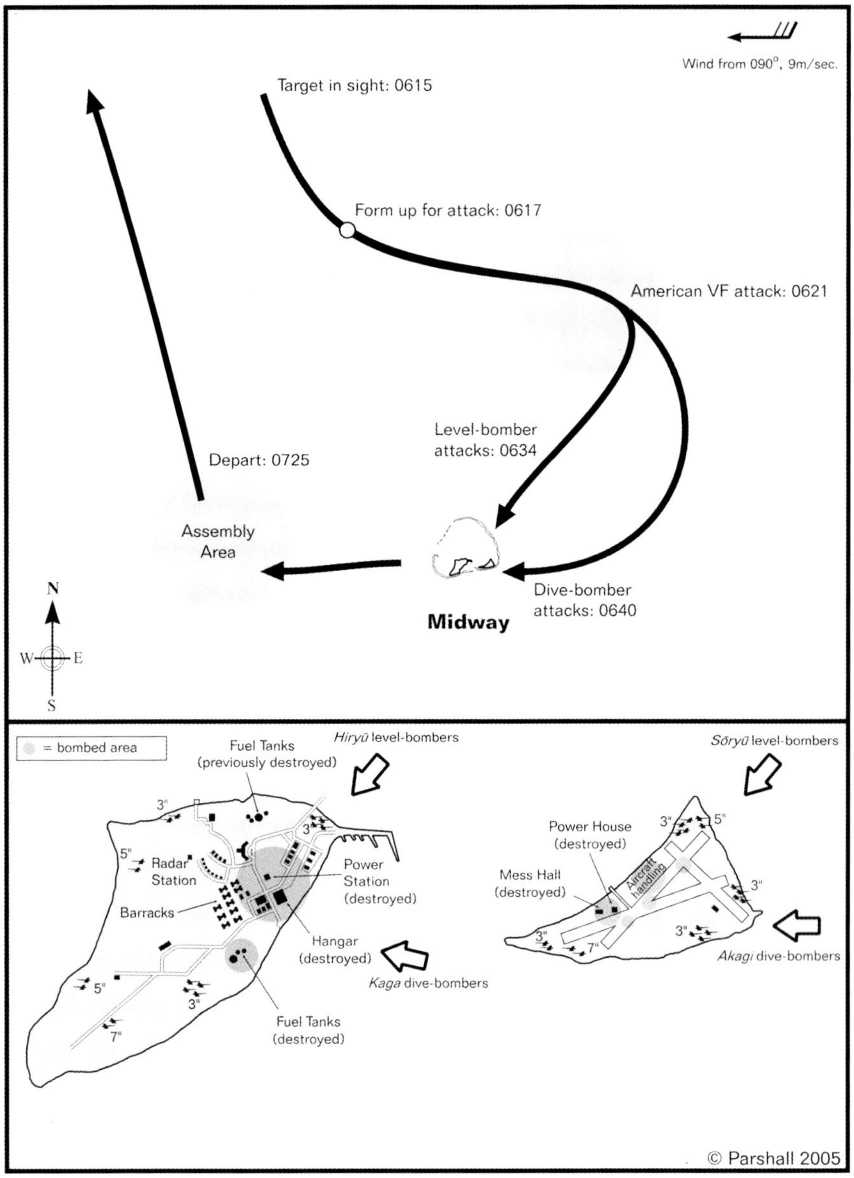

The Japanese Navy's air attack on Midway Atoll. (Jonathan Parshall)

The burning oil tanks on Sand Island after the Japanese morning air strike on Midway Atoll. Note the island's famous Laysan Albatross "Gooney Bird" chicks in the foreground. (NA)

The torpedo and bombsight maintenance sheds were destroyed, several of the barracks badly damaged, and the seaplane hangar was burned down to the bare steel skeleton.[8]

We went back to *Akagi*, *Sōryū*, and *Hiryū*. However, at that time B-17 bombers were attacking our carriers, so we were not able to land immediately. I flew away and waited until the attack was over. After the enemy aircraft left the area, I landed back on our carrier. Luckily, every *Akagi* airplane returned safely, and the enemy fighters didn't hit my formation. Our carrier wasn't damaged from the high-level bombing attack; it turned into the wind so we could land, and I landed first after receiving the order to land. After landing, I put my Type 99 into the hangar, and people brought food to us. While I was eating my lunch, American torpedo planes began to attack. I saw the airplanes and said "They are coming." Zero fighters were above our fleet doing combat air patrols, and other airplanes were ready to take off on the deck. They took off quickly and shot down the torpedo planes one after another. As far as I could see, the enemy planes were completely destroyed by our Zeros. Our fighter pilots were very skilled, and we didn't suffer any damage from the enemy aircraft.

Vice Admiral Chūchi Nagumo and his staff thought that the planes must be coming from an enemy carrier, so he ordered us to prepare our airplanes for the next strike. Because I was a senior pilot, I told the younger airmen to go to the hangar and help ready the airplanes. They did this, and finished loading the bombs and torpedoes on the aircraft. The mechanics then poured fuel into the airplanes and took them to the deck. We were supposed to take off shortly after this, and when we finished working on the airplanes, it was very hot. So, I told the other people to open up the hangar windows to get some air, and I let some others go outside. I also went outside to cool off.

Suddenly I saw, probably 1,500-2,000 meters (4,921-6,562 feet) away from our ship, the carrier *Kaga* being attacked by dive-bombers. I thought that this was a real emergency, and two or three bombs hit the ship, causing a big fire. I thought to myself "Oh, my god." After seeing this attack, I thought it was best to urinate, because I probably would be flying another mission very shortly. While I was in the head, a bomb hit the deck of our carrier and there was a big explosion. I thought "We are hit!" Then, while I was still in the head, another bomb hit toward the rear side of the *Akagi*. I felt that this was a very bad situation, because at that time our airplanes were fueled up and loaded with ammunition. The bombs created a big fire, and we couldn't do anything about it. Inside our hangar our bombs blew up one after another, so it became a blazing cauldron.

After I finished urinating I went to the flight deck, but it was difficult to get there because many hatches were closed. Several bombs hit *Kaga*, two bombs hit our carrier *Akagi*, and *Sōryū* also

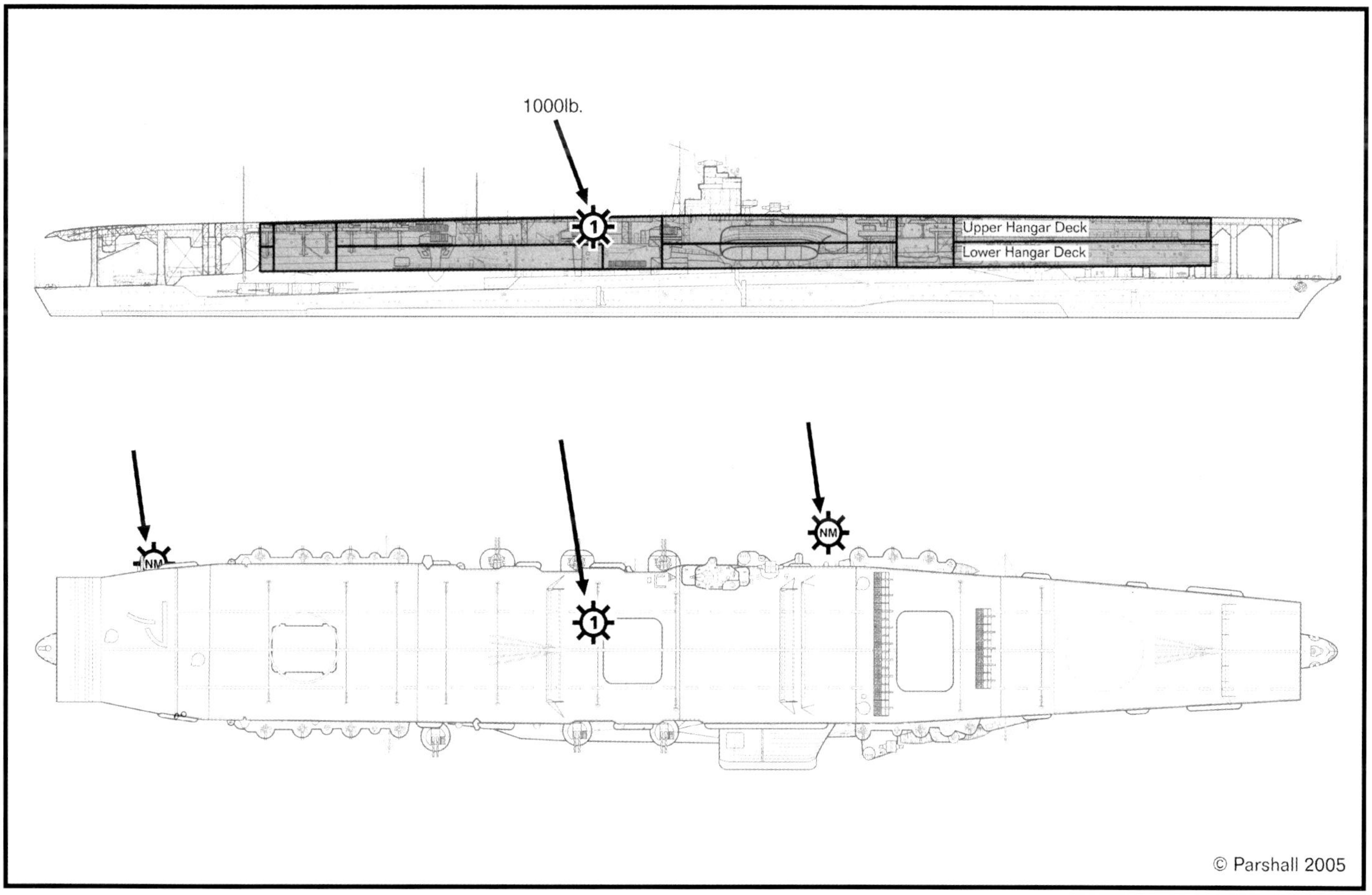

The bomb hit locations on the *Akagi* during the Battle of Midway. (Jonathan Parshall)

was hit. Every ship was loaded with highly explosive things, such as bombs and torpedoes, and three of them were now engulfed in flames. In essence, our own bombs sunk our carriers, and there was nothing that we could do. If there were no bombs or torpedoes loaded on our ships, it probably would not have destroyed our carriers.

I ended up going to the flight deck because I was ordered to help put out a fire. A sailor showed me a big handle which, when opened, would release a large amount of water into the bottom of *Akagi*. We were concerned about the fire reaching the room where the ammunition was stored. If the fire spread to this area, our carrier would be split into two parts. I helped the sailor douse water on the fire. Nevertheless, as I mentioned before, the ammunition in the hangar continued to blow up one after another. *Akagi* was an inferno, and the electricity was cut off. Because electricity was lost, our fire extinguishing pump didn't work, and even if it worked, the pump would not have put out this inferno. So we just gave up trying to put out the blaze.

At 1026, the carrier Akagi *was attacked by three SBD Dauntless dive-bombers of VB-6 from the USS* Enterprise. *The trio of dive-bombers was led by Lieutenant Richard Best, who scored a direct hit on the enemy carrier, which struck amidships in the vicinity of the island. The other two bombs were near misses, with one hitting the port-side forward and the third hitting near the fantail (but didn't detonate on the flight deck).*

Because the Akagi *was preparing its aircraft for another strike, some were already armed and fueled, so remarkably even with just being struck by one bomb she was doomed. The rudder on the carrier also was jammed at twenty degrees port, which caused the* Akagi *to go in wide circles.*[9]

Vice Admiral Chūichi Nagumo moved his command to the destroyer *Nowaki* (then later the light cruiser *Nagara*) and didn't stay on the carrier. However, in those days, the captain of the ship was supposed to stay with his ship until the end. The mechanics on *Akagi* tried to escape the fire and were divided into two groups. One group went to the bow of the ship, while the other group went to the stern of the ship. They had to escape the heat. Captain Taijirō Aoki came down to the bow section and ordered everyone to gather around him. He said that the pilots on board should be saved, and that we had to go back to Japan alive. Captain Aoki also said that pilots were so precious because it took twenty years (from birth to manhood) to become a skilled aviator. He also said that if we had a new carrier we could fly again soon.

There was one boat in the bow section, and it was lowered. After this, about forty people including myself transferred via this boat to a nearby destroyer. At this point, it didn't seem that *Akagi* was sinking. Nevertheless, the carrier was bright red because it was on fire everywhere. The carrier *Kaga* looked like this as well. The *Akagi* was originally designed to be a battlecruiser, so it was built very strongly. We couldn't leave the carrier alone because America could capture it. Instead, early the next day, we decided to scuttle it using torpedoes from our destroyers. Before scuttling the *Akagi*, we made sure that nobody was left on the ship, including the captain, who was supposed to go down with it. Luckily, a group of people pulled him off the ship, and he survived. As for our carrier, it sank quickly.

At 0520 on 5 June, Admiral Yamamoto's beloved Akagi *was scuttled by two or three torpedoes fired from the destroyers* Arashio, Hagikaze, Maikaze, *and* Nowaki. *Only 263 men perished out of a crew of more 1,070, and as Furuta-san states, Captain Aoki was one of the fortunate survivors of the engagement.*[10]

In retrospect, I feel that we shouldn't have attacked Midway Atoll. Instead, we should have tried to find and sink the enemy aircraft carriers because we had a hunch that they were probably in the area. It should have been a battle between our carriers, and I believe if we sank some of the enemy's carriers, we could have easily captured Midway Atoll. Nevertheless, we attacked an airfield, but there were no planes, so it was a mistake by the upper echelon of the navy. We just did what we were ordered to do, and I felt that we had a meaningless mission. I didn't know what our Japanese commanders were thinking. To me, the best idea would have been to locate and engage the enemy's carriers, capture Midway Atoll, then advance to Hawaii.

Prior to the Battle of Midway we won many battles. However, we lost four of our carriers at Midway. If the Japanese Navy would have been smarter, things would have been different. We sank several battleships during the Pearl Harbor attack, but we didn't sink any carriers. However, I believe that we ignored this fact and focused on attacking Midway Atoll instead. Later in the war we lost all of our carriers, so I think we didn't fight well against American carriers. New pilots were younger and less skillful; then, in the end, we lost the war.

Action after Midway

After the battle of Midway, I joined the Type 99 *kanbaku* group on board the carrier *Shōkaku*. I participated in both the Battle of the Eastern Solomons on 24 August 1942 and the Battle of Santa Cruz on 26 October of that same year. My partner, Lieutenant Commander Keiichi Arima, was the radioman/observer for my aircraft. Unfortunately our carrier, *Shōkaku*, was severely damaged by American bombs during the Battle of Santa Cruz, so I returned to Japan. After returning home, I became a flight instructor for dive-bomber pilots with the 17th *Kōkūtai* and later the Kaikō (Haihow) *Kōkūtai*.

The end of the war

Towards the end of the war I transferred to Usa *Kōkūtai* and served as a flight instructor again. However, at this base, most of the airplanes were destroyed, so I transferred to Hyakurigahara. After completing training, many of my students died while doing *tokkō* missions. They died one after another on these missions, and we had very few aircraft left at Hyakurigahara Air Base. We had very little gasoline, and it was being conserved for flying *tokkō* missions. My new group did *tokkō* missions, but I survived because the war ended on 15 August 1945.

At the end of the war, I felt that Japan was annihilated by America. I didn't know what the United States military would do to us when the occupation troops arrived. I thought that Japan

CPO Furuta in his dress uniform with medals and good conduct chevron. (Furuta Collection)

became a pathetic country because we lost the war. Contrary to what I expected, the Americans were very good to the Japanese people after the war. For example, when we were running out of food, they gave food to us. In normal circumstances, Japanese people would have hated the United States. Nevertheless, once the war ended, we didn't have any hateful feelings towards the United States as an enemy of Japan. My final rank in the Imperial Japanese Navy was lieutenant, junior grade, and I flew 5,000 hours while serving in the military.

Postwar

Shortly after the war ended I went back to my hometown. Luckily, because my father was a farmer, we had food to eat. I initially helped him, but I couldn't make a living doing this. When I was I still in the navy, I hoped to become a pilot in the private sector once I was discharged. However, if you became a high rank in the navy, such as commander, you had to dedicate your life to serving your country. Because I did not want to do this, I asked my superior officers not to promote me after becoming a lieutenant, junior grade. However, after America occupied Japan, they said that Japanese people were not able to fly airplanes again for eight years. After that time passed I was too old to fly, so I decided to start my own orchard. I have such fruit as pears and grapes, and I invite customers to pick their own produce. People come from all over Japan to visit my orchard, and I have been doing this a long time now.

As for my family, I was married in 1940. My wife and I had three sons and one daughter, but my second son died shortly after childbirth. My wife died seventeen years ago, and now my eldest son and his wife run my orchard.

Reflections

In general, (during the wartime years) the Japanese Army usually viewed Russia as its potential enemy. The army did its training in Manchuria and focused their efforts on a potential engagement with Russia. In the case of the navy, during the war our enemy was the United States. So whenever you flew a mission, you had to think about how to attack your adversary. The navy trained very hard every day to fight the American ships, which was our goal. During the war, I personally never felt any hatred against the United States or its people. Nevertheless, once you were a member of the Japanese armed forces your objective was to fight for our nation.

A recent picture of the fit, ninety-two year old Kiyoto Furuta. (Werneth)

In regards to why some Japanese military men committed suicide instead of being taken prisoner, I think each man determined his own personal fate according to what he wanted most: to live or die. A person who thought that becoming a prisoner would be shameful chose to commit suicide. Men who inherited the idea from the old ethic code of *bushido* (the discipline and soul of Japanese warriors) might choose suicide as well. One who wanted to survive would choose to be taken prisoner instead.

How do I feel about Pearl Harbor today? During the war, we had no choice but to follow our orders, as we were taught that one must absolutely obey "any" order from his superior officer. I had to follow my orders and had no choice. It all happened sixty-four years ago, and I think it is unbelievable in this "freethinking" era. However, the attack really happened sixty-four years ago, and there is no doubt that the event earned a chapter in history. I appreciate the peace that Japan has today because we fought so many wars since the Meiji Period, such as the Russo-Japanese War, the Sino-Japanese War, and World War II. So it has been sixty years since Japan fought in a war, and I feel that this is a wonderful era of peace.

Lieutenant Commander Keiichi Arima

"I simply wanted to accomplish my duty."

During my stay in Japan, I had a chance to meet Keiichi Arima, one of the last surviving senior officers who served as a naval aviator during both the Sino-Japanese War and World War II. He was in the same class as the well-known Type 99 pilot Zenji Abe at the Naval Academy. In his postwar years, Arima-san also participated in a symposium at the National Museum of the Pacific War in Fredericksburg, Texas.

When I met him, I could not believe that he was eighty-seven years old, because he looked so physically fit and much younger. Furthermore, he was very sharp and had excellent command of English. Arima-san currently lives in Tokyo.

Naval Academy Days

I was born on 26 November 1916, in Tokyo. My father worked at a trading company, and I had one younger brother and one younger sister. The Japanese middle school system is a little different than the American system. Normally, if someone went to an excellent middle school, after graduating, they went on to an elite university. In my case, I chose to go to the Naval Academy. I was impressed by a relative of mine who was about six years older than I and he was in the navy. The entrance test was very difficult, but fortunately I passed, and was admitted into the Naval Academy. Only 160 people were admitted to the Naval Academy for each term, but ten people from my middle school entered the academy, which was extraordinary.

I joined the navy in April 1933 as a 64th Term student, and this was my usual schedule at the academy. Early in the morning we had breakfast, which was followed by lectures until lunch. After lunch we had additional lectures and then physical training. We did training such as rhythmic gymnastics, sumo wrestling, kendo, and judo. We also did cutter rowing, and practiced thrusting with a rifle and bayonet. After this we had dinner, and after eating our meal, we went to a self-study room and studied until 2100. On the weekends, we often went mountain climbing and rode horses.

I graduated on 23 March 1937, then went on a six-month training cruise. We were the last class to go to Europe. We went on ships that were used in the Russo-Japanese War, the *Yakumo* and *Iwate*. I was on board the *Yakumo* and studied mainly navigation, but also learned how to fire a cannon and range finding. I studied how to defend the ship and rescue the vessel in emergency situations. In those days, I got up two hours before dawn and checked the directions and places of the stars along with studying charts. The whole package was called "usage training." Back then we didn't have passenger planes that went to Paris. During our cruise we went to many places, such as Southeast Asia, France, Turkey, and Italy.

After our cruise we were appointed to many different ships, and I went to *Sōryū* and did communication related work. After this I was chosen to do flight training, and went to Kasumigaura to study in August 1938. In March 1939 I went to Yokosuka and Saeki Air Bases to study to be an observer, not a pilot. I felt there were very few people who were officers that chose to be observers. A lot of people wanted to be pilots, but I thought that there should be some high-level observers. I subsequently went to Kyūshū and did some additional flight training for three months, and then was sent to China.

Action in China

I was in China from 21 October 1939 until 3 November 1940, as a member of the 12th *Kōkūtai*. I was based at different places, such as Anking and Hankow. In Hankow, there also was the 13th *Kōkūtai*, which did combat missions deep inside China. Initially, I flew the Type 96 biplane carrier bomber (Allied code name "Susie"), and then later the Type 99 *kanbaku* as an observer. Prior to the Type 99 being used in Japan, it was tested in combat in China.

My *kōkūtai* was the first group to bomb Chungking with the Type 99. At that time, the city was the Chinese nationalist capitol. I normally had no specific targets, but they were basically around the Yangtze River. We did attack missions at least four times a week. Sometimes, the target was a small transport or boat. Other times we received information from an army unit, which told us which areas to hit. So every day was different. Usually we flew very low, about 50 meters (164 feet) above the ground, and commenced our attacks. At that time, there were no Chinese fighters that came to

A wartime picture of Lieutenant Commander Keiichi Arima in his flight gear. (Arima collection)

The carrier USS *Enterprise* was Arima's "target" during the Battle of Eastern Solomons and the Battle of Santa Cruz. (NA)

the central part of China, where I flew my missions. However, in other areas of the country our Zero fighters fought against the enemy's fighters.

The Battle of the Eastern Solomons

During the beginning of the war, I was an instructor at Suzuka *Kōkūtai* and stayed there for about one year, and then I joined the carrier *Shōkaku* on 25 June 1942. On 24 August 1942 I attacked the U.S. Task Force. I was the number one *chūtaichō* and flew as an observer, but my position in the formation was actually second. Our group flew behind Lieutenant Commander Mamoru Seki's group.[11] One *chūtai* consisted of nine planes, and we had three *chūtais*.

The pilot of my aircraft, PO1c Kiyoto Furuta, was very skillful. He was very calm and an excellent pilot. Furuta-san is still alive, and we meet each other once a year. We took off at 1450 in the afternoon. During this mission, our group of planes flew higher than we usually did. We flew at about 8,000 meters (24,000 feet). On normal occasions we would fly at 5,000-5,500 meters (16,404-18,045 feet), but we flew higher for this mission to try to avoid Grumman F4F Wildcat fighters. I hid in a cloud, so my Type 99 wasn't attacked by enemy fighters prior to commencing my attack. I then dove into the ring-shaped enemy ship formation and probably bombed the *Enterprise*. I'm not one-hundred percent sure that I hit the carrier, because it is hard to tell from above. The area on the ship that my bomb probably hit was in the middle. It was difficult to see how extensive the damage was, but I saw smoke coming from the ship.

While escaping the ring formation, our aircraft was shot at by a lot of anti-aircraft guns, but none hit my plane. It was a very tough fight, but I didn't have time to be scared because I was focused on what I was doing. However, my mission was not finished yet. My role after the attack was to wait for our other aircraft and help them get back to the carrier. At that time, there were two other Japanese planes with our aircraft. Suddenly I saw four airplanes, which I thought were Japanese fighters coming towards me. I wanted to help them return to our ship, but they were enemy Grumman F4F Wildcat fighters! When you see those airplanes from far away, you cannot identify them properly. However, when the Grummans came close, I was able to see the shape of their wings, which were different from the wings of our aircraft. I tried to escape the enemy fighters, but only had one 7.7 mm machine gun to defend myself. I shot my machine gun, but it had no effect on them.

The *Enterprise* being attacked by *Shōkaku's* Type 99s on 24 August 1942. This shot shows one of the doomed Type 99 carrier bombers during the attack. (NA)

A Japanese bomb exploding on the flight deck of the *Enterprise* just aft of the island during the Battle of Eastern Solomons. (NA)

We were flying very low, maybe less than 10 meters (33 feet) above the water, and tried to get back to our carrier at full speed. The sun was setting, so I decided to fly towards it. I thought the sun would obstruct their view, and they would stop chasing my aircraft. I landed after sunset, because it took longer to return to our carrier because of the engagement with the Wildcat fighters. A moment after landing on *Shōkaku*, the engine of my Type 99 carrier bomber stopped due to a lack of fuel. I returned with only two airplanes from my group, and maybe five or six planes from the other groups came back, so I was lucky to come back alive.

The carrier Enterprise *was hit by three bombs during the above mission.*[12] *Arima-san, flying with his pilot, PO1c Kiyoto Furuta, scored the first ever hit on the carrier at 1644, and about thirty seconds later it was struck by a bomb dropped from the Type 99 carrier bomber flown by PO1c Tamotsu Akimoto and his partner, PO1c Hiroshi Koitabashi. The third bomb subsequently hit the carrier at 1646.*

The official damage reports of the Enterprise *and* Enterprise *CV-6 Association website go into detail about what happened during the attack.*[13] *According to these sources, the carrier was struck by three direct hits and four near misses. The first bomb went through the number three elevator and detonated between the second and third decks (42 feet below). It also caused the hangar deck to bulge two feet upward and made the aft elevator useless. Thirty-five men lost their lives in an instant. The second bomb blew up only fifteen feet away from the first bomb. This bomb obliterated the aft starboard 5" gun galley and killed thirty-eight men. The third and final bomb made a ten foot hole through the flight deck and disabled the number two elevator. On board the damaged carrier, seventy-four men died and an additional ninety-one were wounded. As for the* Enterprise, *she was repaired at Pearl Harbor and lived on to fight another day.*

The official Japanese records state that out of the strike group of twenty-seven Type 99 kanbaku *(from the carriers* Shōkaku *and* Zuikaku*), nineteen aircraft failed to return.*[14] *However, the crew of one of these bombers ditched and survived, while another crew ditched at Malaita. Out of the ten escorting Zero fighters, three pilots perished: PO2c Goro Sakaida, PO2c Toshiharu Okubo, and PO1c Shigeru Makino. Well-known Zero ace PO3c Sadamu Komachi also was shot down, but he was rescued. Finally, Sea1c Shigeru Hayashi also ditched but survived.*

After the battle we went to Tinian Island, which is part of the Marianas Islands. A lot of people died in the previous battle, so we were waiting for replacements to come. In September the replacements came, and we started to do training for our next operation.

The Battle of Santa Cruz

My next mission, which occurred on 26 October 1942, was very similar to the previous battle. We searched for the American Task Force, but we weren't able to locate them. The Japanese Navy searched for them on three occasions, moving north to south, which we called the "piston movement." Our aircraft found the enemy almost at the same time they found us. Of course, it was ideal when we had a battle that we found the enemy and they didn't locate our force. However, usually when we fought one another they also found us.

I took off in the morning from my carrier *Shōkaku*, and we found the U.S. Task Force under the clouds. We tried to attack with

The *Enterprise* "in action" during the Battle of Santa Cruz. Note the heavy anti-aircraft fire that the Japanese attackers faced during the engagement. (NA)

A Japanese bomb explodes off the port side of *Enterprise* on 26 October 1942. (NA)

twenty-seven airplanes, with three *chūtais* of nine airplanes each. Once again, I was the number one *chūtaichō*, but our group flew behind the first group and my plane was at the top. The overall strike leader, Lieutenant Commander Mamoru Seki, was shot down during the attack by anti-aircraft fire. My target was once again the carrier *Enterprise*, and I hit it somewhere in the middle. However, because of the black smoke around my target ship, it was hard to determine the damage. I was able to see it because I was in the observer's position in the back of the aircraft. While we were trying to bomb our target, we went in a line one by one. Because of this I was only able to see a little in the front and a little to the rear of my aircraft.

During the battle, a fighter directly above shot down my comrade; however, I personally wasn't involved in any air battles. The anti-aircraft fire was enormous, so probably many Japanese airplanes were shot because of this rather than air battles. I saw several airplanes from Seki's group go down in flames. The anti-aircraft came from the carrier, and I saw the shells right in front of my airplane. It looked like fireworks coming right toward me. This all lasted for several minutes, and I was wondering why the shells were not hitting my plane because there were so many. Our Type 99 was heavily damaged and had several dozen holes. The oxygen tank also was damaged. I thought that the airplane probably couldn't fly again without being repaired. I was surprised that we were able to land in the first place. Because my carrier *Shōkaku* was heavily damaged they sent me a message to land on the carrier *Zuikaku*.

The official damage reports and Enterprise *CV-6 Association website once again go into great detail about what happened during this mission.*[15] *The carrier suffered two direct hits and one near miss. The first bomb penetrated through the flight deck at 1017 and then reemerged to explode in the air, close to the ship's bow section. This bomb also put 160 shrapnel holes between the waterline and forecastle of the ship, alighted a Dauntless dive-bomber, and put another over the side.*

Moments later a second bomb struck just aft of the forward elevator and may have broken into two parts, because there were two separate holes in the hangar deck. However, one of the holes may have been caused by one of the bombs which were being loaded on aircraft forward of the hangar deck. Nevertheless, this second Japanese bomb caused an explosion at hangar deck level, which caused casualties and damage at that level. This bomb also caused a second explosion on the third deck that killed a lot of men, wounding many others and causing overall heavy damage in that section of the carrier.

A third bomb, which was a near miss, exploded near the starboard side of the ship. This caused damage to the hull plating, flooding two empty fuel tanks and opening a third one that was full. It also rocked the carrier violently, which caused one plane to go over the side. The ship casualties for this day were forty-four men killed and seventy-five wounded.[16]

According to the official Japanese records, the brave Japanese aviators paid a heavy toll for this mission; out of the nineteen Type 99 kanbaku *that participated in the mission, ten were lost, including the one flown by the overall commander, Lieutenant Commander Mamoru Seki. However, the records don't indicate if any other aircraft were lost due to ditching. Finally, out of the escorting five Zero fighters, none were lost during this mission.* [17]

Arima-san remembers Lieutenant Commander Seki as a fine officer. He said that his ex-commander was very calm and

Lieutenant Commander Seki led the *Shōkaku's kanbaku* in the attack on the Enterprise on 26 October 1942. He was one of the Japanese casualties of this battle. (Arima Collection)

easygoing. Arima-san felt that Lieutenant Commander Seki knew his subordinates very well. Seki was born on 8 March 1909 and graduated from the Naval Academy on 18 November 1930 as a member of the 58th class.

After doing a few non-aviation related positions in the navy, he started his flight training on 1 April 1933. Seki's first aviation assignment was with the Tateyama Kōkūtai *beginning on 28 November of that same year.*

Throughout the 1930s until the Pearl Harbor attack, (at that time) Lieutenant Seki gained a lot of flying experience while in land-based aviation positions and operating from the carriers Ryūjō, Sōryū, *and* Akagi. *During the first half of 1942 he served as the* hikōtaichō *of the Usa* Kōkūtai. *On 1 July 1942 Seki joined the carrier* Shōkaku *as a* hikōtaichō, *and held this position until his death on 26 October 1942 during the Battle of Santa Cruz. His last rank in the navy was lieutenant commander.*[18]

Military duties in Japan

On 18 November 1942 I transferred to Usa *Kōkūtai* in Kyūshū as an instructor. After this I joined the Yokosuka *Kōkūtai* on 31 December 1943, as a *hikōtaichō* teaching navigation and communication. I also was in the research department, and worked on developing such things as radar and communication gear. I feel strongly that Japan was inferior to the United States regarding wireless communication. During the war Japan mainly used Morse code, but American aviators were able to use voice modulation gear. We were not able to use voice modulation gear well, but regarding Morse code we were superior. I stayed at Yokosuka until the end of the war, and my final rank was lieutenant commander. I estimate my total flying hours to be between 1,500-1,600 hours.

Postwar

After the war I started a small photocopying business, which I later passed on to my son. Then I joined a trading company and stayed for two years in Switzerland, retiring once I came back to Japan. My wife and I have one son and one daughter. My daughter married an American and now lives in California. I used to play golf and travel, but recently I enjoy using the Internet. I've been reading the English edition of *Newsweek* magazine for about thirty years, and believe it's very difficult for nations to agree with each other. For example, America and European countries have different opinions on issues, so it is very difficult to unite.

Reflections

During the war, I concentrated on doing my duty and never doubted fighting for our country. My duty was to attack the enemy successfully. I simply wanted to accomplish my duty. At that time, I really didn't have a clear picture on what was happening in Japan and its fight against the United States. Looking back, I don't have any regrets for participating in the war. I chose to fight and contribute to my nation. I did what I had to do. I don't agree with talking aimlessly about the past using your individual feelings. I believe war itself is unavoidable.

Today, some of the left-wing people criticize Japan's previous decision to go to war. I really think that it is regrettable that these days Japan has a lot of left-wing thinking. It may be useless to say, but the postwar education system in Japan was bad. In a way, the American occupational forces were responsible. This is because there were many people who had left-wing thoughts, so the Japanese postwar education system was influenced by them. This is still happening today. In other words, instead of protecting their own nation, Japanese people just criticize everything about it.

Keiichi Arima in his Tokyo home during our interview. He was one of the few Japanese Navy veterans who could speak English. (Werneth)

Lieutenant Commander Zenji Abe

"I don't understand why we had to go to war with the United States."

As we entered the home of Zenji Abe I noticed a dark blue navy officer's cap, black leather belt, and a polished dress dagger hanging near the door. These items, which were typical garb of a wartime Imperial Japanese Navy officer, are a reminder of Abe-san's war years, which occurred over half a century ago and changed the world. Abe-san is probably one of the most well-known navy pilots, because after the war he traveled extensively to attend events such as symposiums and meetings of wartime veterans in both America and Japan. The ex-pilot has dark tan skin, which is accented by a few dark sunspots. He is warm, articulate, well read, and mentally sharp at a young eight-nine years old. Abe-san currently lives in Koga City, in the Ibaraki Prefecture.

This is his story, which was researched for a number of years through numerous interviews and background research. Special thanks to the National Museum of the Pacific War (Fredericksburg, Texas) for allowing me to use some of their materials to write this story, and historian Michael Wenger for reviewing this account.

Abe's Early Years

I was born in Kano, which is in the western portion of Honshu, Japan, on 18 August 1916. After attending primary school for six years in my native town, I entered a middle school in Yamaguchi City and studied there for four years. Yamaguchi City is the capital of Yamaguchi Prefecture, the most western portion of Honshu. This particular school was the number one middle school at that time. Many prime ministers also had attended that middle school. I also studied military subjects at the same time.

Usually there was only one year of military training, but because my grades were very good, I studied for two years. After one year I tried to pass a test to get into the army, and my score was the best in my school. However, there was another student from my school whose score was not as good as mine. Nevertheless, I found that he passed the test because his father was a high-ranking officer who died in combat. So I thought that the army was not fair and decided not to go there.

I was trained to be a soldier, and passed the test to join the navy. I thought that joining the navy was the only way to advance my career, because I already had two years of military training. Most students studied for five or six years in middle school before entering the Naval Academy, but I entered after four years of study.

Life in the Naval Academy

I entered the Naval Academy on 1 April 1933 and graduated on 23 March 1937, as a member of the 64th Term class. At the academy we studied math, science, foreign languages, and of course, military subjects such as communication and military armament. We also practiced doing physical activities like judo, kendo, and sumo. On Saturdays we had boat training and pole fighting. The pole fighting was really physical, and the men were divided into red and white teams. During that situation, it was permissible to punch or kick to get the pole even if our opponent was a senior. The fourth year students were like my brothers, or even parents to me when I attended the academy. Most of the time, students got three to three and a half years school experience, but in a few classes, including my own, they increased the length of schooling to four years. The increased time was not spent on studying military matters; instead, it was for general knowledge.

After graduation at the academy we had sea training. We served in a training squadron and visited some countries in the Mediterranean. I was on board the *Iwate*, an old cruiser used for training. We traveled to the Sea of Japan, Korea, Mukden (Shenyang), Shanghai, Formosa (now called Taiwan), and once came back to Japan to meet the Emperor. After this our ship sailed out towards Europe. We were cruising in the Indian Ocean in the west when the incident happened in China on 7 July 1937. This was the beginning of the war. We also visited Singapore, Bombay, and Colombo, but I don't remember these places. Then we went to Aden, at the northeastern end of Africa at the entrance of the Red Sea. Our ship went through the Red Sea, the Suez Canal, and

Lieutenant (junior grade) Zenji Abe relaxing in his flight suit. (Abe Collection)

The young Navy officer Zenji Abe in his dress uniform. (Abe Collection)

then into the Mediterranean Sea. During this time we visited Cairo, Greece, Turkey, Italy, and Marseille, France. Half of us also took a one-week trip to Paris.

Our class of one hundred cadets graduated together from the Naval Academy in 1937, and were assigned as midshipmen. After we came back from the training cruise in autumn, perhaps in October, we entered Yokosuka, and all of us went to Kasumigaura—which was an air training school—for one month of flight training and testing.

An important mission of that school was the selection and testing of potential aviators, which was a very difficult process. The navy headquarters employed very special technicians, who made the decision on who would be suitable to become a pilot. During this one month of training they selected from the 160 candidates: those who would be a navigator of a seaplane, a pilot of a bomber or fighter on an aircraft carrier, or a pilot of a twin-engine bombers based on land.

Then I was assigned. In March 1938 we were promoted to ensign from midshipmen. My first assignment was on a new cruiser called the *Kumano* with seven other classmates. In April, one month after being promoted to ensign, I was transferred to *Uzuki*, a destroyer. My assignment on the destroyer was to be an assistant to both the navigator and the communications officer.

Flight Training

In August of that year, I was assigned to Kasumigaura again. Along with trainees from battleships, cruisers, and carriers, I entered school. About thirty or forty of them trained for seaplane duty. An additional thirty were trained for fighters, dive-bombers, and level-bombers. The training was done separately, and lasted for about four months at Kasumigaura.

After four months of basic training on aircraft, I was assigned to be a pilot of a two-seat dive-bomber, and others became fighter pilots. Ten of my classmates were assigned to be pilots of carrier-based fighters, while only four were assigned as carrier-based *kanbaku*. I was one of the four pilots of the two-seat dive-bomber. Ten others were assigned to the Nakajima Type 97 *kankō*, which was used for torpedo attacks. Finally, another group of ten men were trained to be navigators on carrier-based aircraft.

After we finished the training course I went to Kyūshū for special training for dive-bomber pilots with the Ōmura *Kōkūtai*. After doing specialized dive-bomber training for four or five months my training was finished. Then I was promoted from ensign to lieutenant junior grade and assigned to Saeki Air Base. Following this, on 1 November 1940 I went on board the *Sōryū*, which was the first aircraft carrier I was assigned to. On 20 August of the following year (1941) I transferred from *Sōryū* to *Akagi* as the

An illustration of the typical dive-bombing technique utilized by Japanese Navy pilots during the war. (George Zielinski A.G.P.)

Zenji Abe with his first wife, Kuniko. She passed away in 1984. (Abe Collection)

buntaichō of the second *chūtai* of dive-bombers, and was promoted to the rank of full lieutenant. Finally, in late October or November the Imperial Navy rotated personnel. So from December to March or April was the first step of training for many rookie pilots.

We trained for the massed use of these planes. In ship battles, always the champion was the big gun, the battleship. This was the idea of the old Imperial Japanese Navy. However, Admiral Isoroku Yamamoto believed in order to fight against the United States we had to attack by massed power of aircraft carriers and planes, so we massed and assembled the same types of aircraft from the six carriers.

Training for Pearl Harbor

In my recollections before the formation of the First Air Fleet in April 1941, each carrier or squadron had its own training for carrier-based planes.[19] After April 1941, all the air groups under the First Air Fleet left from the command of carrier captains and were separated by types: Mitsubishi Type 0 carrier fighters, Aichi Type 99 carrier bombers and Nakajima Type 97 carrier attack planes. This type of training was different than the previous training. They gathered in certain air bases to undergo joint training. After October, the number of night exercises decreased and daytime exercises of large mixed groups of fighters, carrier bombers and carrier attack planes were more emphasized.

Our *kanbaku* pilots trained on the east coast of Kyūshū (Tomitaka, in Miyazaki Prefecture), and concentrated on improving our accuracy rate. Usually dive-bombers went down at a 55-degree angle from 800 meters (2,624 feet) to try to drop a bomb, but it was usually inaccurate. Hence, we tried to lower the altitude to 600 meters (1,968 feet), but it still was not accurate. I was good at flying, so I was able to do this technique from 400 meters (1,312 feet). I also needed to use the air brakes so the wing wouldn't break apart. There is a lot of gravity (5-6Gs), and it's a split second decision.

When I dove down all the blood went out of my brain, and I was momentarily blind. At this time I was 20-30 meters (66-99 feet) above sea level, and my bomb, although small, was usually effective against an aircraft carrier. So if you were late less than one second, you would crash into the sea. During training there were many accidents, as well. Our target was usually a white ship painted on the beach. We once had a moving target, and also used a dummy bomb two or three times. We practiced every day, but at the time, there were no electronic systems to use for flying on a rainy or foggy day, so we could not fly. Instead, we did self-study on those days.

I also got married in 1940, and my first son was born in 15 May 1941, on the same day that I was promoted to lieutenant. The Japanese Imperial Navy actually did a background check of my wife before we could get married.

Feelings toward Japanese Naval Airplanes

The Aichi Type 99 *kanbaku* was a good plane at that time. I think carrier bomber design was often a step behind fighter and carrier attack plane designs because it was more difficult to develop and manufacture. The Aichi Type 96 carrier bomber was a biplane, while the Mitsubishi Type 96 carrier fighter was a low wing monoplane. The Nakajima Type 97 *kankō* was a monoplane with retractable undercarriage. We finally got a monoplane with the Type 99, but it had a fixed undercarriage.

Dive-bombers had to be rugged for dives, and also had to be able to engage in air to air combat like a two-seat fighter. Having a multi-role requirement made it more difficult for designers. I became very comfortable flying the Type 99, so it was a good aircraft to fly, although I wished it was faster. Of course, that was solved with the Yokosuka *Suisei kanbaku*. That was a very advanced design, and for the first time, dive-bomber design was more advanced than a fighter or carrier attack plane. It was even faster than the Mitsubishi Type 0 *kansen*.[20] In general, Japanese Navy aircraft were characterized by the lack of self-sealing tanks and armor plates. It was not that the designers did not care for the crew. Instead, more priority was put on the aircraft's performance and flying range than survival of the crew. Therefore, one advantage we had compared to allied aircraft was an excellent flying range.

Skills for being a good pilot

In order to be a good pilot, you have to be able to pay attention to many things at one time. For example, you have to always keep an eye on the people flying beside and behind your aircraft. There also are many things to look at in the cockpit, such as the altimeter and engine temperature gauge, but you can't always look at these things and fly at the same time. Hence, you had to know these things without looking. Sometimes, you have to check these gauges, but at any given moment you have to know many things off the top of your head.

The Pearl Harbor attack

I heard for the first time about the proposed Pearl Harbor attack in October 1941, but didn't feel excited or scared. I didn't think much at that time. I actually thought that it was going to happen, because ten years prior to this, Japan was in a difficult financial situation, and many men died fighting in China. The whole situation was gloomy, so I thought something was going to happen.

On the day of the attack I woke up between 0330-0400, and our carriers were about 200 miles north-northeast of Oahu. I didn't have any excitement or special emotion prior to my sortie. I was calm, just as if I was going on a training mission. It seemed to me that my men realized that it was an honor to be a member of a great operation in this century. Morale was quite high, especially among the *kanbaku* units, and there was nothing more that could be desired for the group. They also were extremely confident in their skills.

The airplanes were lined up after getting them out of the hangar. There were two attack waves, because they could not fit all the airplanes on the deck at the same time due to limited space. It took about ten to fifteen minutes to warm up the first wave of aircraft. The aircraft of the first wave were sent to the rear of the carrier in accordance to the flight order, then the aircraft carriers turned into the wind, which was coming from a little to the northeast.

We had to think of the speed of the wind and the speed of the carrier and put them together. For example, if your ship was traveling at twenty knots, it meant ten meters per second speed. This speed, combined with the wind speed of 10 meters (33 feet) per second, meant an overall speed of 20 meters (66 feet) per second. With an overall speed of twenty meters per second, it was an ideal situation for our airplanes to take off, because on a carrier we had a short runway compared to airfields that were land-based.

We also were thinking about the timing to take off. If I tried to take off from land, it might take eight hundred meters, but considering the wind and speed, I might be able to take off within eighty to a hundred meters. So it was 0600 and dark when the planes of the first wave took off from the six aircraft carriers. I was in the second wave, so I was watching them take off from a middle section between the deck and the bridge. Of course, everyone couldn't be on the deck when the planes were taking off, so they were watching from the side of the ship. The aircraft carrier also was pitching and rolling at this time. Since the fighters were the first airplanes to take off, they only had a short distance to do so and it was very difficult. When the first airplane took off it momentarily disappeared, so we felt relieved when it reappeared.

They took off first in small groups, then gathered up in a medium-sized group before finally forming a large group. There were 183 planes, and it took fifteen minutes to join a formation. I saw blue on the right and red on the left, so it looked like a firebug that was circling—and it was beautiful. The aircraft carrier was going to the east, so it went back to the south and began to prepare the next wave. The second wave started about one hour later after the launch of the first wave. At 0750 the first wave attacked, and at 0730 Japan was supposed to declare war, but it didn't happen. I had previously written letters to my wife and children, and left them in my private chamber before I took off for the attack. However, I didn't feel any special sadness or excitement. During the attack I carried a handgun, and it is my understanding that it would be used to kill myself if I had to land in an enemy-held territory.

After the second wave took off, it took about one hour and twenty minutes to reach Oahu, because we were flying about 125 knots indicated airspeed. I thought that I was in a privileged position, because I was looking at the scene from behind as the leader of the tail end group of Type 99 *kanbaku*. The total group was comprised of 167 airplanes, and eight airplanes were following me. So about 150 airplanes were in front of me. For example, if the first group of fighters were flying at 3,000 meters (9,842 feet), then the airplanes following them should be a little above the proceeding airplanes because of "prop wash." I was looking at the proceeding airplanes from above and felt like a sheep herder. Our group was going to the south towards Oahu Island, but it was very cloudy, and I couldn't see the island. I was worried if we were going in the right direction.

The *Akagi's* second wave aircraft with their engines being warmed up. (Makiel Collection via Wenger)

An *Akagi kanbaku* takes off during the second wave. (Makiel Collection via Wenger)

When I was flying I received a Morse code message, "Tora! Tora! Tora!" which meant it was a successful surprise attack. It also meant that the torpedo bombers should attack first. If there wasn't this message, the fighters and carrier bombers were to attack first, but it didn't happen. The radioman received the message and told me it was a success. At this time, I also saw the first wave for the first time, and while I was looking ahead, I saw clouds. Right above the clouds, at about 3,000 meters (9,842 feet), I saw many flashes from anti-aircraft guns, which were gradually coming closer to us. For a moment I felt a chill go through my spine, since this was the first time that enemy fire was directed at me. It was a very quick response from America, so I was worried if the attack was really a surprise, because the enemy responded so quickly. This wouldn't have happened if Japan had to respond to an American attack. After looking at the seventy-eight Type 99 carrier bombers led by our leader, Lieutenant Commander Takashige Egusa, continually flying in a tight, unwavering formation toward Diamond Head, I immediately regained my composure.

My flight route for the mission was the following: first to Kaneohe, then to Diamond Head, afterwards to Honolulu, and finally to Ford Island, where the aircraft carriers would be located. After we started to attack, I had to focus my attention on sighting and confirming our targets, so it became impossible to think about anything else.

Before taking off I received the final information about our attack. I was part of the Type 99 *kanbaku* group from the second wave attack. This group was flying higher than the other groups. I learned that there were no aircraft carriers, so I was told to attack the same targets as the first wave. Many people thought that 250 kilogram (551 pound) bombs could not sink capital ships, such as battleships or cruisers, so the original plan for the dive-bombers was to attack the carriers. However, I was disappointed because there were no aircraft carriers to attack.

I believe I attacked the *Arizona*, but at that time, I didn't know what ship I was attacking.[21] All I was thinking about was the two paired-up ships on the east side of the island that I heard about. I was looking at the ship from above and didn't know that it was the *Arizona*, but I clearly remember seeing the shape of the *Vestal*, which was anchored near the outer side of the *Arizona*. However, when I attacked the ship was sinking, because it was attacked by the first wave. I confirmed an outline of a huge warship prior to dropping my bomb; however, I didn't see any upper structures, flames, or smoke. As soon as I dropped my bomb I had to escape from the location quickly. Our group scattered momentarily, and then we had to have a place to meet again. The meeting point was twenty miles west of Kaena Point. The altitude was 1,000 meters (3,281 feet) at the rendezvous point after the attack. When I arrived back on *Akagi* some people had died, and I realized the war had really begun.

I believe that the reason why Japan attacked Pearl Harbor was because it wanted several Asian countries to get their independence from European countries, such as England, and co-exist in the world community. Japan also didn't have enough food for itself, so it had to survive for trading purposes. Our nation also depended on the United States for fifty percent of its food and energy at that time. Japan needed four months to free these Asian countries, and it also had to stop America from attacking our country. Pearl Harbor was chosen because it would prevent America from getting into Asia. This is what a lot of historians say is the rationale for attacking Pearl Harbor. I think Japan should not have attacked Pearl Harbor; it was such a waste. Because of Pearl Harbor, the war escalated into the Pacific war.

Lieutenant Abe on the flight deck of *Akagi*. (Abe Collection via Wenger)

Life on board *Akagi*

Regarding the living conditions on *Akagi*, I was an officer, so I had a cook. However, one month or so before going on board the carrier I had to buy my food supplies. I had to pay for it myself because the government didn't pay for the officers' food. In the morning I used to eat *miso shiru* and fish. In the afternoon, I used to eat western food like soup and coffee. At night, I would eat raw fish. I thought the food tasted pretty good on *Akagi*. I was a lieutenant, so I had my own cabin. After dinner I could have read books, but since I was a leader, I played *Go* and card games.

When I was not flying I went to the airplane hangar and into the cockpit of my airplane. Then I looked at the instrument panel and mentally simulated the situation. Also, there was simulation training, but it was not effective. This is because we were looking at the enemy from a horizontal view, but in combat, I looked at my target from above. The perspective was different, so it was not effective. I sometimes read an old Chinese military book. There was a small library on the aircraft carrier, and I read some books.

I believe both the officers and the enlisted men were connected mentally. Even though the food and places to sleep were separated and different, there was no friction. For example, my radioman, WO Chiaki Saitō (who participated in the Pearl Harbor attack with me), was a gentleman. Even though he was older than I and had two or three years more experience, Saitō-san helped me. We spent one year in Kyūshū together before attacking Pearl Harbor, and my flying partner gave me some presents. He made a battle scarf for me, which was made from silk, and a belt. Sadly, Saitō-san later died in action on 15 June 1944 in the Marianas.

Action in the Indian Ocean

At that time Britain and America were supporting Burma, and the location was in the Bengal Bay, near Ceylon. On 5 April 1942, a reconnaissance plane found the British ships about 200 miles away. The *chūtaichō* (Lieutenant Takehiko Chihaya) was sick at that time, so he asked me to lead the group. There were seventeen airplanes in my group, and fifteen were successful. There were

Abe-san and a Type 99 *kanbaku* at Iwakuni Air Base in January 1942. (Abe Collection via Wenger)

Abe-san noted every combat mission he flew on this scarf, which is on display at the National Museum of the Pacific War (Fredericksburg, Texas). (National Museum of the Pacific War Collection)

three aircraft carriers: *Akagi*, *Sōryū*, and *Hiryū*, and each carrier had eighteen planes, except my group from *Akagi*. Prior to this attack nobody thought our bombs could sink a cruiser, but we hit them many times.

The usual attack for our dive-bombers was done this way. The commander led the group, and when we started to attack, we made one line. The commander was at the top, and he figured out the timing and went down to 2,500 meters (8,202 feet). At that time the angle was twenty to thirty degrees. Then he went down to 400 meters (1,312 feet), and we commenced our attack at a fifty-five degree angle.

I personally hit the HMS *Dorsetshire*, which was trying to escape, and they turned the ship suddenly.[22] I don't remember well, but I saw smoke but no fire on the ship. It was trying to escape at full speed, so there was a large wake because the ship was going so fast. The ship was shooting its guns as well. It took fifteen minutes for the ship to sink, and men were swimming around it. Our dive-bombers had an amazing 86% successful hit rate for this attack.[23]

On 9 April, we flew the same formation as above to attack the *Hermes*, but aircraft from *Zuikaku* and *Shōkaku* joined so they flew first, then the aircraft from *Sōryū*, *Hiryū*, and *Akagi*. *Hermes* didn't have any escorts, so it tried to escape to the south. The ship sank quickly compared to the HMS *Cornwall* and HMS *Dorsetshire*. We also attacked using more airplanes. Some people later said we should change the way we attack because if we lined up, they tried to shoot the same position, and it was easier to target us. In those days, however, we just lined up 100-150 meters (328-492 feet) apart and didn't think about what would happen to us. Our attack was successful because our skills were very high at that time, the weather was calm, and the *Hermes* didn't have any escorts.

The Dutch Harbor Attack

After finishing the Indian Ocean operation in April 1942 I returned to the mainland at Yokosuka. I was transferred from *Akagi* to *Junyō* as a *buntaichō*. In late April 1942, I focused all of my efforts on the training of my two *chūtais* of Type 99s. Later, the carrier *Junyō* joined Carrier Division 4 and participated in the second phase of Japan's war operations. The first phase began with the Pearl Harbor attack and the occupation of the Southeast Asia area, which lasted three or four months. In the second phase of operations, the headquarters didn't have an exact idea of what to do next, because the first phase had achieved more than they ever expected.

The *Junyō* was the second ship of Carrier Division 4, which took part in the second phase of operations on 20 May 1942.

Akagi's strike aircraft on 5 April 1942 getting ready to launch. (Wenger Collection)

Above: The British heavy cruisers HMS *Dorsetshire* and HMS *Cornwall* being attacked by Type 99 carrier bombers from the *Sōryū*, *Hiryū*, and *Akagi* on 5 April 1942. (NHC – Pineau Collection via Wenger) Below: The British aircraft carrier *Hermes* sinking after being hit by the Japanese strike group on 9 April 1942. (NA via Wenger)

We went on board the carrier, but fifty percent of this group was trainee pilots, and their training period was too short to join the actual operation. They were also deficient in maneuvering tactics. While on the *Junyō*, my part in the Midway operation was the attack on the Aleutians. The Aleutians campaign was planned for two reasons. First, to secure Imperial Japanese held islands, such as Attu and Kiska. Secondly, from the fear that the Americans and the Russians would join hands through the Aleutians—that was the ultimate nightmare. However, I realized that all that was totally unnecessary when I got there and saw the weather conditions of the islands. June was one of the better times of the year to be in the Aleutians, but it still was very foggy.

During this time the only data that we had on Dutch Harbor was an old map that had been published thirty years prior, and a photograph that was taken by a Japanese fishing boat in the Bering Sea. We didn't have any recent intelligence data, and nobody knew if there was an airfield or not. So there was nothing that we could study, and I didn't know where Dutch Harbor was located. On 26 May we left Ominato bound for the Aleutians, and several hours later our task force was in the fog. From this time until we returned to Ominato in the middle of June our sight was very limited due to low heavy clouds and thick fog outside. There was only one occasion that I recall seeing a blue sky.

Our Carrier Division 4 reached the vicinity of Dutch Harbor, which was about 200 miles south of Unalaska Island, on 3 June 1942. After this we received our orders to commence the air attack. At 0240 I took off, leading two *chūtais* of Type 99 *kanbaku*. We reached the target area, but heavy clouds prevented us from accomplishing our objectives. At 0945 we tried to approach the target again, but due to terrible weather we were once again forced to return to the carrier. On our way back we encountered an American PBY Catalina at low altitude under the clouds.

Fort Mears after being attacked by *Ryūjō's* Type 97 *kankō* level-bombers (Dutch Harbor, Unalaska Island). (NA via Cressman/Wenger)

In the afternoon of the following day, 4 June 1942, Admiral Kakuta ordered me to bomb Dutch Harbor, which was our third try. He was a gunnery man, and did not know much about air operations. When I returned from two abortive missions because of fog, an unhappy Kakuta (who was aboard the carrier *Ryūjō*) pressured me by sending a message saying that the *Ryūjō* planes had bombed their targets. I was very angry with this, because *Ryūjō* did not carry Type 99 *kanbaku*. Level bombing can be done even under somewhat cloudy situations. Dive-bombers could not do so because they had to dive through the clouds instead of just flying over them, and that was very dangerous if the cloud level was very low. Prior to getting the radio message I had suggested that it was not possible to dive-bomb, but Admiral Kakuta refused to be convinced. For Kakuta-san, this was the first time he had dive-bomber units under his command (he only had the *Ryūjō*, with Zero fighters and Type 97 *kankō* (being used as level bombers)), and was dying to use the famed dive-bombers that showed amazing accuracy in the Indian Ocean Campaign.

The *Akagi* dive-bombers recorded fifteen hits out of seventeen bombs released; this was magic to any gunnery man, because heavy batteries could record only a 1 or 2% hit rate. This accuracy was achieved through the intense training before Pearl Harbor. Japanese dive-bombers would dive at 50-60 degrees and release at 400 meters (1,312 feet). Then they pulled out hard and would almost black out, and they would be barely 30 meters (99 feet) above the water by the time they leveled out. At any rate, the commanding staff remarked that the *Ryūjō* Type 97s had already bombed targets, and implicitly said that I was a coward after I returned with my unit without bombing anything for two consecutive missions, making "excuses" about weather. So I was angry and determined to fulfill my mission at the next possible opportunity.

On 4 June I believed that, due to foul weather and thick clouds covering Unalaska Island, our attack would be thwarted once again, and it would not be possible for us to make an accurate bombing. It also would be difficult to fly in formation. In lieu of the above situation, I intentionally decreased the number of attack aircraft for

The barracks ship *Northwestern* ablaze after being bombed on 4 June 1942. (NA via Cressman/Wenger)

this operation. The first *chūtai* had six planes, and the second *chūtai* had five planes, which excluded the young, unskilled pilots from the mission. I selected eleven experienced pilots out of eighteen men who would be able to handle the poor weather conditions, and we took off at 1430 bound for Dutch Harbor.

While flying at 2000 meters (6,561 feet), we were circling above the clouds, looking for a patch of clear sky that we could dive through. Somehow the escorting Zero fighters led by Lieutenant Yoshio Shiga had disappeared. I had only my "*kōgeki-seishin*" (attacking spirit) and nothing else. My morale was low, because I knew that the Aleutian fleet was a decoy. I had no idea what military installations were there, and basically told my subordinates to find a hole in the clouds, dive, and drop their bombs on anything that came into view.

With these eleven planes we found our target through a small hole in the clouds. Flak from the anti-aircraft guns covered the sky around us. After I finished my bombing attack, I flew west of Unalaska Island, but noted that just two of the aircraft from my group had followed me. The cloud ceiling also was as low as 300 meters (984 feet), and after our bombing attack we crept along until we came into the Bering Sea. The group leaders, PO1c Hajime Numata and WO Nobuo Harano, were very close to me, but the other aircraft were out of sight. Our three planes flew along the northern part of the Unalaska Islands.

According to our operation plan, we were supposed to go to a rendezvous point, which we called "*Maru Nishi*" by transmitter as a signaling code over the western cape of Unalaska Island.[24] I decided to wait for our Zero escorts at "*Maru Nishi*" along with the other dive-bombers. I began to get impatient, and wanted to return to my carrier with the rest of my men. After a while, I noticed something bright on my left side and believed that it must be the Umnak Channel. Then we went through the south of the channel. I thought that we had arrived at "*Maru Nishi*," and could see several smaller aircraft under the clouds. Around the channel area there were little clouds, and we flew at 300 meters (984 feet) altitude. I thought that these airplanes must be Zero fighters and felt relieved. I became very optimistic at that moment, and hoped to be able to rendezvous with my comrades' aircraft at "*Maru Nishi*" and return to the *Junyō*. For a moment, I thought that these were the Zero escorts that were lost before the bombing, but that couldn't be, because there were only four Zeros to start with. After this, I was shocked that what I thought to be Zeros' drop tanks were actually the radiators on nine enemy P-40 fighters. I then knew that our group had been ambushed.

This occurred while I was flying towards the direction of the Umnak Channel over the Bering Strait, with clouds down to 100 meters (328 feet) above the sea. To the east of us was Unalaska Island, and to the west was the Umnak Islands. I figured that there was no other way of returning to my carrier some 200 miles away to the south without going through the channel. The first thought in my mind was to run into the clouds. However, it occurred to me that one of my classmates was killed in a mid-air collision when he led a formation of Zeros into a cloud.[25] The Type 99 *kanbaku* was equipped with forward firing 7.7 mm machine guns, and dive-bomber pilots did get air to air combat training, and since my aircraft was very agile at low altitude, I decided to fight it out.

All of a sudden, I was attacked by P-40s from both sides. I threw my Type 99 into a tight turn, and soon my group's *kanbaku* and the enemy P-40s were going after each other in circles. I knew that the low ceiling would not allow the quick P-40s to zoom down on the dive-bombers like they usually do, so I thought that I would have a chance in a dogfight. I fought back against one of them, but another one shot at me. My comrade, WO Nobuo Harano, chased after it. So the air battle became a confusing aerial melee. I saw another comrade, PO1c Hajime Numata, engaged in a dogfight with a P-40 about 300 meters (984 feet) above the sea in some low clouds. They were circling vertically, each trying to get on the other's tail. I was sweating profusely, and time seemed to stand still, but it was only a few seconds. A little later, I found that both WO Harano and PO1c Numata were shot down and crashed into the sea.

Several P-40s were still flying around, and I figured that they were based on the east side of the Umnak Islands. I also noted that the Americans had steel plates over the tundra to make an airfield, on which there were parked more P-40s.[26] Our aircraft did put up a good fight, but I saw three trails of smoke go down, and I could no longer see other Type 99s, so I figured I was now alone, and escaped into the clouds. I also am certain our group shot one of the P-40s down, probably jointly.

The second group leader, WO Hiroshi Yamamoto, transmitted a message that he had just run out of fuel and was going to ditch in the water. A little later, PO2c Takeshi Sugie transmitted the following message, "I shot down an enemy plane and am returning to the ship." PO2c Sugie and PO3c Okada were with us on our first battle campaign and the youngest amongst us. They also were members of Yamamoto's group.

About thirty minutes later I received his message, which stated, "I am flying over 200 degrees, but cannot see the aircraft carrier, so please generate smoke for confirmation use." My understanding was that he was alone and lost. The carrier continually transmitted a message to PO2c Sugie to start sending a long wave message, but he did not respond to *Junyō*. So, it is possible that his radio receiving equipment wasn't working properly. He reported to the aircraft carrier, "I turned my plane over twenty degrees north." Sugie-san did this because our task force was maneuvering about 200 miles down south from Unalaska Island and was flying towards this position. However, he could not find *Junyō*, and the young aviator thought that he passed by the carrier because of the clouds and fog. After this he turned up north and said, "Turn on your searchlight! I cannot find the aircraft carrier. Please release smoke. Please turn on your searchlight!" He asked this while I had my radio on.

I don't remember how many anti-aircraft shells hit my aircraft, but several did hit my plane. There was a big hole in my wing, and the hydraulic oil pump on the flap was damaged, so it was very difficult to land. On the aircraft carrier there were many wires to stop my plane, but I went all the way to the end of the deck and almost fell overboard.

Immediately upon landing I ran to the radio room and ordered the operator to send a long wave message to PO2c Sugie right now.

The remains of Second Lieutenant Winfield McIntyre's Curtiss P-40E fighter, which was shot down on 4 June 1942, awaiting restoration at the Alaskan Aviation Heritage Museum (Anchorage, Alaska). (Alaskan Aviation Heritage Museum)

Group photo of the *Junyō kanbaku-tai* prior to the Dutch Harbor attack in May 1942. Last row (standing), from the left: second person, Kaichi Harada; fourth person, PO3c Kunio Osemoto; and tenth person, PO3c Shinsaku Yamakawa. Middle row, from the left: third person, Lieutenant (junior grade) Kazuya Kurihara; fourth person, Lieutenant Commander Yoshiro Sakinaga (*hikōchō*); fifth person, Lieutenant Zenji Abe; and next person, PO1c Hajime Numata. (Abe collection)

He transmitted this message, "Do your best until you run out of the last drop of fuel." This was the only thing I could do for him at that time, though I knew that Sugie-san would never hear me.

Looking back at the various events of World War II, I am absolutely convinced that the Aleutian campaign in 1942 was unnecessary. It also did not make any sense to occupy the Attu and Kiska Islands. If Midway was our primary objective, I really wonder why our headquarters did not concentrate the majority of our forces there. Instead, we divided our forces into two separate groups. In my opinion, the Aleutian campaign should not have been carried out.

Abe-san and the other Japanese Navy pilots fought against eight Curtiss P-40 fighters flown by members of the 11th Fighter Squadron.[27] *Their airbase was located at Otter Point, Umnak Island. Second Lieutenants Lester Chancellor, James Dale, and Herbert White were credited with shooting down a Type 99 "Val" dive-bomber. Second Lieutenant John Cape Jr. also received credit for shooting down a Zero fighter.*[28] *Unfortunately, Cape was subsequently shot down by a group of Zero fighters and crashed into the ocean. Nothing of him or his aircraft were ever found. Second Lieutenant Winfield McIntyre was also shot down in his P-40E fighter over another part of the island, but he later was rescued and arrived back at his base with a bad gash on his forehead.*[29]

The following Japanese aviators died during the above attack mission that Abe-san described: pilots PO1c Yukio Ōishi, PO3c Tadao Okada, PO1c Hajime Numata, and WO Nobuo Harano. The reconnaissance men who died with their pilots were WO Hiroshi Yamamoto, PO2c Takeshi Sugie, PO2c Yoshio Takano, and PO1c Ichirō Nakajima. The Japanese air attacks resulted in forty-three American casualties and fifty wounded. The attacks also destroyed four oil tanks, 20,000 barrels of fuel oil, two barracks, four huts, one 20mm gun and emplacement, and one Navy PBY-5A Catalina flying boat was destroyed on the ground. They also damaged the Northwestern, *a barracks ship, one warehouse, and one hangar.*[30]

Landing on board a Carrier

This is what it was like to fly an airplane off a carrier: Before landing we circled around the carrier, and there was a large circular ring painted on the deck near the second and third wire (on the center line) which meant a perfect landing.[31] Then, we did our final turn and were flying at a level of 200 meters (656 feet). Japanese Navy pilots had to adjust our aircraft to a seven-degree angle because the main wheels were bigger than the tail wheel. We did this so we could make a level landing.

The goal at 200 meters was to gradually reduce the speed by adjusting the throttle and flaps, but we didn't want to stall the engine. So if the engine looked like it would stall, we had to adjust the throttle. The ship also was pitching and rolling. There were green and red lamps on the left, and we glanced at these while landing. The *hikōchō* calculated the position of the lamps, and if they merged together, it was the right angle to land. There were about ten wires to stop our airplanes on the deck of a carrier. The first wire was on the edge of the boat, so it was impossible to use. If we landed using the second wire our landing was perfect. When we landed the wires stretched for about 20-30 meters (66-98 feet), and the aircraft stopped.

I was very good at landing, and if I could stop at the second wire and do a perfect landing, I could get a five yen bonus. In those days sixty yen was the monthly salary. The maximum was six bonuses per month. In the navy flight hours were important, but also the quality and number of times you landed on a carrier. I landed on a carrier 440 times, which was probably the most in the navy. I believe this is a very honorable thing. I worked only on a carrier, and in my opinion, only carrier pilots are real pilots.

On 11 November 1942, Lieutenant Abe's Type 99 carrier bombers from the carrier *Hiyō* attacked the transport USS *Zeilin* (AP-9), which was anchored north of Guadalcanal Island. (NA via Cressman/Wenger)

Take off is the most difficult thing about flying from a carrier. On land, for example, we needed 500 meters (1,640 feet) to take off, but on a carrier there were about thirty airplanes, and the length was only 200 meters (656 feet). So if thirty airplanes were on board, the first airplane had less than 100 meters to take off. What made it possible was that we used the wind, and we adjusted our direction towards the wind. When we adjusted the direction, there was a hole at the front of the ship that released steam. The *hikōtaichō* looked at the steam and a white line on the deck, then made his calculations according to the way steam moved towards it. Also, we had the speed of the ship. For example, if it was moving at 20 knots, it had a speed of 10 meters per second. So we mixed this together, and it was called the relative speed. After this the *hikōtaichō* calculated how fast the ship should go to make adjustments. However, in the case of *Junyō*, one of my ships, it was not originally designed as a carrier, so it had only a top speed of 25 knots, while a carrier should have over 30 knots.

Guadalcanal Strike

On 31 July 1942 I became the *buntaichō* on *Hiyō*. In September and October we operated near Southeast Asia, and *Hiyō* became part of Carrier Division 2 after we had lost four aircraft carriers at Midway. We conducted combat operations in the Solomon Islands. For *Hiyō* it was the carrier's first cruise after it was manufactured, and the carrier had engine trouble. They couldn't run, so I left *Hiyō* for Buin, which is located on the south end of Bougainville Island. The island was a part of the Solomon Islands, and it is the most western one. My group of aircraft landed there, and we were supposed to attack a transport ship group anchored north of Guadalcanal. Lieutenant Commander Tadashi Kaneko, a *Hiyō* fighter pilot, escorted us with eighteen Zeros.[32] They said later that our Zeros shot down twenty airplanes.

In my case, we had two *chūtais* flying at 6,000 meters (19,685 feet). Thirty Grumman F4F Wildcat fighters were waiting for us in the air because they used radar. So shortly after we engaged the enemy fighters, and I saw a dogfight in the air above me. After I bombed a ship, I could see only four airplanes following me. Out of my group of nine airplanes, five airplanes were shot down, but one of the five crash-landed on an island, and the pilot was picked up after several days.

This mission took place on 11 November 1942. Lieutenant Tadashi Kaneko commanded eighteen Zero escort fighters from the Hiyō Hikōkitai *and 204* Kōkūtai, *while Lieutenant Abe led nine* Hiyō *Type 99* kanbaku. *Their opponents were twenty-one Grumman F4F Wildcats from VMF-121, VMF-212, VMO-251, and VMF-112. Anti-aircraft was heavy, but Abe's carrier bombers scored three near misses near the transport USS* Zeilin *(AP-9) that caused a hold to flood. They also slightly damaged two other transports. A total of five of the Type 99s were lost, but one crew was rescued after crash landing. Two* Hiyō *Zero fighters flown by PO2c Isamu Yoshiwara and PO2c Toshio Morita also were shot down. American losses consisted of four F4F pilots: Second Lieutenants Joseph L. Narr, Roy M.A. Ruddell, and Robert F. Simpson, all of VMF-121, and Master Technical Sgt. William H. Coahran, Jr., of VMF-112.*[33]

Shore Duty

After this I was transferred back to Japan. I guess the reason I was transferred to inland shore duty from the aircraft carrier was due to a rather simple rotation procedure, which was managed by the Administrative Division of the Naval Ministry. Because of this reason I did not receive any special training or mission. Generally the Imperial Japanese Navy, in peacetime, rotated our carrier pilots under the following working formula: one-year duty on an aircraft carrier, and then one or two years of shore duty. I served continuously for two years on aircraft carriers. I also came down with malaria, and returned to Japan on board a destroyer. Therefore, it was quite natural that I was assigned to shore duty in November 1942, and became the *buntaichō* and flight instructor at Tsukuba *Kōkūtai*.

By this time we had sent millions of troops to China. We didn't have any resources, such as fuel, iron, tin, and natural rubber. In the past, Japan bought iron and more than fifty percent of its fuel from America. Since war broke out in China, Japan was exhausted by the never-ending battles, one after another, with no sign of improvement. In fact, there was a shortage of goods and materials, and even our meals were controlled by special distribution procedures. By this time everyone in Japan felt very disheartened. We saw our great losses, such as the death of our Commander-in-chief, Admiral Isoroku Yamamoto.[34] In addition to this, there was a suicidal attack on Attu Island by 3,000 or 4,000 of our troops. So, we were so worn down and could not initiate an effective battle strategy against Allied forces.

Action in the Marianas

On 10 March 1944 I was appointed as group leader of Carrier Division 2. Then I started organizing four *chūtais* of carrier bombers consisting of three *chūtais* of nine planes each of the Type 99s and one *chūtai* (nine planes) of *Suisei kanbaku*. The total number of airplanes was thirty-six, and training was done off Iwakuni Air Base.

Each *hikōtai* was instructed to get together on their respective carriers on 10 May, to move to an advanced base in the southern territory. The reason for this was that the quantity of petroleum saved in Japan was being reduced, so we became unable to supply fuel for flight training. Furthermore, we needed to prepare for any future battles with the U.S. Navy, which was advancing with great force in the Pacific.

We went to Tawi Tawi, which is very close to Borneo. It is located on the southwestern end of the Philippines. Since Borneo had an abundant supply of oil we went there, but we still couldn't do proper training for our aviators. This is because the *Junyō* was converted to an aircraft carrier, and its speed was slow. In that season, the Pacific Ocean didn't have enough natural wind. In order to take off or land on an aircraft carrier for the *Suisei* carrier bombers, at least eighteen meters per second was necessary, but the natural winds in that season were less than five meters per second. So we couldn't take off, and had no training after we left Japan from early May until 19 June, when the big American task force came over to the Marianas to attack Guam and Saipan. I attacked on 19 June, but we came over there in the middle of May 1944. So for forty or fifty days, we had no training flights at all.

After nearly one month of staying in Tawi Tawi, we received information that the U.S. Navy was advancing in the area. Then, at last on 13 June 1944, we departed toward the battle area. Immediately after that we heard that U.S. Task Force 58 commenced its attack on the Mariana Islands. As commander of the second attack group of Carrier Division 2, I was assigned to attack one of the enemy's carrier formations with our four squadrons of our carrier bombers. The target was reported by our reconnaissance floatplane to be approximately 400 miles from our take off point. Our carrier-based aircraft had a combat flying radius of about 250 miles or so, we would have no fuel to return. Therefore, an unusual instruction was given to us that we would refuel on Guam after the attack. Then, on the following day, we were to return to our carriers again. We had a basic problem of the flying speed between two different types of *kanbaku*, the Type 99 and the *Suisei*. The Type 99 flew at about 145 knots, and the *Suisei* flew at 180 knots, so we were unable to keep the same formation.

On 19 June I took off from the carrier *Junyō* at 1145, and was accompanied by six Zero fighters under my command. While flying amongst our group of *Suisei* carrier bombers, I could not hear my navigator Ensign Nakajima's voice through a voice tube, perhaps because of engine noise. It seemed that he also could not hear me either. I was suffering from a very unusual physical condition caused by prolonged fatigue, and felt I was in a plane being flown by somebody else. I was sure that all of the other aviators were feeling the same way. Suddenly, the second bomber (from my lead section) and the third section leader had to return to the carrier because their landing gear failed to retract. One Zero fighter had an engine problem, so it also returned. Now I was flying at 6,000 meters (19,685 feet) toward the east, and after one hour passed, I was surprised to see that one *Suisei* and three Zeros had disappeared. I really wondered if they left the formation due to mechanical trouble or dove into the sea from mental confusion. That's why our formation ended up being only six *Suisei* carrier bombers and two Zero fighters.

We continued flying an additional hour, and arrived in the target area. However, we could not find the enemy fleet or Lieutenant Yasunori Miyauchi's group of Type 99s. Because of this I was forced to give up the originally assigned attack plan, and flew down to about 4,000 meters (13,123 feet) while still looking for enemy forces. All of a sudden Ensign Nakajima said, "Sir, big enemy formation, left forward." I saw a circular disposition with distinct white wakes over the left part of my engine cowling. Then the command was given to all aircraft to commence their attacks, and I myself began to accelerate my airplane. It was my understanding that the enemy caught us well in advance, so they had several enemy Grumman F6F Hellcat fighters preparing to engage us from the opposite direction. I could see that the ships were making broad white wakes. Although it was almost too late to reach the best point of diving towards this big formation, I realized we could not wait even a few more seconds. Otherwise, we would have been shot by the Grumman fighters. I started swooping towards a large aircraft carrier in the middle of the ring disposition and commenced my attack. During my attack I dove through a lot of black smoke, which was caused by anti-aircraft fire, and dropped my bomb.

Abe's unit attacked at about 1426. They had three near misses on the carrier Wasp *that caused a small internal fire and injured two men on the flight deck. A fourth bomb exploded about 300 feet above the flight deck, possibly hit by anti-aircraft fire, and dispersed bits of flammable phosphorus on the carrier. Two* Suisei *carrier bombers attacked the* Bunker Hill, *which resulted in two near misses. One bomb killed three men and wounded seventy-five others. Flames erupted and temporarily knocked out the gasoline system in the hangar.*[35]

After this I could see some of the F6Fs flying in the air, and I escaped by just skimming over them. I barely escaped while being pursued by four aggressive enemy fighters. There were not many large clouds, so even if we hid in them, we would pop out very soon and be found. We played hide and seek with these four persistent enemy fighters for about an hour. The enemy held the air above Guam, so we could not land there. I thought I had finally gotten rid of the Grummans, and then realized I was very low on gas. It was then I found a small island named Rota on which there seemed to be some kind of an airstrip, and it was starting to get dark. I approached it, banking my plane left and right to indicate I was not the enemy.

I landed the plane, and while it was still taxiing I got shot. For a moment I thought that the enemy had taken the island, but my navigator yelled "Enemy aircraft!" so I realized the Grummans were back. Shrapnel hit my left wrist, but I'm glad the American pilots were not very good shots! The navy tried to rescue me, but it was impossible to do so without having air superiority. I was ordered to be the commanding officer of some 1700 navy men left on that island (Rota Island), and I stayed there until the end of the war.[36]

Abe's Suisei *was probably strafed at Rota Island by eight Grumman F6F-3s from VF-24 that were launched from the carrier* Belleau Wood *(CV-24) at 1725.*[37]

In the Marianas, the Japanese tactic was to strike the United States' fleet from outside the combat radius of its aircraft. That was a good idea if our pilots were good enough, but at that time most of our airmen were rookies. I doubt if it would have been successful even if our crew were like those at Pearl Harbor. The ability of an aircrew deteriorates as fatigue sets in because of the long duration of time strapped to their seats. That tactic was a mistake. We should have struck at close range even if it meant losing our carriers, and maybe then even the men the Americans called "turkeys" could have reached and struck at the U.S. fleet. The official Japanese name of this operation was "A"-Gō, but many people say that it should be called "*Aho*," which means stupid in Japanese slang.

The End of the War

We surrendered to Colonel Howard N. Stint, USMC, on 4 September at 1100 hours, one mile offshore Rota Island. I then spent a year and a half on Guam as a POW. I'm glad I was a POW with the Americans (and not the Russians). By the way, I ate cheese for the first time in my life while I was a POW! We didn't know where we would go, but we were disarmed by the commander of the American authorities, and three or four LSTs came ashore on the morning of 4 September 1945.[38] The next day we landed on Guam and went to the camp stockade. I stayed there for fifteen months, from September 1945 until I got home in late November 1946.

The Americans thought we would be prisoners of war for only a few months, so they built temporary housing for us. We had tents in areas where the coconut trees had been cut. I wondered why we had to stay so long, and after I came back to Japan, I found out why. The Japanese government asked MacArthur's headquarters if they could bring food instead of prisoners of war to Japan. My total flying hours during my military years were about 2,000 hours, and my final rank was lieutenant commander.

Return to Japan

Since I left in May 1944, almost two-and-a half years had passed. In July 1944 Saipan had a suicide attack, and in September of that year on Guam, the Japanese garrison, both army and navy, made a final suicide attack. So people thought that I was dead, too. My wife didn't receive any official notification, but she wondered whether I was alive or dead. Another reason for the uncertainty is that before I left Japan, I asked the paymaster to send my monthly salary to my wife, instead of me. Money was not necessary on board an aircraft carrier. That was the kind of system we had. Several years later we were talking about that, and we found out that my wife never received any salary. My brother, Kihachi Miyazaki, an army pilot, died during a training mission in 1943, and I also found out that my father had died.

Postwar

After the war ended, I couldn't have an official job by MacArthur's order, so I worked doing salvage work in the Inland Sea. Very shortly, I also worked for the Toyota Motor Company. Then, in 1950, the Korean War started, and MacArthur ordered Japan to organize the National Police Reserve. At that time the headquarters of the National Police Reserve invited me to join as an officer, a major. We trained with the U.S. Army. At Yokosuka, under American instructors, we studied a couple of months to be officers of the new Japanese Army. Very shortly I was assigned to Regiment S-1, which was headquartered in the Yamaguchi Prefecture. The headquarters of the National Police Reserve planned to send forty-five students to train to be young officers in the infantry. So we went to an area close to Tokyo and entered a language school to learn English, to prepare to study in the United States.

The author and Zenji Abe during one of his visits to his home. (Werneth)

Zenji Abe with his brother Kihachi Miyazaki, who was an army pilot during the war. (Abe Collection)

After retiring from the military in 1967 I worked for a plastics company, Ube Plastics, as a senior managing director, and retired in October 1983. My first wife, Kuniko, passed away on 1 March 1984, and I later remarried. We had two sons and one daughter together, but my eldest son passed away at thirty-three years old due to cancer.

Reflections

I have to say something about the war. Japanese leaders made the wrong choice. Japan started off as a modern nation with the Meiji Restoration. However, Japanese agriculture could not support its population of eighty million people. We had no oil, and half of our oil was imported from the United States. Iron was imported from the United States. Other important materials like aluminum, rubber, and zinc all had to be imported.

The Europeans had colonized Southeast Asia. Had we just fought the British, the French, and the Dutch, then our rationale to free Asia would have been legitimate.

I don't understand why we had to go to war with the United States. We didn't have to hit Pearl Harbor. I feel sorry for making that attack. However, if you ask me if I think the atomic bombs were used because of the Pearl Harbor attack, I really don't think that's comparable, because with those lethal bombs, you are talking about 320,000 Japanese, Korean, and Taiwanese civilians killed or suffering aftereffects of radiation. The "sneak attack" at Pearl Harbor was the fault of the diplomats. They should have apologized for their blunder through a neutral nation even as we were fighting the war.

In conclusion, 1.5 million people visit the museum at Pearl Harbor every year, but they are American. Japanese people don't know the facts of Pearl Harbor well. Because we sacrificed so much, younger people should know more about it. I want the media to do their best to show how these things happened; for example, the Hollywood film, which came out a few years ago about Pearl Harbor. Future generations also should do everything possible to stop needless wars from happening in the future.

Abe-san passed away on 6 April 2007. He will be missed by many people.

Ensign Kenji Hori

"I thought we did something extraordinary."

When I visited the home of naval aviator veteran Kenji Hori, I had no idea what to expect, because of a previous phone conversation with my translator. On the phone, he spoke with a strong, unfriendly tone, but in person he was much different. Although Hori-san spoke with a loud, firm voice, he was very friendly and kind. Unfortunately, for the past few years his body has been weak, but mentally he is very sharp, and remembers well even little details.

When one of my Japanese friends saw a letter from Hori-san, she said, "He is a traditional gentleman because he writes so politely." During the war, Hori-san had several near death experiences and is a real lucky survivor of World War II. Remarkably, according to him, he was never interviewed much by historians, even though he saw a lot of action during the war. Hori-san currently lives in Nishinomiya City, Ōsaka.

Hori's Early Days

I was born on 29 October 1920, and grew up in Nishinomiya City with my father, mother, and older brother. My older brother served in China with the army and survived the war. Before the war, everybody thought they should die for the Emperor, and that was the way to do something for your nation. I joined the Imperial Japanese Navy on 1 October 1938 at Yokosuka.[39] I did my training in several places, such as Kasumigaura and on the ships *Kongō* and *Akagi*. I graduated at Kasumigaura on 1 April 1940 and went to Tsukuba and Yatabe. After this I served with the Usa *Kōkūtai*, 12th *Kōkūtai*, and Saeki *Kōkūtai*, before joining *Zuikaku* on 26 September 1941.

A young Kenji Hori when he was in a judo club. Hori-san is in the back row, far left. (Hori Collection)

Ensign Kenji Hori in his tropical service dress uniform in September 1944. (Hori Collection)

Above: Hori's flight training class, but the exact date of the photo is unknown. (Hori Collection) Below: *Zuikaku* while anchored in Hitokappu Bay. (*Maru* magazine via Wenger)

Pearl Harbor

During my training to prepare for the Pearl Harbor attack I tried to hit a target in Saeki Bay. We used that area, and made it look like Pearl Harbor, but at that time I didn't know we were going to attack Pearl Harbor. Instead, I thought I was going to fight against the Soviet Union in the Kamchatka area. On 18 November 1941 our ship left Ōita, Japan, bound for Hitokappu Bay, in the Kurile Islands, where our fleet was being gathered together. Then, on the 24th, I learned for the first time from a commanding officer that I was going to attack Pearl Harbor. We used a northern sea route to Hawaii in order to avoid being recognized by other commercial ships.

Hori-san was the pilot of a Type 99 carrier bomber, and his flying partner for the mission was Lieutenant (junior grade) Reijirō Ōtsuka. They were a part of the first wave attack from the carrier Zuikaku. *At 0755 Hori's group, consisting of twenty-five Type 99s led by Lieutenant Akira Sakamoto and eight* Sōryū *Type 0 carrier fighters struck Wheeler Field.*[40] *During the second wave, possibly eight Kaga Zero fighters (out of nine from the group) did a strafing attack of Wheeler Field.*[41] *The American aircraft were quite literally "sitting ducks" because they were parked outside closely together. Lieutenant General Walter C. Short, the army commander at Pearl Harbor, ordered this because he was concerned about sabotage from the local Japanese residents. Nevertheless this was a major blunder, and the aircraft were easy pickings for the Japanese attackers.*

During my flight to Oahu Island the weather was sunny, but I saw some scattered clouds at the altitude of 2,500 meters to 3,000 meters (8,202-9,842 feet), which was the altitude that I was flying at. However, by the time I arrived, Pearl Harbor was under the clouds. Then, after turning left, I was able to see Oahu Island well. The island had a lot of greenery and looked beautiful. It looked like a miniature garden. I also thought our formation of airplanes was simply grand and powerful. I thought that the area surrounding Wheeler Field was like a fantasy land. Down below, I could see houses with beautiful gardens and trees. When I thought that this place would become a place of chaos, I felt regret.

A group of *Zuikaku's* dive-bomber pilots before the Pearl Harbor attack. Front row, from the left: second person, WO Masataka Fukunaga; third person, Lieutenant (junior grade) Reijirō Ōtsuka; fourth person, Lieutenant Tamotsu Ema; and fifth person, WO Tohichi Azuma. Second row, fourth person from the left is PO2c Kenji Hori. (*Arizona* Memorial via Wenger)

Over Wheeler Field there was no heavy anti-aircraft fire, but we did have small arms fire, which came from the barracks. Luckily, none of *Zuikaku's* airplanes were shot down during the attack. Wheeler Field was a big airfield with large hangars, and I could see a lot of parked aircraft. We attacked the fighters first because we didn't want them to take off. I saw many fighters lined up and dropped my bomb on them; there would be a chain reaction explosion. After I finished my bombing, I started strafing with my machine guns at an altitude of 1,500-2,000 meters (4,921-6,562 feet).

My partner, Lieutenant (junior grade) Reijirō Ōtsuka, was usually calm and quiet, but in an emergency situation he lost his calmness and got panicky. At this time he saw an airplane behind us, and said that an enemy aircraft was getting ready to attack. When I looked at the airplane, I saw a red stripe and *hinomaru*, which showed that it was one of our fighters from *Akagi*. Ōtsuka-san was born in Fukui Prefecture. He was a classmate of veteran Takeshi Maeda in junior high school. Unfortunately, Lieutenant (junior grade) Ōtsuka later died in the Battle of the Eastern Solomons on 24 August 1942.

On my way back, I attacked some fuel tanks on the road going to Schofield Barracks. The tanks were lined up along the west side. We attacked them several times but they didn't ignite. It seems they must have had some sort of armor, and it was too thick. After returning to my carrier from my mission, I thought we did something extraordinary, and I was very lucky to survive. At that time the water was very calm and totally different from the turbulent sea that we encountered earlier. I was so excited that my lips became very dry, and when I rubbed them with my flying gloves, I felt that my skin might be rubbed away.

There were no aircraft carriers at Pearl Harbor, so I thought it was a superficial attack. Nevertheless, other pilots were enthusiastic and excited. Some people even wanted to go all the way to the west coast and bomb more places, so we could finish the war quickly. We arrived back at Hashira Jima, Japan, on 23 December.

A burning Wheeler Field during the first wave of the Pearl Harbor attack. (Matsumura Collection)

Above: The aftermath of the Japanese attack on Wheeler Field. This is the apron near Hangar 3. (NA via Wenger) Below: An angry Captain George S. Boyer, U.S. Army Medical Corps, with some aircraft wreckage. (NA via Wenger)

As a result of the Wheeler Field attack on 7 December 1941, thirty-five people perished (thirty-one enlisted men and four officers) and sixty-nine men (sixty-seven enlisted men and two officers) were wounded in action. Please note that the four officers who died during the attack were lost in aerial combat, not on the ground.[42] *Losses for aircraft based at Wheeler Field consisted of eighty-three aircraft destroyed and twenty-six damaged but repairable.*[43]

Flying the Type 99 carrier bomber

My aircraft, the Type 99 carrier bomber, was very easy to fly and had very good performance. I thought that it was a great aircraft for dive-bombing, but had very little protection for the crew. The Type 99 was very stable to maneuver, so the Imperial Navy used it for a long period of time. The aircraft also was very easy to land on a carrier. I can only say one negative thing about it, which was the oil leakage from the engine cylinders. This sometimes made the aircraft difficult to fly. In this situation oil smeared on the windshield, so I had to wipe it using a towel or my glove, but it was difficult to do because of the strong wind. I had to do this, because otherwise I couldn't see well.

Rabaul Attack

I attacked Rabaul, New Britain Island, on 20 January 1942.[44] In the beginning the battle in Rabaul was very carefree and relaxed. The Japanese Army sent men to install communication wires at Rabaul and didn't want them to be attacked. Initially there was a Union Jack flag flying, and they tried to hit us with anti-aircraft guns. However, they didn't calculate correctly and missed us. Because of this I didn't feel tense at all, and as I looked down, it just looked like tobacco smoke. When I went over the harbor there also were five or six ships sunk. Enemy airplanes also didn't try to attack us. After our attacks, the Australians retreated to the south.

Action in the Indian Ocean

On 5 April 1942 we flew over the warehouses in Colombo Harbor at an altitude of between 2000-3000 meters (6,562-9,842 feet).[45] Suddenly, our aircraft were attacked by a large group of Hurricane fighters at the altitude of about 2500 meters (8,202 feet). This occurred before I commenced my attack dive. Our mission was to bomb the harbor facilities and ships with 250 kilogram (551 pound) bombs. Unfortunately, it was impossible for our heavy Type 99 *kanbaku* to battle against Hurricane fighters in the air. I

A view from one of the Type 99s, during a mission in the Battle of the Coral Sea on 7 May 1942. (Japanese Defense Agency, War History Section)

dropped my bomb on a warehouse, which exploded. Other people attacked transport ships as well. During this mission I also saw one of our airplanes get shot down.

After this my fuel tank (inside the right wing) started to leak, and it looked like it was about to catch fire. My Type 99 also had thirty-seven bullet holes in the fuel tank, right landing gear, and fuselage. I thought that I would have to crash my airplane into the sea because I could not return to my carrier. However, I was able to switch on the other fuel tank and return safely. On the 9th of that month, Lieutenant Commander Kakuichi Takahashi led the Type 99 carrier bomber group from *Shōkakū*. The attack unit of eighty-five Type 99s from four carriers (*Shōkakū*, *Zuikaku*, *Akagi*, and *Hiryū*) sank the British carrier *Hermes* with a hit probability of 82%. My bomb was the thirteenth to hit the ship, and it was a direct hit.

The Battle of Coral Sea

After raids in the Indian Ocean our fleet went back to Makung, Formosa (now named Taiwan), via Singapore. All carrier-based aircraft landed at Makung Airport. After refueling and servicing our airplanes, we left Makung on 19 April to head for the Coral Sea via Truk Island. At 0800 on 7 May, after receiving a report of a sighting of some enemy ships from one of our search aircraft, the 5th Carrier Division (consisting of the carriers *Zuikaku* and *Shōkaku*) launched seventy-eight aircraft for an attack. When our aircraft arrived at the destination, we discovered that the ship was not a carrier, but an oiler and a destroyer. It became clear that our search plane had made a mistake. This fact was transmitted back to our carriers. The Type 99s were ordered to attack these ships, while the rest were ordered back to our carriers. However, I personally took part in this attack on the destroyer and oiler, but had no air to air combat during this mission. *Zuikaku's* Type 99 *kanbaku* unit did their attacks from 1126-1140.[46] The destroyer *Sims* split in two and went down with a violent explosion. The oil tanker *Neosho* was burning, but didn't sink.

While bombing the *Neosho*, my classmate, PO2c Shigeo Ishizuka, from Niigata Prefecture, was hit while diving and burst into flames at 1000 meters altitude. Ishizuka's Type 99 was very close to my aircraft, so I could see his face. I could also clearly identify the rear-seat observer, PO3c Masayoshi Kawazoe, from the Nagasaki Prefecture. Suddenly the plane turned and crashed into the bridge of the oil tanker. I confirmed the loss of this crew, and later, during funeral rites on board the carrier, I read the eulogy.

The stricken Type 99 carrier bomber flown by Ishizuka and Kawazoe slammed into the Gun No. 4 enclosure of the oiler, which was a prelude to the organized kamikaze *attacks later in the war. The* Neosho *was hit by seven bombs, but remained afloat, listing at an angle of about thirty degrees without power.*[47] *The majority of the survivors clung to the damaged oiler until they were rescued on 11 May by the USS* Henley. *The USS* Neosho *was subsequently scuttled by the USS* Henley *and sank stern first at 1522 that same day.*[48] *As a result of the air attacks on the oiler 177 men perished with the doomed ship.*[49]

The oil tanker *Neosho* burning after being attacked by a group of Type 99 carrier bombers. (Japanese Defense Agency, War History Section)

Around 1215 the destroyer Sims *took the first of three bomb hits that went through the deck and exploded in the after engine room. The* Sims *was then hit by two more bombs, one on the after deck house, port side forward that caused only minimal damage. The last bomb struck the #4 Gun, but only caused local damage. Nevertheless, this doomed the destroyer, and afterwards the boilers blew up, followed by a smaller explosion.*[50] *It then broke into two parts and sank at 1230 on 7 May 1942.*[51] *Loss of life was immense for the destroyer's crew, with 225 men lost (including the* Sim's *Captain, Lieutenant Commander Wilford M. Hyman).*[52]

On 7 May the reports came from different directions that the enemy fleet had been located, which confused us, and we did not know what to do. Meanwhile, we were approaching closer to the enemy. In the evening we knew that we were pretty close to the enemy aircraft carriers, but we could not attack them because of the poor weather, and it was getting very dark. So the decisive battle was postponed until the next day; however, the *Shōhō* was sunk, and a lot of our aircraft were already lost.

In the early morning of 8 May one of our airplanes (a Type 97 carrier attack plane) from the *Shōkaku* found the enemy mobile fleet at 0822. It sent a message, which stated the enemy's position and provided us with vital information. My classmate, PO2c Seijirō Kishida, was on board as the radioman. His message was sent all in code; though he must have been very busy in the aircraft, his message was textbook-quality. It was quite different from the message sent from the search plane on the previous day. This was their message:

0822: Have sighted the enemy carriers. Location of enemy carriers 205 degrees and 235 miles from your position, course 170 degrees, speed 16 knots.
0825: The weather is good. Wind velocity, 7 meters. Height, 800 meters. Visibility, 15 Km.
0854: The enemy changed the course to 130 degrees.
0855: Approaching the enemy from the east. It's easy.
0910: The size and formation of the enemy are unchanged.
0940: Thirty enemy planes are heading to our fleet.
0950: Additional planes are heading to our fleet, height, 2000 meters. The enemy has a direct escort.
0955: We will return.

This was a beautiful report. On their way back to their carrier, the plane met the Japanese aircraft that were heading towards the enemy. It then changed directions in order to lead our aircraft to the enemy ships. The airmen on this airplane must have known that their fuel was low. After leading our aircraft to the enemy ships, this aircraft flew away and never returned to its carrier. They could have perished because of a lack of fuel, or were shot down by an enemy aircraft.

The above Shōkaku *Type 97* kankō *was flown by pilot PO1c Tsuguo Gotō, observer WO Kenzō Kanno, and radioman PO2c Seijirō Kishida. The brave aviators were shot down by two F4F Wildcat fighter pilots of the Yorktown Air Group, Lieutenant (junior grade) William S. Woolen and Ensign John P. Adams. For their heroic action during the Battle of Coral Sea on 1 January 1943, the Imperial Navy awarded the three men a posthumous letter of commendation personally signed by Admiral Yamamoto.*[53]

At 0910 on 8 May 1942, the carriers Shōkaku *and* Zuikaku *launched a strike force led by Lieutenant Commander Kakuichi Takahashi. The group consisted of eighteen Type 0 carrier fighters, thirty-three Type 99 carrier bombers (armed with 250 kilogram bombs), and eighteen Type 97 carrier attack planes (armed with torpedoes).*[54] *Hori-san was the pilot of one of the Type 99s flying from the carrier* Zuikaku.

Responding to this self-sacrificing work of our reconnaissance plane, our aircraft went to engage the enemy carriers. Our aircraft tried to attack the carriers without being shot down by their fighters or anti-aircraft fire. The enemy carrier *Lexington* was hit by two bombs and two torpedoes, while the carrier *Yorktown* was hit by one bomb and had two near misses from our bombs. *Lexington* completely stopped shortly after and sank after being scuttled by

An explosion on the doomed *Lexington* launches an aircraft off the deck. (NA)

torpedoes from the destroyer *Phelps*. *Yorktown* also was damaged and left the Coral Sea.

Frederick C. Sherman, who was the captain of *Lexington* at that time, wrote in his book about this Japanese attack, "It was a beautiful coordinated attack. I saw the enemy aircraft from the bridge swooping down from every direction. Torpedo planes rushed to the bow from both sides of the vessel simultaneously." In the official Japanese records of the 5th Carrier Division, the section about the enemy anti-aircraft fire during this mission says that it was extremely heavy. During the strikes on the American aircraft carriers we lost twenty-two planes, either due to being shot down or ditching. The aircraft consisted of eleven Type 97 *kankō*, ten Type 99 *kanbaku*, and one Type 0 *kansen*.

During this battle the Lexington *was hit by two torpedoes, three bombs, and several near misses. As Hori-san states, it was scuttled several hours later; nevertheless, out of a total complement of 2951 men, only 115 perished (including eighteen marines) during the battle.*[55] *The* Yorktown, *which skillfully dodged eight torpedoes, was subsequently hit by one bomb that penetrated the flight deck and exploded below decks. The personnel losses of the latter ship consisted of forty-three men and twenty-seven wounded-in-action.*[56] *The damage, due to the Japanese air attacks, prompted the carrier to leave the Coral Sea.*

As Hori-san mentions, the Japanese side lost a number of highly-experienced aviators during this mission, including the beloved Lieutenant Commander Kakuichi Takahashi, the strike leader and senior hikōtaichō *from the carrier* Shōkaku. *Kenji Hori was one of the lucky Japanese aviators that managed to survive this bloody battle.*

The Imperial Navy lost the carrier Shōhō, *and the* Shōkaku *was damaged. Although* Shōkaku's *division mate* Zuikaku *escaped major damage, it suffered heavy losses of both personnel and aircraft during the battle. Because of this both carriers could not participate in the Battle of Midway, which occurred just one month later.*

As for the American side, it lost the oiler Neosho, *destroyer* Sims, *and the carrier* Lexington. *The* Yorktown *also was damaged, but remarkably able to participate in the Battle of Midway, due to the intense effort of around-the-clock maintenance work shortly before the battle.*

In retrospect, I feel the Battle of the Coral Sea was a big fiasco. Our forces suffered a great deal, and the positive results were minimal. Our aviators suffered heavy losses during the battles on 7-8 May. Even the carrier *Shōkaku* had to leave the combat zone after being bombed.[57] So the 5th Carrier Division went to port at Truk Island. As a result of this battle, an attack from the sea against Port Moresby had to be postponed. I also believe this really changed the tide of the war (in favor of the United States).

Daily Life on board *Zuikaku*

On my carrier *Zuikaku*, the first floor was for the pilots of the Type 0 *kansen* and Type 99 *kanbaku*, and the second floor, which had a lot of space, was for the Type 97 *kankō* aviators. In general the living conditions were very bad, because you couldn't control the temperature. Because of this when it was hot, people gathered around a fan to get some air. There were no air conditioners or heaters on the ship, so it could be sometimes either really hot or freezing on board our carrier. For example, when we crossed the equator, my bed was soaking wet from my sweat.

During the war I didn't think too seriously about fighting the United States and its allies. I just felt that Japan had to win the war, and I really didn't have time to think about other issues. When I was flying combat missions, I only thought about hitting my target and focused only on this. As a pilot you had to focus on doing your duties, and you couldn't be scared while engaging the enemy. Regarding the relationships between the officers and lower-ranking personnel I think there was some tension. Nevertheless, I think we were still able to focus on our missions. Performing our duties was the most important thing for us.

The Battle of Santa Cruz

During 20-25 October 1942, the Japanese Army planned a major ground offensive with the hope of finally taking control of the strategically important island Guadalcanal. Henderson Field, the airfield on the island, was vital to Allied air operations for the counter-offensive against Japan. The Japanese Army's October offensive was repelled by Allied ground troops and it suffered heavy casualties.

However, at the same time a large contingent of Imperial Japanese Navy vessels, including the carriers Zuikaku, Shōkaku, Zuihō, *and* Junyō *were still in the area, and they hoped to defeat the Allied naval forces once and for all. The U.S. Navy also had the carriers* Hornet *and* Enterprise, *along with several other ships in the same waters, so an engagement between them was to be anticipated.*

On 26 October at 1315, Hori-san took off as a member of the First Carrier Division's third attack wave. The group consisted of a "mixed" batch of two Type 99s (one from Shōkaku *and the other from* Zuikaku*—Hori-san), five Type 0* kansen *(three* Zuikaku, *two* Shōkaku*), and seven Type 97* kankō *(five* Zuihō, *two* Zuikaku*). Six of the Type 97s were armed with 800 kilogram bombs for level bombing, and the overall strike leader was Lieutenant (junior grade) Ichirō Tanaka (*Zuihō*).*[58]

When this strike group spotted the Hornet, *the carrier was already damaged by several bombs and torpedoes from prior Japanese attacks. At 1540, Hori's Type 99 and the other Type 99 (*Shōkaku*) engaged the carrier* Hornet *and its screening ships. Hori-san and his partner may have scored a near miss on the cruiser* San Diego, *while the other Type 99 crew did likewise on the beleaguered* Hornet.[59] *As for the Type 97s, they dropped their bombs on the* Hornet *fifteen minutes later and scored one hit on the flight deck aft, but it caused very little damage.*[60]

During my mission on 26 October 1942 the weather was really clear and sunny. The *Hornet* was already damaged from our attacks but didn't sink. The carrier had no power, so the cruiser *Northampton* was pulling it. I got hit by anti-aircraft shells that went through my parachute pack and the fragments went into my leg. However, I don't know exactly which ship fired at me, but while it occurred, the *Hornet* couldn't move and a cruiser was pulling it. I was wounded prior to making my attack. There were many

Ensign Kenji Hori in his flight gear while at Saeki Air Base in November 1943. (Hori Collection)

ships escorting the *Hornet*, so the anti-aircraft probably came from them. I hit one of the ships protecting the carrier, which I think was a cruiser (*San Diego*). It wasn't a direct hit, but my bomb hit the edge of the ship. The ship suffered minor damage, and it was not the kind of damage which would cause a vessel to sink.

My airplane was damaged during the attack, and my right wing had a big hole. My observer, PO2c Masaaki Negishi, also was wounded in the right side of his chest and bleeding very badly. So I was very concerned about him. The speed of my aircraft was less than 100 knots and it was very difficult to fly. The fuel gauge also showed that my plane was almost out of gas. Fortunately, I saw the carrier *Junyō* and was able to land around dusk. Since Negishi-san was badly wounded, it was not until I landed that I realized that my right leg was hurt as well. I received word that my partner for the mission (Negishi-san) recovered from his wounds. Sadly, he died later in the war.[61]

After the battle *Junyō* went to Truk Island. Due to radio silence we were not able to send messages to *Zuikaku*. Because of this, right after entering the port there was a report transmitted via a light signal to *Zuikaku* regarding our emergency landing. Since there was no surgeon on *Zuikaku* I was transferred to the heavy cruiser *Kumano* with a guy named Kishi-san. I went into surgery to remove a shell fragment, which was embedded in my thigh. By grasping a ring above my head, I energized myself before the surgery. Because no anesthesia was used everything went blurry, and I was semi-conscious for about thirty minutes. During the operation a nurse held me down, and the surgery was completed successfully; then the *Kumano* left for Japan. After the operation I was recuperating and transferred to Beppu Navy Hospital. I spent three months recovering there before flying again.

The Hornet *lost 118 officers and men during the battle.*[62] *After being hit by numerous bombs and torpedoes, the stricken carrier was considered lost. So the crew of the* Hornet *evacuated by 1627, and the decision was made to scuttle the ship.*[63] *The U.S. Navy destroyers* Mustin *and* Anderson *scored numerous torpedo hits and gunfire, but the* Hornet *didn't sink. When Japanese forces approached the area, the burning hulk of the once proud carrier still didn't sink. The* Hornet *finally went down at 0130 the following morning, after being struck by four additional Japanese torpedoes.*[64] *As a result of the Battle of Santa Cruz the carrier* Enterprise *also was damaged, but still participated in the Naval Battle of Guadalcanal on 13-15 November that same year.*

As for the Japanese Imperial Navy, the carriers Shōkaku *and* Zuihō *were severely damaged and wouldn't participate in combat operations for several months. However, more importantly, Japan lost 148 experienced naval aviators, including two Type 99* kanbaku *leaders and three Type 97* kankō *leaders.*[65] *These battle-seasoned veteran pilots simply couldn't be replaced easily. In retrospect, The Battle of Santa Cruz can be considered a tactical win, but a strategic loss for Japan.*

Back to Japan

I then joined the Saeki *Kōkūtai* on 26 December and did dive-bombing training day and night. I also achieved my long-time dream of becoming an ensign in the navy. I started to be able to walk well, and was ordered to join the 702 *Kōkūtai* in Mobara, Chiba. However, the group's main unit was located in Hokkaido. The beach name was "Beach 99," and our headquarters was near the beach in a pine forest. One runway was from south to north, and we used the Type 99 *kanbaku*. The daytime and nighttime training was very intense.

After this I was transferred to Kasumagaira *Kōkūtai* because our leader, Ema-san, said that I should work as an instructor because of my combat injuries. Lieutenant Sakamoto led the *kōkūtai*, and I instructed some graduates from the Navy Academy. One of my counterparts there was Lieutenant Yukio Seki, who would later lead the first *tokkō* mission in the Philippines.[66] At that time he had just gotten married, and his wife came from Kamakura to visit him. During one of these training flights, shortly after take off, the aircraft's speed went down to almost zero! Luckily, I took control of the airplane and the engine started again, but by that time we were flying very close to a wheat field.

Action in the Philippines

After being an instructor for twenty-three days, I told my commanding officer that "I almost died during a training flight and this is not a suitable job for an experienced war veteran." I also said that I wanted to be transferred to the frontlines and fly combat

Hori flew an early model of the *Suisei* carrier bomber, similar to the one pictured here, during combat missions in the Philippines. (Werneth Collection)

Ensign Hori while he was a member of the 702 *Kōkūtai* in Mobara, Chiba, in February 1944. (Hori Collection)

missions again. Due to the shortage of skilled pilots on the frontline, after only one week I received an order to board the battleship *Ise*. However, in October 1944 the war was progressing very badly for Japan, and our frontlines became Taiwan and Okinawa. So, we organized the 634 *Kōkūtai* at Ōita (Kyūshū) quickly and left for Mabalacat, in the Philippines.

Before leaving for the Philippines we did training with the *Suisei* carrier bomber at Iwakuni Air Base using a catapult with gunpowder. However, we never used this in actual combat. The *Suisei* was an excellent airplane but it wasn't mass-produced, so the older model, the Type 99 *kanbaku*, was used more often. It also was fast and stable. This aircraft also carried 500-800 kilograms worth of bombs compared to the usual load of one 250 kilogram bomb on a Type 99. I loved the *Suisei*; it was very maneuverable, just like the Zero fighter, and the engine had a lot of horsepower. Unfortunately, at that time we only had 100 octane gasoline, and the *Suisei* couldn't perform to its maximum capabilities because the aircraft needed 120 octane to do so.

I went to the Philippines with my *kōkūtai* in late November 1944, and was stationed at Mabalacat East Airfield. Suddenly, at Leyte during the night numerous American ships arrived, and troops began landing in the Philippines. I thought we couldn't compete against the vast industrial might of the United States and its military forces. The number of enemy troops multiplied like mice, while we had very few airplanes left at Mabalacat Air Base. After arriving there, every day we were very busy bombing Leyte. Our target was Tacloban Air Base, and the troops that were conducting landing operations. I did my daytime attack missions almost daily until early January.

A Deadly Accident for Hori-san

Our 634 *Kōkūtai* lost every flyable airplane, and a group of experienced airmen were supposed to return to Japan to get more aircraft for our group. On 2 January 1945 we were planning to leave Clark Air Base, but our airplane never made it out. It was nighttime, and we used a 4,000 meter runway there. In Japan they used lights to illuminate the runway, but this was the frontlines, so we avoided doing this. Sometimes we used to light a candle-like substance in a can with a wick to illuminate the runway. Unfortunately, on this occasion we didn't use anything to light up the runway, and it was pitch dark.

We were flying in a Mitsubishi Type 1 *Rikkō* bomber that was modified to carry people. I was a pilot, so I was in the cockpit giving a pep talk to the other aviators on board to encourage them. Soon after the engines roared to life we left quickly, because we were worried about getting hit by the enemy. While we were getting ready to take off, the night-fighting aircraft were returning after long missions, and they collided with us while trying to land. During the collision I was thrown out of the aircraft and everyone else on board died. Sadly, a lot of good men died because of this terrible accident.

I was unconscious, and stayed in a Manila hospital for one month; I don't remember what happened. In hindsight, during my navy days I practiced judo, and should have used a judo technique to protect myself from getting hurt. When I awoke, I saw my burnt flight uniform near my pillow and that very night received an order from Yokosuka to go to Formosa. I then flew to Tainan Air Base, but we were attacked, so I returned to Japan. I was so sick that my commanding officer told me to go to Beppu (in Kyūshū). Other people who weren't sick became members of the *tokkō* groups. Therefore, I probably would have died if I wasn't ill. Regarding joining the *tokkō-tai*, officers were ordered to join, but petty officers were asked how they felt about joining an air group that would be flying suicide missions. The men had two choices: I have second thoughts about joining a *tokkō* group, or I really want to join a *tokkō* group. Everyone chose the latter option, and naturally officers were needed, because someone had to lead the group.

A recent photo of Kenji Hori during one of our interviews in his home. (Werneth)

The end of the war

After my stay in Beppu I transferred to a hospital in Matsuyama, and stayed there until the end of the war. Once the fighting stopped, I felt that I had to commit suicide because we lost. Initially everyone was very disillusioned, and thought they had to kill themselves to accept the responsibility for losing the war. However, after that we cooled down. My flying hours during the war years were between 2,000 to 2,500 hours, and my final rank was ensign.

Postwar

My wife and I had one son and one daughter. We now also have five grandchildren. After the war I established a post office in Nishinomiya City and became the manager. I retired in 1989, and my daughter's husband now runs it.

Reflections

I think the younger Japanese people of today have too much freedom, so they don't have any perseverance, and don't think about the security of their nation. Sometimes they are too selfish, and only care about themselves. Somewhere in the world there always must be a war, which is something that you might not be able to avoid. It also could happen in Asia, so Japanese people have to care more about the long-term security of our country. If they can't protect our nation, then Japan's future could be very bad.

In retrospect, sixty years ago Japanese people were very nationalistic, and tried to make Japan a better nation. In those days we were obligated to fight for Japan, and this also meant dying for the Emperor. During the war I think that I was brainwashed. Nevertheless, I still feel proud for having fought for my country.

Maintenance Warrant Officer Hachirō Miyashita

"We trained very hard so I was ready to attack."

While I lived in Japan, I really hoped to interview a former aviation mechanic who served on board a carrier during the war. However, I looked for several years without success until I had a chance to meet Hachirō Miyashita. Miyashita-san is one of the few survivors of this breed of mechanics, and he served throughout the war, from the conflict in China until the final months of the war when aviators flew tokkō *attack missions (*kamikaze*) against American ships. The veteran aviation mechanic saw a lot of combat while serving on board the carrier* Shōkaku *during engagements such as the Battle of Coral Sea and the Battle of Santa Cruz. He also worked on several different navy aircraft, such as the Type 99 and* Suisei kanbaku.

Miyashita-san was very kind to me, and always took a lot of time to explain the background of several battles and the key personnel who were involved. We met together in his home, which had many war related mementoes, such as his battle flags, and models of the airplanes which he worked on. He was energetic and vibrant while talking with my translator and me. Miyashita-san currently lives with his extended family in Tokyo.

Miyashita's Early Days

I was born in Tokyo on 25 May 1918. I had four older brothers and one sister, and I was the youngest in our family. During my childhood I was wild, and a bully in our neighborhood. One day when I came home from kindergarten the great Kantō earthquake occurred, and I was evacuated to the square in front of the Imperial Palace.[67] At that time my house was completely burnt down.

During my school days I played baseball and was a pitcher. An American baseball team came to Japan for a goodwill tour and came to Tsukishima, a reclaimed baseball park, which is now called Harumi. Lou Gehrig, the home run king, donated money to a boys' baseball team. The famous slugger Babe Ruth also came with them. I was very impressed that these well-known major league baseball players came to Japan.

On one occasion, the battleship *Nagato* was anchored in the waters off Shibaura and my father took me to see it.[68] I met Captain Sonoda, and was given lemonade and dumplings with sweet beans. While looking inside this grand battleship I was impressed. Captain Sonoda said that if I wanted to join the navy, I should go to the Naval Academy. I entered a private junior high school and tried to enter the Naval Academy, but I wasn't smart enough to be admitted to that prestigious school. I was able to join the navy in a unique way. The one-year anniversary for Admiral Togo's death was held at Tama Cemetery, and I went there with my father to help. At the service was an acquaintance of my father, and he asked me, "Do you really want to enter the navy?" I was excited and said yes. My father's acquaintance then talked to the Rear Admiral Shibayama on my behalf.[69] That's how I got a telegram to join the navy!

Life in the Imperial Japanese Navy

On 1 June 1935 I entered the navy at Yokosuka and finished the new recruits' training course in six months. Then, in November (of the same year) I was ordered to the *Yamashiro*, which was the flagship of the Combined Fleet. The commander of the ship was Admiral Miyoshi Takahashi.[70] I was a member of the 15th Auxiliary Cannon Division. The training was harsh, and we had to constantly lift heavy shells while onboard the ship. Due to the intense training it was nicknamed the "The Hell of *Yamashiro*," which became kind of a song, and the ship was famous for having tough discipline standards. Every night after a round of checks in front of the cannon we had to line up on the deck.

Upon completing the first part of training we went to Beppu for some rest.[71] The next morning we went to a port in Shikoku and dropped anchor. Suddenly a trumpet blew, and we had to leave the port. Then there was an announcement by the captain to gather on the deck. He said "This morning there was a revolt by younger officers of the army, and Prime Minister Keisuke Okada, Finance Minister Korekiyo Takahashi, Lord Privy Seal Makoto Saito, and Jotaro Watanabe (Inspector General of Military Education) were assassinated. We are going to Tokyo to suppress this uprising." I got very nervous after hearing the news.

At this time, each ship of the Combined Fleet was going side by side and going at full speed. Usually those ships traveled in a single file line. In the meantime, on our ship, we formed a land fighting group and did machine gun and small arms training on deck. The next day, on the 27th, we arrived off Shibaura. Usually

Maintenance Warrant Officer Hachirō Miyashita when he was a member of the 601 *Kōkūtai* in May 1945. (Miyashita Collection)

it took two full days and nights, but this time we arrived in one full day and night. Immediately we formed some groups at the navy accounting school in Tsukiji. We patrolled and relaxed as civilians for about ten days before returning to Yokosuka.

This event, which occurred on 26 February 1936, is very famous, and taught today in history classes in Japanese schools. Prime Minister Okada was not killed during the revolt, but the other three Japanese government officials lost their lives. Okada, who was sleeping at his official residence elsewhere, wasn't harmed. Due to mistaken identity, his brother-in-law was killed instead. Lord Chamberlain Kantaro Suzuki also was wounded very badly. Four days later, the army personnel responsible for their deaths were captured.[72]

Action in China

In February 1937 I went to Kasumigaura Air Base (in Japan) and became a 38th Term Maintenance Student, finishing a six-month class. After this I was then promoted to the rank of Maintenance Sea3c, and then assigned to the Kasumigaura (water unit). During the summer we had a fifteen day vacation, and I went back to my home. While I was on vacation I enjoyed visiting my family and friends. On 7 July 1937 in China, a Japanese military group and Chinese group clashed. Then the Sino-Japanese War started, so the rest of my summer vacation was canceled. Nevertheless, even after war broke out in China we were allowed to leave our base the same as before.

Once the Sino-Japanese War began I longed to go there and fight, but they didn't send me. I felt very disappointed that some of my comrades were sent to China to fight, but I was still stuck in Japan. In 1939 Rear Admiral Ono was put in charge of the Kasumigaura *Kōkūtai*.[73] One day he invited me to his room and said "Fighting on the frontlines is very tough, so I will send you after you become a petty officer. So please be patient." I was finally transferred to the 13th *Kōkūtai*, and Ono-san gave me a Japanese flag as a present. I boarded an express train and arrived at Sasebo. There I joined the Sasebo Navy Engine Group and I had a terrible time. One of the group's petty officers was a very negative person, and said, "Since you are going to the frontlines, I will give you energy to fight." Then he let the petty officers, who were waiting for ships to Shanghai, change into their uniforms, complete with dress daggers. After this he ordered us to run fifty laps around the practice field. I tried very hard not to fall behind, but I became very exhausted. Fortunately every day we had a chance to get out, so the men were able to relieve their stress on the streets of Sasebo. Ten days later I got on a ship bound for Shanghai. After arriving there I temporarily joined a Shanghai land-based battle group. I looked around the streets of the city and saw battlefield remains. Next, I then got on a Chinese passenger ship bound for Hankow and cruised on the Yangtze River. The ship's hull was reinforced with logs to protect it from the floating mines in the river. After about a one week journey we arrived at Hankow, and soon went to the 13th *Kōkūtai*.

We lived in a former Chinese prison, which was a building made of bricks, complete with iron bars. The door was thick with a small window, and the walls were thick and dirty. It made me sick thinking about the prisoners that were once inside this prison. The 13th *Kōkūtai* was equipped with Mitsubishi G3M2 Type 96 land-attack airplanes (Allied code name "Nell"), and the 45th

While Miyashita was in China, he did maintenance work on the Mitsubishi G3M2 Type 96 land-attack airplane (Allied code name "Nell"), like the ones depicted in this wartime photo. (Werneth Collection)

bombing operation started. The targets of the operation were the cities Chengdu and Chungking. Between operations, we went by truck to Hankow to get some rest. The mid-summer of Hankow was terribly hot, and there was a saying that "Birds that perched on telephone lines instantly dropped dead to the ground, deep fried." On top of that the barracks had thick walls, so when it was hot it was like a heated room. So even at night, because of the heat, I could not fall asleep until midnight.

I went to the airfield with the pilots and started to remove the camouflage Type 96s until they became silver. This was done to make the aircraft faster. I also could do any type of work on the Type 96, such as engine or fuselage related tasks. During airplane test flights we put many *saké* bottles filled with water on board. At high altitudes we did many tests to evaluate the generators, heat pressure, and oxygen systems. At 5,000 meters (16,404 feet), when you breathe in the oxygen your eyesight greatly improved, and the view was incredible. On the ground everyone enjoyed the water in *saké* bottles, which was now chilled from the flight, and also drank some Japanese cider.

In October 1940 the operation was over, and our *kōkūtai* was dissolved. In my case, I was assigned to the Kizarazu *Kōkūtai* at Hankow. I then took a ten day vacation in Tokyo, but on my flight back to Japan my aircraft almost crashed. While we were flying over the eastern China Sea one of our engines began losing oil pressure. Fortunately, the oil pressure returned to the normal level and we made it to Japan safely.

On 11 November our nation had a ceremony to celebrate the 2,600th anniversary of the founding of the Empire.[74] Present at the event were high-ranking army and navy officers, wearing their formal uniforms with their badges, which made for a grand atmosphere.

Carrier Duty

I transferred to the carrier *Akagi* as an aviation mechanic of the Type 99 *kanbaku* group in February 1941. We did intense training at several places in Japan, such as Kagoshima, Kasumihara, Saeki, Usa, and Ōita. In August, when I was training at Tomitaka Air Base, the carrier *Shōkaku* became a part of the Fifth Carrier Division. So some experienced people from *Akagi* were transferred to *Shōkaku*, and I was one of them. I transferred to that carrier in late August. *Shōkaku* picked us up by sea, and we went to Yokosuka. At Yokosuka people were collected from land-based units, and a new group was created.

Pearl Harbor

In late August we began working hard during training at Ōita Air Base. This lasted for less than three months and ended in November. Some personnel from the carrier *Akagi* were doing training at the same air base, so we were able to go out with them at night. Since their group was just formed, the airmen practiced doing landings and flying during the day and night. It was a really rigorous training program, and we didn't have much time to sleep.

Veteran Hachirō Miyashita participated in numerous combat operations while he was assigned to the *Shōkaku* from August 1941 until late 1943. (NHC via Wenger)

Sometimes pilots died during the training, and it was our job to find their bodies. Aviators didn't have to worry about doing this unpleasant duty because there were more mechanics, so we had to do this job.

During the training we didn't know that there would be an operation in December. There was a problem with the Soviet Union regarding fishing rights, so I thought we were going to deal with the Russians on this issue. On 19 November 1941 we left Ōita, and on the 22nd arrived at Hitokappu Bay, off Etorofu Island (in the Kurile Islands). At that time I was told that we were going to patrol the northern area. By the 24th there were carriers, battleships, and cruisers anchored in Hitokappu Bay. A lot of ships were busy loading magazines, fuel, and winter uniforms. We loaded our ammunition there because spies would see if we did this in Japan. On the morning of the 23rd, each ship commander and pilots were told to go to *Akagi,* and were given the details about the upcoming operation. At that time we still didn't know what was going on. In the afternoon the sea became very turbulent, and it was impossible for the men to go to back to their ships. Everyone was forced to stay on board *Akagi* for the night.

On the 26th we left Hitokappu Bay, and everyone was told to gather; this was the first time I heard that we were going to America. Captain Jōjima said "From now on we are going to take action against America.[75] The date of the attack is called 'X' day, and we are going to follow strict radio silence." *Akagi* celebrated by firing its 20-centimeter main cannon toward the cape, which filled us with fighting spirit. Since we had such good training we were ready to fight, even though the United States was a very powerful country.

The weather was bad moving north, and there was heavy fog, so we could not see in front of us. Our carrier was behind *Hiryū*. In order to avoid colliding with *Hiryū* we put a bell, which was mounted above a float (made of wood) and attached to wire between our ships. The float and bell assembly was floating on the water, and it was attached to 50 meters (164 feet) of wire on each side. On *Shōkaku* we put a man on watch on the front deck, and he reported to the bridge saying, "We are going within 50 meters," and that way we avoided any collisions during the voyage. There was not much work going on because the weather was bad in the area around the Aleutian Islands. During the voyage we also received

A view from the flight deck of *Shōkaku* when it launched some Zero fighters to do CAP (Combat Air Patrol) over the carriers during the Pearl Harbor attack. (Wenger Collection)

oil from one of our oilers. I remember a tense moment when we saw a Russian commercial ship with shining lights heading north. Luckily they passed our group of ships without seeing us.

If my memory is correct, the night before the Pearl Harbor attack we went to bed at 1500 in the afternoon, and woke up at 2000 at night. Everyone was forced to wake up and put the airplanes out in the dark. On 7 December, at 0100, the airplanes were ready to fly, and it was dawn. Nevertheless we still followed Japanese time, and because it was different than local time we had "jet lag." On that day everyone was wearing a headband with a red *hinomaru*, which is something that only pilots did. However, maintenance personnel also wore these headbands on this occasion. When the airplanes took off they also waved their caps to say goodbye.

When the airplanes returned from their mission and landed, they stopped when their tail hooks caught a wire on the deck of the carrier. The aircraft then moved a little forward, and we had to remove the seat belt and check if the pilot was okay. We also tested the engine of the aircraft after a mission was completed. The airmen had bloodshot eyes because they had to concentrate so intensely, and blood rushed to their heads after doing the dive-bombing attacks. We felt good when our comrades came back safely and said things like "Good job!" to them.

However, we didn't know if we would have to do another attack. We already had completed two attack waves, but different aircraft flew each time. So we didn't know if the first wave airplanes would have to fly again. We also thought that we were going to have an enemy attack and that they would follow us, so we were very tense. Our ship did a zigzag motion to avoid enemy attacks, and we didn't take a direct route back to Japan. Prior to the attack, we never imagined that it would go so well for our side. After the battle we didn't have a big party, but there were small gatherings. We really didn't feel like we won the battle at that time.

We went back to Japan on 24 December to Kure and took a rest on the mainland. Our airmen went to the hot springs in Beppu. We couldn't talk about the attack, even though civilians already knew about it. The newspapers already stated that we attacked Pearl Harbor, but the details, such as what airplanes and ships participated, were not reported to the Japanese people. During the New Year's holidays civilians gave us *mochi* and *saké*, and we probably left for duty on the 4th. It was too short and I wanted to stay longer.

Maintenance Duties

We could not put the airplanes outside unless they were perfect, so we did our maintenance work on the aircraft in the hangar. One day before a mission we had to check everything on the airplane, such as the engine, fuselage, etc. We usually did this at night, and couldn't sleep until our jobs were done. Once an aircraft was on the flight deck we could not lower it again. Because of this, we checked out the entire airplane in the dark hangar. Even though it was dark, we did our best. We checked various parts on the engines, such as carburetors and magnetos. The mechanics also tested the operation of the flaps and components in the cockpit, such as the control stick.

In those days we didn't use microphones, so we had to use our own voice or a megaphone to give directions as to where the airplanes should be placed. For example, we did this when the aircraft were loaded on the elevators to be taken up to the flight deck. After the airplanes were lifted to the flight deck via the elevators they were lined up. It was one of my duties to give directions so that all of the strike aircraft were placed in the proper position, and my voice became very hoarse.

We pushed the airplanes by hand, and the area on the flight deck was very small. All of the aircraft had to placed very tightly on the flight deck, so it was very difficult duty for me. You only could use a few places on the airplanes to push them, including the front of the wings and the tail, so you had to be careful at all times. While pushing them you had to avoid touching the delicate parts, such as the aircraft's control surfaces.

The aviation mechanics used a device with a lever that could be attached to an airplane's tail so it could be moved more easily to the proper place. I directed the men as to where to put the airplanes, and once they were put in the right place, this device was put away. Without this device the strike aircraft couldn't be moved very well. Because they were heavy, we actually needed about ten people to push one airplane. After this about five people remained with the aircraft. Two people were doing the wheel chocks, two additional mechanics were on the sides of the aircraft, and there was one more person, who was usually a leader checking out the cockpit.

Next, the engines on the aircraft were started at the same time. Aviators didn't get on their aircraft until the mechanics said that it was okay. It usually took about fifteen minutes to warm up the aircraft. The mechanics on the sides of the plane held ropes made of hemp, which were connected from the wings to the deck of the carrier. These ropes were important because of the strong wind from the swirling propellers and the swaying of the carrier due to turbulence. After the pilots climbed into their aircraft, only the men doing the wheel chocks stayed with the planes. The rest of the mechanics went to the walkways along the sides of the flight deck. This was because the flight deck was very small, and the swirling propellers were very dangerous. On some occasions people died or lost their arms due to accidents with propellers. One of my duties was to warn the mechanics of any dangers on the flight deck. Lastly, a *buntaichō* used a final flag, which told the men with the wheel chocks to get away, and the airplanes took off.

Our maintenance group was run this way. A *buntaichō* commanded a group of 120-150 men, and the personnel were divided into smaller groups, which were usually led by three *buntaishi*, but sometimes there were five of them. A *buntaichō* was usually a lieutenant or lieutenant commander, whereas a *buntaishi* was a lieutenant (junior grade) or warrant officer. On *Shōkaku*, I was the *buntaishi* of the Type 99 *kanbaku* maintenance group. The men worked on the same airplanes all the time. I supervised the maintenance of usually nine aircraft. However, five lower-ranking people took care of only one airplane.

We normally had no holidays and worked every day. We woke up at 0600, washed up, then ate breakfast at 0700. After this we started working at 0800. Then the mechanics ate lunch, and we started working again at 1330. Maintenance work stopped at 1600, and 1700 was dinner time. At 2000 trumpet sounded, which was a signal to go to sleep.

Working on the Type 99

Regarding the Kinsei engine in the Type 99 *kanbaku*, I was able to assemble and reassemble it from scratch. I could fix just about any problem with these engines. The Type 99 was not difficult to maintain, but it was hard to start in hot weather. I also worked on the magnetos and the carburetors on the engines. My other tasks included checking the landing gear and adjusting the flaps, rudder, and pilot's foot-bar (in the cockpit). I also checked the variable pitch mechanism on the propeller hub. Inside there was a piston, and hydraulic oil was used. Sometimes there was oil leakage from this area, and if that occurred, the pilot couldn't use the pitch well. This is very important, because when a plane took off it needed a lot of power, and the aviator had to adjust the pitch accordingly. As an interesting sidenote, during the war the Japanese Navy continued to use English a lot, but the army didn't like to use English. For example, we often used words like choke, switch off, and make contact.

Relationships between Pilots and Mechanics

Regarding our relationships with the pilots, our livings quarters on board the carrier were separate, and the aviators were treated better. For example, their rooms were more comfortable than ours. There was a place outside to smoke, and sometimes we were able to talk with the pilots there. If we personally knew any of the aviators, we could visit and talk with them in the pilot's room. When we were working on their aircraft, the pilots would come to clean their beloved airplanes. At that time we talked with them about things like Japan or our families. In general, I feel they treated us well because we took care of their airplanes. One pilot in particular, Lieutenant Commander Kakuichi Takahashi, a Type 99 *kanbaku* leader, was very kind to me.[76]

A Surprise Flight

On a carrier, aircraft mechanics were not supposed to get on an airplane during a test flight. However, on one occasion, right before taking off, Lieutenant Hisayoshi Fujita said, "Unless a mechanic gets on my airplane, I can't understand the condition of it." Normally during a test flight, a pilot usually flew with his flying partner, an observer/radioman. Since I was the *buntaishi* of our maintenance group, I wasn't able to refuse when Fujita-san requested me to fly with him. So I put on a flying suit over my mechanic's uniform and got on board his Type 99 carrier bomber.

During the test flight he did many amazing maneuvers in the air. Below us there were a lot of clouds, and I couldn't see our ship. Suddenly *Shōkaku* appeared right below us, as we descended out of the clouds. I was impressed, because Fujita-san predicted the position perfectly. I believe I was the first mechanic from a carrier to fly during a test flight. On some occasions, mechanics flew aboard an aircraft when they were going to the air bases (on land). This is because they were needed to do work at the base.

Type 99 pilot Lieutenant Hisayoshi Fujita and his partner, WO Mitsuo Cho, died after the 5 April 1942 raid on the British held territory of Columbo. Another Type 99 carrier bomber pilot, PO2c Toshio Suzuki, witnessed his final moments, which happened about ten miles away from the island. During the raid Fujita's plane was hit by anti-aircraft, and fuel was leaking from his aircraft. Because Lieutenant Fujita was over enemy held territory and couldn't go back to Shōkaku, *he decided to crash his airplane into the sea. However, before doing this he wrote on a blackboard the directions back to the carrier and showed this to PO2c Suzuki, who was flying near his aircraft. Fujita then yelled "Banzai" and shot his pistol many times to say goodbye. After this he crashed his aircraft into the water. His comrade, Suzuki-san, circled in the air above the crash site after he went down. From his position, PO2c Suzuki could see things such as food rations floating in the sea and a small boat with native people who were trying to pick them up. Because of this Suzuki-san strafed the boat, so they wouldn't touch anything from the crash site. He told Miyashita-san about the incident soon after it occurred during the war. Toshio Suzuki survived the war, but died a few years ago.*

When I asked Fujita's comrade, Zenji Abe, about him, he said "Fujita-san had fair skin and big eyes. I thought he was cheerful and intelligent. I think Lieutenant Fujita would have survived, if he decided to bail out, because our ships controlled the waters in that area. However, Fujita-san elected not to."

The Battle of Coral Sea

I remember *Shōkaku's* crewmen manning their gun batteries and being ready to engage any possible enemy aircraft that would come to attack our ship. Once our airplanes took off the mechanics didn't have any jobs to do. All we had to do was to be in a safe place. But if a fire broke out (due to an enemy attack), we had to put it out with foam because there was a lot of fuel on the ship. During an enemy air attack the flight deck was a dangerous place, so we tried to stay on one of the lower decks once our maintenance duties were completed. If you were on a lower deck it was hard to know what was happening in the battle, but you still heard the sounds of combat, such as the anti-aircraft batteries firing on the enemy aircraft. However, our crewmen near the flight deck and the higher-ranking personnel on the bridge could see exactly what was happening in the battle.

This was the first time that I experienced being bombed, so it was a very memorable experience for me. I thought that we were being attacked, because I could hear our gunners starting to shoot. At that time I was at the stern section of *Shōkaku* in the motor adjusting room. This room was used to test and repair engines. Everything was destroyed in that area of the ship. A fragment from the bomb hit my toolbox during the bombing, and I still have it as a memento today. There was no place to escape to because the ship was cruising in the middle of the ocean. Only two petty officers, including myself, were unscathed from this bomb blast.

During the bombing of *Shōkaku* some people died and others were injured. Above the motor adjusting room was a storage space. There were many flammable aircraft parts in that room, and the enemy's bomb exploded in that area. At that time I was trying to put out another fire on the flight deck. From the motor adjusting room you go up to the storage room by ladder, but that room started to emit smoke because some aircraft parts caught fire. Some people died from carbon monoxide poisoning when they went up the ladder and tried to enter that room.

After this, I cooled down the room with a water hose from the flight deck. While I was doing that, the cruisers and destroyers started to shoot their guns again. When I looked up I saw an enemy airplane, which was carrying a bomb, right above me, and it was diving down. Usually our carrier tried to evade the bombs by swerving left or right, and I felt the bridge area was a safe place to go during this time. So when I saw that airplane diving with a bomb, I dropped my water hose immediately and tried to go towards the bridge. Suddenly there was a column of fire right in front of me, and I was blown over a little because of the wind after the explosion. Nearby one of my comrades died when he was hit by some bomb fragments.

As I mentioned earlier, the first bomb hit the rear part of the ship, and this was the second bomb that hit us. Normally you fill up the airplanes with fuel in the hangar, but sometimes you need additional fuel when you go up to the flight deck. Because the second bomb hit a small gasoline container on a small cart, it created a column of fire. By this time the second attack was over.

I wasn't able to eat because I was busy taking care of the injured and the dead. I helped out until late at night. During the air attack Lieutenant Sao Noda, the leader of my maintenance group, was hit by numerous bomb fragments all over his body.[77] There were so many fragments in Noda's body that the doctor said that removing them was like "picking potatoes from the soil." I donated four pints of blood to him, which was a lot of blood. Normally a person would give only 200cc of blood, but I gave 400cc because it was a lot of trouble for another person to do this procedure again. After this I was treated to red wine. We had to take care of several other wounded and bury the casualties from the attack. Watanabe-san, who was one of my men, had fragments in his face. He said that I saved his life. At that time there was no anesthetic, but right after someone was injured, it was okay to perform an operation because he was somewhat paralyzed due to shock. However, if the operation took a long time, it could be painful.

On 8 May 1942, between 0907-0915, the carrier Shōkaku *was severely damaged by three bomb hits. One tore open the port bow and started a fire in the forecastle. The second struck the end of the flight deck to starboard. The third hit the starboard side of the rear of the island, damaging gun tubs and the mainmast. Large fires broke out, but the carrier evaded all the torpedoes successfully. The damaged carrier was escorted by the destroyers* Ushio *and* Yugure, *and was detached at once. Because of this it was able to evacuate the battle area at full speed. Personnel losses for the carrier included 108 officers and men killed by the fires and explosions, and another forty wounded.*[78]

Burying the dead at sea

During the battle three bombs hit *Shōkaku*. On the way back to Kure we had a funeral for the 107 people who died. We did services for the fallen men and then buried them at sea. We covered their faces with gauze and wrapped their bodies in blankets. Then we placed a practice (non-explosive) 30 kilogram (66 pound) bomb between their legs in the crotch area in order to weigh down the body for burial at sea. However, after being put in the water, the caskets later broke up due to water pressure, and the dead bodies floated back up to the surface. So the next time, when we had to bury 150 men at sea after the Battle of Santa Cruz (26 October 1942), we did it differently. Instead of placing the bodies in coffins, we wrapped them in blankets and attached a practice bomb to their legs for weight. Then we attached each body to a ladder and buried them at sea. This time the bodies didn't float back to the surface.

The Battle of Santa Cruz

After the Battle of Coral Sea, the damaged parts of the carrier were repaired at Kure, in Japan. On 25 May Captain Masafumi Arima was appointed as the new captain of *Shōkaku*.[79] On 24 August the Battle of the Eastern Solomons occurred. Then, on 26 October 1942, during the Battle of Santa Cruz, we were hit by four bombs and 150 people died.

During the American bombing attack, I was on a lower deck in the rear section of *Shōkaku*. One deck above me was hit, and I couldn't open the door. The bomb missed the lower deck area. After this I used a passageway to go to the front of the ship and reached the pilots' sleeping quarters. At that time I had several people with me, but there was smoke coming from the front and rear of us. So I ordered one person to check out the area in front of us and another man to check out the area to the rear of us.

In the end one person found some stairs that led to the upper deck and bridge area, and we went up. The rear portion of the flight deck was damaged, but I don't recall seeing any fires or dead bodies at that time. We once again did services for our comrades and buried them at sea. After this we went back to Yokosuka, and the ship was repaired.

During the battle Shōkaku *was heavily damaged by bombs. Four, possibly even six bombs struck the flight deck, one aft of the island, and the rest all grouped around the amidships and aft elevators. Large fires started, and the flight deck was heavily damaged. Though sixty officers and men were killed, since no aircraft were aboard no fuel was active, and damage control was able to extinguish the fires and save the carrier. Vice-Admiral Nagumo transferred his flag to the destroyer* Arashi. *Then, with the also-bombed light carrier* Zuihō, *the carrier was detached and ordered home to Truk escorted by the destroyers* Hatsukaze *and* Maikaze.[80]

In November 1943 there was an air battle off of the island of Bougainville, and the Type 99 *kanbaku* group went to Rabaul. Due to losses in combat there were no airplanes left, so we returned to Yokosuka on 17 December. Around this time I also did ten days of training at Yokosuka for the *Suisei* carrier bomber, and engineers taught me about the new aircraft.

Working as a Maintenance Instructor
My next assignment was as an instructor for the 14th Term mechanic students at Okazaki. I stayed here until early the following year, when I joined the newly formed 601 *Kōkūtai*. When I was in Okazaki, near Nagoya City, American B-29 bombers bombed the city very heavily. I was stunned to see the body of a young American pilot that must have slammed into the ground because he wasn't wearing a parachute. Because of the high-speed impact his body made an impression in the soil.

601 *Kōkūtai* Days
In February 1944 the 601 *Kōkūtai* was formed at Kanoya Air Base. The mechanics went to the Aichi Factory (in Aichi Prefecture) to inspect the new airplanes before the aviators arrived. We mechanics stayed at the factory, and the pilots flew the new airplanes, one by one, to Kanoya. Then, after the *kōkūtai* was formed in Kanoya, we went to Iwakuni. The carriers *Shōkaku* and *Zuikaku* were at Iwakuni, and we loaded our aircraft on the ships using derricks. Then we left Iwakuni and went to Singapore for training, because at that time there was no fuel in Japan to do flight training. That formation went to Singapore and had training at bases in Seletar, Sembawang, and Tanga. I stayed at each base for about one month while our group was doing training. Our aircraft were divided into smaller groups, and we had intensive, hard training at those bases until mid-May. Then the various smaller groups came back together at Tawi Tawi.

The "A"- Gō Operation (the defense of several crucial areas close to the mainland of Japan, such as the Marianas Islands) started, and the 601 *Kōkūtai* participated in this operation. Our group was attached to Vice Admiral Jisaburō Ozawa's First Mobile Fleet, which had the carriers *Taihō*, *Shōkaku*, and *Zuikaku*. I was on board *Zuikaku*, and at that time I was the most experienced aircraft maintenance man of the *kanbaku* group. During the Battle of the Philippine Sea on 19-20 June, the carriers *Taihō* and *Shōkaku* were sunk by enemy submarines. We lost a lot of men and airplanes from those carriers, so the unit was reorganized at Matsuyama Base in Shikoku. The new *Suisei* carrier bombers (Type 33 models) were sent from the Aichi Factory in Nagoya, and we did intense training. Since the Japanese Navy didn't have any aircraft carriers that we could use, the 601 *Kōkūtai* had to be land-based for future operations.

In February 1945, Vice-Admiral Kimpei Teraoka ordered a *tokkō* operation to start. His order stated that the 601 *Kōkūtai* should now be stationed at Katori Air Base. The commander of our air group was Captain Toshikazu Sugiyama. I was an aircraft maintenance *buntaishi* of the 601 *Kōkūtai*, *Hikōtai #1*, *Suisei* carrier bombers. The overall leader of the carrier bomber unit was Lieutenant Kozō Nomura. On 16 February the first American mobile fleet air raid occurred over the Kantō area. About sixty enemy airplanes strafed and dropped bombs on Katori Air Base. Immediately we counterattacked, and our Zero fighters took off one after another. After the air raid six *Suisei kanbaku* took off to do a reconnaissance/attack mission.

These raids were done on 16-17 February by Task Force 58. They were done for two full days with the purpose of diverting Japan's attention away from the upcoming landings (scheduled for 19 February) on Iwo Jima. The other goal was to neutralize Japan's ground-based air force. Remarkably, over 1,000 carrier-based aircraft took part in the raids and were credited with destroying over 500 enemy planes and sinking several ships and boats.[81]

After this, a large enemy invasion force appeared off Iwo Jima. In response we organized the 2nd *Mitate-tai* ("Imperial Shield Unit"). On 21 February Lieutenant Hiroshi Murakawa led twelve *Suisei* carrier bombers, eight *Tenzan* carrier attack planes, and twelve escorting Type 0 carrier fighters to attack enemy warships off Iwo Jima. They took off from Katori Air Base, stopped and refueled at Hachijō Jima, then did *tokkō* attacks on the American vessels. The results were the following (according to Japanese accounts): one enemy carrier sunk, two enemy battleships immediately sunk, one carrier destroyed, and two cruisers on fire. They also destroyed two other ships, and four transport ships immediately sank.

Two of the Japanese attackers smashed into the escort carrier Bismarck Sea *(CVE-94), which caused heavy damage and two large explosions. Once the fire spread to the magazines they blew up one by one, then an enormous explosion tore off the stern.*[82] *The* Bismarck Sea *subsequently sunk, and 318 men perished during the engagement.*[83] *Around 1700, six Japanese aircraft struck the carrier* Saratoga *(CV-3) and scored five hits on the ship within three minutes.* Saratoga *suffered damage in the flight deck forward, its starboard side was hit twice, and there were also large fires in the hangar deck. Due to this attack, 123 men were dead or missing.*[84] *About two hours after this lethal first attack, the carrier was struck by one additional aircraft. After the crew got the fires under control and the aircraft were recovered,* Saratoga *departed the combat zone and was sent to Bremerton, Washington, for repairs. Because of this damage the carrier wasn't able to resume combat operations until late May 1945.*[85]

On the same day, in the vicinity of Iwo Jima, four other American vessels were damaged by suicide attacks from Japanese aircraft: the escort carrier Lunga Point *(CVE-94), the net cargo ship* Keokuk *(AKN-4), LST-477, and LST-809.*[86] *As a result of this engagement seventeen men died on board* Keokuk.[87]

Rear Admiral Toshinosuke Ichimaru stated, "Our Japanese airplanes did a brave *tokkō* attack." Because of their successful attack mission, the men became optimistic that we still may have a chance to win the war. I personally felt certain that we were not going to lose this conflict. We promised each other to fight courageously against these enemy forces approaching our bases in the Pacific. I received a confidential telegram that stated that there were nineteen fire columns coming from Iwo Jima. The 601 *Kōkūtai* had used up a lot of its aircraft and men conducting these *tokkō* attacks, so we went to Hyakurigahara Air Base (in Ibaraki Prefecture) to regroup and re-equip our unit. After we arrived there we did maintenance work and pilot training.

On 23 March American forces launched intense attacks on Okinawa. *Kikusui* ("Floating Chrysanthemum") Operation #1 was thus initiated, and some aircraft were sent to Kokobu Air Base (in Kyūshū). This operation mostly consisted of *tokkō* aircraft attacking targets off Okinawa. After these sorties were completed *Kikusui* Operations #2 and #3 were conducted. During the month

Iwo Jima in February 1945; the final resting spot for numerous American and Japanese men while engaging in brutal combat. (NA)

The USS *Bismarck Sea* after being struck by Japanese *tokkō* aircraft of the 601 *Kōkūtai*. (NA)

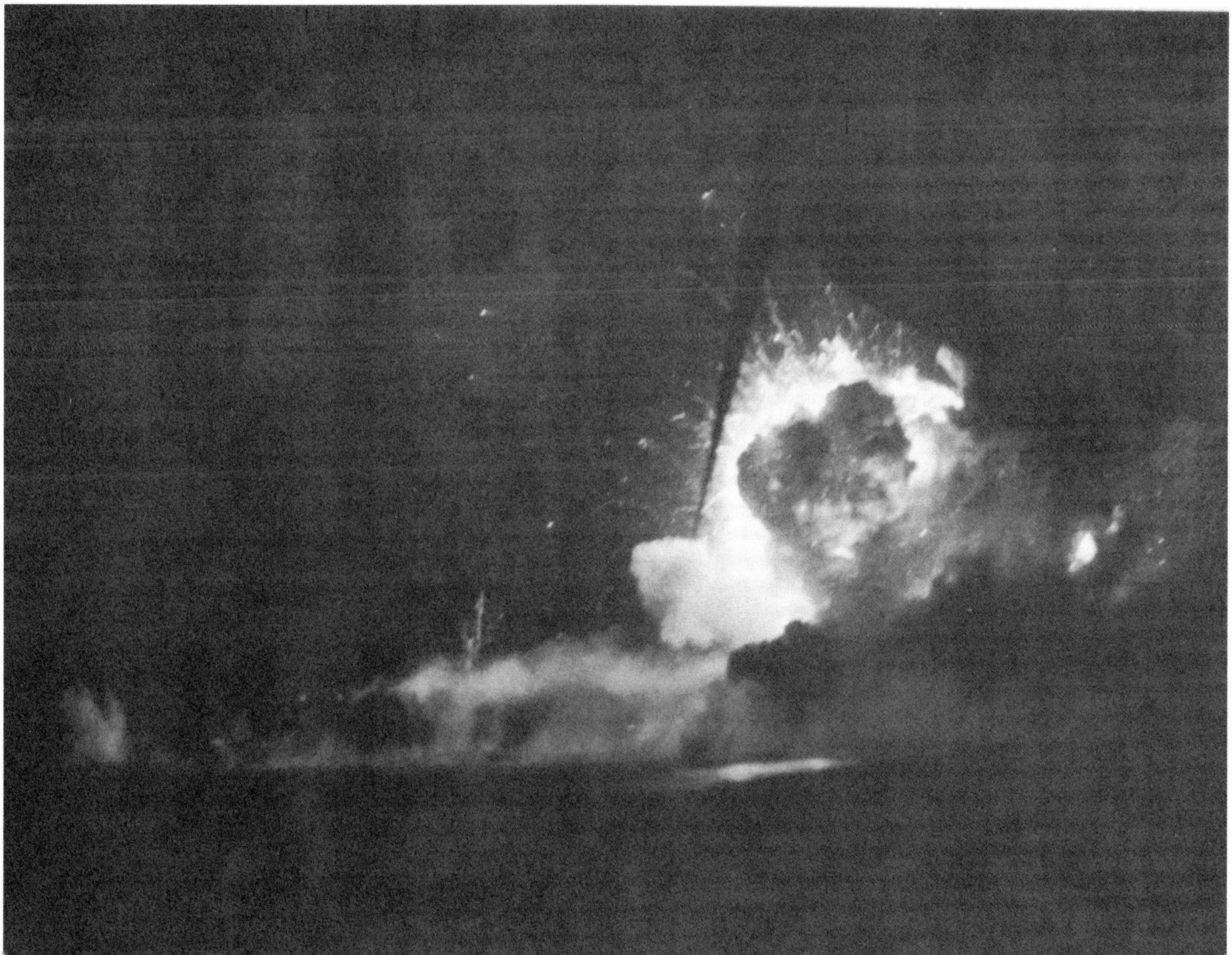

One of the 601 *Kōkūtai's* D4Y4 *Suisei* (Model 43) carrier bombers under maintenance about one or two kilometers away from Hyakurigahara Air Base, which protected the aircraft during Allied air attacks. The D4Y4 *Suisei* (Model 43) was equipped with three RATOG auxiliary rockets, which enabled the aircraft to do take offs on short runways or give extra power during a *tokkō* attack. (Miyashita Collection)

A group photo of the 601 *Kōkūtai* taken in front of the command post at Hyakurigahara Air Base just prior to *Kikusui* Operation #1. This operation consisted of lethal *tokkō* attacks on U.S. Navy ships off Okinawa. Captain Toshikazu Sugiyama, the commander of this air group, is sitting in the second row, sixth from the right (in the tropical service dress uniform). (Miyashita Collection)

of April they did the following attacks: on the 2nd, four airplanes; the 3rd, eighteen airplanes; the 6th, four airplanes; the 7th, eleven airplanes; and on the 17th, five airplanes. At Kokobu Air Base we lost a lot of aircraft and men, so once again we retreated to Hyakurigahara Air Base and tried to rebuild our group.

As a result of these operations the unit lost twenty-six Zero fighters and twenty-three Suisei *carrier bombers, so they returned to Hyakurigahara.*[88]

Initially, the 601 *Kōkūtai* was not formed with the purpose of doing *tokkō* missions. Instead, if our pilots found the enemy they were to attack. However, if the enemy could not be found, the pilots were supposed to return. In the case of the Iwo Jima and Okinawa operations, the pilots were told not to come back. During June 1945 seventy *Suisei kanbaku* and one hundred Type 0 *kansen* were usable and prepared for the mainland defense. Beginning in late July, American mobile fleet airplanes began to attack many places. *Kikusui* Operation #4 was planned so we could retaliate against this new enemy threat. On 9 August Lieutenant Watanabe became the commander, and twelve *Suisei* carrier bombers took off to attack the American mobile unit off Kinkazan Island, in Miyagi Prefecture. After this, on 13 August twelve *Suisei* were dispatched to attack the enemy's mobile unit near the Kantō area.

Maintenance Warrant Officer Hachirō Miyashita on 5 May 1945. (Miyashita Collection)

The Last Day of the War

On 15 August there was an order to do a general attack at noon. However, before doing that there was an order to attack an enemy carrier, so experienced aviators were selected to do it. I was preparing the *Suisei* carrier bombers early in the morning when I saw enemy airplanes flying towards us, so all I could do was escape into a bunker of the command post. I also heard the sound of machine guns. It was like hail falling from the sky. Nearby there were aircraft, which were armed with 500 kilogram (1,102 pound) bombs and full of fuel. They were not hidden, so I was relieved that they were not found.

After the enemy attack was over the commander, Lieutenant Saito, and WO Yo Tawara took off at 1000, but didn't fly in formation with the ten other aircraft participating in the mission. WO Tawara joined the navy the same year I did. I waved my cap to see them off. Then there was preparation for the general attack, and the target would once again be the carrier. The earlier mission specifically was to target the flight deck of the carrier, but for the second attack there was no specific target.

I heard that at noon there was going to be an announcement by the Emperor, and we were supposed to attack after the announcement was over. I heard the announcement from an

9 August 1945: a D4Y4 *Suisei* (Model 43) about to take off to attack the American mobile unit off Kinkazan Island. (Miyashita Collection)

airplane's radio receiver, but because of a lot of noise, I was not able to hear it well. I was expecting that the Emperor was going to encourage us to continue fighting because there was going to be a battle for the mainland. As a result of the morning mission six airplanes were lost, and the remaining six planes did forced landings at many different places. So right before the end of the war sixteen people died, which was really sad. Lieutenant Shinichi Tokuya hurried by bicycle and said that the war was over. When I learned that Japan had surrendered unconditionally, I simply couldn't believe it.

At the command post I felt very distraught, and I couldn't stop crying. Dumplings were served for lunch, but because I was so busy I didn't have time to eat. Then our mission was canceled. Later, I ate but I couldn't taste anything. I wasn't able to eat at all because it was too much to bear. I was energetic before that, but I became depressed and couldn't concentrate on my job. I also couldn't believe that the war ended, and was waiting at the airfield to prepare for the attack; then it started to get dark. At 01900, when I heard the news, I finally could believe that war was over.

On the previous night, it was pitch dark outside because all of the buildings were "blacked out" due to the possibility of enemy air attacks. However, on that night, even the farmhouses lit their lights. The sky was full of stars, and a lot of lights were shining. I felt that the war was over and I survived. However, I was still worried what was going to happen to Japan and what was going to happen to us. There was a lot of speculation going around; for example, every pilot should go to Okinawa, and maintenance workers should gather in Nagoya and work as servants.

On the 16th every airplane was ready to attack. The aircraft were filled up with fuel, and the engines were in excellent condition. So we were able to leave at any moment. Pilots were saying that every airplane should go to Iwo Jima and do *tokkō* attacks. Mechanics were talking about blowing themselves up in the middle of the airfield by taping a tube on the bomb. Because of this we were waiting at the airfield all day.

Then, on the 17th, a Zero fighter from the 302 *Kōkūtai* landed at our air base, and a lieutenant climbed out of the cockpit and said "Why don't we fight until the end?" On the evening of the 18th some higher-ranking people gathered together and had a meeting to discuss the situation. The second highest ranking person there, Commander Kanji Yoshitomi, said, "Since the Emperor made an announcement that Japan would surrender, we can't continue fighting because it could cause a lot of suffering for Japanese civilians.

I want your men to be calm and refrain from doing something stupid." We agreed with him and decided not to continue fighting.

As Miyashita-san states, some members of the 302 Kōkūtai *led by their commander, Captain Yasuna Kozono, a distinguished navy officer, wanted to continue fighting even after the Emperor's radio announcement for Japan to surrender on 15 August. Fortunately calm later prevailed in this group, so they agreed not to fight anymore against the occupying Allied forces.*

From the 19th we lined up the *Suisei kanbaku* on the airfield and removed the propellers from the aircraft. American airplanes also came, and their pilots checked out the situation. On 24 August we started to retire from the navy. I personally retired on 25 August. My final rank in the navy was maintenance, warrant officer.

When I look back on the 601 *Kōkūtai*, I think of its *tokkō* missions and the young men that I sent off on their one-way missions. I did this on many occasions, and recall these times with a lot of sorrow. I thought that it was a last resort because there was nothing else we could do. During that stage of the war the United States controlled both the air and sea, so unless we did something extraordinary, we couldn't win. At that time nobody said that it was bad doing these missions because of the desperate situation we were in. They did *tokkō* mission after *tokkō* mission. Since I was a mechanic, it was very hard and sad to prepare their aircraft because I knew they were going to die. I believe that it's our responsibility to pay our respects to those aviators who perished in the war, and tell the next generation of people about how they were sacrificed fighting for Japan. I hope they are at peace now.

Postwar

My home in Ginza, Tokyo, was destroyed during the 24 May 1945 nighttime B-29 bombing raid, so I had no place to live after the war was over. For a while I was allowed to stay at a farmhouse near Hyakurigahara Air Base. Thereafter, I moved to Tokyo and worked for my oldest brother, who was running an art business. I then joined a papermaking company, which later merged with other companies and became Fuji Paper Company. In 1970 several firms joined together again, and became Japan Paper Pulp Trading Company. After this it became the number one paper company in Japan at that time.

I retired at the age of fifty-five years old in 1973, but later worked as a supervisor at the Yokohama service center of a paint company. After this I worked for the largest navy-related publishing group, and still continue to edit their newspaper, because I'm one of the last surviving navy veterans who saw a lot of combat during World War II. My wife and I had three daughters, but sadly my second daughter died. We now live with my two granddaughters.

Reflections

In regards to my feelings about fighting against the United States during the war, we trained very hard, so I was ready to attack and did my utmost to do my duty well. It's a matter of life or death, so unless you attack, you will be killed. So you have to fight against the enemy. I feel that American pilots were very brave, and their fighting spirit was high. When our carrier was attacked, American aircraft came so close I could clearly see the pilots' faces. I felt that the Japanese people fought for our country and families, while Americans felt the war was like a challenge to them.

I served mostly on carriers and on a few land bases, so I didn't fight the enemy face to face. Instead, I only received their bombs; so there was no personal hatred. When you experience being bombed for the first time, you don't know what to expect. After the first attack you see many people die; so the second time it happens, you are scared. However, there is no place to escape on a ship, so you can't be scared; you have to be brave.

Today, in Japan, many people are opposed to our military forces being deployed overseas. However, as long as we have a security treaty with the United States it is unavoidable. I recently read in the newspaper that if a Japanese soldier died in combat, his family would receive 100 million yen. Today we have to compensate the family of the dead soldier. However, in my navy days, we were considered to be "expendable," and could be replaced quickly. Because of this, very little compensation would be sent to our families if we died during the war. Our Prime Minister Koizumi cannot refuse to send our military, if America requests this, because they protect us. However, other countries probably won't attack our nation because we have the support of the military forces of the United States.

It's hard for me to answer how I feel about fighting in World War II. There is no simple answer for me. We veterans go every year to the Yasukuni Shrine for a memorial service. I believe that whether people die or survive is only a slight difference. I could have died, and if I was told to go and die, I would have done it. Today the educational system is different, and I feel American people are brave.

The Yasukuni Shrine is a Shinto shrine located in Tokyo, Japan. The shrine is dedicated to all of Japan's "war dead," including several war criminals. The facility also has a museum with war-related artifacts from several conflicts. During the war, Japan's military men were taught that if they died in battle their souls would go to the Yasukuni Shrine. Hence, this is a special place for many of Japan's surviving World War II veterans. Several veterans' groups in Japan have their annual meetings and memorial services here, including the surviving tokkō-tai, *or suicide-attack veterans. To many of the veterans that I have met, they visit the Yasukuni Shrine to remember their comrades who died in battle and get together with their wartime buddies. This shrine is also a very controversial place, because other Asian countries, such as China and Korea, protest every time a Japanese politician visits this facility, because they believe this action demonstrates that Japan's previous military actions are justifiable, and the nation is now absolved of what it did during the war. Debate and controversy continues to this day in both Japan and other Asian countries about this complex issue.*

Maintenance Lieutenant Hiroshi Suzuki

"I felt no hatred towards the enemy."

During my three year stay in Japan, the last veteran that I interviewed was a distinguished aircraft mechanic named Hiroshi Suzuki. This particular gentleman was a fortunate survivor of several battles, including Midway and the Battle of the Philippine Sea. Suzuki-san is one of the few higher-ranking maintenance men still alive who served on board a carrier during the war, but I believe he was never before interviewed by other historians.

Suzuki-san currently lives in Toride City, in Ibaraki Prefecture. This city is located about 40 kilometers (25 miles) away from the center of Tokyo. Once my translator "Hammer" and I arrived at his house, we were moved by the beauty of the roses in his large garden. This interesting man is one of a few Japanese Navy veterans that I met who has excellent command of English. Even though he is well into his 80s, Suzuki-san is both mentally and physically very fit. He and his family were very kind to us, and they even gave me some beautiful roses to take home to my wife.

Suzuki's Early Days

I was born in the famous navy port of Yokosuka, Japan, on 24 March 1920. I had two brothers and three sisters. When I was born my father, Sosaburō Suzuki, was in the navy, and stationed at Yokosuka. During his time in the service he served on several warships, including the carrier *Akagi*. The four large navy bases were Yokosuka, Maizuru, Kure, and Sasebo. When our ships were not out to sea, they were stationed in their respective home ports. For example, my father's ship *Akagi* was based at Yokosuka Navy Base.

I joined the navy on 1 April 1937, and attended Maizuru Naval Engineering College. I graduated three years later on 7 August 1940. Normally the curriculum took four years to complete, but due to war it was shortened by one year. Three days after graduation I joined the *Kashima* and did my midshipmen cruise. I stayed on board this ship until transferring to the heavy cruiser *Kumano* on 20 September 1940.

War Breaks Out in 1941

During the first half of 1941 the *Kumano* supported the army's operations in French Indochina. On 1 October 1941 I was ordered to attend aircraft maintenance school, and did this for six months. While I was in this training course war broke out with the United States and her allies. Next, on 28 April 1942, I transferred to the carrier *Akagi*, where I served as a mechanic and a *buntaishi* of the Type 99 *kanbaku* maintenance group.

Maintenance Duties on board *Akagi*

On board the carrier we had three squadrons, and each group had eighteen aircraft and three spares. One squadron used the Type 99 *kanbaku*, the second one operated the Type 97 *kankō*, and the last group flew the Type 0 *kansen*. Each squadron was divided into six sections, and each section was responsible for three aircraft. So all together there were eighteen planes in each squadron (as I mentioned above). Normally one aircraft was maintained by five or six mechanics, but only two or three men actually did the work. The other engineers did miscellaneous work.

One of my duties was to help arrange all of our strike aircraft on the flight deck, which was a real tough job. Spacing between each aircraft was very important. Normally we had a distance of nine meters between each Zero fighter, about ten meters (thirty-three feet) separating each Type 99, and nine meters (thirty feet) between every Type 97. The pilot who was in the leading aircraft had the shortest distance to take off. For land-based flight operations, Zero fighters normally had about 300 meters (984 feet) to take off, but on a carrier the entire flight deck was only 171 meters (561 feet). We mechanics had really tight working conditions on a flight deck that was filled with aircraft, and if just one plane moved abruptly, we could be killed. I remember that a man was killed when he went to help another mechanic with the wheel chucks. This poor guy must have forgotten about the spinning propeller and was instantly killed.

While the strike aircraft were being warmed up, fix or six men were assigned to each plane. However, for take off only two men did the wheel chucks for each aircraft, then scurried to the walkways along the flight deck after it took off. Prior to the take off of our strike group, I had the arduous and stressful task of climbing up on each aircraft to confirm that everything was okay, and to say goodbye to each pilot. Keep in mind, some of these

Hiroshi Suzuki in March 1942. After the Battle of Midway, the Suzuki family thought that he died in the engagement, so they made an 8x10 version of this photo as a memorial to him. They were surprised when they later learned that he survived the battle. (Suzuki Collection)

aviators probably wouldn't return, and I had to do this for every aircraft that would participate in the mission. After that I gave my report to the *hikōchō* to state that our entire strike group was ready to launch. Sometimes, the leading aircraft stalled and crashed into the sea, so if that plane took off safely, the pilots in the following ones felt relieved.

Prior to the Battle of Midway all of the *Akagi* Type 99s had their engines overhauled, which was hard work. Before our carrier left for a combat operation all of the aircraft had to be in top mechanical shape in every respect, but just in case we took along additional spare aircraft and engines. After the engines were reinstalled every plane had to be test flown. On these test flights, I usually flew on the aircraft to make sure everything was okay. Every time a Type 99 *kanbaku* went up, the pilot went through a number of maneuvers, including loops and slow rolls, which made me very sick. Then the aviator practiced doing dives at 45 degrees, but it felt like 90 degrees to me! During each dive the aviator pulled up at 400 meters (1,312 feet). I remember when one guy hit the ground while practicing his dive-bombing technique. The following day I tried to do all of my test flights before lunch, but I still got sick to my stomach. Nevertheless, after doing numerous test-flights, day in and day out, I didn't get sick anymore, and it was easy to recognize the skill level of each pilot.

The Battle of Midway

My first combat experience was the Battle of Midway in June 1942. While we were eating rice balls for breakfast there was an announcement that enemy aircraft were coming to attack our ship. Then a trumpet also was blown to warn our crew of the incoming planes. Immediately we stopped eating, and I saw about nine B-26 medium bombers trying to attack our carriers. I thought several of them were shot down by our Type 0 carrier fighters, which were doing combat air patrols over our carriers. Next our Zeros returned to *Akagi* to be refueled and rearmed for their next mission. Then,

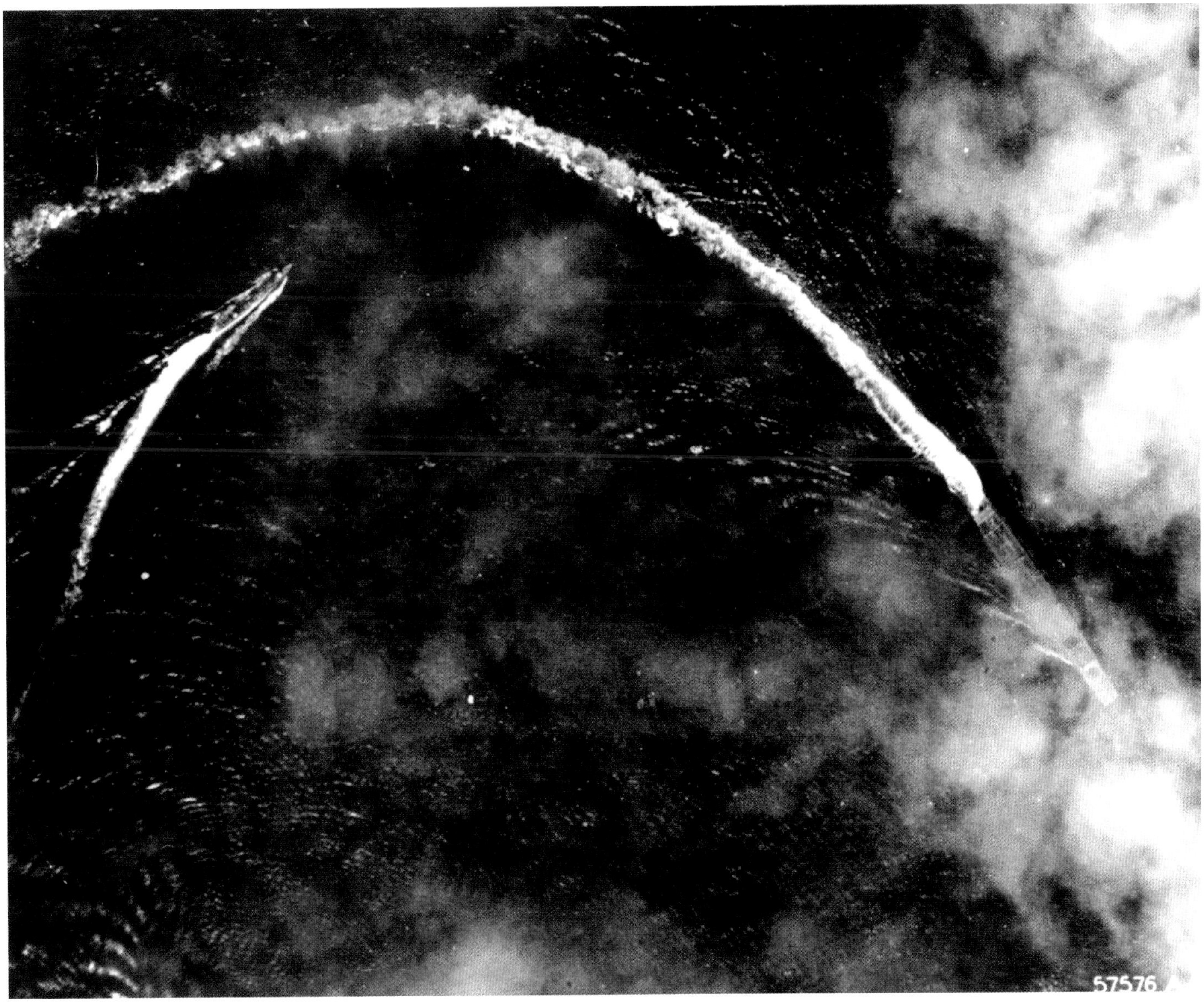

B-17 "Flying Fortress" bombers try to drop bombs on the *Akagi* from high altitude. (NHC via Jonathan Parshall)

after all the maintenance work was complete on the fighters, we did a final inspection of the aircraft before they flew again. We were so busy trying to get all this work done under such strenuous combat conditions.

Enemy B-17 bombers, which were flying at high altitude, also tried to drop bombs on the carriers *Hiryū* and *Sōryū*. Geysers of water engulfed the *Sōryū* and, since I couldn't see the carrier, I thought it must have been hit very badly. However, after the water went back down it looked like the ship was okay. As I looked at the water, it was filled with both Japanese and American aviators who were shot down during the aerial melees. I thought it was funny that you could tell the difference between the pilots of the two nations because they used different swimming strokes. The sea was warm and calm, so downed aviators had a good chance to survive.

During this battle, the situation changed so rapidly that I constantly went back and forth to the operations center to hear what was happening and to get my orders. I was there when the SBD Dauntless dive-bombers swooped down to attack our carrier. Once again, a warning blared out that we were being attacked. The first bomb was a near miss, but I was knocked down by the force of the blast. I stood up and checked my body for any wounds. Fortunately I wasn't hurt, except that my face was all black. Then there was a direct hit on our carrier that caused a big explosion. This bomb landed squarely on the Zero fighters sitting on the flight deck. As the aircraft ignited a big fire rose up, and then the 20 mm shells from the aircraft started to crack off. I thought that the *Akagi* would split in half due to the big explosions, but it was a very strong warship. Due to the intense heat, the rivets from the steel plates started to pop out like they were bullets. One of my classmates was wounded because he was hit by some of these lethal rivets flying through the air.

Gradually the blaze began to spread, and everything was on fire. In the beginning the engine room was able to still operate normally, but later in the evening when the fire spread, the engines stopped. I went down to the lower deck; then the order was given to abandon ship. I jumped into the water and was rescued by a small boat that was sent from the destroyer *Arashi*. Each of our carriers was escorted by three destroyers, and the *Arashi* was one of our escorts. As I looked at the doomed carrier it looked fine from the side, but the flight deck and center of the ship were burning out of control. I was rescued by the destroyer just after dark, but the *Arashi* was so crowded that there was nowhere to sit. I hadn't eaten since breakfast and was starving. I was very happy to finally eat something, and the food tasted delicious.

During the night the *Arashi* circled around *Akagi* to protect it from additional enemy attacks. After sunrise the order was given to scuttle the carrier with our torpedoes. The torpedo specialist, who was ordered to launch the torpedoes, was weeping while he had to carry out this unpleasant task. Prior to this time he had trained very hard to do this job, but never had to fire any torpedoes in combat. So his first combat experience was firing torpedoes at one of his own ships. Two torpedoes hit the *Akagi*, and there was a big explosion after the second one hit the carrier. Gradually, our once magnificent ship began to tilt over and sank very slowly. With the *Akagi* almost completely underwater, the rays of the sun illuminated the chrysanthemum (The Imperial Seal of Japan) on the bow of the ship, and it became very bright. After the carrier was completely submerged underwater there was a very big explosion, and *Akagi* was gone.

We lost four carriers during the Battle of Midway, but the newspapers were not allowed to print what actually happened. Nevertheless, my family thought that I died because my father heard what really happened in the battle while stationed at Kasumigaura Air Base. Some of the Midway survivors told him that *Akagi* sunk, so he thought I perished in the battle. Once a week my father went home to Yokosuka, hoping to hear some official news about my fate; but the navy didn't say a word to my family. Since they thought I died, my family paid a lot of money to make an 8x10 picture of me, which would be displayed in our home as a memorial. Later my family was shocked to see me return home safely from this disastrous battle.

Personally, I learned some important lessons because of the intense combat which occurred during the Battle of Midway. Remarkably, prior to this battle, we never used ear plugs on the flight deck while spotting the strike aircraft. It was very difficult to do this job while our ships were under attack, and there was a lot of noise around us. So, after this battle, I recommended the use of ear plugs. Secondly, before June 1942 we didn't use megaphones on the flight deck, so it was very difficult to give orders. Therefore, I used a megaphone for future operations. Thirdly, I recommended the use of a small flashlight to help navigate through the dark passageways on board our carrier. Lastly, I thought it was important for maintenance officers to wear two white sashes over their uniform (while in combat) and to always have a whistle. I felt that it would be easier for my men to identify and locate their superiors if these items were utilized.

Another important development was the use of hand signals by our aircraft maintenance men. Although they were commonly used in the engine section (*kikan-ka*), hand signals were not used by our aircraft mechanics. I became aware of the need for hand signals during the Battle of Midway, and began using them when I was later appointed to be the *buntaichō* of the maintenance group for the Type-97 *kankō* and *Suisei* on the *Zuikaku*. Every morning for fifteen minutes we practiced sending messages by hand signals, both individually and in a "relay" method with several people. This new communication method enabled us to communicate with each other well, even when the aircraft engines were running on the flight deck.

As I mentioned earlier, one of my most difficult duties was to do the last check to make sure everything was okay for each and every aviator and their aircraft prior to take off. However, after we adopted the use of hand signals on the flight deck to convey messages, this job was done in a better fashion. Later in the war we did it this way. One mechanic stood on the wing of each aircraft, and he gave me a signal that the plane was ready to go. At this time I would be looking at all of the flight deck operations via my binoculars to make sure everything was all right. If there was a problem, such as a bad spark plug, the mechanic of that respective aircraft would notify me by doing a hand signal, and we would do whatever was necessary to fix the issue prior to launch.

Action in the Solomon Islands

After the Battle of Midway on 25 July 1942, I was ordered to the Yokosuka *Kōkūtai* and served as a *buntaishi* for the maintenance group. On 20 January 1943 I was assigned to the carrier *Zuikaku* as a *buntaichō* of the *kankō* maintenance group. First, our aviators flew the Type 97 carrier attack plane, then switched over to the *Tenzan*. Our carrier went to Truk Island, then to Rabaul, on New Britain Island. I thought the overall living conditions on Rabaul were poor, but we couldn't complain. Our base was attacked almost every day, but our supplies were usually safe, because everything was stored in underground tunnels. In November 1943 our group's aircraft participated in combat operations off Bougainville Island.

The Battle of the Philippine Sea

On 11 February 1944 I became the *buntaichō* of the maintenance division of the 601 *Kōkūtai*. Then, on 7 May 1944, I was appointed to the same position on the carrier *Zuikaku*. Our group went to Singapore for three months of training because there was no fuel in Japan. At that time we changed our aircraft from the Type 97 *kankō* to the *Tenzan*, and the Type 99 *kanbaku* to the *Suisei*. We used three different bases at Singapore to do our training: one base was for fighters, one for dive-bombers, and the last for *kankō*. The training was intense, and almost every day there was an accident. There were a lot of crashes because the pilots and mechanics were mostly rookies, and they were flying new aircraft. Besides that, the weather in Singapore was usually very bad, and we had a lot of rain. Due to all of these reasons there were a lot of accidents.

Our new aircraft, the *Tenzan*, had a very powerful 2,000 horsepower engine. There was a problem with the rudders coming off the aircraft during take off, probably due to the turbulence from the powerful engines. So we had to ask the factory to redesign the rudder, to make the aircraft safe for flight operations.

The 601 *Kōkūtai* went aboard three carriers (*Zuikaku*, *Shōkaku*, and *Taihō*), and participated in the Battle of the Philippine Sea during June 1944. During the battle I was on *Zuikaku*, and the two other carriers were sunk. Several enemy aircraft, which looked like fighters, flew over *Zuikaku*. At that time I was in the command post, located at the rear of the middle portion of the bridge. Our fighters were getting ready for take off on the flight deck to protect our ships. The enemy aircraft strafed our flight deck, which damaged some of our planes, and right in front of my eyes several mechanics were killed. Fortunately the flight deck still could be used for air operations, and we had no other damage on board the carrier.

A formation of 601 *Kōkūtai's Tenzan* carrier attack planes flying a training mission prior to the Battle of the Philippine Sea. (Nakamura Collection via Lansdale)

Most of our aircraft that participated in combat operations during this battle didn't return; there was only a handful of survivors. This is because our aviators didn't have enough time to become familiar with the new aircraft onboard our carrier. They had just started using the *Suisei*, which replaced the Type 99 *kanbaku* and the *Tenzan*, the successor to the Type 97 *kankō*. At this stage in the war a lot of our pilots were not experienced, so when the navy changed their aircraft, it was very difficult for them to fly these new models in combat for the first time. On the other hand, we mechanics didn't have much trouble doing maintenance work on these new aircraft. In all, we had sufficient time to get our planes ready for their first strike mission, and they were able to take off safely.

During this battle the Zuikaku *took one direct bomb hit aft of the island. It penetrated the flight deck and started a fire in the hangar. There also were five bombs that were near misses. Luckily for the carrier's crew the fire was extinguished, and damage was very moderate.*[89]

Back to Japan

Once *Zuikaku* returned to Japan on 24 June I went to Yokosuka again. There I was assigned to be the temporary equipment officer for the construction of the carriers *Unryū* and *Shinano*. While the latter carrier was being built, I made some suggestions for the design of the aircraft hangar, based on my experiences during the Battle of Midway. For example, I wanted the *Shinano* to have a system that made it easy to have fuel pumped out of the aircraft into a storage tank prior to when they were lowered into the aircraft hangar.

Both the Unryū *and* Shinano *were later sunk during the war. On 19 December 1944 the* Unryū *was the last Japanese fleet carrier sunk in the war, by a torpedo from the American submarine USS* Redfish. *It sank within seven minutes and 1,238 men perished, including the captain. The carrier's precious cargo, thirty* "Ohka" *suicide rocket planes, which were bound for the Philippines, went down with the ship.*[90] *The* Shinano *sank on 29 November 1944, after being struck by four torpedoes from the USS* Archerfish. *The*

Zuikaku (center) with two destroyers under attack by U.S. Navy carrier-based aircraft from Task Force 58, during the late afternoon of 20 June 1944. (NA)

carrier's cargo also contained fifty "Ohka" *suicide rocket planes and six* "Shinyo" *suicide boats, which were going be used in the Philippines. Captain Toshio Abe (by his choice) and 1,435 men perished when the carrier sank.*[91]

The Last Year of the War

My next assignment was to serve as instructor and *buntaichō* for aircraft maintenance with the Yokosuka *Kōkūtai*; then I had this same position with the 1st Sagano *Kōkūtai*. I was at Yokosuka when the war ended. My final rank in the navy was maintenance lieutenant, and I was officially discharged on 15 September 1945.

Postwar

After the war I worked for a trading company, and in the 1950s transferred to our office in New York City. After I retired from this firm I started my own trading company, which I have run from my home for the past twenty-five years.

I got married to my wife Etsuko on 19 June 1945, just one year after the Battle of the Philippine Sea. I was intent on working harder, because I never dreamed that the war would end just two months later. We have two daughters, Kyoko and Yoko. Yoko, my younger daughter, is now working for the National Medical Clinic located in Hiroo, Tokyo, as a head nurse. Most of the clinic's patients are foreign nationals living around the Hiroo area, many of whom are Americans. I think this is a unique fate for a member of our family because of my past experience in World War II.

Suzuki-san's Passion

When I went on a field trip to Yokohama as a 5th grader of Tsurukubo Elementary School (Yokosuka City) and visited a rose garden in the *Minato-no-Mieru-oka* Park, I became intrigued with roses for the first time. Of course, I had no knowledge of roses at that time; I was just deeply impressed by their exquisite beauty. In the 1990s, when I had more free time, I started gardening and focused on growing roses. I began with twelve rose bushes; now I have sixty of them. I became a member of the Ibaraki Rose Society several years ago and learned how to take care of my rose bushes. For example, they taught us how to prune the bushes, spray insecticides on them, and properly fertilize them. After learning all of these new techniques I started to grow more beautiful roses. As a result, now I win prizes from time to time at the contests held during the bi-annual rose fairs.

If I get lazy and don't take care of my roses, they won't become beautiful. On the contrary, beautiful roses will only bloom if I make every effort to take care of them. I always work hard towards my goal of winning a prize at the next contest, which makes me forget my old age. So that is my way of keeping fit, and it gives me a new sense of purpose in life.

Reflections

During the war I felt no hatred toward the enemy. I just carried out my duties to the best of my ability. I had no special feeling toward the enemy because, unlike army soldiers, we Navy men never saw the faces of our enemy during a battle. I feel so fortunate to have survived several near-death experiences while in the Navy. During the Battle of Midway I could have perished during the air attack and the eventual sinking of the carrier *Akagi*. On another occasion, while getting ready to land in a *Tenzan kankō*, my aircraft almost collided with another one, but managed to swerve off the runway in time. My last near-death experience occurred during a flight to Singapore on a Douglas DC-2 transport aircraft. While we were flying above some really rough mountainous terrain one of the DC-2's engines stopped, but miraculously restarted just 50 meters (164 feet) above the ground—that was a close call! The pilot of this DC-2 didn't even realize right away that one engine had stopped, so we were really fortunate not to crash. I consider myself one lucky survivor of World War II.

Part 2

The second section of this book covers all the veterans involved with flying or maintaining the *kankō*, or carrier attack planes (in English). The full Japanese name is *kanjō kōgekiki*. To help make my text user-friendly and still utilize some original Japanese terminology, I chose to use either *kankō*, or in English, torpedo bomber or carrier attack plane. During the war members of the Japanese Navy didn't use western code names like "Kate" to describe the Nakajima Type 97 *kankō*, so I chose not to use them in this work as well. This particular type of aircraft was used for level-bombing missions, torpedo attack sorties, and sometimes utilized for reconnaissance duties. It was manned by a crew of three men: a pilot, an observer/navigator, and a radioman/rear gunner.

The Nakajima B5N1 Type 97 *kankō* was initially assigned to an operational unit in late spring-early summer 1938. In August 1938 B5N1s began flying combat missions in China, and joined the fleet that same year. This *kankō*, like many of Japan's wartime aircraft, didn't have self-sealing fuel tanks, and had only one flexible 7.7 mm Type 92 machine gun (mounted in the rear part of the fuselage) as protection. It was powered by one Nakajima Hikari 3 nine-cylinder, air-cooled radial engine rated at 770 horsepower for take off. Because the B5N1 was a bit underpowered for flying combat missions, an updated Type 97 *kankō* was redesignated B5N2 and fitted with a 1,000 horsepower, Nakajima NK1B Sakae 11, fourteen-cylinder, air cooled radial engine. Armament for all models consisted of either one 800 kilogram (1,764 pound) torpedo or 800 kilograms of bombs.

During the Pearl Harbor attack and combat missions throughout the first half of the Pacific War, the B5N2 Type 97 *kankō* was a workhorse, and performed very well in combat. In the beginning of World War II, this aircraft was flown by some of the most highly skilled naval aviators in the world, who were capable of doing very difficult low-level torpedo attacks and level-bombing. However, because of limited performance, no self-sealing tanks, and only one 7.7 mm machine gun, this aircraft also suffered very heavy losses in combat.

The B5N2 Type 97 carrier attack plane was replaced by the Nakajima B6N1 *Tenzan* (Allied code name "Jill") in late 1943/early 1944. This new *kankō* wasn't assigned to an operational group until early Fall 1943. The first combat for the *Tenzan* occurred during Operation Ro against Allied landings on Bougainville in November 1943, when carrier units were land-based at Rabaul (New Britain Island).

The first model of this *kankō*, the B6N1 (model 11), was powered by a Nakajima NK7A Mamoru 11, fourteen-cylinder, air-cooled radial engine rated at 1,800 horsepower for take off. The next version, the B6N2, was fitted with a Mitsubishi MK4T Kasei 25, fourteen-cylinder, air-cooled radial engine, which had 1,850 horsepower for take off.

B6N1s and B6N2s (model 12) were fitted with one flexible rear-firing 7.7 mm, Type 97 machine gun, and another 7.7 mm (of the same type) that fired through the ventral tunnel. The only difference in armament on later models was that the rear-firing 7.7 mm machine gun was swapped with a 13 mm, Type 2 machine gun. Bomb load for all the *Tenzan* consisted of 800 kilograms (1,764 pounds) of bombs or one torpedo.

A final version of the breed (the B6N3) was intended to be manufactured, but the war ended before it could be produced. The B6N3 was going to incorporate a strengthened undercarriage with larger wheels, which would make the aircraft better suited to operate from land bases, because by the summer of 1945 Japan didn't really have a viable amount of aircraft carriers to fight allied forces in the Pacific. During the last two years of the war the *Tenzan* carrier attack plane saw a lot of combat in such engagements as the Battle of the Philippine Sea, the Philippines Campaign, the Okinawa Campaign, and lastly was an aircraft used for *tokkō* attacks against allied ships.

One last aircraft that should be noted in this section is the Aichi B7A1 *Ryusei* (Allied code name "Grace"), although none of the veterans in this book flew this aircraft. The *Ryusei* was the largest and heaviest carrier-based aircraft ever operated by the Imperial Japanese Navy during World War II. This particular aircraft was designed to be a replacement for both the *Tenzan* (a *kankō*) and the *Suisei* (a *kanbaku*). It was powered by a Nakajima NK9C Homare 12, eighteen cylinder, air-cooled, radial engine, which had 1,825 horsepower at take off. Armament on the *Ryusei* was two-wing mounted 20 mm cannons, and either one flexible, rear-facing 7.92 mm or 13 mm machine gun. It could carry up to 800 kilograms worth of bombs (in an enclosed bomb bay) or one torpedo. Only 108 of these unique aircraft were produced, and they saw limited service towards the end of the war. [92]

Ensign Takeshi Maeda

"Japan lost the war, but we were still lucky."

When I did my first research trip to Japan in the spring of 1999, one of the first veterans I was able to meet was Takeshi Maeda. At that time he was the president of Unabarakai, *the Japanese veterans' group. Maeda-san was one of the men who understood the purpose of my research, and did everything he could to support my work with the Japanese Navy veterans. The image the ex-Navy aviator projected to me was that he was very proud of his long Navy career, but still humble. He also stressed on numerous occasions that it was important to get all my stories "right," and take time to research everything properly, so future generations would know what really happened in the war.*

I was surprised to learn later that when this ex-Navy aviator was a child, he dreamed about being a painter, not a pilot; but his family discouraged him. Maeda-san was truly lucky to survive World War II. Early in the war he participated in numerous combat missions, including Pearl Harbor, the Rabaul attack, and Midway. He was severely wounded during the Battle of Midway, but luckily was rescued and eventually recovered. Later in the war Maeda-san flew dangerous torpedo attack missions off Okinawa.

During my stay in Japan we met on several occasions and talked a great deal about his wartime experiences. He also gave me his private memoir "Tsukubasan Yosoro," *which was written in 1979, and allowed me to publish it in this book, for the first time for the general public (in both the western world and Japan). Maeda's book is a treasure-trove of stories covering his wartime career and memories of so many fallen comrades. Part of his story about the Battle of Midway, which follows, was an excerpt from the speech that he wrote for a Midway symposium held at the National Museum of Naval Aviation (Pensacola, Florida) a few years ago.*

This distinguished veteran is well into his 80s, but is still very sharp. At first he seemed reluctant to talk about his personal feelings about fighting for Japan, but as we got to know each other better, Maeda-san began to open up more about how he really felt. He still enjoys socializing and drinking alcohol to relax. He currently lives with his wife in Tokyo. On a personal note, one of the highlights of my stay in Japan was walking with this accomplished aviator through the gates of the Yasukuni Shrine, to attend a veterans' memorial service with him.

Maeda's Early Years

I was born on 31 March 1921, in a small town called Ono, in Fukui Prefecture. I had two older brothers who joined the army and fought in China. I learned that my mother died soon after my birth. My father was a construction engineer, and our family was financially well-off. I graduated from middle school, and volunteered for the flying corps of the Navy at the age of seventeen. I joined the navy because I loved airplanes, especially navy aircraft. Unfortunately, my father died of lung cancer on 14 September 1939 when I was in the navy, leaving three sons behind.

Training Days in the Navy

On 23 September 1938 I arrived at Yokosuka, which was still hot. Every time a train arrived I saw a group of people in junior high school uniforms get off the train. Waiting to greet them was a group of Navy petty officers, who would then escort them to a local inn. These young men, including me, who came to Yokosuka, were required to take a secondary check up test before being admitted into the Navy.

The following day we were supposed to attend school. There was a large room in the inn, and the petty officers were explaining to us how to take the test. After that we were divided into groups and socialized with each other. I found it strange that quite a few applicants were accompanied by their parents, and one guy came with both his father and mother. I thought that this wasn't a kindergarten entrance ceremony and found this disdainful. I just relaxed and did some "people watching." Some of the potential trainees were still students and wore their caps, while others looked older, because they had already graduated from school.

I gradually lost my confidence after seeing so many other able-bodied young men hoping to join the Navy. What surprised me was a guy wearing Japanese clogs and speaking a Kyūshū dialect. He seemed to be very macho, and his name was Yoshiyasu Ōtsuka. This guy passed the entrance test but didn't graduate, because he was considered unsuitable for the Navy. In general, people with Kyūshū dialects looked tough, and when I listened to them, it sounded like they were speaking another language. The school that I came from had very few students who were in the Army or Navy.

Maeda-san in his dress uniform while he was a member of the Tateyama *Kōkūtai*. This photo was taken on 3 November 1942. (Maeda Collection)

Instead, most of my school classmates who had good grades went on to elite high schools, not the military.

After dinner at the inn, I talked with the young man who came with his parents. He introduced me to them; his father was a church pastor. This was my first encounter with Shirō Sakai. His brother was a fighter pilot who died in action at Matsuyama Base. So the Sakai family had two boys who would later become Navy pilots. I felt sorry for his mother, who must have felt a lot of sadness because of the war.

I moved to a barracks at Yokosuka Base and was tested for one month to see if I met all the qualifications to be in the Navy. The people who didn't pass went home, and gradually there were more and more empty bunks. In the end, only Sakai-san and I passed the final test. Sakai's parents were pleased, but also concerned. They probably realized that they wouldn't see their son for a long time. Out of the 3000 potential applicants, only 260 of us passed the entrance exam. The people who passed participated in an entrance ceremony the following day; then we went on to live as Navy men.

The formal announcement that we passed the test was made on 1 October in an ugly, wooden military barracks. We were provided with Navy uniforms, and our personal belongings were sent home. I was excited about getting my uniform, but at the same time I felt shocked. Everyone was disgusted that they gave us these ugly sailors' uniforms, instead of the sharp uniforms that officers wore in the Navy.

Suddenly, a tough looking guy with a loud voice appeared. He had a long stick, and tapped the floor with it as he walked. This guy was huge and spelled trouble. He said, "I am the senior instructor named Santoki." He held that stick all the time, and constantly gestured with it. Besides this senior instructor, there were two additional Navy officers standing proudly with their Navy daggers. Later I learned that one of the officers was a lieutenant commander and a *buntaichō*. Santoki-san said, "As of today, you are Navy personnel, and you have to think before you speak, not like civilian people who can say whatever they want. If you act like an old woman, you are going to be strictly reprimanded." His comments were very malicious, and everyone felt very intimidated by him.

Lieutenant Akira Sakamoto, *Zuikaku* Type 99 dive-bomber group *buntaichōs* during the Pearl Harbor attack. He also was a good friend of Maeda's eldest brother. (Prange Collection via Wenger)

Later I tried on a pair of oversized trousers and a shirt. I thought that this was a temporary uniform, and I would get a more formal one after they adjusted the size. I guess I was too hopeful at that time. I imagined getting a sharp uniform, like Sakamoto-san wore during the summer when he came back for vacation. He was a person from my alma mater and lived near my house. Lieutenant Akira Sakamoto was a 63rd term graduate of the Navy Academy, and later participated in the Pearl Harbor attack as a *buntaichō* of the *Zuikaku* Type 99 dive-bomber group.

On 5 October there was an entrance ceremony, but I didn't have time to think about how we would be treated. The following evening I was summoned to the barracks. There was Sakamoto-san, with a round face and slight smile. He asked what is my brother doing now? At that time, my eldest brother was fighting in China. Lieutenant Sakamoto was one year older than my eldest brother. They were close friends, and both men were black belts in judo. I asked Sakamoto-san, "What is my position in the Navy?" He looked puzzled. I was shocked to see an instructor standing behind me, trying to overhear our conversation. Therefore, he couldn't tell me the truth. Lieutenant Sakamoto just said, "You just have to be patient until you get used to it." He went on to say that he would be transferring to a frontline unit in China very soon, then said goodbye.[93]

Our basic training lasted one and a half years, but had nothing to do with learning how to fly. During this time I studied such things as ground combat and cutter boat training. All of this intense training made me realize that I wasn't a Japanese civilian anymore, and I really started to be "aware" of the environment we were in. I also learned that in the Japanese Navy, it was the years that counted, not the ranks. Even if you were promoted, having a good conduct chevron was even more important. At that time it was difficult for me to understand, but I started to realize that I now had to follow some Navy regulations and customs.

Every day there was hard training; especially the cutter boat training, which was the hardest activity for my small body. During the winter the sea around Yokosuka was very windy, and when we circled around a nearby island, we were hit by strong waves. So if you weren't careful you could lose your oar. Due to the intense rowing calluses on my body opened up, and my flesh became visible. Because of the friction between my body and the seat my pants were covered with blood. After that your flesh became infected, and it produced yellow puss. Even if the *hanchō* was aware of your condition he ignored it. I would go to the infirmary, and they treated my wounds by applying ointment and gauze. The following day, when I did cutter boat training, the same thing would happen again, and my old wounds would reopen, which was very painful.

During training my classmate Seijirō Kishida (who later died in the Battle of the Coral Sea as an observer on a Type 97 *kankō*) was in my *buntai*.[94] He was the first one to get the initiation of being hit by a baseball bat. Kishida-san was small in stature, and when you saw him, he looked very weak. He received a lot of love from his parents, and looked like a guy that grew up in a good family. Kishida-san looked like he couldn't take it anymore. One night he complained about his hardships to an instructor and said he wanted to quit. The following day he was hit with a baseball bat in front of our entire class. We witnessed this terrible abuse, and felt anger and hatred building inside us. How could a human being hit another with a baseball bat?

We were hit with a baseball bat for a number of reasons. The Japanese Army adopted the German style of training and, beginning in the Meiji era, our Navy began to follow a British style of training. For example, a Japanese Naval aviator would get hit if he failed to land his aircraft properly or drank too much alcohol. Another aspect of this discipline system was that if one person in a group did something wrong, everyone in the group was hit. This is because it was our responsibility to work as a group, and you had to pay attention to what each person did. I thought this form of discipline was very bad, and I am sure the United States Navy would never beat servicemen like the Japanese Navy did.

In flight training, the trainee pilot sat in the front seat and the instructor was in the cockpit behind him. If a rookie aviator did something wrong, he would be hit in the back of the head with a wooden stick. One way we dealt with this abuse was by wrapping a towel under our flight helmets. Our instructors caught on quickly and, once we landed, they made us take off our flight helmets, then struck us on our heads with the sticks.

As a child I was often disciplined physically by my father, so I didn't complain about the calluses on my palms and feet. I was born in snow country, and during my primary school days my father never allowed me to wear socks throughout the winter and summer. I felt ashamed, because at one time I despised my parents, since I thought that they were too unconventional. When I came home for vacation I gave my father a massage, but the New Year's holiday passed too quickly.

1939 – Training Continues

One day in February there was some talk in my group about our classmate Akira Igawa, of the 12th *Buntai*. I heard that he was hospitalized because of a cold. I thought it was a rumor, but it turned out to be true. According to our instructors, Igawa-san was diagnosed with a chest disease, and the young man realized that he couldn't dedicate his life to his country, so he committed suicide. We had a memorial service for him at a temple in Yokosuka. Physically, Igawa-san was plump, but he had a fair complexion, so he looked weak. I think the hard training really affected him. When his sister attended the memorial service, I told her about our intense training regime, and she thought the Navy had killed him. Normally whenever someone dies, we honor them with kind words. However, in his eulogy for Igawa-san, Mr. F, the *buntaichō*, really didn't want to believe that this young trainee stuck a fruit knife in his stomach because of his diagnosis.

On 17 April, during training on board a ship, Commander Yoshio Furuta left our group. Since we had joined the Navy everyone respected him. He was small in stature and had a mustache. When Furuta-san spoke he was very persuasive and logical. Commander Furuta also had great hopes for the graduates of our training class. During gunnery school he appointed well-qualified people to be instructors, and did his best to give an educational foundation for us. Just like the old saying that children don't understand their

通信兵器の發達は軍用航空機の活動に大きな貢献をもたらせてゐる。文字通りコツコツと、地味ではあるが無電もまた重要な課業の一つである

年は若いが體は大人並、一丼の汁粉ぐらゐでは胃袋が承知しないといふ。この旺盛な食慾こそ少年兵たちの健康のバロメーターだ

短艇下ろしの練習をする少年兵たち。洗濯したばかりの真白な作業服に海上を

An excellent series of wartime photos that illustrate basic training for a young man in the Imperial Japanese Navy. (Werneth Collection)

parents' feelings, we criticized Navy policies at any chance we could get. We disliked our arrogant instructors. Our instructors also noted that we didn't like our sailor-type uniforms, and this information must have reached Commander Furuta. We had no way of knowing what happened exactly, but Furuta-san must have expressed his feelings very strongly regarding this matter. In fact, there were many students who told their alma maters not to take the test to join the Navy. Those letters were censored, and when this information got back to the trainees, things got nasty. It went so far as people boycotting nighttime classroom study, so I can clearly understand how Commander Furuta must have felt. So in this unfortunate chain of events Furuta-san may have thought that he must take the responsibility for these issues, and after seven months he left. His contribution was great, because he convinced the Navy to adopt a seven button tunic, but at that time there was opposition from the supply department. Furuta's idea was finally adopted in 1942. I would like to take this time to apologize to Furuta-san and to say thank you.

In July 1939 I temporarily joined the Tsukuba *Kōkūtai*. Prior to that, I trained on a flight simulator at Kasumigaura, and then I took my pilot qualification test. Before this time I received a certain amount of flight training, but this was the first time for me to get on an airplane and control it. So I forgot all about my earlier painful experiences, such as land-fighting and cutter boat training.

I joined the Tsukuba *Kōkūtai* gladly; however, it was a place where some demons lived, including Mr. O and Mr. K., along with a bunch of other instructors. When I was flying in a training aircraft, behind me was an instructor saying, "You're so stupid!" while at the same time whacking me in the back of my head with a stick. Right in front of us was Mt. Tsukuba, and our aircraft swayed to the left and right, so our course couldn't be fixed. When I landed, he used many kinds of reasons to criticize and beat me. This instructor also ordered me to run one lap around the airfield with my parachute pack dangling behind me. Keep in mind, this was during the summer. We ran along the outer fence of the airfield, and behind us (on bicycles) were instructors. They chased us with sticks, just like wolves chasing a herd of sheep. I thought those instructors abused us because they thought it helped them get promoted quickly.

One day when I was preparing to eat a meal, I saw Ichirō Kobayashi washing with a dirty rag the dishes and tea cup of Mr. O, one of our most intimidating teachers. Kobayashi-san was a graduate of Azabu Junior High School and much older than us. He also was familiar with many worldly things, and spoke Tokyo street language quite well. So a country boy like me had a lot of things to learn from him. Long after the war I learned that his father was an excellent western-style painter. I was afraid when I saw Mr. O's shadow lurking right behind Kobayashi-san. The young trainee then poured tea in Mr. O's cup, and he noticed everyone was looking at him. Kobayashi-san turned pale and exchanged the instructor's dishes with well cleaned ones. Next, he drank from Mr. O's cup and smiled. All of our faces turned blue, and we thought that there would be hell to pay for this incident. Nevertheless, Mr. O didn't say anything and went to the teachers' lounge. After this occurrence he didn't beat us as much.

Memories of People from Maeda's Small Group

On 1 October our training group was divided into two groups: pilots and observers. Exactly one year had passed since we entered the Navy and we said goodbye to our friends, feeling both happy and sad at the same time. We were together for one year through good and bad times. Some of the trainees were able to be pilots as they wished, while others became observers, which they didn't want to be. The *hanchō* of our small group held a party with good food at his home for twelve of us. He let us drink beer, and we toasted and prayed for good luck. We really appreciated his kindness, and thought that he was a good *hanchō*. When I look at a photo from this party everyone looks happy, and we had high hopes for the future. Sadly, I am the only person still alive (in this picture). PO2c Tamotsu Shibata was on *Kaga* at one time, and he was a guy with few words.[95] He really was an introvert, which was rare for a person from Fukuoka Prefecture. Shibata-san had excellent skills as a pilot, and on many occasions while landing on an aircraft carrier, he put the tail on the fourth wire. Unfortunately, he is now in the deep ocean at Midway.

Another member of my group was WO Masahide Izaki, who I met (later in the war) again while I was doing training at Yokosuka (as a member of the Tateyama *Kōkūtai*). While I was there I saw WO Sadayoshi Takehara (who also was on *Kaga* earlier in the war). When I saw him he was coming off his aircraft (after a mission), and behind him was a stout looking guy with a mustache; surprisingly this was Izaki-san. At that time he was teamed up with Takahara-san as the crew of a leading aircraft for the level-bombers. Izaki-san was very pale and had a big head that looked like a rice ball upside down. During training he made fun of other members of our group. We drank together at Yokosuka, and that was the last night I saw him alive. Izaki-san died on 13 October 1944 during the Taiwan Sea Battle. He was a member of K-762 and a pilot of a Mitsubishi Type 1 *Rikkō* bomber. Izaki-san was an excellent pilot, and had good leadership skills. His final rank in the Navy was warrant officer.

One other member of my group was PO1c Toshio Yamada from Nagoya. He was small in stature, quiet, and had dark skin and a soft smile. Yamada-san was the kind of person everyone liked, and he never spoke anything unnecessarily. When I learned how he died in the war I became very angry. I saw his flight records from 24 August 1942 until the day he died on 5 September 1942. During those fifteen days there was only one day when Yamada-san didn't fly (probably because there was no mission). On 25-26 August he did daytime attacks on Guadalcanal Island; then, on 27-29 of that month PO1c Yamada did nighttime attacks off the same target. Next, on 30 August, the young aviator attacked enemy warships off Guadalcanal, and from 1-5 September participated in bombing missions on Guadalcanal Island. At 0600 on 5 September, he took off from Rabaul in a nine-aircraft formation. Yamada's aircraft was in the second position of the 3rd *Chūtai*, and he was the pilot in command. At 0904 the group finished the attack, but on the way home Yamada's aircraft engaged an enemy Grumman F4F Wildcat fighter. The fighter hit the right engine of my buddy's plane; they fought back, but didn't return from the mission.

I assume PO1c Yamada would have flown dangerous combat missions without complaint with his signature smile. I still wonder why he flew such a lethal schedule of combat missions. I once heard a story from another *chūkō* pilot that some experienced aviators didn't agree with such an arduous mission schedule, and they drank soy sauce, which raised their body temperature, so the men could pretend they had a fever. Can you imagine flying dangerous seven-hour (roundtrip) missions, day in and day out? No matter how strong you are spiritually, there is a limit if you're a human being.

Maeda's Flight Training

On 1 April 1940, after one year and six months of *Yokaren* curriculum classes, we graduated. Altogether 248 people (out of the original group of 260 members) actually graduated. 126 men out of the graduating class became observers and transferred to Suzuka *Kōkūtai*. We were now called 1st term flight practice students. From this time on the previous names (used in the *Yokaren* training system) for pilots and observers, such as *Kō* and *Otsu*, were abolished, and a number system (according to the time the men entered) started.

Some of our instructors were pilots, while others were radio, weapons, or signal specialists. My *hanchō* was PO2c Koji Ohjino. He was warm-hearted and took care of me well. Later Ohjino-san was one of my flying partners (in my Type 97 *kankō*) for the Pearl Harbor attack. At that time I never thought I would one day fly combat missions with him. Another person that I can never forget from my Suzuka days is Instructor Igawa of the *Hikō Buntai*. From the beginning he was so supportive of us, even when we made mistakes. Igawa-san had dark skin and looked good.

Young Takeshi Maeda in flying gear during December 1940. (Maeda Collection)

There is one incident that I remember well from this time period. Many of the students in my group were beaten by a young assistant teacher of the *Hikō Buntai*. Instructor Igawa heard about this, and one day ordered everyone to line up in the auditorium. In front of all of us, Igawa-san and the senior instructor Todoroki-san hit this guy with a baseball bat. After that he didn't bother us anymore.

We studied navigation, bombing technique, gunnery, and communication. We also learned about the weather and photography. All of these classes were for our duties as an observer or radioman/rear gunner. We did the actual flight training in the afternoon, unless the weather was bad. Gunnery also was a very important subject, because our guns protected us during combat. We fired live ammunition at a sleeve target being pulled by a teacher's plane, but rarely hit the target.

On 1 June we finally became petty officers third class, and we could say goodbye to our sailor uniforms. Then our last course was maintenance training, which was done at the Mitsubishi factory in Nagoya. On 24 December we graduated from this training program and were divided into two groups for "practical training." So we left Suzuka and went to Ōmura and Usa air bases. Right before I finished my practical training at Usa Air Base, Hajime Arakawa didn't return from a nighttime navigation training sortie. It seemed that he went down in the Hime Jima area, and this was the first time a classmate died due to an accident.

Maizuru *Kōkūtai* Days

I finished this last training class on 24 March 1941 and was transferred to Maizuru *Kōkūtai* as an observer for a seaplane group. When we heard the announcement for our next assignments, some people felt sad and others were joyful. Men who were chosen to fly "big" airplanes (such as a Mitsubishi Type 1 *Rikkō* bomber) and had to take training at Kizarazu were especially disappointed. Maizuru *Kōkūtai* was a small group, and we were like a family. Our base faced Kurita Bay. I have many good memories from this time period. I remember doing nighttime take off and landings from the water. Then, after we took off and turned to the left, we saw *Amanohashidate*, and opposite this was the Nihama Prostitutes Quarters.[96] It was very beautiful because the red lanterns cast shadows on the sea. My aircraft, the Kawanishi Type 94 Reconnaissance Seaplane, had good balance, and even a control stick for the observer. One day when I was with Ohashi-san I asked him a difficult question, "Would you let me fly for a while?" He said yes, and I took the controls and flew.

During this time there was one incident that I can never forget. We landed (in the sea) off a beach in Tottori Prefecture. We had lunch, and I went to a fisherman's shack. I lay down to relax a bit and fell asleep. While I was sleeping, I heard the roar of aircraft engines but didn't care. When I woke up I was shocked that nobody else was there! When I looked at my watch one hour had passed, so I asked a fisherman, where did my comrades go? He said that they flew to Ōita. Luckily, when I went to the beach I was relieved to see one aircraft still there. I also could see the *buntaichō* standing on the wing of his aircraft and looking around with binoculars. The original plan was to fly to a large lake and stay overnight at a nearby hot spring called "Tamazo." Because of my terrible mistake I thought something bad would happen to me. Strangely enough there was no punishment, and it became a good story to tell when we were drinking. Even now I get a cold sweat thinking about this incident.

Maeda-san Joins *Kaga*

I was a member of Maizuru *Kōkūtai* for five enjoyable months. On 18 September 1941 I transferred to the carrier *Kaga*, and couldn't understand why I was going to now fly a "land" airplane (not a seaplane). There was nothing that I could do, and I said goodbye to my group and departed for Kyūshū. I arrived at Sasebo and went on board the *Kaga*. Shortly afterward I left the carrier and went by train to Kagoshima. At Kagoshima Station I asked for directions to Kōnoike Air Base, and the person said in local dialect, "Oh, it is a horse racing track." He also said that a lot of Navy aircraft came to this facility, which was converted to a military base from a city-owned horse racing track. When I arrived at the base there was a plate on the gate that read "Hashiguchi *Butai*."[97]

The living quarters for the aviators were a quickly made one floor barracks. It was very simple and had only *tatami*. The senior man there was PO1c Hirotake Iwata, who had a thick beard. During dinner time we all gathered together and introduced ourselves. Four same term students (from my class): Yoichi Tanaka, Isamu Matsuda, Hajime Yonezawa, and Seiichirō Hirano welcomed me to the group. PO1c Tatsuya Sugihara was the "Deck Petty Officer," and he announced the following day's flight roster. He was a big guy who spoke in a loud voice and laughed a lot. There also were many other petty officers first class in rank with two-lined good conduct badges in the *Kaga Kankō-tai*. I wondered why PO1c Sugihara was chosen to be our "Deck Petty Officer." I later learned that he was a specially trained pilot who teamed up with PO1c Shizu Yamamoto. Sugihara-san was the pilot who flew the leading aircraft for a level-bombing mission. I thought he had excellent flying skills and a brilliant mind. Sugihara-san was trusted by the senior pilot PO1c Iwata, who was the pilot for the leader of our group, Lieutenant Commander Takashi Hashiguchi. What's important in the world of naval aviators are your flying abilities, not your rank or number of lines on your good conduct badge. If you don't have good skills as an aviator, people would laugh behind your back. You may get proper respect "on the surface," but people will still talk about you.

PO2c Yoichi Tanaka was from Kumamoto Prefecture and an interesting guy. He was a close friend of mine. Whenever we started to hang out together he started to date the bar hostess girls (or madams) who worked there. We always drank at a bar when we went out which I think was called "*Print Temps*."[98] On one occasion when I went to a brothel in the village, Tanaka-san pointed to a prostitute's house on the left and said it was the home of our comrade Hajime Yonezawa. If I remember correctly this area was called "Matsushima Row."

Flight Training with the *Kaga Kankō-tai*

Our flight training mainly focused on launching torpedoes toward non-moving targets. Before breakfast we took off from Kōnoike

Air Base and turned to the right above Ikeyama Park. After we changed our direction, we flew higher and went over the city. Then we flew right above the prostitutes' village off the sea, and once we were over the water, we launched our torpedoes 400 meters (1,312 feet) ahead. At that time we were flying at just 10 meters (33 feet), so we were able to see the prostitutes' houses well. We also saw the licensed prostitutes who were opening their storm windows still in their sexy outfits after saying goodbye to their customers. I could see them very clearly from the air. In fact, these ladies even knew the tail numbers of the aircraft of their regular customers! So when they saw the airplane flying overhead, they waved and screamed.

The hard training continued from morning until night every day. When I looked at my flight records for that time period in October alone I flew 128 hours. Nighttime training focused mainly on landing on the carrier in pitch black and doing torpedo attacks. We had only one day off every week, so our training was really intense.

On 1 October I received a good conduct chevron, which I had wanted for a long time. Prior to this, whenever Tanaka-san left the base, he pulled out a good conduct chevron and attached it to his uniform with rice, which really worried me. Now we could finally walk around town feeling proud. Having this badge really made you look like a higher-ranking person.

Pearl Harbor

In mid-November the *Kaga Kankō-tai* left Kōnoike Air Base in Kagoshima and went to Tomitaka Air Base (in Miyazaki Prefecture). The prostitutes from the village off the beach tried to meet us one last time. They visited in groups of three to five women at a time. The ladies came to our gate with neatly made boxed lunches. Every time they arrived, there was a phone call from the guard saying petty officer your sister has come to visit. Keep in mind the guard always said "sister," not prostitute. The *buntaishi* made fun of them and said, "How many sisters do you have?" When I think about it now, I have to pay my respects to the women, who had pure hearts and, in some cases, even gave us their hair as good luck charms.

A wartime example of a "three stripe" good conduct chevron. Maeda-san talked about the importance about getting these badges which gave you respect from other navy personnel. (Werneth Collection)

Tomitaka Air Base was a small facility facing Toyogo waterway and located a little south of Nobeoka City. During this time many engineers were sent from the Navy factory, and they installed cold-resistant gear for our Type 97 *kankō*. The fuselages of our aircraft also were painted in a bluish-black camouflage paint scheme. We were told to go over the paint with fine sandpaper. At that time I had a hunch something significant was about to happen. Then, after the maintenance work on our Type 97s was completed, we were given three days of leave to relax before leaving Japan. Our *taichō* said that the people who lived nearby should visit their homes as much as possible, and that we should take our personal belongings off our carrier. In my case three days was not long enough to go to my home, so I just hopped on a train to Kagoshima.

After the holidays the carrier *Kaga* appeared outside the bay and all of the men from the *Kankō-tai* boarded the carrier. Then the Type 99 *kanbaku* and Zero fighters flew from Saeki Air Base, and all of the aircraft were loaded on the *Kaga*. Throughout the night there was a lot of work to be done because we were leaving the base. Later I learned that there was a delay in the production of our modified torpedoes. On the day they arrived, instead of the torpedoes being armed with the usual training warhead, which was red in color, these "live" ones had black warheads. To me they looked grotesque.

In the early morning hours we finished loading everything and the carrier left port immediately. After leaving Toyogo waterway we headed east. Then all of the aviators from our carrier gathered together in the pilot's ready room, and it was the first time we ever did that. There was an announcement about two hours after we left port that we should go to the flight deck. All of us gathered in front of the bridge and on the left of the carrier was Shikoku Island, but it looked a little blurry. Captain Jisaku Okada, *Kaga's* commanding officer, pointed and said "That is Shikoku. This ship is cruising to a certain place and has a significant assignment. So there is a possibility that some people among you or all of you may not see the Japanese mainland again. We are now going to say farewell to Japan." That was his speech. Actually, about one month prior to this time I felt in my whole body that we would go to war because of the unusual atmosphere (around us). Nevertheless, when I heard Captain Okada's formal declaration I felt my body become tense, and mentally prepared myself for possible combat in the near future.

Early in the morning on 23 November the *Kaga* dropped anchor. When I looked out the porthole I could see the *Akagi*, *Hiryū*, *Sōryū*, *Shōkaku*, and *Zuikaku* against a beautiful snow backdrop. I also saw the battleships *Hiei* and *Kirishima*. As for the cruisers, I could see the sleek *Tone* and *Chikuma*. After seeing

PO2c Maeda was assigned to the carrier *Kaga* from September 1941 until it was sunk in June 1942 during the Battle of Midway. (Maru magazine via Wenger)

all these other ships, I figured *Kaga* was the last ship to arrive at this meeting spot. Under gray skies this huge armada of Japanese Navy ships secretly gathered together and wondered, where are we going? Nobody thought that we would attack Pearl Harbor; this was beyond our imagination. Considering all the "winter" gear that we had on board there was a good possibility that we would attack Dutch Harbor. We all thought a lot about our potential destination over breakfast.

On 24 November all of the aviators from each carrier went to the carrier *Akagi* via a launch for a meeting. On board *Akagi* I saw one after another of my classmates (which were from the other carriers). Commander Minoru Genda explained the Pearl Harbor plan in great detail to us. After his explanation, I finally learned that our ships were now in Hitokappu Bay, at Etorofu Island (in the Kuriles). I also heard that nobody stayed here in the winter. In the middle of the room there was a huge diorama of Pearl Harbor, which was probably 4.5 *tatami* in size.[99] Then a naval staff officer stood up and started to explain while pointing to this diorama. He told us the precise locations of the anti-aircraft batteries, airfields, and ships. Each group of pilots learned what their targets would be during the attack. For example, I was a member of the Type 97 *kankō* group which was armed with torpedoes, and our targets were the ships located on the right side of Ford Island.

Two days later on the 26th at 0600 a trumpet blared out which indicated we were now leaving Hitokappu Bay. Prior to sailing each ship test-fired its guns, and the target was the cape (to the left of us). The shells blew up the island's iced-up mountains, and it was simply spectacular. For some time I just looked at this sight in sheer amazement.

On 3 December, during the voyage to Hawaii, we had a strong south wind with huge waves, and this shook our large carrier like it was a leaf. We couldn't even eat our rice balls because of this storm. Before dawn one man was swept away by the high waves and disappeared into the ocean. He was the first war casualty for us.

When the ocean was calm, the flight crew of the lead Type 97 carrier attack plane were on the flight deck and did their best to practice shooting with small arms. I heard this method was excellent to sharpen your concentration and raise your spirits. Because of all the shooting, aviators who were taking naps woke up and went to walkways along the flight deck to watch the men practicing. Gradually the temperature became warmer, so it was too hot to wear our winter gear.

6 December was the first day that we were allowed to take a bath since leaving Hitokappu Bay. We were finally able to wash our filthy bodies. After this we had a farewell party in the pilot's room with a lot of key personnel from the carrier, including Captain Okada, the captain's aide, mechanics, and weapons specialists. We all celebrated and toasted, because it was really life or death for the aviators who were going to participate in the forthcoming mission. Our *hikōtaichō*, Lieutenant Commander Hashiguchi, then said, "After this drinking party, I prohibit consuming any alcohol

This is the setting that Maeda is describing at Hitokappu Bay on 23 November 1942, going (left to right) *Kirishima*, *Kaga*, and *Hiei*. (Maru magazine via Wenger)

Above: *Kaga* and *Zuikaku* during the turbulent voyage to Hawaii. (NA via Wenger) Below: On 6 December 1941, Lieutenant Ichirō Kitajima's briefing on *Kaga's* flight deck about the forthcoming Pearl Harbor raid. (Chihaya Collection via Wenger)

until after the mission. However, tonight you can drink as much as you want. I want you to get energized after drinking." Hashiguchi-san sincerely appreciated the efforts of everyone, and this drinking party was simply extraordinary. I felt like we were washing the deck with spilled beer. We also were allowed the rare opportunity to be frank with some of the higher-ranking people on our carrier, including Captain Okada and Lieutenant Commander Hashiguchi. I think most aviators drank a lot to help relieve the stress of flying dangerous combat missions. Since we probably had only two days to live, you can imagine how much we enjoyed drinking that night. Ordinarily the paymaster of our ship was bothered by the pilots' conduct. However, on this particular night he was always smiling and trying to encourage us. The paymaster said, "I'm counting on you to do a good job," and he then poured *saké* for everyone. The drinking went on and on until we collapsed.

Personally, I didn't want to go to war with the United States. I wanted our governments to settle their differences peacefully. But I was a military man who was ordered to participate in the attack, so I really had no choice in the matter. Prior to the mission I felt calm. Since both of my parents were deceased, I didn't even bother writing a will. The only thing that I did was organize my personal belongings. There was no confusion on our carrier prior to the Pearl Harbor attack, and we were ready to fight. Furthermore, the morale of our crew also was very high. I felt it was a great honor to be chosen to participate in the attack of Pearl Harbor. The other pilots who were not selected to fly on this historic mission thought that they must be incompetent aviators. They felt dejected, and it was hard for me to see my comrades so depressed.

Regarding the aviators that I flew with during the Pearl Harbor attack, PO3c Yōshirō Yoshikawa, the pilot, was skilled in doing torpedo attacks, and PO2c Koji Ohjino, the navigator, was the plane captain. Although I was assigned to be the radioman/rear gunner on the day of the attack, the three of us had been trained as a team and always worked together. Yoshikawa-san was an excellent pilot even though he was one rank lower than me. In addition, he was a hearty drinker. PO3c Yoshikawa used to go to the downtown section of Kagoshima City and enjoyed drinking almost every holiday. He survived the war, but unfortunately died shortly after the war at his home due to illness. Ohjino-san was our teacher at Suzuka *Kōkūtai* and was very gentle. I think he never reprimanded me. Unfortunately, Ohjino-san, while flying as a as a commander of a torpedo plane, was killed in action on 17 October 1942 during a battle near the Solomon Islands.

Early in the morning on 7 December I woke up and changed into new underwear. For breakfast we ate fish with its head and tail and red rice with beans, which was usually just eaten for special occasions. Then we went to the *Kaga* shrine and prayed. After this everyone went to the flight deck, where all of the attack planes were already lined up. You also could hear the roar of aircraft engines that were being tested.

All of the aviators from my group—the *Raigeki-tai*, who were flying Type 97 *kankō* armed with torpedoes—went to observe the torpedoes being tested after they were installed on aircraft. After the testing was completed, the torpedo specialist said, "Test completed," and he held my hands and then said, "Hit the target." At this time the sun hadn't come up yet, and I could see the moon fading away along with some clouds. The water also had strong waves and was turbulent. At 0120 the carrier's bow turned east by northeast. Next the Zero fighters took off, followed by the Type 99 carrier bombers, and lastly the Type 97 carrier attack planes. The moment the wheels of each aircraft left the deck, each plane looked like it was sinking then momentarily disappeared. This surprised me, but I was relieved to see each aircraft with its landing gears pulled up reappear against the backdrop of the eastern skies. One after another the attacking aircraft took off and gained altitude very quickly. Then came the *Raigeki-tai's* turn to take off, and I saw *chūtaichō* Lieutenant Kitajima's Type 97 pass the bow of the ship. However, it looked like his aircraft "kicked the deck" with a strong motion and then quickly sank down because of the weight of the torpedo. Kitajima's *kankō* then reappeared, and the next moment the landing gears were pulled up.

The beloved pilot of my aircraft, PO3c Yōshirō Yoshikawa, was a superb aviator. Before take off he stepped on the brakes, then (when it was our turn to go) Yoshikawa-san let go of the brakes and gunned the throttle. He kept the nose down and the Type 97 parallel to the deck, while at the same time the flaps were lowered (so the nose wouldn't go up). Once we took off, our aircraft lumbered to gain altitude because of the heavy torpedo, and PO3c Yoshikawa retracted the landing gears.

While I was in the air I looked behind me, and could see our carrier below filled with crewmen in white uniforms waving their hats to see us off. As we flew on the people became smaller and smaller, then faded away from my sight. In my mind I just said, "Goodbye *Kaga*, return to Japan safely. We will probably never land on you again." Our aircraft then banked right and went into formation with Lieutenant Kitajima's Type 97. We were flying in the second aircraft position (to the left of his aircraft). The Type 97 flown by PO2c Yoshiyuki Hirata caught up with us and joined our formation.

One after another more planes joined us and followed our group, so we were all set. As I looked at the horizon (to the left of us), the sun rose and illuminated the morning sky. We continued on to Hawaii with supreme confidence. I saw to the right and left of our formation escorting Zero fighters, which flew along in a snake motion. This was very comforting to me. At 0310 there was a flare fired that was a signal for us to get into formation for a "surprise" attack, and nine minutes later we received the radio signal "To, To, To." The *chūtaichō* ordered us to get into a single-file formation and to prepare to attack. At this moment, I already could see bomb smoke from Wheeler Field, which was the beginning of the dive-bombers' attack. Then we flew close to a mountain range, and to the right of us I could see Barbers Point and an airfield. The enemy's airfield was filled with aircraft, lined up very tightly.

The enemy battleships looked like silhouettes floating on the water below. However, all of a sudden I saw water columns rise up, and it looked like the silhouettes disappeared. Already at this early stage of our mission, *Akagi's* Type 97 torpedo planes began to attack Battleship Row. Our airplanes went right above the water, then turned around above the east side of Hickam Field before heading towards Pearl Harbor. At Hickam Field there were many large planes that were lined up on the base. Then at 0322 we received the radio signal "Tora! Tora! Tora!" which meant that our surprise attack was successful. We lowered the altitude of our Type 97 while watching the *chūtaichō's* aircraft, which was 400 meters ahead of us. Lieutenant Kitajima was heading for a California-class battleship right in the middle of the row of ships.

The pilot of my aircraft, PO3c Yōshirō Yoshikawa, said very calmly "*Yōi*," just like it was a training mission. He flew very close to the height of the battleship's mast, and lots of anti-aircraft fire was coming from both sides of our Type 97 *kankō*. When the anti-aircraft shells hit our plane it sounded like someone was banging on a bucket. Then I heard the command "*Tei*," and we launched our torpedo, which made our Type 97 rise up because now our aircraft was much lighter in weight. I didn't know the name of the ship that I attacked, but it was a *California* class ship. In 1991 at the 50th Anniversary Pearl Harbor Memorial Service, I recognized for the first time my target was the battleship *West Virginia*.

Maeda's target during the mission was the battleship West Virginia, *which was hit by at least seven torpedoes and two bombs during the attack. Eventually settling on the bottom, salvage and yard personnel later raised, repaired, and modernized her. As a result of the Pearl Harbor attack 106 men were lost, including the Captain Mervyn S. Bennion.*[100] *Because of his heroism the Captain was posthumously awarded the Medal of Honor. The proud ship later served with distinction in the Pacific Theatre from October 1944 until the Japanese surrender.*[101]

After dropping the torpedo the commander of the aircraft decided whether to bank either left or right. If you banked right, there was heavy anti-aircraft fire; going left was much safer. I banked left because I wanted to hide our aircraft in the smoke. We did get some anti-aircraft hits in one of the wings though. Our aircraft flew close to the bridge of our target ship, and when I looked behind us, I could see a water column heading towards the battleship. Beyond that I also could see PO2c Hirata's aircraft, which was flying very close to the water.

West Virginia, the battleship that Maeda's crew attacked during the first wave, sits sunk but upright due to effective counterflooding efforts. The Japanese attackers inflicted serious damage to the ship, but it returned to fight again during the fall of 1944. (NA via Wenger)

We flew very low over land, which had a pineapple field, and went to the predetermined rendezvous point. Near this meeting spot there was a submarine that was supposed to rescue any downed aviators. After some time a *Hiryū* Type 97 carrier attack plane (with a dangling torpedo wire) flew near us. This aircraft had a hole (from anti-aircraft fire) in the left wing, but was still able to fly back to the carrier. One after another our Type 97 *kankō* arrived with dangling torpedo wires, and we gathered together at this spot. A Type 97 with a stripe on the aircraft, which indicated it was a *shōtaichō's* plane, also arrived on the scene. Our group decided to use this particular Type 97 as a lead aircraft to go back to our carriers. On the horizon (a far distance away from us) I saw some of the *Kidō Butai's* aircraft, which meant we were in good shape, so I was relieved.

Once we found the *Kaga* our planes began to land back on the carrier. As for my aircraft, while we were getting ready to land, a Type 97 flown by PO2c Kazunori Tanaka suddenly cut in front of us. I could see PO2c Toyohiro Nakamura (who was an observer) waving his scarf, which was covered with blood.[102] He was doing this to ask for permission to do an emergency landing. Sadly, we lost five Type 97 carrier attack planes and fifteen men during the Pearl Harbor attack. The Type 99 *kanbaku* and Zero fighters (from the second wave) then returned to our carrier. Several of our aircraft were trying to land at the same time. The engine of one Type 99 carrier bomber stopped running once it landed. Upon closer inspection of this particular aircraft I saw a whopping twenty-two bullet holes, and the propeller looked like the teeth of a saw. Every person who saw this Type 99 was shocked that it came back. Prior to the attack all of our pilots ate breakfast at the same table, but when we returned in the afternoon some seats were empty. That night we couldn't sleep without drinking some alcohol.

In all, during the first wave attack Kaga *lost five Type 97 (torpedo planes) and two Zero fighters. The carrier also lost six Type 99s and two Zero fighters during the second wave.*[103]

At 0630 on 22 December I took off to do a patrol mission for the safety of the ships from the *Kidō Butai* and headed towards Kanoya (on the island of Kyūshū). I didn't see the mainland of Japan for one month, so I felt relieved and very lucky to be alive. In December 1941 the *Kaga Kankō-tai* had some rest and training at Iwakuni Air Base. Then, on the 24th of that month, the *buntaichō* and I went to Suzuka on business. When we arrived, many students ran towards our aircraft and crowded around us because they knew we were from the distinguished *Kaga* group. My old instructor Igawa-san was in the front row and ran towards to me. He said many times to me, "You did a good job." We drank together all night, and when I awoke I was still wearing my uniform. In those days Suzuka had old-fashioned instructors.

In retrospect, we should have done a third wave during the Pearl Harbor attack to destroy the fuel tanks and docks. If we did this, the U.S. Navy may have retreated to the United States mainland. Furthermore, Japan should not have attacked Pearl Harbor before formally declaring war on America; then it wouldn't have been a "sneak" attack

Daily Life on board a Carrier

Normally, when we were not flying we had nothing special to do. Flying was our only job. But after going back to a land base we did training every day; otherwise we would lose our instinct. For example, we practiced doing "touch and go" landings.

On board our carrier officers ate *ginmeshi* (white steamed rice) at every meal, and sailors took care of them during the meals. The officers sometimes ate elegant meals that had appetizers, soup, bread, and beef. These kinds of meals could never be served to the petty officers or to the sailors because there were too many men. The meals for us consisted mostly of *mugimeshi* (steamed rice blended with barley), accompanied by Japanese soup and a couple of poor side dishes. Our meals were tasteless, but nourishing. At least people who smoked were able to get cigarettes on board the carrier.

1942 - Flying Combat Missions Again

I spent New Year's Day at Iwakuni Air Base without having any time to relax; instead we prepared for our next operation. Our group did its utmost to maintain our aircraft and do formation bombing training. On 9 January 1942 *Kaga* left Iwakuni bound for Truk Island. After arriving at Truk Island on the 15th we were allowed to go on land.

As Maeda-san states, he participated in the 20 January 1942 air attack on Rabaul (New Britain Island). According to the Japanese war records, his carrier Kaga *launched nine Type 0 carrier fighters and twenty-seven Type 97* kankō *(level-bombers) at 1115. Around the same time nine* kansen *and eighteen Type 97s (level-bombers) took off from the carrier* Akagi. Shōkaku *also contributed nineteen Type 99* kanbaku *for this mission. As for* Zuikaku, *at 1100 it launched three Zero fighters, which may have been used for CAP (Combat Air Patrols) over the carriers. Lastly, at 1240 that same day nineteen more Type 99 carrier bombers took off from* Zuikaku *to attack this same target.*[104]

Our next assignment was to support the troops landing on Papua New Guinea and New Britain Island. Before daybreak on 20 January we took off in our Type 97 *kankō,* which was armed with one 800 kilogram bomb. There would be intense fighting in skies over Rabaul later in the war; however, at this time none of us were familiar with this place. It had thick jungle bordering a small town along the harbor. All of sudden the Type 99 *kanbaku* swooped down and attacked a warehouse and anti-aircraft batteries. Commercial ships also were inside the harbor, and anti-aircraft fire started coming from the ground. Our group went over the eastern beach area towards our target area. The *taichō's kankō*, which was initially flying in the lead position, signaled the second aircraft (which had a specially trained bombardier and pilot) to take his spot in the formation. As usual, the Type 97 flown by PO1c Tatsuyasu Sugihara went to the lead position of our formation (to lead us during the level-bombing). My aircraft was flying in the third position and, after seeing these Type 97s switch position, I pulled the safety device off my bombing equipment.

The first Japanese Navy aviators lost over Rabaul

PO1c Tatsuyasu Sugihara (Wenger Collection)

PO1c Katsuo Yamamoto (Wenger Collection)

PO2c Yoichi Tanaka (Wenger Collection)

As we began our "bomb run," there was a lot of anti-aircraft fire to the left and right of our formation. Our aircraft shook a lot from all this anti-aircraft fire. I paid attention to the leading Type 97 and released our bomb, which caused our aircraft to rise up. Suddenly, Sugihara's aircraft was hit by anti-aircraft fire and dropped out of our formation. Then it became engulfed in flames and slammed straight into the mid-slope of Mt. Hanasaki, a volcano on Rabaul. I believe this was a direct hit, and everything happened in just a matter of seconds. If it had not been on the "bomb run," the *taichō's* Type 97 and our aircraft would have been in danger. The men who perished on the leading aircraft were PO1c Tatsuya Sugihara, PO1c Katsuo Yamamoto, and PO2c Yoichi Tanaka. They were together as a "team" since the Pearl Harbor attack. Long after the end of the war, Tanaka's older brother visited Rabaul and visited the crash site of his brother's aircraft. While visiting Rabaul he dedicated a poem to the souls of the three lost aviators. In 1980 I visited Tanaka's birthplace and grave in Kumamoto (located in Kyūshū). In retrospect, these men were the first Japanese losses at Rabaul. Later in the war a lot of men perished in countless air battles that continued endlessly.

On 1 February we received an emergency signal that said that our bases in the Marshall Islands were being attacked by enemy carrier-based planes. We departed Truk Island and went north to search for the enemy carriers but couldn't locate them; it was too late. Then, on 19 February 1942, 188 aircraft from the carriers *Akagi* and *Kaga* did an air raid on Port Darwin, Australia, which had a lot of military facilities. Once again (like the Rabaul attack) my Type 97 *kankō* was armed with one 800 kilogram bomb. This was the first time I saw Australia, which had deep green foliage and peaceful blue water. I saw red-roofed buildings that surrounded the harbor area. Inside the harbor were enemy destroyers and transports, but they became the prey for our Type 99 *kanbaku*, so our Type 97s had no target to attack. I saw a hospital ship, but we couldn't attack it. Therefore, our commander had no choice but to attack some land-based facilities. Suddenly about twenty enemy P-40s came to engage us. Nevertheless, the Zero fighters that were escorting our group began to dog-fight with the enemy defenders. In no time I saw some enemy aircraft spiraling downwards in balls of fire, and some of them had lost one wing. They were simply annihilated by our powerful Zero fighters.

A rare photo of the ill-fated Type 97 *kankō* flown by PO1c Tatsuyasu Sugihara, PO1c Katsuo Yamamoto, and PO2c Yoichi Tanaka that was lost during the 20 January 1942 Rabaul attack. (Bill MacGowan, courtesy Ken MacGowan via Peter Stone)

After we dropped our bombs I thought the city of Darwin was blown away. Once the brown colored smoke (from our bombs) quelled I saw no fires below. Personally, I thought it was really a psychological attack, because we didn't have to drop our bombs on the city. I then flew back to the carrier *Kaga*, and after I landed I heard a story from my classmate, PO1c Kenji Noda. He said that during the mission one of his comrades (a Type 99 *kanbaku* pilot) was getting ready to attack the hospital ship, but a P-40 fighter chased after him, so he couldn't drop his bomb. Since the Type 99 carrier bomber still had its bomb the aircraft was slow. Because of this the enemy fighter sped past him and clipped a palm tree with his wing, then blew up.

Next we went to Staring Bay (in the Celebe Islands), but other than patrol aircraft flying some sorties we didn't fly. Instead, our planes flew to Kendari for maintenance, and the pilots did flight training there. On 25 February I was on the carrier *Kaga*, and we searched for a group of enemy ships that was going towards the southern sea of Java. So, once again we were in the Indian Ocean, and one destroyer and fifteen commercial ships became the prey of our *Kanbaku-tai*.

On 5 March we did an air attack against Tjilatjap, which devastated its land-based facilities and sank nineteen commercial ships. Carrier Division 1 (*Akagi* and *Kaga*) temporarily returned to Kendari, and the aviators from the two carriers went back on land. One day I flew an anti-submarine patrol mission near the mouth of Staring Bay, and I was shocked to see *Akagi* and *Kaga* traveling very close together. I thought that the stern sections of the two carriers might collide, so I dove into a spot between them to notify the men on board of this dangerous situation. Luckily, they didn't hit each other and everything was okay. Nevertheless, there were many parts of Staring Bay that were shallow, and I heard that the bottom of *Kaga's* hull got damaged. Therefore, we couldn't participate in the next operation in the Indian Ocean and returned alone to Sasebo, Japan, to be repaired. So *Kaga* went to Sasebo, and our aircraft took off from the carrier and went to Kanoya. Next, we went to Tateyama (on the southern tip of Chiba Prefecture), and it became our new base. When I look back, this was the beginning of my connection with the Tateyama *Kōkūtai*.

The Doolittle Raid

On 18 April 1942 the United States did its first air attack on the Japanese home islands in a very unconventional way. Lieutenant Colonel Jimmy Doolittle and his men, who were flying a group of sixteen B-25B Mitchell twin-engine bombers, took off from the carrier Hornet *with their aircraft, which was the first and only time this was ever attempted during the war. This bold mission alarmed Japan, because it demonstrated for the first time that the United States could attack their homeland. The B-25B bombers had to be modified for this particular mission. The aircraft were fitted with self-sealing fuel tanks in the fuselage, while the bottom turret was removed and a sixty gallon fuel tank took its place. Because of these modifications these B-25Bs added five hundred miles to their normal range of 2,000 miles. Two black broomsticks were installed in the tail with the hope that they would scare off enemy fighters.*

The innovative plan was to launch these sixteen bombers from the deck of the Hornet, *and then they would bomb military targets in Japan and land the aircraft in China. However, the task force was spotted by a Japanese picket boat that was able to send out a warning about the approaching American ships. Even though the picket boat was engaged and sunk, it was decided to launch the B-25Bs immediately. However, because of this engagement, at 0820 ship time the aircraft began to take off about 650 miles from Japan. Due to the decision to launch the B-25Bs earlier than expected they had to fly 200 hundred miles further in their mission, which could lead to problems later on, such as fuel starvation.*[105] *The sixteen medium-bombers proceeded to attack their assigned targets in Tokyo, Yokohama, Kobe, Osaka, and Nagoya. None of the American aircraft were damaged or shot down during the raid.*[106]

Around this time in 1942 there was a report that the United States Navy was possibly planning an operation in the eastern Pacific, so we had to protect our urban areas (such as Tokyo). Hence, we were stationed near Tokyo Bay. Regardless of the reason why we went there, I was very happy to be able to see the cherry blossoms in full bloom. One month later the above report became a reality when, on 18 April, American aircraft carriers appeared about 700 nautical miles east of Kinkazan Island (in Miyagi Prefecture). We got ready in a hurry to attack these ships, but our carrier was still at Sasebo, so all we could do was wait until the enemy came closer. We evaluated the situation and felt that there wouldn't be an enemy air raid until the following day, the 19th.

At Kizarazu, *chukōs* started to fly sorties to locate the enemy carriers and attack them. Every one of the *Kaga's* Zero fighters took off to escort the above attack unit. On this occasion for lunch we ate *norimaki*, which was considered to be battle provisions. I saw two enemy airplanes going north and flying low. They were twin-engine planes and went close to the western edge of our airfield. It was common sense that a twin-engine aircraft couldn't be carried-based. Still, our anti-aircraft batteries started firing at these planes, so we knew that they were enemy aircraft. Everyone at our airfield was in a state of shock, but there was nothing we could do about it. All of our airplanes were lined up on the airfield, but the enemy aircraft didn't even take a look at them. Instead the attackers disappeared and flew towards the Yokohama area.

Evening came, and by this time ten hours had passed since the Zeros took off. We began to worry that they ran out of fuel or something may have happened. At that time our airfield wasn't lit up because we didn't want the enemy aircraft to attack us. Miraculously, all of the eighteen Zero fighters returned safely. They had very little fuel left and had to land in the dark. Because of this every airplane looked for the nearest airfield to land on. Later, I learned that sixteen twin-engine B-25 medium bombers were launched from the aircraft carrier *Hornet*. Fifteen of the B-25s landed in China, while the last one went to an area near Vladivostok, Russia. The crew of the B-25 that landed in Russia was captured by the Russians. As for our side, the enemy carriers were too far away for our aircraft to reach them.

As Maeda-san states, fifteen of the B-25Bs headed for China, and the sixteenth landed safely in Russia. However, because of the early launch of the aircraft the crews of the China-bound aircraft either had to bail out over the mountains or crash offshore. Two men died while swimming to shore, while one man perished during the bailout. During the ditching four other men were seriously wounded and eight others became prisoners of war. Sadly, out of the eight aviators who became POWs three were executed, one died of malnutrition, and the other four men were mistreated but survived the war. As for the B-25 crew who landed in Russia, they were held by the Russians for fourteen months before escaping via Iran.[107]

The Battle of Midway

Our training at Tateyama Air Base was wrapping up, and at the same time the repairs on *Kaga* were completed at Sasebo. The carrier was ready to take our group back on board. In late April we left Tateyama and went to Kanoya. On the day we left a lot of local female performers came to see us off, and they stood by the fence around the airfield. Wherever there were pilots, there were women and alcohol. Each man said goodbye and waved to the lady they knew well. Then we took off from Tateyama. During this time period many new aviators joined our group on the carrier, so there were some changes to the flight crews that in the past had flown together. All of the experienced pilots had nighttime landing practice on just two occasions.

I personally felt angry, because in Kure, Japanese Navy officers talked about our secret plans for the upcoming Midway operation to the prostitutes in the red-light district. Prior to our departure everyone was talking about our Midway plans, so it wasn't a secretive mission like the Pearl Harbor attack. Personally I thought this operation wouldn't be as easy as Pearl Harbor. I also felt that since everyone seemed to know our Midway plans ahead of time this was a bad omen.

We left for the Midway Operation on 27 May from Hashira Jima on Navy Memorial Day, so we were sent off with military marching songs being played. The Carrier Divisions 1 and 2 left Japan in a very dignified manner. As for Carrier Division 5 (*Shōkakō* and *Zuikaku*), they couldn't participate in this operation because of the damage and aircraft losses suffered during the Battle of Coral Sea. Just as we set our course for Midway there was very rough weather. It was *Kaga's* day to do patrol duties for our ships. On

The remarkable sight of B-25 medium-bombers being launched from the carrier *Hornet* to do the first air attack on the Japanese mainland. (NA)

30 May 1942 two Type 97 *kankō* took off at 0800 and covered the right and left sectors near our ships. My flying partners and I had to cover the left sector. The pilot of my aircraft was PO3c Kameo Sasaki, and PO2c Keisuke Sakata flew as radioman/rear gunner. I flew as the plane captain and observer during this mission. The visibility that day was very bad, and the height of the clouds was only 500 meters. Our carriers were now traveling near an area where the enemy did reconnaissance missions, so we continued on and did our duty.

While talking about Midway, I briefly want to mention our navigation technique (over water). After we took off from the carrier it actually continued to move while we were flying. Because of this, the farther you flew away from your ship to do a reconnaissance mission, the less margin of error you had at the tip (or the furthest point of the area you flew in). Hence, inferred navigation becomes more difficult the further you flew away from the carrier. So prior to take off you had to do three things. First, mark on your chart the location of the carrier at take off. Second, we talked in detail about the speed and direction that the carrier would be traveling (after take off). Lastly, you had to synchronize your watch with the carrier's clock. Once we departed from the ship we flew along a predetermined flight route, then calculated both the wind direction and the velocity at that altitude. After this we could make adjustments for navigational purposes.

We also had to determine a few other things while navigating over water, such as the distance we flew and the arrival time to the furthest point of our route. Still, wind direction and velocity can change from place to place as well as the altitude, so calculations had to be done in small time intervals. We didn't have any markers on the sea except being able to look at the spray off the whitecaps, which indicated wind direction and (to an extent) velocity. While flying a reconnaissance mission it was useless to fly above the clouds, so we had to fly whenever possible underneath them. However, if we flew under the clouds the airflow was very bad, and wind direction would frequently change. Under these difficult conditions simply controlling the aircraft would be difficult. Because of this there was no time to relax, and we had to pay attention to the spray off the whitecaps (from the waves).

While operating at 135 knots, the Type 97 *kankō* could fly for 1300 nautical miles. So suppose our mission was to cover 300 nautical miles with a "dog-leg" of 60 nautical miles; it would take about five hours to return back to our carrier. But our total flying time would vary because of wind direction and wind speed. After we took off it was about two and a half hours once the aircraft arrived at the tip of our flight. Then we did our "dog-leg" for about forty minutes before setting our course to return back to the carrier. This was a crucial time, because up until this time you had to know exactly where your carrier traveled (while you were flying). From all the information you had, the observer had to use his "hunch" to determine where the mother ship was. Quite naturally, if your calculations for wind direction and velocity were incorrect it would be difficult to plot the correct course back to the carrier. Other important factors were correcting the deviation of the magnetic compass and making adjustments for a time zone difference. It was very important for the pilot of the aircraft to continually listen to his observer's directions (during the flight).

On this particular day the visibility (both coming and returning to the carrier) was only 5,000 meters (16,404 feet). Our flying altitude was between 500-800 meters (1,640-2,624 feet). This was really the best we could do, but it still wasn't an optimal situation. As estimated arrival time to *Kaga* became closer, all three of us on board the Type 97 started to get very nervous. I said (to my flying partners) that we will arrive back to our carrier in five more minutes. I tried to look everywhere with my binoculars, but with visibility being so bad, I had no luck. Then I checked the chart and looked at my watch.

Now, if your vessel had to zig-zag to avoid an enemy air attack, for example, it may be in a different location than you first thought. In that case, the standard procedure if we couldn't see your carrier at the estimated arrival time was to go from the estimated point where our ship was supposed to be (in the center), and gradually expand a wider radius around this area to search for it. If we were panicky at this moment, we would lose the position of our aircraft and ultimately run out of fuel. If that happened it would be the end of us.

Moreover, at this time in the mission we had only four hours of fuel left, so we thought that it would be okay to increase the area near the estimated position of our carrier. I told PO3c Sasaki to continue flying in the same direction for fifteen minutes and he agreed with me. However, this was the first time we flew together, so the trust level between us was low, but this was a perfect situation to gain his trust. When I used my binoculars again I saw a ship's mast on the horizon. I felt, I did it! I really couldn't say anything yet, because the ship was probably one of the escorting destroyers. I still had a good feeling that we would find our carrier, and told Sasaki-san to head a little bit to the left. Suddenly PO2c Sakata spoiled it for me and blurted in a loud voice, "I can see a mast!" So my plan was ruined by his comment.

Once we came close to our ships, the procedure was to send a signal to indicate who you were; otherwise, you might get shot down by friendly fire. So we lowered our landing gears and banked, but just as I originally thought, it was a destroyer. Then we found *Kaga* and went to the bridge to give our report. After this I was scolded by *hikōchō* Commander Takahisa Amagai and he said, "You flew in such lousy weather! Did you still think it was good to do a reconnaissance mission?" My response to him was that I did my best to "complete my assigned mission." I felt Amagai-san was a useless *hikōchō*, and he was just transferred to our carrier in April 1942, so this was his first combat operation with us.[108] While I was being reprimanded, I saw our *buntaichō* Lieutenant Kitajima looking at me sympathetically. Later I heard that the other aircraft (that was supposed to patrol the other sector) returned to the carrier within fifteen minutes due to bad weather. The pilot of this aircraft was a graduate of the Naval Academy, and this was his first time to serve on a carrier. The observer on this aircraft was PO1c Hideo Morisaki, and he said that Mr. K, the pilot, lacked confidence and didn't listen to him. Then Mr. K gave up quickly and said, "We're going back to the carrier." This mission was a lot of hard work, but still a useless one. Sadly, because the Japanese Navy didn't value doing reconnaissance missions enough, this ultimately led to our loss during the Battle of Midway.

During the Midway Operation, every day from the time we left Japan until 4 June we had bad weather. 3 June was especially bad because there was thick fog. Because of this our ships had to use search lights to avoid hitting another friendly vessel; it was that bad. At 0430 on 4 June, our first wave attack consisting of 108 aircraft from the carriers *Akagi*, *Kaga*, *Sōryū*, and *Hiryū* took off to attack Midway Island. Immediately after this, *Akagi* and *Kaga* prepared thirty-six Type 97 carrier attack planes so they could be used for torpedo attacks on enemy ships. The two carriers also launched two Type 97 *kankō* to do reconnaissance, while the heavy cruisers *Tone* and *Chikuma* dispatched two seaplanes for this purpose. A battleship also sent out one two-seat patrol plane for the same reason. I think there was poor planning in regards to doing reconnaissance for the Midway Operation because our side did only seven search lines with twenty-three degree intervals. Furthermore, Vice-Admiral Nagumo's staff really believed that there couldn't be a U.S. task force in the vicinity of Midway Island, and this predetermined assessment was one of the factors that led to our loss of the Battle of Midway.

A malfunction of the catapult on the *Tone* caused a thirty minute delay in the launch of the patrol aircraft. Ironically, it was this very aircraft that later located some enemy ships. At 0728 it sent a radio message stating that they sighted ten enemy vessels, but the ships were actually five cruisers and five destroyers. However, back on our carriers (at 0715) there was an order given to remove the torpedoes and install 800 kilogram (1,760 pound) bombs on our aircraft. This was because the commander of the first wave attack on Midway Island sent a radio message that another attack on the atoll would be necessary. Therefore, when the abovementioned ten enemy ships were spotted, the crew members of *Akagi* and *Kaga* were already busy shuttling our Type 97 *kankō* to the hangar and were now installing 800 kilogram bombs on the aircraft. On the *Hiryū* and *Sōryū*, thirty-six Type 99 carrier bombers were being armed with 250 kilogram (550 pound) bombs as well. A very serious tactical error, and the loss of precious operational time was about to unfold.

The Japanese Navy could not anticipate that the carrier *Yorktown*, which was heavily damaged just one month earlier during the Battle of Coral Sea, would be operational again after just three days of maintenance work. Then it would rejoin the carriers *Hornet* and *Enterprise* in the Pacific Theatre. We also didn't know that our messages were being decoded by the enemy. Therefore, American intelligence personnel were able to learn about our upcoming Midway Operation. During the Indian Ocean Operation two months prior to this time an important lesson should have been learned. Commander Mitsuo Fuchida, who led the first wave attack group, sent a radio message stating that a second wave would be necessary. Because of Fuchida's message, Nagumo's staff authorized the swapping of torpedoes with land-use bombs (on our aircraft still on the carriers). Then our reconnaissance plane radioed the sighting of two enemy ships, so once again torpedoes were put back on our aircraft. Due to this snafu, two and half hours of precious time were lost. Whether it is war or a game of golf, you have to be more decisive in your judgment. I believe that, during the Battle of Midway, if Nagumo's staff hadn't authorized our strike aircraft to change their armament so quickly, then the outcome of the balance of the operation may have been different.

By 0728 or so the American aircraft that were going to hit the Japanese aircraft carriers were already in the air, so the changing of the armament may not have ultimately made the difference between winning and losing the battle.[109]

I later learned that six TBF Avengers, four B-26 medium-bombers, sixteen SBD Dauntless dive-bombers, fifteen B-17 bombers, and eleven SB2U Vindicators came from Midway Island to attack our carriers. In addition, thirty-two PBY Catalinas were based on the island but didn't participate in the attacks, which began at 0705 and lasted until 0840. Our Zero fighters either shot down or damaged these attacking enemy aircraft, so our carriers were virtually untouched. I was on the carrier *Kaga* during these attacks and had a good view of the air battles occurring right in front of my eyes. The land-based B-26s came in low and dropped their torpedoes from a long distance (from our ships), and none of them were hits. I saw two of the four medium-bombers get shot down. As for the low-flying TBFs, five out of the six planes also were shot down. We were very impressed by the enemy aviator's sheer determination to fight, as they kept on coming to attack us.

At 0820 the *Tone* patrol plane sent a message stating that there was an enemy carrier "in the rear." Yes, this was the U.S. Task Force. By this time I was in the hangar deck area and helping out with the loading of our torpedoes, but I felt apprehensive about what was happening. Because *Kaga* was turning to the left and right to avoid the enemy torpedo attack, our task was not an easy one. The intercom blared out, "Speed up the loading of the torpedoes!" At this time our carrier was being attacked not only by torpedo planes, but also some of the other land-based bombers. So our Zero fighters took off to engage these enemy aircraft and started to dog-fight with them. Then our first-wave attack planes returned and we needed to recover them, because they were low on fuel. To me things looked pretty dim. Nevertheless, by 0840 the enemy air attacks started to subside, and all of returning strike aircraft were recovered by 0900.

According to the research done by Midway historian Jonathan Parshall, the carrier Kaga *finished recovery operations at 0850, while the entire force was finished with recovery at 0910.*

On board *Kaga* the eighteen Type 99 *kanbaku* (from the first wave) were taken down to the hangar and immediately prepared to fly for the proposed second wave. Our ordinance men worked very hard to load 250 kilogram bombs on these planes, and all of the aircraft needed to be refueled. The hot working conditions in the hangar prompted me to get some fresh air. Once I was outside the difference was like day and night. Everything was so quiet because all of our anti-aircraft had gone silent, but just for a short period. Next, at 0918 American carrier-based aircraft came to attack our ships. Looking through my binoculars I could see about eighteen Devastator torpedo bombers, and they were all heading towards the *Sōryū*. Our Zero fighters went after them and shot the enemy aircraft down one after another.

When I spoke with Parshall about situation on Kaga *he stated, "My strong impression is that at this time, the* kanbaku *were not being rearmed and refueled, because the reserve strike aircraft (i.e. the Type 97s) were the current center of attention. Even if the* kanbaku *were being refueled and rearmed, I doubt that they would have been included in the upcoming counterattack. That would have gone against their current spotting / launching / strike doctrine, which called for deckload strike packages of one attack community (i.e. either Type 97 or Type 99) We know that the Type 97s were slated to go with the first counterstrike. So it's my strong opinion that the Type 99s would have gone on a subsequent wave, even if it was to be launched very shortly thereafter."*

The Kidō Butai *was initially attacked at 0918 by fifteen Douglas TBD-1 Devastators of VT-8 from the carrier* Hornet; *however, only one American pilot, Ensign George Gay, survived the engagement. After this, between 0940-1000 fourteen Devastators of VT-6 attacked the* Kaga, *but only four aircraft returned back to the carrier* Enterprise. *A fifth TBD of the latter group, which was flown by Machinist A. Walter Winchell and gunner ARM3c Douglas M. Cossitt, ditched, and the men were rescued seventeen days later by a Midway-based PBY Catalina.*[110] *During the two torpedo attacks of the Japanese carriers no hits were scored, and a lot of brave American aviators lost their lives.*

Then, at 1022 SBD Dauntless dive-bombers came right through our fierce anti-aircraft fire, but some of them were shot down by Zero fighters. I also saw one Dauntless without a bomb circle above our carrier close to the deck; this could have been the commander of the group. The area around the base of the bridge was no longer safe, so I decided to take shelter at the stern's lower deck near the rescue boat station. I ran to the pilots' living quarters and shouted, "It is dangerous here, get the hell out!" to two shipmates resting on an upper bunk. I kept scurrying down a ladder, but *Kaga* suddenly listed to the port side. Then I heard an explosion at the starboard rear of the carrier, and suddenly I was hit by a blast of air and sea water. I felt something strike the upper part of my left thigh and then fell to the landing area (along with two other men). A piece of shrapnel was lodged in my thigh and I began to bleed very heavily. Quickly I took the muffler from my neck and made a tourniquet for the wound. Luckily none of my bones were broken.

After this there was an enormous explosion and piercing sound, followed by an air blast hitting my face. To me it sounded like a direct hit; then two other bombs struck the carrier, piercing through the flight deck into the hangar area. In the hangar there were eighteen fueled Type 97s armed with torpedoes and a mass of 800 kilogram land bombs scattered on the nearby deck. Remarkably, *Kaga* was still operating at full speed. One of my comrades helped me go to the stern section because it was safer there. Postwar

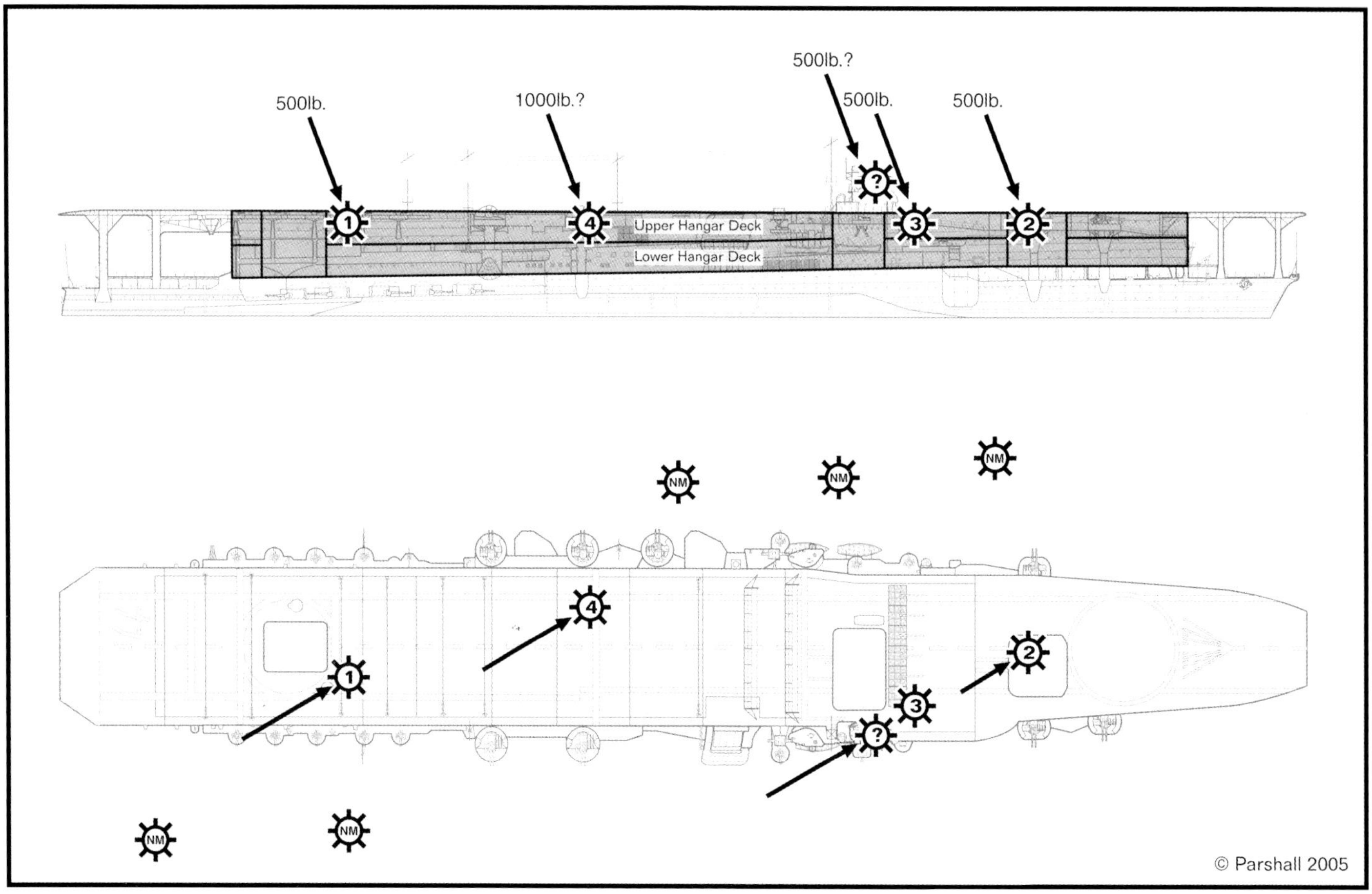

The bomb hit locations on the carrier *Kaga*. (Jonathan Parshall)

American records indicate that SBD Dauntless dive-bombers from the carrier *Enterprise* scored at least four hits on our carrier with 500 and 1000 pound bombs. Prior to these four hits there were three near misses. Then the next one hit the starboard rear (pilots' living quarters); after that two more bombs hit the front half of the bridge, which killed the skipper and his staff. The last bomb was a direct hit on the flight deck, and this sealed the fate of *Kaga*. Because of this last bomb hit all of our munitions, such as the torpedoes and bombs, along with the gasoline started to ignite, and then blew up in a chain-reaction. A lot of maintenance and ordinance personnel perished because of this last bomb blast.

During the Battle of Midway Kaga's *total casualties were 811 men, and out of that number 212 were engineers. Most of the ship's fatalities were the 261 seamen and 268 mechanics who probably perished on the hangar decks.* [111]

The crew members who escaped the fire sought shelter at the rescue boat staging area, which was still relatively safe at that time. Hence, at 1400 the order was given to abandon ship. *Kaga's* engines stopped and we began to drift. I had no idea what time it was.[112] I laid down, trying to ease the pain. I also was hungry, because I hadn't eaten anything since breakfast. Then a series of secondary explosions caused sudden jerks on the doomed carrier. The destroyer *Hagikaze* was unable to get close to *Kaga* because of all the fires. Someone then shouted, "Send a boat for the wounded!" Many wounded men were waiting for help. My watch stopped, and I thought it was around 1500 but wasn't sure. I heard a voice, "A boat is coming!" A shipmate then shouted in my ear, "Maeda-san, hang in there just a little bit longer." I must have lost consciousness, but then I heard another voice, "Move the injured personnel quickly to the boat!" Since the lower deck of the stern section of the carrier sat high above the water, you had to jump into the sea before climbing onto the rescue boat. So my shipmates lifted my body, then threw me overboard. Still, I ended up spending about two hours in the water before being rescued. Once a launch came close I struggled to reach the rope, which was thrown to me and, having reached it, I managed to get on the boat. They took me to the *Hagikaze* around 1600.

On the destroyer the deck was covered with spent shells, some of which were still hot. Since my socks were wet I could feel the hot shells. On the deck there were numerous men who were burned or wounded. I was in pain, but had to wait a long time before a surgeon tended my wound. There was only one surgeon on the entire ship, and he didn't have any proper medical supplies and equipment to help the wounded men. I received twenty-eight stitches in my left leg without anesthesia. It was a rough operation, because the doctor used a twisted needle (normally for sewing canvas) and a non-medical string to stitch my wounds, but the bleeding didn't stop. Later in the afternoon my comrade told me that *Kaga* would be scuttled by our destroyer's torpedoes. He carried me up to the deck so I could see the last moments of our beloved carrier, which was nearby. Even though I was in pain tears started to run down my cheeks, and everyone around me was crying; it was a very sad sight.

As Maeda-san states, Kaga *was hit by a shower of both 500 and 1,000 pound bombs from the SBD Dauntless dive-bombers of VB-6 from the USS* Enterprise. *They arrived over* Kaga *around 1022 and subsequently scored at least four hits and several near misses on the now-doomed carrier. One of the bombs wiped out a number of high-ranking officers on* Kaga, *including Captain Okada, chief gunnery officer Lieutenant Commander Toyosaburō Miyano, navigator Commander Ichiji Monden, and communications officer Lieutenant Commander Hidekazu Takahashi. All of the surviving* Kaga *veterans who fought during the Battle of Midway talked about munitions (bombs, torpedoes) lying on the hangar deck and mounted on fueled aircraft which annihilated the crew and the carrier itself. A quick snapshot of this can be ascertained by these numbers: an estimated 80,000 pounds of explosives were strewed in the hangar or already installed on aircraft, and approximately 10,000 gallons of fuel was in the aircraft during the time of the dive-bombing attack.*[113] Kaga *also was hit by one torpedo in her starboard quarter, which was launched from the submarine USS* Nautilus, *but it failed to explode.*[114] *Nevertheless, this would be the last battle for* Kaga, *the carrier which fought so valiantly during the early phase of World War II.*

After the *Hagikaze* left the combat zone three days later I transferred to the battleship *Nagato*. Once I was on board this ship they gave me proper medical treatment. Then, on the 13th I was transferred to the hospital ship *Hikawa Maru*. Commander Mitsuo Fuchida, the well-known Pearl Harbor attack leader, also was on board; we were all lost soldiers. After returning to Japan I was taken to Kure Naval Hospital. I was carried on a stretcher, which was covered with thick cloth, through the hospital gate late at night. To conceal the loss of our four carriers, wounded men from the battle stayed in virtual isolation in the same building for over a month, while healthy pilots were not allowed to leave Kanoya Air Base. The survivors didn't have any money and couldn't even smoke cigarettes.

Lieutenant Hideo Maki of *Kaga's Kankō-tai* also was in Kure Naval Hospital with me. He had been burned very badly during the battle, and his face was covered with bandages. One day Admiral Yamamoto came to visit us in the hospital. He stood in front of each bed and met each wounded Midway survivor. I was very impressed when he said, "I want you to get well soon." Finally, after being hospitalized for three months, we were allowed "normal" contact with the outside world.

I asked a nurse who was leaving the hospital to buy me some alcohol. There was a nurse that used to give me *saké* in a medicine bottle and handed it to me under my blanket. Normally these sympathetic nurses, who understood our needs, were middle-aged women. During my hospitalization I was promoted to the rank of chief petty officer, and the name plate near my pillow was changed. Since I was appointed as the "room chief" it became easier to get alcohol. Sometimes a nurse gave me alcohol mixed with glucose, which was normally used for cleansing. She put some color into the drink and called it "*saké* acid storm." Pilots also were popular with the women at the hospital. A *Sōryū* mechanic in the bed next to mine became jealous of us, so I gave him *saké* so he would stop reporting about our drinking habits. After the war I received a letter from this guy, who lived in Kagoshima Prefecture.

When I look back on this time period while I was in the hospital, battles raged on and on in the South Pacific. The men on board the carriers *Zuikaku*, *Shōkaku*, *Junyō*, *Hiyō*, and *Zuihō* were fighting very hard to avenge our loss at Midway. During this time they sank the carrier *Hornet* and damaged the *Enterprise*. Sadly, several of my classmates died during these bloody battles. Combat went on day and night in the Solomon Islands. About ninety of my classmates died in the Solomon Islands area alone.

At this time I still wasn't able to walk well, but remember getting information about the results of each engagement. Naturally, if it was good news I was happy, and if it was bad news I became depressed. In November, Kure Naval Hospital received a lot of new patients who were wounded in combat, so we didn't have enough beds. Because of this I was transferred to Maizuru Naval Hospital.

At that time I was beginning to walk again with crutches. I still didn't have a uniform so I asked the head nurse for one. She brought me a tunic that had a good conduct badge with three lines that was from a higher-ranking petty officer. I heard that the original owner of this tunic just died, but I had no choice. Then I boarded a train for the first time in many months. However, I really couldn't enjoy the trip because it was a wartime atmosphere on board the train. Maizuru Naval Hospital was a newly built wooden structure. It had a more relaxed atmosphere than Kure. When they saw me wearing this "adopted" uniform I got the best bed there; I was pleased. However, I pretended that it wasn't a big deal. I was the only aviator at the hospital, and the rest of the patients were paratroopers and soldiers. Since some of the men were from Niigata and Kukuriko I felt like it was home, and this was very comforting. I was visited by the sisters who ran a small restaurant that I used to go drinking at back in my Maizuru *Kōkūtai* days. They put *saké* into a medicine bottle, so I could drink whenever I wanted. Finally, in late December I was able to leave the hospital.

After leaving the hospital I became a member of the marine group at Maizuru on a temporary basis. There were no special duties all day, and I just marched endlessly. During this time I was able to see a movie *Hawai Malay Oki Kaisen* (Hawaii and Malaysia Sea Battle), which was made by Toho Films. While we watched the film in a theatre everyone started to clap and cheer, so I felt like I was being recognized for participating in the Pearl Harbor attack.

Hawai Malay Oki Kaisen *was produced in 1942, essentially as a wartime propaganda movie, by Toho Films. The movie has some interesting footage that shows the training of WWII Japanese Navy aviators, and features some wartime aircraft "in action." It chronicles Japan's early wartime exploits, and the film is sometimes played on Japanese television. I actually saw this movie on television when I lived in Japan. Note the Japanese spell Hawaii with only one "I," not two.*

Maeda-san Flies Again

On 22 December 1942 I finally received the order to be transferred to the Tateyama *Kōkūtai*. I requested to be a member of this group on several occasions because the weather at Tateyama was very warm. The effects of the cold weather caused more pain in my still bandaged left leg. I arrived there on the 26th, but at that time all of the pilots were gone because they were busy doing flight training. I went to the airfield and was shocked to see my classmate, PO1c Takayuki Hori. He was very happy to see me and said, "I thought you were a goner on board *Kaga*. It is amazing that you are still alive!" I said to him, "I thought you died on *Akagi*!" We both laughed exuberantly and talked about what happened during the Battle of Midway. On 4 June Hori-san was flying in the Type 97 *kankō* and doing reconnaissance duties for the *Kidō Butai*. When he returned *Akagi* was on fire, so PO1c Hori did an emergency landing on the undamaged *Hiryū*. While on board the *Hiryū* he flew in the second wave attack against the carrier *Yorktown*, consisting of ten Type 97s and six Zero fighters. The young aviator was very lucky to survive; only five Type 97s returned from the mission. After the mission he also managed to survive the enemy air attack on *Hiryū*; Hori-san was fortunate to be alive.

PO1c Hori, a Tokyo native, was very simple-minded. Right after we joined the Navy we were introduced to our *hanchō*. Do you know what Hori-san said to him? In very impolite Japanese he said, "You're my *hanchō*?" Because of this wisecrack the trainee was beaten, and it became a well-known story in the Navy. He liked to drink a lot, but really couldn't hold his liquor well, and when Hori was a warrant officer he had a habit of taking off his shoes and hitting people with them.

The *buntaichō* of Tateyama *Kōkūtai* was Lieutenant Toruo Morimoto, and he was a pilot. He was very bright and easygoing. Morimoto-san said he cared about our feelings, and that we didn't have to push ourselves too hard. I was bored after being six months in the hospital, so I said to him, "Please don't hesitate to use me as much as you can."

Another aviator that I knew from previous assignments was WO Takeyasu Kanai. He also was a pilot on the carrier *Sōryū*. Kanai-san said, "I'm glad you're alive. We both had a rough time during the Battle of Midway." Hori-san joined our conversation, and together we talked about the battle and enjoyed drinking on the second floor of the command post. During this time I became a *hanchō* for the first time since entering the Navy. I did my best not to discriminate against any of our group members, because I recalled my painful memories from my early days in the service. I didn't want the men to experience what I did.

On the night of 29 December 1942 I was able to finally fly again after six months of being stuck on the ground. Prior to being wounded, I flew so much at night on board a carrier that I grew tired of it. However, on this occasion I felt nervous while taking off. The pilot of my plane was PO1c Toshio Iijima. Our duty was to escort a group of ships that was cruising 100 nautical miles off Hachijō Jima. In those days there were a lot of enemy submarines that attacked our ships that were sailing south, and Japan suffered heavy losses. At any given time at Tateyama *Kōkūtai* there were *kankōs* and *rikkōs* armed with two 250 kilogram anti-submarine bombs ready to take off. We had three shifts and stayed in the command post. When we received a radio report stating that some enemy submarines were located, we went to engage them even if it was bad weather or nighttime.

One guy that I will never forget is a pilot named WO Tokoro. He had messy long hair, and always had dandruff on his shoulders. Aside from this, however, Tokoro-san was very strong, both in character and fighting spirit. He was always ready to fight a powerful enemy and very brave. This young warrant officer also criticized openly his superior officers without hesitation. In our group there was a Lieutenant "M," who was a Naval Academy graduate but didn't fly because of an ailment in his chest. This lieutenant didn't have the proper personality to be a pilot, and was a stark contrast from Lieutenant Morimoto. After Morimoto-san was promoted to lieutenant commander he was transferred to the Philippines, and Lieutenant "M" became our *buntaichō*. This lieutenant constantly started problems with the airmen in our group and WO Tokoro criticized him, whenever he had the chance. Hence, Tokoro-san was ordered to transfer from our group.

During the summer a really unique individual, WO Ryōichi Domoto, joined our group. His character and personality were totally different than most other guys I met in the service. One of the duties for a "Deck Petty Officer" was to take care of any people who were transferred into our group. When Domoto-san arrived, I saw that he had the rank of chief petty officer with a one line good conduct badge. He had sharp eyes, a fair complexion, and a strange mustache which was "turned up" at each end. Normally, when a new person joined our group they weren't arrogant, and kept to themselves. This guy was different though, and he came across as being too proud of himself.

Later I learned more about WO Domoto. He once bit an officer and lost his good conduct badge because of his actions. Domoto-san told me that the reason he appeared so pale is because he was put in solitary confinement due to his poor conduct. As I hung out with him I learned more about this unique fellow. Regardless of how he looked, this guy was a good person and had a strong sense of justice. Every day he put egg whites on his mustache to make it look good. Personally, I thought WO Domoto's appearance would have improved without this strange mustache. Later I met him at Kisarazu, when he was a warrant officer, and thought at first that he was different person because his mustache was gone. As I imagined, Domoto-san looked a lot better without his mustache. Sadly, I found out that he died in combat off Taiwan and didn't survive the war.

On 1 November 1943 I was promoted to the rank of warrant officer. There were eight warrant officers, but we didn't have enough individual rooms for each man. Because of this we put partitions in the barracks and made a big fuss about carrying beds into that area. Other than the time when there was a high-ranking officer on duty, we were able to go out and enjoy ourselves. So just about every day we enjoyed drinking and partying, but gradually ran out of money. I ended up getting an advance of my salary from the paymaster so I could have some cash.

Building an Airfield at Hachijō Jima

Sometime in December 1943 we decided to build an advance base at Hachijō Jima, so I flew there with *buntaichō* Lieutenant Morimoto to take some photographs of the island.[115] I saw an area near the foot of a mountain called Hachijō Fuji where we thought of building a runway. We flew back and forth several times over this area, and took sequential pictures in order to make an aerial photo map. Once we returned the photos were pasted together, and after calculating the altitude the shots were taken from, we could make an accurate aerial photo map.

On another occasion when I flew with the *buntaichō* in a Type 96 *kankō*, we tried to do the first landing on Hachijō Jima. There was a lot of turbulence and a strong west wind, so landing was very difficult. Furthermore, nearby our landing site there was a big mountain of jagged rocks, but after two failed attempts we were able to land on the third try. We used the technique for landing on a carrier and estimated the altitude and speed while passing over this rock mountain. However, we almost hit this rock mountain while touching down. The runway was short, but in the end we were able to make ten successful landings on this primitive landing strip. In order to complete this base our group transported materials to the island, and engineers blew up that mountain of rocks. Lastly, the runway was smoothed out and resurfaced so it would be safe for aircraft operations. By March 1944 Hachijō Jima began to resemble an air base. With local native islanders looking on, three Type 96 *kankōs* were able to land safely. In the winter patrol flights couldn't have been more difficult, but while I was there our group had no accidents.

Around this time my classmate, PO2c Yuzo Watanabe, was transferred to our group. Prior to joining the Tateyama *Kōkūtai* he was in the 582 *Kōkūtai*, based in Rabaul. As I mentioned before, in the beginning of the war he was on the carrier *Sōryū* as a member of the *Kankō-tai*.[116] Watanabe-san stayed on this carrier until it was sunk during the Battle of Midway. After this he transferred to the carrier *Junyō* and flew numerous combat sorties, including the 17 October 1942 Guadalcanal strike.[117] During this mission, one of his comrades, PO1c Mori, had his right hand blown off, and he was very badly hurt. After the war Mori-san wrote a book called *Miracle Torpedo Unit*. This wounded aviator thought that he was history, but managed to crash-land on the western beach of Guadalcanal Island. PO1c Mori was badly hurt, but managed to survive in the jungle for twenty days before being rescued by one of our destroyers.

Furthermore, our fellow classmate Hori-san and I had a welcome party for Watanabe-san after he arrived. Shortly after this Hori-san transferred to serve as the *buntaishi* in the recently formed 551 *Kōkūtai*. Sadly, he died in action on 15 June 1944, on a torpedo attack mission against an American aircraft carrier during the Battle of the Philippine Sea.

A Deadly Accident for Maeda's Classmate

As the war situation worsened for Japan, Tateyama Air Base became a stop-over base for fighter units that were going to Iwo Jima. A lot of junior fighter pilots also were temporarily assigned to our group. One day my old classmate, WO Kaoru Shimazaki, piloted the leading aircraft for a group of fighter planes. He and I were from the same prefecture, but didn't see each other since flight training, because we flew different types of aircraft.

On the day that WO Shimazaki and the group of Zero fighters were supposed to leave for Hachijō Jima there was bad weather. I really thought that it was very dangerous for inexperienced aviators to fly in such poor weather, but they had to go. Shimazaki-san said that they would still go even though a bad storm was approaching our area. He would be flying in a *rikkō* (to guide the group) and I saw him off. I was worried until I saw every aircraft take off and join the formation safely.

About one hour after they left the sky became very dark and it started to rain very heavily. Suddenly Shimazaki's *rikkō* appeared, and since it was flying so low, the aircraft looked like it was crawling on the ground. I heard that the pilot of his plane was an experienced warrant officer, so I was not very concerned. I don't know what happened, but the aircraft was still coming in too low while trying to land. Several people in the command post commented that this looked like a very "dangerous" landing. The moment the *rikkō* touched the ground the aircraft jumped up again, then landed in a very awkward position. The belly of Shimazaki's plane burst into flames that quickly engulfed the *rikkō* before it finally to stop about 100 meters (31 feet) from a hangar. Everything happened so quickly that I don't remember the details, but I managed to rescue my buddy from the inferno. By the time I found him he was unconscious, and his face and hands were burned. I carried him to the hospital, and he received immediate medical help. In the meantime, one after another of the Zero fighters started to return. However, due to heavy turbulence in the air several fighters had to do crash-landings on the runway. It was a very sad thing to watch for someone who has seen (on numerous occasions) seasoned Zero pilots flying from our carriers.

Combat in Late 1944

While the fighting came closer and closer to the Japanese mainland, more of our men went to the southern part of Kyūshū and the Philippines. Since Saipan was now lost to the enemy Iwo Jima became our frontlines. One of the hard-working and very experienced aviators on Iwo Jima was CPO Reiji Miyanaga. He didn't get promoted to warrant officer because of his suicide attempt while on board the carrier *Shōkaku*. I thought Miyanaga-san was a very passionate and wild guy. I knew he was in love with a woman at Tateyama, and she wrote him a letter. After I gave CPO Miyanaga the letter he read it very carefully. Then he asked me, "Sir, I have to go back to Japan, no matter what. Would you give me a good excuse to go home?" I asked him why he needed to go back, and he said that the woman was finally able to marry him. Prior to this time both of her parents were deceased, and her brother would not allow them to get married. I explained the situation to the base commander, Lieutenant Shinji Numura, and he agreed to let Miyanaga-san go to Kisarazu, under the pretext that he had some duties there. I helped take care of all the arrangements for the wedding, which was a simple one. Four days later we had a reception at a Japanese restaurant at Tateyama. I thought Miyanaga's wife also was pregnant at the time.

Around this time a young lieutenant (junior grade) with red cheeks, Mr. S, joined our group. Another change in the Tateyama *Kōkūtai* was that our *buntaichō* Lieutenant Morimoto was transferred to a unit in the Philippines, and a Lieutenant Mr. M took his place. I simply couldn't put up with a lot of things that both of these men did. For example, this Lieutenant (junior grade) Mr. S forced us to use this "new" navigation technique, which he probably just learned in flight training, but never actually used. One day we flew in a group of three aircraft led by this Mr. S from Tateyama to Iwo Jima. He was in the leading aircraft, and my aircraft, along with a third plane flown by my classmate PO2c Yuzo Watanabe, followed him. All year long our pilots were flying this route, which was about 600 nautical miles to Iwo Jima, and usually covered by clouds. Nevertheless, it was impossible to get there using this "new" navigation technique that Mr. S insisted on using. The only way to get there safely was to use our traditional inferred navigation method which was done this way: first we set our course bound for the Borne Islands; then, once you got there, you looked for Chichi Jima and Haha Jima. When you were able to see the latter islands, it was easy to locate Iwo Jima, which was nearby.

Mr. S was very excited about going to Iwo Jima because this was his first time to go to the island; but we didn't tell him anything beforehand. I felt some satisfaction when this guy couldn't find the island and was lost. However, both PO2c Watanabe and I knew exactly where Iwo Jima was, but we didn't tell him! Mr. S got more and more worried because he couldn't see anything; especially while flying at the altitude of 1,500 meters over water. We thought that it wouldn't be prudent to waste anymore fuel, so after a while I signaled to Mr. S and took the lead. We turned around, and Mr. S reluctantly followed us. Then, after doing some calculations, we lowered our altitude and saw a flat piece of land that almost looked like an aircraft carrier. On the island there was a large mountain which looked like a carrier's bridge; we had found Iwo Jima. After we landed, I said sarcastically to Mr. S, "Your navigation technique worked very well today." Then his face turned red and he looked embarrassed. I thought he wanted to hide in a cave somewhere! After that Mr. S really started to harass Watanabe-san and me.

One night, while I was drinking in a local restaurant, Mr. S started to argue with WO Sojirō Kojima. Kojima-san, who joined the Navy in 1933, was chubby and had a fair complexion. This guy was a very well-known *chukō-tai* navigator, and if you didn't know of his exploits, you had to be an "outsider." His nickname was "Fighting Sobe." He looked very soft, but once WO Kojima started to drink his behavior was totally different. After a few drinks this well-known aviator wouldn't hesitate to fight someone that he disliked, especially officers. Because of his tendency to start fights it took him a long time to get promoted through the ranks. Nevertheless, Kojima-san knew about Mr. S' bad reputation and didn't hesitate to use his fists on him. They fought in front of Mr. M, so he always had a grudge against this young warrant officer because of this incident. Since Mr. M couldn't drink he was sober at the time. As for Mr. S, he was drunk while they fought, so it wasn't a big deal to him. As for Kojima-san, I saw him once after the war but he is now deceased. After the above fight Mr. M started to act differently towards Watanabe-san and me. I thought that after he got promoted to the rank of lieutenant commander and Mr. S. became a lieutenant they would surely retaliate against us.

Mr. M, now a lieutenant commander, seemed to get his revenge on people he didn't like by transferring them to a combat unit on the frontlines.

The experienced pilots from Tateyama *Kōkūtai* began to be transferred one after another, and finally came my turn to leave the group. I don't know why, but I was appointed to the 932 *Kōkūtai* on 12 December 1944, and became a part of the detachment based at Toyohashi. One of the reasons I may have been transferred to this group was because I once attended a lecture on the use of radar. Perhaps someone thought that I was an expert in this field. In fact, on one mission, which occurred in December 1943, I saw some purple smoke that was coming from an enemy submarine recharging its batteries on the surface. At that time I was flying in a Type 96 *rikkō* that had radar, and we engaged the submarine around 100 nautical miles north of Chichi Jima. We dropped two twenty-five kilogram bombs on the submarine, which quickly went down in the water, but we couldn't confirm if it sank. The 903 *Kōkūtai* was an anti-submarine specialist group, and the commander of the unit was Lieutenant Yoshitake. He was a warm-hearted individual; I also served with him at Iwo Jima.

After a while the base changed from Toyohashi to Ōhi. One day, around this time, I went to Kisarazu Air Base to get radar installed on my aircraft. In December my good buddy and classmate, PO2c Yuzo Watanabe, transferred to K-252, a group that flew the *Tenzan kankō*. I felt depressed at his farewell party because he was the last man (in my group) that flew on aircraft carriers earlier in the war. By this time all of my other buddies from my early days in the Navy, like Lieutenant (junior grade) Haruo Yoshino, had already transferred to other groups. PO2c Watanabe had a girlfriend in Tateyama that he loved very much. The following year, while he was on his way to a new base in southern Kyūshū, Watanabe-san stopped by her home in Kamakura to say goodbye. Later, I heard that he told her family very calmly, "I don't think that I will survive this mission, so please take care if I don't return." On 13 April 1945, while flying from Kushira Air Base, he participated in a torpedo night attack mission against American ships and died in action.

1945 – The Last Year of the War

On 6 January 1945 I transferred to K-256, a group that flew the Tenzan *kankō*. By this stage in the war I knew nobody close to me in my group, so there was no farewell party for me. However, I did go back to my hometown, which had a lot of snow at this time, and got married. We exchanged our vows at my home, surrounded by family and friends. The following day I left my wife at my home and boarded a train bound for Kyūshū.

Two days later, on the 8th, I arrived at Kokubu Base in Kagoshima Prefecture, but this wasn't my base. My new base, named Kushira, actually used to be an auxiliary strip for emergency landings, and was located southeast of Kanoya. The *taichō* of my new group was Lieutenant Akira Chosokabe, and the men of K-256 had very high morale. This was my first time to fly on a *Tenzan kankō*, which was larger than my usual aircraft, the Type 97. The *Tenzan* had a very wide landing gear system and a powerful engine. I heard that the maximum speed of the aircraft was 270 knots, but the engine was unreliable and frequently broke down. To tell you the truth, I felt a bit worried flying in the *Tenzan*, but it really didn't matter because the aircraft would probably be my coffin. The pilot who was my flying partner was WO Keiji Hayakawa, and we started to do test flights together. There also were some officer pilots in this unit that were graduates of the 69th and 70th term classes from the Naval Academy. Our usual spot for drinking was at a restaurant (inside a hotel) that was in front of the train station. Since K-256 had the lethal job of doing torpedo attacks, most of the guys in our group really didn't think they had much longer to live. Because of this the men enjoyed themselves and drank a lot.

At the end of January I was told to go to Saeki Air Base for a lecture on radar. After the lecture was over a pilot was chosen from our group to be a member of the *shōtaichō's* crew that was going to participate in a nighttime torpedo attack. During our lesson we learned about enemy fighters that were fitted with small, yet very efficient radar units. The hit ratio of the enemy night-fighters was excellent. So it was very difficult for us to attack enemy ships at night. We learned about *giman-shi*, which could be used to block enemy radar. Lastly, the lecture also covered how to use a radar unit while flying combat missions.

Giman-shi *literally means "radar cheating paper," which was similar to the chaff that was used by Allied pilots to confuse radar controlled guns. According to the book* Kōkū Gijutsu no Zenbo *by Hozo Terai, studies showed that strips of tinfoil cut to 1 meter and 2 meter lengths gave the best results. They were most often simply tossed by hand out of the back of the plane, although a parachute-equipped dispensing tube was also developed.*

By the time I returned from Saeki the allied forces were winning the war in the Philippines, and Formosa was attacked by an enemy mobile unit. I didn't tell this to anyone, but I thought that the war was in its final stages. The younger men had different reasons to join the Navy than I did, and they wanted to do something for our nation. All of them looked so young, and it seemed like they enjoyed the training. The focus of our training was taking off, landing, and doing torpedo attacks. However, there were very few people in our group that had experience flying at night. The veteran aviators (including me) didn't have a chance to fly much because we were low on both airplanes and fuel. Our group did have a lot of aviators, but we really couldn't train them to their fullest potential. The training was sufficient to improve their basic skills, and they became better aviators.

As I mentioned, the morale of the junior pilots was very high, even though they were facing death. Frequently the men sang songs like the "Dandelion Song," which had nothing to do with war, because I believe they had hope for peace. These young guys were not career soldiers from the Naval Academy. Instead, they left college in order to join the Navy. I felt that the same thing would have happened to me if I had chosen to go college, instead of joining the Navy. Because of this I felt a kinship with these young men and began to sing with them. Normally they gave me cup after cup of *saké*, and then I got drunk and feel asleep (in my uniform).

Rookie pilots flew missions only in the daytime, while experienced veteran aviators flew at night. During this time I flew three missions at night, and our aircraft flew alone (with no escorts or other *Tenzans*). Enemy fighters always were waiting for us so it was very dangerous. The *taichō* said to take the direct flight route going south from Kyūshū, but if we always flew the same pattern every day we would be shot down. In order to survive we had to fly a totally different flight route, and our targets were the American ships anchored off Okinawa. However, since it was night, it was difficult to confirm if we scored any "hits" or not. Returning home also was very dangerous, and normally we stayed overnight at islands such as Miyakō Jima before going back to our base the following day.

Around this time in February I also participated in a "group" nighttime attack mission against American ships off Okinawa. I flew in the leading aircraft and dropped flares to illuminate the area around our targets. After dropping these flares our pilots could see the silhouettes of the enemy ships for about thirty minutes, almost like it was daytime. The drop point of the flares was very crucial for the success of the mission, and only experienced aviators could do this important task. Furthermore, most of the other navigators in our group were rookies, so my job for this mission was very important. I was shocked to see the battleship *West Virginia* in action again, because I thought my torpedo sank that ship at Pearl Harbor in 1941!

As I mentioned before, the *Tenzan kankō* had very strong landing gears and they rarely ever broke. However, because of the large size of the engine, while landing our view was obstructed by the large engine cowling. Since it was so tough to see well most of the pilots jacked up their seats to get a better view. Furthermore, the people who had short legs had a difficult time reaching the foot bar, so it was difficult to make a three-point landing with this aircraft. One night in early February 1945 I went on a nighttime navigation training mission and tested the Type 19 radar, which was just installed in my aircraft. My job was to check the accuracy of this radar gear as well. The Type 19 radar was developed at the end of 1944, and it weighed about sixty kilograms.

*Historian Osamu Tagaya explains more about this radar set: "The Type 19 would be 19-*Shi Ku Denpa Tanshin-Gi *(i.e. radar) Mark 1 Model 2, also known by its short code designation FK-3. This was largely a scaled down version of the Type 2 Ku Mark 6, designed for use on small and medium-sized aircraft. Test results were said to be good, and much was expected of it, but it is reported that the war ended before production versions of the set reached combat units."*[118]

It seemed to me that the pilot (WO Hayakawa) who flew my aircraft didn't have much experience flying at night. He came in too high while we were landing, so our aircraft came down with a big thump, then bounced up. Because of this landing mishap the rubber wire which held the radar gear was severed, but luckily we didn't crash.

Due to this bad landing the old wound on my leg opened up and starting bleeding. The military doctor worked on my wound and stopped the bleeding. He said after the wound healed I could get a skin graft, and it would finally heal properly. I didn't think that my 26th birthday would be spent in a hospital, but that's what happened.

While I was in the hospital I met PO2c Akira Okinaka of K-251. He was the pilot of an aircraft that dropped flares during a nighttime torpedo attack. Okinaka's plane crashed during landing and he was burned on his face and hands. According to him, his job was to guide a group of twelve aircraft to the target and drop flares (to illuminate the attack area). However, Okinaka's group was ambushed by enemy night-fighters and completely annihilated. When PO2c Okinaka was landing his aircraft it fell into a bomb crater on the runway and flipped over, then burst into flames. His face was covered with bandages, and he felt very bad about what happened during that mission. Since the hospital was very close to the war front there were air raids. Wounded men filled up the hospital, so I was transferred to Maizuru Hospital. Finally I was discharged from the hospital on 1 May and promoted to the rank of ensign.

I was told to go to Katori Air Base (Chiba Prefecture) and went there by train. On the way to Katori I stopped at my hometown for one night, then took a train (Sobu Line) to my new base. I arrived there on 4 May and began my last military assignment of the war. By the summer of 1945 anyone could see that the war would be ending soon, but nobody thought we could end it on "even" ground with the Allied forces. The young pilots in our group were still very energetic and tried to keep a positive attitude. Nevertheless, both aircraft and fuel were in short supply, so we couldn't do enough training. There were frequent enemy air raids, so our aircraft were dispersed in ditches around the airfield, and we had to live in farmers' houses along the beach.

On 10 August 1945 we put bombs on every aircraft, and veteran pilots were told to be ready to fly *tokkō* attack missions. So I thought my last day would be coming soon. If the war would have lasted one month longer all of us would have died. I believe the atomic bombs really saved my life. Navy pilots felt obligated to fly *tokkō* missions whether they wanted to or not, and their rank really didn't make a difference.

The End of the War

On 15 August about forty of us gathered together in a farmer's yard to hear the Emperor's radio address to the nation. But it was hard to hear his message because of the noisy cicadas. Under the hot August sun we tried our best to listen, but it was very difficult. I thought the men looked worried, and once they learned what happened, there was almost a low moan from the group; it seemed like the cicadas stopped making noise momentarily. We were all in a state of disbelief and stunned.

The following day Nakajima J1N *Gekkō* fighters (Allied code name "Irving") from the 302 *Kōkūtai* dropped flyers on our airfield, urging us to not surrender. Then, on the 17th, most of the members of our group went home feeling that they didn't do enough during the war, or some still wanted to stay at the air base. As for me, on 22 August I took off in a *Tenzan kankō* with my flying partner, WO Hayakawa, for our final flight to Suzuka Air Base. Our job was to transport the aircraft to this particular base. From the air Tokyo looked like it was one big burned field, and the cities of

Kawasaki and Yokohama also were badly damaged because of the intense bombing raids on Japan. I could see only one train running, the Tokkaido Line, which was a symbol that our nation was still alive.

Seven years of Navy life ended when I landed at Suzuka Air Base. When I thought about my years in the service it seemed like a long time, but it passed quickly. I kept on thinking about my comrades who died, like quick flashes of fire; then they were gone. I thought over and over about the deaths of so many of my classmates in the war. Why did they have to die? After thinking about all of this, I simply couldn't stop my tears of sadness. My last rank in the Imperial Japanese Navy was ensign, and my total flying time was 3,800 hours.

Postwar

After the war I passed a test to become an inspector for the construction of air base facilities on Okinawa. In those days you couldn't go to Okinawa without a passport, and I stayed there for ten years. Next, I started a construction company and specialized in overseas projects; in places such as North America, South America, Indonesia, and Africa. My wife and I had two sons, who are both now married. We also have two grandchildren.

Reflections

One day, in the summer of 1991, I received a letter from someone in the United States requesting me to attend a symposium, which would commemorate the 50th anniversary of the Pearl Harbor attack. My family didn't want me to go to the symposium because they knew that the American public thought that it was a "sneak attack" on their country. However, I still wanted to attend the symposium being held in Hawaii. After I arrived there someone from a television company contacted me, and said that a Pearl Harbor survivor from the battleship *West Virginia* wanted to meet me. On the night of 5 December 1991 I met Mr. Richard Fiske at the *Arizona* Memorial. I said to him, "I am very sorry about attacking Pearl Harbor." Then Mr. Fiske waved his hand and said, "Don't be sorry, all military men had to follow orders. It was not your fault." During the war he was a bugler on board the *West Virginia*, and later fought in the Battle of Iwo Jima. We became friends, and the following year he came to Japan with his wife to visit me. Sadly, after being ill for some time, Mr. Fiske died on 2 April 2004.

Prior to the war I thought America was not united, because there were so many different kinds of people living there. My idea was wrong, because everyone in the country joined together as one nation after Pearl Harbor. Even if Japan would have beaten the United States during the Battle of Midway, in the end we would still have lost the war. This is because our nation had a flawed war strategy and limited natural resources.

Lastly, I can't forget Admiral Isoruko Yamamoto, because he made every effort to avoid going to war with the United States, but in the end he had no choice. Yamamoto-san lived in America while serving as a naval attaché, so he understood the power of its economy and industry. This realistic Navy admiral realized that Japan could not beat the United States, so he did everything possible to avoid fighting this powerful western country. Then, some right-

The author with *Kaga* veterans Haruo Yoshino (left) and Takeshi Maeda (right) in Tokyo, 2002. (Werneth)

Admiral Isoruko Yamamoto was an important Japanese Naval aviation pioneer and leader. He died on 18 April 1943 when his aircraft was shot down by P-38 fighters. (NHC via Wenger)

wing activists said that Admiral Yamamoto was a turncoat, and a group of extremists wanted to kill him. The pro-war faction of the Japanese Army supported their actions. I believe Yamamoto-san really had no choice in the matter once Japan decided to fight the United States.

During Japan's wartime years we were taught at home and school that the Emperor was a god. However, I did not believe that. I thought that the Emperor was a human being just like everybody else. Over sixty years ago I thought we were fighting for our country, not the Emperor. My friends who survived the war tell me that they felt the same way I did. Having served as an aviator during the war made me mentally stronger as a person, and this helped me throughout my postwar years.

In 1945 Japan accepted the Potsdam Declaration, and American troops helped rebuild our country after the war. During the war the United States suffered heavy casualties during the battles of Okinawa and Iwo Jima; yet these territories were returned to our country in the postwar years. I really appreciate that America did this. I can't imagine the fate of Japan if the Russians would have occupied our country after the war. Japan lost the war, but we were still lucky. As the honorary president of the veterans' group *Unabarakai* I can never forget the war, and always have to attend many memorial services across Japan. I personally have no hatred of the United States or the American people. I believe America's big challenge now is fighting terrorism around the globe.

Ensign Haruo Yoshino

"We thought that they were the enemy and nothing else."

When I think of my friend Haruo Yoshino I think of a cat. He is like a cat with nine lives. During the war the young Navy aviator was fortunate to survive several dangerous battles, including the Pearl Harbor attack, the Battle of Midway, and the Battle of Santa Cruz, as well as many others. Yoshino-san always flew as an observer for several different three-place carrier attack planes, such as the Type 97 and Tenzan. *He flew repeatedly in battles where countless men died, yet Yoshino-san was always fortunate to survive. In the last few years the old warhorse fought and survived another type of battle, with cancer. Fortunately, he made a complete recovery from this illness. I met the distinguished veteran for the first time in the spring of 1999. During our meeting he made me feel at ease with his laid back, warm personality. Because of this I felt like I knew the man for many years. After this initial meeting we met again on several occasions over the past seven years and became good friends.*

Sitting in an express train bound for Yoshino's house, which was located in the rural town of Mobara, Chiba, I began to discover a Japan that I never saw before. After about thirty minutes on the train my window was filled with a sea of rolling hills and trees. It was beautiful. What a refreshing change from the "concrete jungle" of Tokyo to see such natural beauty in Japan. I arrived at my destination after about fifty minutes of train travel. As soon as I arrived at the train station gates I spotted him. He was dressed casually in a baseball cap and sweater. As usual, he greeted me with a warm smile, and we were on our way. Besides the beautiful hills, the area near the ex-aviator's home was filled with flooded rice paddy fields and farmers busily tending them. To me, this was truly a look into the Japan of the past.

After a short ride we arrived at the gate of Mr. Yoshino's home, which is over one hundred years old. His family has lived there for about the past eight decades. The outside of his home is simple, but the interior of his house is breathtaking. It is filled with traditional Japanese furnishings and tatami. *After seeing the rural area of his town, and the exquisite old house, I began to feel as though I had traveled back into time. As we sat together, feet crossed, in front of one of the low Japanese style tables, he began to tell his tale.*

Yoshino's Early Years

The place where I grew up was a very rural area with a lot of farms and rice paddies. It was mainly a rice producing area and very poor. My family owned our farm, a house, and some land. I had two younger brothers and one younger sister. After I graduated from elementary school I went to a junior high school that was located near my town. I spent five years as a student at that junior high school, which had one hundred students. It was about eight kilometers from my house to school. In those days the streets were all gravel, not paved. I rode to school on my bicycle. Even on a rainy or windy day I attended school. I wore a Japanese student's uniform with knitted shoes and gaiters. To our teachers and seniors we saluted, so the atmosphere was just like a military academy. Military training was a part of the curriculum. Students also were able to take martial arts classes, such as Kendo and Judo, to strengthen their bodies. Army officers were assigned to the school to instill discipline in the students. Under them were retired warrant officers and petty officers who made up the faculty. There also was a bugler, who used to play military songs. The army supplied the school with Type 38 rifles. We would line up outside and walk like soldiers with military trumpets. It was a very grand atmosphere.

Once a year, higher-ranking Japanese Army officers observed us to see the results of our training. However, on this day, if I remember correctly, there was tension among the officers and the school's faculty. When we became seniors we had a chance to experience what military life was really like for one day. The assigned officer for us was Lieutenant Colonel Sano of the 15th Cavalry Regiment. We experienced the army life of his group and stayed overnight in Narashino City.

In 1937 the Navy created a system to increase the number of naval aviators. The program was designed to have a student complete all his flight training in two years. During the late 1930s, if you were a man who was healthy, both mentally and physically, it was your obligation to be a member of Japan's armed forces. So, sooner or later, you would be drafted in the military. Practically everyone around here (my hometown) joined the Sakura Regiment, and their specialty was marching. I was poor at marching; becoming

A wartime picture of Ensign Haruo Yoshino in his flying gear. (Yoshino Collection)

The rice paddies and beauty of rural Mobara, Chiba. This is where Yoshino-san grew up and still resides today. (Werneth)

Haruo Yoshino when he was a middle school student prior to joining the Navy in 1937. (Yoshino Collection)

a naval aviator was a much better choice for me. In March 1938 I graduated from junior high school, and in April I joined the Navy as a Second Term Student.

Training Days

Basic training lasted one year and two months. I entered the Navy at Yokosuka on 1 April 1938, and later trained on the battleship *Hyōga* from 7 December through 31 October of that year. Then, on 1 March 1939 I transferred to Kasumigaura *Kōkūtai*, which later was renamed Tsuchiura. Some of my basic training included boat rowing, flag signals, light signals, and communication. Other notable subjects included airplane maintenance and learning about the weather. I started my flying courses on 31 May 1939 at Suzuka *Kōkūtai* and completed them in ten months time.

During training we had no holidays, and practiced seven days a week. There was no regular schedule and no regulations about the time that we worked. We trained the entire day from morning until night, and worked hard to become skilled airmen. Once or twice a month we were allowed to go out, for example, on a rainy day. The place for the training was mainly at an air base. First, let me explain the training for the landing on an aircraft carrier. We started the training by doing regular landings, then advanced to landings on spots by looking at a guiding panel, which showed the instructions from the control tower. Looking at the panel, we were trained to land on those spots at a land air base. An observer's job was to notify the pilots of the altitude and speed.

After completion of the different types of landings we began training for landings on a carrier. The waiting place in the air was the right side of the ship. I circled around that area and waited for the okay signal to land. After this I lowered the hook, and the carrier increased its speed and turned into the wind. If the flag signal was raised to show the speed of the wind on the deck it meant that I should land. On both sides of the ship there were landing lights. I went down to the ship following these lights. After repeating "touch and go" landings, we trained again by stopping with a series of wires. We trained thoroughly, but still some people were not able to land with these maneuvers on the paths with guiding lights, so they were excluded from carrier duty. The aircraft were gathered at the bow of the ship after landing because it would take too much time if we lowered each one in the elevator. There was a barricade at the front part of the ship, so even if an airplane failed its landing it would not collide with other aircraft on the flight deck.

At nighttime the control tower was different from the daytime. The signal code was the old Japanese alphabet, which was attached to each aircraft. We flew under the direction of a commander on land. From the point of lining up the airplanes until landing a commander on land controlled everything.

Doing formation level-bombing exercises was one of the objectives of our training. Typically, when we flew in a formation of aircraft, the leading plane was usually the commander of the group. However, during a bomb run the number two aircraft in the formation, flown by a "crack" team of a specially trained pilot and observer, switched positions with the commander's *kankō*. Then, the aviators in this "crack" team signaled to the rest of the aircraft when to drop our bombs. After this all of the *kankō* dropped their bombs simultaneously on the target.

An illustration of the typical torpedo attack technique utilized by *kankō* airmen during the war. These highly skilled crews suffered heavy losses during dangerous low-level missions. (George Zielinski A.G.P.)

Torpedo Training

There are two types of attacks by carrier-attack planes (*kankō*): one is level-bombing, and the other is by torpedo. Torpedo training was regarded as the most important attack on vessels. A daytime attack would be done at 100 meters (328 feet), while a night attack would be done at 200 meters (656 feet) altitude. The distance of the target varied depending on the direction of the ship. The usual attack procedure, when a ship was going directly towards you, was 1,000 meters (3,281 feet). When the target ship was turning toward you it was 1,200 meters (3,937 feet), and finally, when it was going away from you, 800 meters (2,625 feet). The target was our mother ship. We did this training exercise flying in both large and small aircraft formations. Our group did these exercises as much as possible, whenever we had the chance.

You had to be very skilled to drop your torpedo properly. We loaded torpedoes for training and (during a practice mission) released them so they went under the bottom of the carrier, which was the target. Hence, it was obvious to see whether or not it actually hit the target from the airplane. This exercise was used to evaluate the skills of the aviators who flew the Type 97s, which were armed with torpedoes. At the same time, however, it also was an exercise for the carrier to practice avoiding a torpedo attack. In a real torpedo there is a black torpedo head, which contains gunpowder. For the exercise a red torpedo head was installed, which contained water instead of gunpowder. With the water inside the practice torpedo weighed the same as a real one. The released torpedo had an electric light, so it was easy to see at night. After the torpedo came to a stop water from the head was pushed out by pressured air, so when it became empty the torpedo floated up. At the same time it emitted light and gave out smoke. Therefore, during both day and night it was easy to identify the location of the submerged top and get it back to reload again.

Doing nighttime torpedo drops was probably the most technical part of our training. It was the final part of the training during the year and gave us a chance to show our skills.. Three different groups did their torpedo attacks, which were coordinated. After completing my flight training I served with the Tateyama *Kōkūtai* on 30 March 1940, but later transferred to the Ōmura *Kōkūtai* on 1 July of that year. In November I was promoted to the rank of PO2c and transferred to the carrier *Kaga* on 18 December 1940. While on board *Kaga* I participated in one attack on a southern area of China.

Since our carrier was a member of the *Kidō Butai* we had very vigorous drills every day. There were no days off, including weekends. My aircraft was the Type 97 *kankō* equipped with one 800 kilogram (1,764 pound) torpedo, or a bomb load of one of the following arrangements: one 800 kilogram (1,764 pound) bomb, one 250 kilogram (551 pound) bomb, or six 60 kilogram (132 pound) bombs. We had enough practice doing attacking and bombing missions by the end of August 1941, especially for night attacks, using an illuminator. At this time we were training at Kanoya Air Base, in Kyūshū. *Kaga's* Type 97 *kankō* were having training here, and up until that time we were training only at sea. I believe it was in early September when torpedo launching training from low flying positions started, replacing night attack drills. The practice was introduced to make shallow water torpedo attacks possible. During daylight drops you should be 100 meters (328 feet) above the water, or at night, 200 meters (656 feet) above. The torpedo, when launched, usually plunged down to 60 meters (197 feet) before its propulsion gear activated, and it rose to its set depth and sped on to strike its target. Hence, if the water was too shallow (such as Pearl Harbor), the torpedo would stick in the sea bottom. So we practiced dropping from only 10 meters (33 feet) to prevent the torpedo from diving too deep, so the attack would be successful.

There were some changes made on the torpedoes, and fins were added to the rear end of the torpedo. On the original, unmodified torpedoes, when they were launched, they hit the surface of the water horizontally and bounced up. For the torpedoes to penetrate into the water at an appropriate angle, a box made of plywood was manufactured and installed on the rear portion of it. The minute the torpedo hit the water the plywood fin box would detach so it didn't affect the movement of the torpedo in the water.

The training was done in Kagoshima Bay. The area of the sea we used for the shallow water practice was a small fisherman's harbor called Furue, in Kagoshima Bay, to the west of Kanoya Air Base. You had to guess to determine the altitude because the altimeters were useless while flying only 10 meters (33 feet) above the water. It took us several days to get the hang of this type of attack, but it was not until I fired a torpedo during the drills with no gunpowder that I finally gained confidence. Our commanders were Lieutenant Ichirō Kitajima and Lieutenant Mimori Suzuki. They checked the height of each aircraft's torpedo drops and took turns doing this. Then they put fishermen's boats on the water, and we launched training torpedoes at these targets. We did this "real" training four times. At first there were many aircraft that flew too low. When a Type 97 *kankō* flew too low during its torpedo drop the plywood box or fin on the tail broke into pieces and hit the tail of their aircraft.

As I mentioned above, we discontinued night attack drills and practiced shallow water torpedo attacks instead. I think we had this shallow water training for about one month. But I believe nobody—at least no lower ranking aviators (enlisted men)—were aware that this training was done in order to prepare for a possible attack on Pearl Harbor. I was no exception; it never even crossed my mind. Prior to Pearl Harbor, our virtual enemies were the United States and Britain. So we were taught in advance about the identifications of American and British battleships, cruisers, and carriers, as well as their speeds before the shallow water training. We also learned the names and types of ships by studying their silhouettes on drawing paper, which were seen through binoculars.

Pearl Harbor

During the beginning of November our *Kaga* Type 97s moved our base to Fudaka. We spent several days over there in a relaxed manner with no special drills. But one day, all of sudden, some of our maintenance men came over and painted dark green camouflage on our planes. Our Type 97 carrier attack planes, which normally had beautiful shiny silver paint, were repainted in a dark crummy color. It was an extremely unpopular color among the pilots.

PO2c Yoshino in January 1941 just after joining the carrier *Kaga*. (Yoshino Collection)

Furthermore, some aviators were concerned that the aircraft might lose speed since the surface was now rough and coarse. Even at this stage nobody was aware that the paint change was made in preparation for an upcoming war.

On 17 November 1941 we entered Saeki Bay, and left for Hitokappu Bay two days later. While the carrier was sailing off of Shikoku Island we were ordered to assemble on the flight deck. Captain Okada spoke to us and said, "If Japan declares war on the United States, we will attack Hawaii. Our gathering place for the fleet will be Hitokappu Bay at Etorofu Island." It was a brief speech, but the most memorable part was that there would be a declaration of war; but if war was not declared we would return. I remember this portion of the speech very well, because his tone of voice was especially strong and emphatic. I gathered from the way Captain Okada spoke to us that he wanted to assure us that the Japanese Navy wasn't acting on its own judgment. Several years back, on 26 February 1936, there was a revolt by servicemen against the Japanese government, and the memory of the incident hadn't yet faded. It would have worried us if the officer had given us the impression that the Navy was ignoring the Japanese government.

One day before the war it was still rough on the sea. Although we made all the necessary preparations and were ready to attack at any moment, I couldn't help going over and over again to my plane, which was tied up and equipped with a torpedo. This was the first time that I ever saw a torpedo with a live black torpedo head. It looked eerie.

I think we were prepared to do whatever was required of us, because the Navy was planning for a possible future attack on Pearl Harbor. We also had no worries about the possible torpedo nets at Pearl Harbor. Rather than worrying about the nets, we practiced for a shallow water attack, so our torpedoes would not get stuck in the sea floor.

According to the information we received, all of the battleships were moored in order inside the bay (Pearl Harbor) exactly as we were told at Hitokappu Bay. We aviators worried the most about whether or not the enemy would be ready to engage us once our aircraft attacked Pearl Harbor. We felt that it was going to be a surprise attack, although the prediction was groundless; other than the fact that we heard lively music being played by a Hawaiian radio station. When I looked at my watch I was disoriented, because we still followed Japanese time. For example, the time shown on my watch was different from the actual local time. I wasn't able to adjust myself to the situation, because when my watch showed 0730 in the morning it was actually lunchtime.

Time in Japan	Local Time
0230	0700
0730	1200
1230	1700

After finishing my dinner, I thought that tomorrow would finally be the day for the Hawaii attack. A shrine called the *Kaga*

The Japanese Navy's lethal Type 91 Kai Model 2 torpedoes (on the deck of *Akagi*) while the powerful strike force was at Hitokappu Bay. (Makiel Collection via Wenger)

A rare unpublished picture of Yoshino's Pearl Harbor crew. He is standing in the center, with PO2c Ichiji Nakagawa (left) and Sea1c Mitsuo Kawasaki (right). Yoshino was the only one from this crew to survive the war. The young pilots included a doll in this picture because it was a Japanese superstition to take a photo with three people. Hence, the doll was a like a fourth person. This photo was taken at Tateyama in May 1942. (Yoshino Collection)

Shrine was dedicated at a place near the bow of our carrier. Pilots went there and placed *saké* before the shrine, and prayed for success during the Pearl Harbor strike. Our three-member team of the same aircraft also went there. After this, we all loaded the *saké* onto our Type 97 and got ready to fly our mission.

I was the observer for my aircraft. The pilot was PO2c Ichiji Nakagawa, and the radioman/rear gunner was Sea1c Mitsuo Kawasaki. Nakagawa-san was from Kumamoto Prefecture, which is located in Kyūshū. In 1936 he joined the Navy and graduated as a 46th term trainee for pilots. His personality was very easygoing, and he was good at maneuvering an airplane. On 6 January 1943, in the middle of training, Nakagawa-san perished, but I am not sure what actually happened. As for Sea1c Kawasaki, I don't know where he came from. In 1937 he joined the Navy as an observer trainee and later graduated as a 50th Term student. He was sensible and considerate. Kawasaki-san also was very charming and popular. On 14 January 1944 he was reportedly killed, but I don't know the details of where he died.

The plane captain, who was the highest ranked person on the aircraft's crew, was the overall leader of the three-man team.[119] He also was responsible for everything that happened on board the airplane. However, if it's in a formation of planes, then the group leader decided. In general, I felt the pilot or the observer should be the plane captain.

My aircraft, which had the tail number AII-305 for the Pearl Harbor attack, was a Type 97 *kankō*. At that time I felt that it was the best plane in the world.[120] The only thing I would have liked was more speed. The Type 97 was an attack aircraft, and had been used frequently since the beginning of the war. It also performed well on reconnaissance missions. Many carrier pilots liked it.

I had no emotional struggles about attacking Pearl Harbor. I wasn't sure if I was able to come back. But in those days we would just do what we were told to do. We never questioned our orders from the higher-ranking Navy personnel. Also, I am not in the position to say my opinion if the attack on Pearl Harbor was right or wrong.

We attacked Pearl Harbor on 7 December 1941. The first attack unit from the carrier *Kaga* consisted of nine Zero fighter planes and a group of twenty-six Type 97 *kankō*; fourteen Type 97s were used for horizontal bombing, and the remaining twelve airplanes were for torpedo attacks.[121] I was in the *Raigeki-tai*. At 0615 (local time), 183 planes of an attack unit from six carriers began to take off toward Oahu Island to attack. We flew at an altitude of 3000 meters (9,842 feet). Because the weather was cloudy on the way to Oahu we flew above the clouds. I was able to discern the shoreline a little after three. It was the northern tip of Oahu Island, called Kahuku Point. My first thought was that the attack was a drill, not war. I also wore no headband during the attack. *Akagi* had twelve airplanes, and another twelve planes from *Kaga* got lined up. I was in the fifth position of the *Kaga* Type 97 torpedo bombers, so from the top of the *Akagi* group I was seventeenth. Following the twelve *Akagi* attack group planes, a twelve-plane *Kaga* torpedo attack group flew along the southwestern shoreline in a single line and lowered our altitude.

We all headed toward Barbers Point. There is a naval base at Barbers Point, so I became very tense. When I came around this area, I was able to see a bunch of battleships in the bay (Pearl Harbor) far ahead. Right at that moment thin columns of water splashed up with great speed high in the sky. They were created by the torpedoes launched by the *Akagi* torpedo group. I was able to identify a water column from a torpedo, which was considered to be from the number one *Akagi* airplane. Before I knew it I was yelling, "Those torpedoes run well" through the voice transmitting tube.

After this, I thought that it took about twenty minutes before I pushed the button to drop the torpedo (from my Type 97). We then flew across Hickam Field at low altitude and entered into the bay. My target was the battleship *Oklahoma*.[122] After this we lowered our flying altitude and prepared to attack. I aimed, waited for the signal from the pilot, and launched the torpedo. Prior to this moment we didn't get any hits from enemy fire.

Until I dropped the torpedo, there was no difference in the training and the real attack. I didn't feel any danger at all. Once I dropped the torpedo it was a different story. The moment I gave the order to break right after dropping the torpedo we received a lot of fire from the ships below. I am amazed how it was possible to respond to our attack so quickly. In my case, I dropped a torpedo then turned north. When my Type 97 *kankō* flew parallel to a group of ships I received a lot of small caliber anti-aircraft fire, which distracted my view with red lines in front of me. Clusters of red lines came in front of us from left to right and obstructed our flight path, so I ordered the pilot to move the aircraft up and down.

I then heard the sound bang, bang, bang, and thought something terrible is happening to me. At that moment a bullet hit the pilot's seat, and another one hit the radioman's seat. The pilot, PO2c Ichiji Nakagawa, had just pulled the control stick up, and the bullet just passed in front of his hand. If Nakagawa-san didn't pull up the control stick he would have lost his hand. The other bullet cut off an electrical cord of a telegraphic instrument and hit the radioman (Sea1c Mitsuo Kawasaki) in the right leg, just under his knee. After the battle six bullet holes were found in the rear part of the fuselage, and an additional two more holes were located near the cockpit; so my aircraft was hit eight times. I thought that it was a surprise attack until we dropped the torpedo. But I never could have imagined that there would be so much anti-aircraft fire right after the torpedo drop. The United States military must have spent a lot of time preparing for a potential Japanese attack, because they responded very quickly. Out of the seven aircraft that were following us, five of them were shot down and two returned. On one of those two planes was a radioman whose chin had been smashed into pieces by enemy gunfire.[123]

During our mission we constantly moved our plane up and down, trying to dodge the gunfire. After we managed to get out of the gunfire, we flew from the north side to the west side of the bay, leaving the island through Barbers Point. After this we headed for a specified gathering point located to the west of Nihau Island.[124] We were told not to fly a direct course back to our carrier. *Kaga* was supposed to be heading north, away from Oahu Island, after

Above: The capsized battleship *Oklahoma* (right) and the *Maryland* on 7 December 1941. Note the burning battleship *West Virginia* behind the *Maryland*. (NA via Wenger) Below: Rescue efforts for the capsized *Oklahoma*, probably on 8 December 1941. (NA via Wenger)

all the aircraft departed the ship. However, they changed the plan, and the ship kept on going south. Although the weather was still bad and stormy around the carrier, everyone landed safely.

The battleship Oklahoma *was struck by an estimated five to seven torpedoes that were launched from Japanese aircraft from the port bow (straight shots) at an estimated range of 200 to 400 yards.*[125] *The doomed ship capsized within twenty minutes after being attacked, and 415 Navy men, along with fourteen members of the United States Marine Corps, perished.*[126] *The United States Navy initially hoped to salvage the battleship, but in the end, the* Oklahoma *was stripped of her vital parts and later sold for scrap in December 1946. However the ship never made it, and sank while under tow from Hawaii to California in May 1947.*[127]

Life on Board a Carrier

As an interesting anecdote, there was a Japanese version of a P/X on the carrier. It was called *Shuho*, which meant "a place where *saké* is kept." We also could buy daily items, noodles, tobacco, and beer at the *Shuho*. Everything was duty free; therefore, tobacco was unbelievably cheap. The brand names were *Hope*, *Sakura*, and *Hikari*. Normally there were only ten cigarettes in a pack, but here it was sold in a large carton, which held fifty cigarettes.

Action after Pearl Harbor

The Japanese military forces planned to occupy Rabaul (New Britain Island) because it had a good natural harbor, and would be an excellent base for us in the Pacific. *Akagi* and *Kaga's* aircraft attacked Rabaul before the Army's invasion forces landed on New Britain Island. On 20 January 1942 twenty-seven Type 97 *kankō* (made up of three *chūtais*) armed with six 60 kilogram (132 pound) bombs apiece, plus nine Type 0 carrier fighters, were involved in the attack. We targeted merchant ships and artillery. The attacks were not so effective, I guess. When we were just about ready to set the course for bombing anti-aircraft shells exploded right above the top *chūtai* (consisting of nine planes), which caused one Type 97 *kankō* to go down and another five planes to receive some damage. The crew on the lost Type 97 was pilot PO1c Tatsuya Sugihara, observer PO1c Katsuo Yamamoto, and radioman/rear gunner PO2c Yoichi Tanaka. Everyone left the formation, and each plane did individual emergency landings on the carrier. The rest of the aircraft didn't receive any damage.

On 19 February 1942 our *Kaga* attack unit delivered a sudden attack on Port Darwin, Australia. We attacked with nine Zero fighters, twenty-seven Type 97s armed with one 800 kilogram (1,764 pound) bomb apiece, and eighteen Type 99s equipped with one 250 kilogram (551 pound) bomb. The Type 97s attacked a government office district and merchant ships in the port, and the Type 99s damaged an airfield, hangars, and merchant ships. I heard that the Zero fighter unit fought an air battle against enemy planes and brought down seven planes. In addition, five planes on the ground were in flames after the Zero fighters strafed them.

On 5 March of the same year, twenty-seven *Kaga* Type 97s equipped with one 800 kilogram bomb apiece, along with nine direct escort Zero fighters, attacked Tjilatjap, the one key harbor on the southern coast of Java Island. The unit bombed merchant ships in the harbor, anti-aircraft batteries, and a warehouse, which did a great deal of damage. Our side didn't suffer any damage and every plane returned safely.[128]

The Battle of Midway

I took off the carrier *Kaga* for a reconnaissance mission on 4 June 1942 at 0430, along with the Midway attack unit consisting of eighteen Type 99 *kanbaku* and nine Type 0 carrier *kansen*. It was a reconnaissance mission to the west of the Midway Atoll at a 158 degree angle; the distance from my carrier was 300 miles, and the dog-leg was sixty miles. I was ordered to do reconnaissance of Kure Island on my way back, which is where the Japanese Navy was planning to do a landing. The weather was fine throughout the mission, with good visibility and a clear horizon; perfect for flying a patrol mission. I flew at 600 meters (1,968 feet) and didn't spot anything unusual on the way. After this I changed my course towards Kure Island, which was fifty miles east of Midway Atoll. I had to keep my eyes open when flying near this small island. Not having seen any man-made structures, I took some pictures and then headed toward the carrier.

About the time when I saw the fleet over the horizon, far ahead I saw some small aircraft flying east, one after another, at a low altitude. They didn't look like our aircraft, which made me very uneasy. Right at that moment I saw an enemy seaplane (possibly a Catalina) with two machine guns that seemed to be watching our fleet closely. Its altitude was about 200 meters (656 feet). I tried to approach it, but the aircraft quickly banked and flew away. We felt relieved that our fleet was safe, without any damage, although it was spread out over a large area. Finally, our Type 97 *kankō* was over *Kaga* and cleared for landing. The time was about 1005.

When I went to give my report to *hikōchō* Commander Takahisa Amagai, he said to me in a loud voice "A formation of enemy aircraft is approaching us. I'll hear your report later." So I went to the pilots' ready room, and a bunch of my fellow aviators were out on the walkway leading to that room. I learned that, before I landed, *Kaga* was attacked by enemy torpedo planes. They all told me excitedly that our carrier dodged the torpedoes and our Zero fighters shot down several enemy aircraft.

I entered the ready room and was taking off my flight uniform when a trumpet blared out; this signaled an impending attack. Then I heard the roar of some anti-aircraft guns, which were directly below the pilots' room. I jumped out to the walkway and saw some enemy torpedo planes attacking us. Our gunners were doing their best to hit the attackers with their 20 mm machine guns. Suddenly, one of our machine gun commanders pointed his baton to the sky and shouted something. When I looked up, several dive-bombers appeared between the clouds and were plunging down on us. The first bomb hit the flight deck by the bridge and a pillar of black smoke went up. According to Japanese records this occurred at 1023. I crouched down in the corner of the walkway and tried to protect my body the best I could during this attack. Four bombs were reported to have hit *Kaga*, but I don't know where the other three bombs hit. A large fire engulfed the hangar because there were numerous (and very flammable) Type 97 *kankō*, Type 99 *kanbaku*, and parts of Zero fighters. All of our aircraft were full of

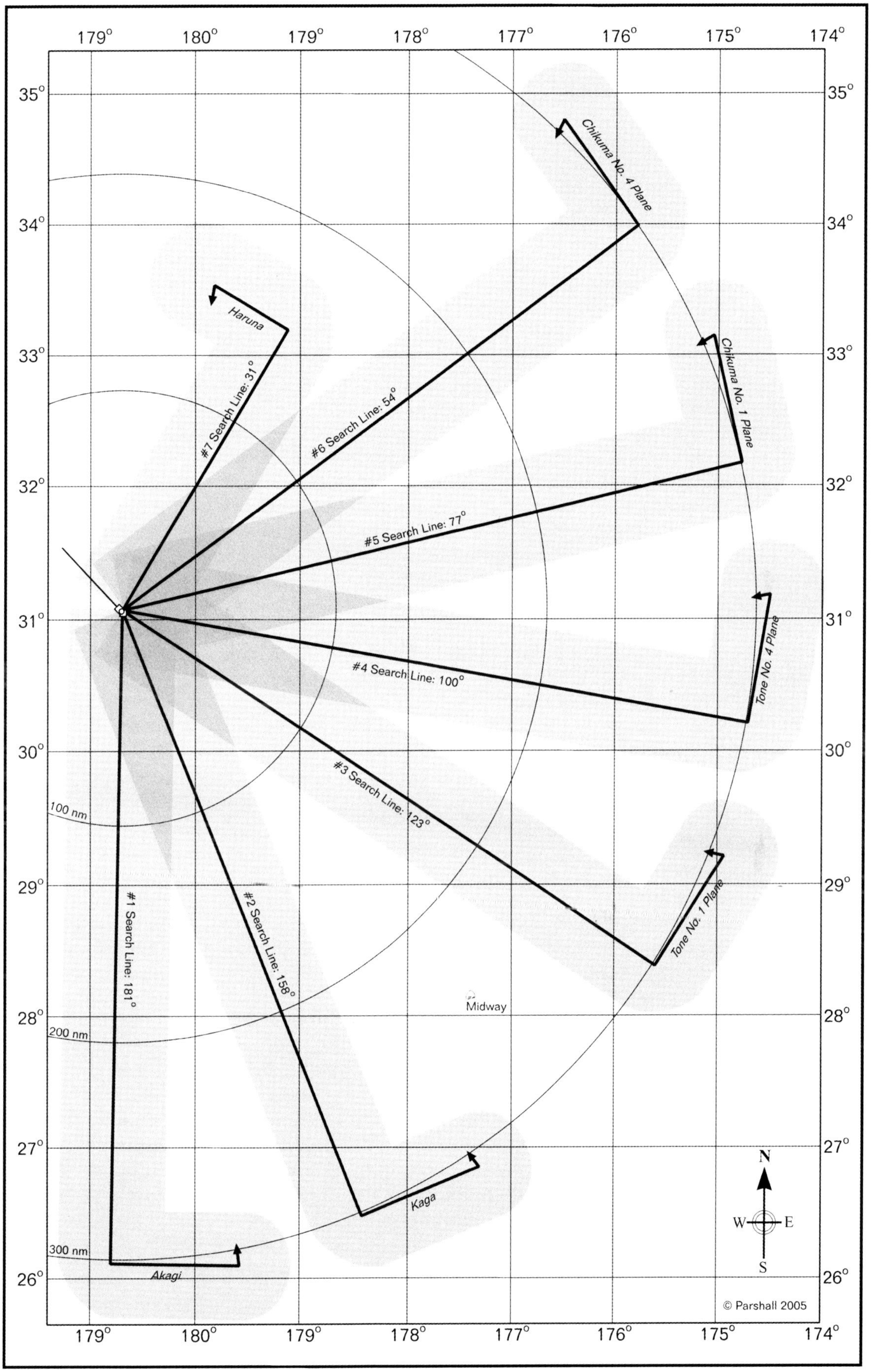

The proposed search plan for 4 June 1942. Yoshino's was #2 Search Line (*Kaga*). (Jonathan Parshall, adapted from the *Senshi Sōsho*)

fuel at that time. The Type 97s were armed with torpedoes, and the Type 99s had 250 kilogram bombs mounted on them. There were several 800 kilogram bombs strewn haphazardly in the hangar.

Everything in the hangar detonated one after another. A fire of some ten thousand liters of fuel, along with the chain reaction of a series of explosions, were beyond my wildest imagination. Numerous explosions rocked *Kaga* over and over. When I came to my senses and looked around, everyone who was there just a moment ago had disappeared. Only a fellow one term junior to me and I remained there. We moved along the outer part of the carrier and managed to come down to somewhere around the upper deck. Explosions were erupting fiercely. After a while the *Kaga* began to lose power to move forward and stopped. It was a terrible situation, and we were both stuck there and could not do anything but wait with the hope of being rescued by one of our escorting ships.

A destroyer approached us, and it stopped about 100 meters (328 feet) along the starboard side of *Kaga*. I mustered enough courage and jumped into the sea, then swam towards the destroyer. But it started to move suddenly, and got out of my sight quickly, leaving white waves in its wake. A lot of people were swimming around me, and I saw many men gathering in the stern section of our carrier. The inside of the hangar was bright red; the series of explosions were still going on. An extraordinary flame appeared with each explosion. All I could do was wait and hope to be rescued by one of our surviving ships. In order to save my energy I held onto a drifting piece of wood. After about two dreaded hours passed the destroyer returned, lowered a boat, and rescued us. I was picked up onto the boat and climbed up a rope ladder of the destroyer *Hagikaze*.

After the destroyer *Hagikaze* finished rescuing the *Kaga* survivors it left the area. I didn't know where I was and couldn't see any other ships. *Hagikaze* came close to *Kaga* at sunset, and it was completely burnt down. My once magnificent carrier was now unrecognizable. The hangar between the bridge and stern was burnt down, but the overall structure of the carrier looked solid and remained intact. Due to all the damage, the Navy must have given up the idea of salvaging *Kaga*.

Hagikaze fired two torpedoes, and *Kaga* sank stern first into the sea. During this time *Kaga* survivors saluted silently from the deck of *Hagikaze* and gave our carrier a final farewell. It had been recorded that "*Kaga* was sunk at 1926." *Hagikaze* then sped up, so it could join up with our main group of ships. We met up with the main force the following day and I boarded the battleship *Nagato*. Around 10 June *Nagato* entered the harbor of Shifuji, and the *Kaga* survivors, including myself, went to Kanoya Air Base. We were treated as prisoners of war and couldn't talk to anyone else. After two weeks our three-man team (from my crew) was ordered to board the aircraft carrier *Shōkaku*. After this *Shōkaku's* airmen had on-base training with the Kanoya *Kōkūtai*.

Yoshino's Feelings During the War

Regarding my feelings towards fighting Americans, I felt the enemy is the enemy. We thought that they were the enemy and nothing else. As naval aviators, we hardly had any face-to-face combat situations, which was fortunate for us. In the case of Iwo Jima many people fought face to face, so either you would eat or be eaten. It would be terrible in that situation. Personally, I was nervous while flying night missions in the Philippines. It was scary being hit by anti-aircraft fire while our aircraft was illuminated in the enemy's searchlights. I had no bad feelings towards the enemy, because I was never physically close to them.

Maybe we were educated to think that the people of the United States were weak. However, during the Battle of Midway I thought that they were very brave, because the attacking enemy planes were not escorted by fighters. Our Japanese torpedo bombers (such as the Type 97) usually had fighters escorting them. It's like being "naked," such as somebody without protection. I thought that it was extraordinary, and Japanese fighters shot down the torpedo planes one after another. Normally, torpedo planes drop their torpedoes at an altitude of 100 meters (328 feet) above the ocean. Since the torpedo bombers flew so low, they were easy "prey" and frequently got shot down.

The Dauntless dive-bombers came from an altitude of over 3,000 meters (9,842 feet), but everybody was focused on the torpedo bombers. This paved the way for the dive-bombers to attack, and the fighters didn't have time to go up and follow them. So it all went very well, because the torpedo bombers sacrificed themselves for the dive-bombers. The dive-bombers swooped down on us easily and dropped their bombs. That's why the Battle of Midway was so successful for the military forces of the United States. American people often ask about the effects of Midway on the rest of the war, but I really don't know. It's just that people believe that Midway turned the tide of the war in favor of the enemy. If the question is did we lose Guadalcanal Island because of it, maybe yes, maybe no. During the Battle of Midway four Japanese carriers were sunk, but the United States Navy only lost the *Yorktown*. Nevertheless, after the battle we still had the carriers *Shōkaku* and *Zuikaku*, so it is really hard to say for sure.

Feelings Towards Officers

I didn't have many problems with higher-ranking officers in the Navy. There were some great people among them. For example, Lieutenant Commander Takashi Hashiguchi was a very respectable man. I was a subordinate under him from October 1940 until April 1942. I flew several missions with him, and Hashiguchi-san didn't say much. However, when Lieutenant Commander Hashiguchi did speak he was concise. Later he participated in the Battle of Midway. Lieutenant Commander Hashiguchi survived the war but is now deceased. Another excellent officer was Lieutenant Minoru Fukuda, who was one of the *Kaga's shōtaichōs*. He was from Hiroshima, and was a very warm-hearted man. However, one of my commanding officers who died during the attack on Pearl Harbor was just terrible. I really hated that guy, and it was terrible to work under him. So, the officers were both good and bad people. Life goes on, and all you can do is think that some are terrible. However, you can't do anything about it. You couldn't say directly to them, I hate you. That's the only way to deal with the situation.

The Battle of Santa Cruz

On 26 October 1942, at 0445, four Type 97 *kankō* took off from a south to southeast direction in order to do reconnaissance. In my case, I took care of the westernmost side, the number one reconnaissance line. I flew 300 miles, and then turned left and flew an additional sixty miles. That was my flight course. Immediately after I took the course to go back to the carrier at 0550 I saw an American carrier-based airplane and sent a message. I found it in the easternmost side, which means the number four reconnaissance line. So, I confirmed the presence of the American mobile force. In my case I didn't see anything unusual, aside from the one enemy aircraft.

Around 0800 I came back to the carrier. After I got the signal to land I put the aircraft in the landing pattern. However, right before I landed the landing lights were turned off. The flight deck swayed to the left very widely because the carrier turned directly to the right. In the sky enemy dive-bombers were getting ready to dive. Then, right in front of me *Shōkaku* was surrounded by smoke and water spouts. Three bombs hit the flight deck directly and a big fire started in the hangar. Nevertheless, most of the airplanes were not in the hangar because they had already left for their mission, so we were able to put out the fire immediately and the smoke disappeared. The carrier *Zuihō* also had a big hole in the rear section.[129] *Zuikaku* didn't immediately give the okay to land, but my Type 97 *kankō* was running out of fuel, so I asked to do an emergency landing. After this I was allowed to land, and my aircraft was put away after landing. Then, on 29 October 1942, if I'm not mistaken, I returned to *Shōkaku* at Truk Island. *Shōkaku* went into a dock at Yokosuka for repairs, and as of 17 November I left the ship and was assigned to the Tateyama *Kōkūtai*.

Anti-submarine Patrols off Japan

I was assigned to protect transport ships against enemy submarines from 17 November 1942 to 17 August 1944, and our division was based at Toyohashi.[130] From the moment I was assigned to the Tateyama *Kōkūtai* I was ordered to work at Toyohashi.[131] My assignment was to do patrol missions for a transport ship group, which was using the waterway from off Cape Omaezaki to the mouth of the Kumanogawa River. In this water area there were ships that carried goods back and forth to Tokyo Bay. The group of ships usually numbered from five to ten vessels, and they traveled in a snake motion. Two submarines protected these ships as well. I would do my patrol missions from sunrise to sunset.

For these patrols I flew a Type 97 *kankō* armed with one 250 kilogram bomb. The method of attack was bombing after a gradual descent. There were two bases for these planes, Toyohashi and Matsushima.[132] We were protecting the transport ships that went along the coast. We received the information by radio beforehand about the ship group, which came into the warning area. When the group of ships came into this area reconnaissance airplanes continued to do patrols in front of them. It was a three-hour shift from dawn to dusk to protect the ships. At the end of 1943 I think there was a movement of enemy submarines. During this time there were several attacks from American submarines, and the time they attacked was around sunrise. On several occasions I just dropped 250 kilogram bombs on the enemy, but wasn't able to determine if they were effective or not. After 1944 I think transport ships received torpedo attacks early in the morning. Finally, on one day around noon, when we were changing shifts of our reconnaissance planes, there was a torpedo attack and one ship sank.

Yoshino Goes to Iwo Jima

On 26 July 1944 I was part of a Toyohashi detachment (consisting of a few Type 97s) that was sent to Iwo Jima. In those days enemy submarines surrounded the island, so transport ships were not able to come close to the island. The strategy was to move our destroyers, which were loaded with supplies, near the beach, and supply our forces on the island. Enemy bombers from Saipan bombed Iwo Jima every day, and the air raids were intense. In the daytime the submarines went out to sea and at night floated back. The Japanese Army gave us information when the submarines came to the surface at night, but when I flew in the morning it was impossible to find them. The air raids from Saipan also became more intense day by day. Iwo Jima, as the name implies, means "Sulfur Island."[133] There was a place where sulfur came out, and we got drinking water by cooling down the steam. Drinking the water caused no stomach pains, but I was bothered by a week long bout of diarrhea. It turned out that we were not able to bring our destroyers near the beach, so after about twenty days we returned to Tateyama.

I got married in July 1944, and we had a wedding ceremony at my house. Nevertheless, I was at Iwo Jima at this time, so my wife got married without a groom! My wife Matsuko and I later had two daughters.

Action in the Philippines

In October 1944 I boarded the carrier *Zuikaku* as a member of the 263 *Hikōtai*, 653 *Kōkūtai*, which was part of the "Ozawa Fleet." This fleet, which was commanded by Vice Admiral Jisaburō Ozawa, was a decoy in order to draw out the U.S. Third Fleet in the Leyte Gulf, so the Allied landing forces would lack air cover. Thus, the landing forces could be destroyed by Japan. On 25 October I took off early in the morning and flew over the water east off Luzon Island to do reconnaissance. After this I advanced to Nicholas Base via Tuguegarao Base. Soon after I took off from carrier *Zuikaku*, and it was attacked by American aircraft and sank.

The carrier Zuikaku *was struck by seven torpedoes and nine bombs. At 1358 the order to "Abandon Ship" was given and the flag lowered. The once proud carrier, a veteran of the Pearl Harbor attack and numerous other wartime operations, slowly rolled over to port and sank bow first at 1414. Captain Takeo Kaizuka, forty-eight officers, and 794 petty officers and men were lost during the sinking of* Zuikaku. *However, forty-seven officers and 815 petty officers and men were rescued by the destroyers* Wakatsuki *and* Kuwa.[134]

As soon as I went to Nicholas Base I was assigned to attack a carrier in Leyte Bay. The plan was to go into the area and attack using three *Zuikaku* aircraft, which were now land-based. At dusk

Yoshino (right) and one of his fellow aviators, which was taken in the spring of 1943 at Toyohashi. This was the same period they were flying patrol missions. (Yoshino Collection)

Twenty-three year old Warrant Officer Yoshino in November 1943. (Yoshino Collection)

The battle-hardened WO Yoshino during the spring of 1944. (Yoshino Collection)

I left and did a nighttime attack, but it was difficult to determine if my mission was successful or not. The next day, on the 26th I went to the North Base of Clark Air Base. In the Clark area there were several bases, including Clark North, Clark Center, Clark South, Mabalacat, and Ban Ban. The North Base was controlled by the Army, but the Navy also utilized this facility. American forces in the Leyte area increased, and in November doing daytime attacks became almost impossible for Japanese aircraft.

On 4 November 1944 at midnight I took off by myself and bombed Tacloban Air Base. When I was flying over Leyte Harbor I was caught in the searchlights and attacked by anti-aircraft fire. The fuselage of my airplane vibrated, and the smell of gunpowder went into the seat area. The anti-aircraft fire was very accurate, so I intuitively felt that it was radar controlled. So I ordered the radioman to drop *giman-shi* and this worked well. Then in no time the noise of the anti-aircraft fire diminished, and we were able to escape.

American forces also started to attack Clark Air Base in the daytime over and over. P-38 fighters did these attacks and Allied forces took control of the air. Several *Tenzan kankō* at Clark North Base were burned as a result of American dive-bomber attacks. However, our *Tenzans* continued to attack Tacloban Airfield at night using only one aircraft at a time. Around 14 November I came back to Ōita Air Base to become part of another group.

In December 1944, while at Ōita Air Base, I was assigned to the 102 *Hikōtai*. Then I went again to the Clark area and stayed at Ban Ban Air Base. At this time there were not many airplanes going to the Philippines, and I arrived there on 25 December. There were only a few airplanes that were able to fly, and after flying only one time I had to leave Ban Ban Air Base. I think then on 6 January American forces landed in the Lingayen area en mass.

On 8 January 1945 the Clark area pilots gathered up on a small hill near Ban Ban Air Base, and we were told to advance to the north. We hopped on five or six trucks and left for the northern tip of Apari, on Luzon. We slept on the road and ate only rice. Finally, after many days we reached Apari. However, we discovered that the submarines that were supposed to transport us were not coming. So we went back to Tuguegarao and were transported back to Takao via a transport plane. From there we went back to Yokohama, Japan.

Feelings while Flying Missions

During my missions I wasn't worried as much as some people might think. When I flew a typical sortie, there were usually three groups consisting of nine planes each, which made a total of twenty-seven airplanes. If you saw the roster of who would fly the next mission, you knew whom you were going to fly with. Furthermore, prior to flying you didn't worry much. I personally wasn't worried about dying because it didn't make any difference. Once the group took off you didn't feel any different. Nobody worries about dying; instead, they think "I will survive." Worrying about things wouldn't help much. The scariest time was when I was returning. On the way back I desperately wanted to return. Everybody felt the same way. For example, if there were vibrations from the engine you started to get scared. Our Type 97 *kankō* received eight anti-aircraft hits over Hawaii and the radioman was wounded. I thought that there might be some other problems with the aircraft, so I worried if I would return to the carrier safely.

On our 20 January 1942 mission to attack Rabaul I also received some hits from anti-aircraft fire in the engine area, which caused vibration. I was really worried because of the vibration and it was a frightful mission. Anti-aircraft shells exploded over my aircraft and one *kankō* went down. I was scared that the engine might stop at any moment because of the vibration. A bunch of electric wires in the engine were hit. Around that area fragments from anti-aircraft shells were scattered inside. So, I thought that there was something in that area that didn't explode yet; I desperately wanted to go back. It was an emergency landing for our Type 97 *kankō* after this mission. Normally we circled the carrier and banked. Then, the carrier turned into the wind to prepare for landing, so once we landed we could stop quickly. It was a scary moment.

In the Philippines I felt the same way when I went to attack Tacloban Airfield a few times. On the way to my target I was not scared, but on the way back I was. After bombing I was caught in the searchlights because the attacks were usually at night. When I was in the searchlights I received American anti-aircraft fire, which was scary. They would locate our planes by radar and try to shoot us down.

How did Japanese Navy pilots feel flying combat missions on a daily basis? It differed from place to place and time to time. It is impossible for me to tell you in general. In the early days of the war until the Battle of Midway, we felt confident and optimistic going into battle. However, things changed as the war progressed. At the end of 1944, while being stationed at Clark Air Base, we flew dangerous missions on a daily basis. I said to the other two aviators on my crew, a young rookie pilot and a radioman, "As long as you are with me you are not going to die, so don't worry." I think, however, they were suspicious or didn't believe one hundred percent what I said about not dying. Of course, you always felt relieved after safely returning to the air base after flying a dangerous nighttime mission. You might have been on a dangerous mission, but I found that there was a strong relationship between my flight crew, and the junior airmen had a lot of faith in me. Furthermore, I didn't fail to notice the shining of their eyes while looking at the flight roster prior to flying our mission. But this story is only about my crew members and me; I don't know about other peoples' feelings toward trust.

In the middle of a losing war, which we could not predict the outcome of, everybody had very little rest between combat, day in and day out, so it was only natural that people were not stable. If we could drink *saké* we could release a lot of our tension. In the Philippines I moved from place to place, such as going from Nichols to Clark Air Base to Ban Ban, but I didn't even drink a drop of *saké*. Our food wasn't good and we had no alcohol to drink. In fact, I think we didn't have *saké* at all. At Clark Air Base alone there were three airfields (North, Middle, and South) that were all connected. Hence, the lodging area was one place for all three airfields. I heard rumors from members of other flying groups, but it was natural that there were not any good stories. It wasn't surprising that there some people were depressed.

Home Defense Duties over Japan

On 10 February 1945 I went to Kisarazu Air Base and became a member of the 102 *Hikōtai*, 752 *Kōkūtai*. We used the Nakajima C6N1 *Saiun* and did reconnaissance missions over the eastern part of Honshu. The Kanoya detachment was assigned to do reconnaissance missions over the Okinawa area. The *Saiun* was completed around the end of the war. It was one of the fastest reconnaissance planes in the Japanese Navy, but due to the pilots' lack of training, from the end of July until August there were many aviators who didn't return from their missions.

The Nakajima C6N1 Sauin *(Allied code name "Myrt") was one of the best reconnaissance aircraft built during the war, but it seems to be largely forgotten, even by aviation enthusiasts. With a top speed of 639 kph (397 mph) and a range of more than 4,830 kilometers (3,000 miles), the versatile* Sauin *could even hold its own against such advanced Allied aircraft as the Grumman F6F Hellcat fighter.*[135] *Today there are only two known survivors: one unrestored C6N1-S, a night-fighter version of the breed, with an oblique-firing 20 mm cannon, which is in storage with the National Air and Space Museum (Washington, DC); and an additional one may still exist "in the bush" on Truk Island. However, the latter aircraft may have been recovered for a private collector a few years ago.*

On 5 August 1945 I went to Hachijō Jima, which was about 1800 miles from Truk Island. This distance was the maximum operating radius of our fuel. It was typhoon season, and I was waiting for information about the enemy, weather, and other reconnaissance related things. However, on 14 August we gave up the idea of delivering four airplanes to Truk Island because two airplanes had engine troubles and returned to Kisarazu Air Base. The next day the war was over, and I was told that the amount of fuel left at Kisarazu Air Base was enough for only one and a half missions if we flew sorties with all of our remaining aircraft. If the planes had returned once, the next time they flew would only be a one-way mission because of a lack of fuel. Hence, we would have survived only for one more month if the war would not have ended.

A group of 102 *Hikōtai's* junior officers around May 1945 at Kisarazu Air Base. Yoshino is wearing the soft cap (far left) in the first row. (Yoshino Collection)

Stars and Bars Replace our *Hinomaru*

Around 10 September I was told to return to Kisarazu Air Base via a telegram from the Kisarazu Air Base Director. American troops had already arrived at the airfield, and some Japanese personnel were still there, such as directors, commanders, and other people to take care of paperwork and business at Otayama. This is also where the barracks was located. We were ordered by the American occupational forces to prepare two *Saiuns* and bring them to Oihama. Oihama used to be the place where the Yokosuka *Kōkūtai* was located. By this time airplane propellers and other parts on our aircraft were removed. Other materials also were gathered up in an old airplane factory. American forces used the old air group building and hangar, so we did the maintenance work in an old airplane factory hangar that was in the northern area airfield. A lot of mechanics and I were involved with repairing the *Saiuns*. It took about one month to do maintenance work, remove the Japanese *hinomarus*, and paint the American star and bar insignias on the aircraft. After the markings were changed we were ready to deliver the aircraft to the American forces.

On the morning of 30 October 1945 the repairs were almost finished, so it was time to have a test flight, which was done over Kisarazu. The number one aircraft was flown by Lieutenant Taemi Ichikawa, Ensign Haruo Yoshino (observer), and PO1c Tokuei Otsuki (radioman). The second aircraft was flown by Lieutenant Chuichi Kadomoto, Ensign Yasuhiko Ogawa (observer), and PO1c Eiji Takeuchi (radioman).

After a successful test flight in the afternoon we flew it to Oihama Air Base, which was located in Yokosuka, and delivered two *Saiuns*. Our aircraft took off after receiving the signal from the control tower. When one *Saiun* took off American fighters took off with it. There were two American airplanes, one in front and one in back. The *Saiun* was between them. When the *Saiun* increased speed the other fighters couldn't keep up with it (when I was in level flight). There also were other fighters above my aircraft. The next group came from above and came close to me. A third group was also there to watch us. Then a pilot used hand signals to direct us not to go toward Tokyo Bay. I think he was afraid that we might make a suicide attack on the ships in the bay. I was stunned when I saw the area between Tokyo and Yokosuka filled with American ships. I was overwhelmed by the sheer number of war materials that the United States had again.

The *Saiun* that was flown by Lieutenant Chuichi Kadomoto had defective brakes and ran into a Corsair fighter on the ground. His plane hit the side of the American plane, and his plane's propeller hit the wing and side of the aircraft. There were no injuries, but the Corsair's wing was severely damaged in the area covered by canvas. We were reprimanded, and the Japanese commander apologized to the men in charge of the base.

One of the *Sauins* with American markings that was delivered on 30 October 1945 to occupation forces at Oihama Air Base. Left to right, back row: Ensign Haruo Yoshino, Ensign Yasuhiko Ogawa, and Commander Keiichi Aoyama (Yoshino couldn't remember the last three mens' names). Middle row: Lieutenant Chuichi Kadomoto, unknown, Lieutenant Taemi Ichikawa, and unknown. Front row: PO1c Eiji Takeuchi and PO1c Tokuei Otsuki. (Yoshino Collection)

Yoshino-san was at Kisarazu Air Base when the war ended, and felt that he was lucky to survive. He felt if the war didn't stop in August, he would not have survived until 1946. Veteran Haruo Yoshino was discharged with the rank of ensign on 30 October 1945 and he returned home. Remarkably, Ensign Yoshino flew about 2,500 hours during the war and survived numerous combat situations. Out of the numerous aircraft he flew, the naval aviator liked the Nakajima Type 97 kankō *the best, but it was noisy because of its air-cooled engine. Yoshino-san didn't like the Nakajima B6N* Tenzan, *which he flew only a few times in the Philippines. The experienced naval aviator didn't like this aircraft because the cockpit was too roomy, but it did have a powerful engine.*

Postwar

In his postwar years Haruo Yoshino worked as a salesman for an electric company, which is now called Tokyo Electric. He worked for that company until retiring several years ago. Today Yoshino-san keeps busy as a member of Unabarakai, *the Japanese Navy veterans' group, and has attended several memorial services in Hawaii to mark the anniversary of Pearl Harbor. During these events he has had an opportunity to meet numerous American veterans, and that has helped him come to terms with his past. In the spring of 1998 the retired naval aviator, along with other World War II Battle of Midway veterans both American and Japanese, participated in the National Geographic Midway expedition. The expedition's goal was to locate the American and Japanese ships lost in the battle. They succeeded in locating the American carrier* Yorktown, *but none of the Japanese ships, including Yoshino's carrier* Kaga, *were located. But a similar 1999 expedition, led by a combined team of the Naval Oceanographic Office and a private firm called Nauticos, located a large section of wreckage from* Kaga. *Yoshino-san helped the historians during their research about his old carrier. The group located a section of his ship, but the main wreck site was not located. Hopefully, in the future there will be another expedition to locate the rest of* Kaga's *remains.*

Reflections

During the war Navy pilots had many kinds of missions. In Hawaii we carried torpedoes, and at Rabaul we used bombs. Each time we had different targets and a specified role to play in that respective mission. In the South Pacific at Midway I was flying alone because I was doing a reconnaissance mission, which usually lasted five or six hours. Three people (on a typical crew) were focusing their attention to look for the enemy's ships or aircraft. This was my mission, so that was the only thing that I was focusing on.

I never questioned the purpose of my missions. I never thought if the war was right or wrong; not at all. I never believed that it was a "wrong" war. It's not for me to say if it was right or wrong;

Veteran Haruo Yoshino in his home with Yukihirō Yamamato (left), a close friend of the author, and Ron Werneth in spring 2002. (Werneth)

that's a historian's job. I have no regrets at all. Today, many people say that the war was wrong, but in those days we didn't have any doubts. Maybe there are some opinions by historians, but it was a conflict between two nations. If a country starts a war the people don't have any choice but to follow the nation's policy. Japanese people fought for Japan, and American people fought for the United States. So, it was a war between two countries. Both Japanese and American military men were fighting for their own nations. That's the "core" part of the mentality common to both nations. In those days we never questioned our government's decision to go to war. Lastly, the industrial might of the United States was stronger than Japan. In the Philippines none of our aircraft, such as the Zero fighter, could compete with the Lockheed P-38 fighter. Furthermore, the United States could manufacture more planes when their aircraft were shot down.

Regrettably, in recent years the Japanese people are not as patriotic as they used to be. History is vitally important and should be learned well. All we know is surrender. Japanese people should not be that way; I feel American people are more patriotic. The Japanese people have no love of country anymore. However, I don't feel the younger generation is bad or anything. Nevertheless, other countries' citizens love their flag, but the Japanese people don't. To me, it is sad that the Japanese people are not patriotic anymore; the reason for this is because we lost World War II.

Ensign Yuji Akamatsu

"There is no question in my mind that attacking Pearl Harbor was the right thing to do."

During my stay in Japan I was fortunate to meet the experienced naval aviator Yuji Akamatsu on two occasions prior to his passing. Like his Kaga *comrades Takeshi Maeda and Haruo Yoshino, he flew several combat sorties from 7 December 1941 until the last days of the war when* tokkō *missions were being ordered. So Akamatsu-san was very lucky to survive the war. During the war his family name was Yamaguchi, but when he got married he adopted his wife's family name Akamatsu. This practice was common; if the woman's family didn't have any sons the groom adopted her family's name after they got married.*

My friend Yukihirō Yamamoto and I decided to travel all the way from Tokyo to Saeki City, in Kyūshū, which was an arduous eight hour journey via several trains. I remember how surprised I was to see the beautiful seashore along our route. I also recall going through numerous long tunnels, which gave me a splitting headache by the time we arrived at our destination. When we met Akamatsu-san he looked very fit for his age and had tanned skin. We spent almost an entire day interviewing this gentleman and touring the Saeki Peace Memorial Hall, which tells the story of Japan's wartime history at Saeki City, and promotes the message of the importance of peace throughout the world.

Akamatsu's early days

I was born on 1 March 1920 in Miyakonojō City, which is located in Miyazaki Prefecture. I had four sisters and four brothers. Since I was a child I had dreamed about becoming a pilot someday. My uncle was a Navy pilot, and whenever I saw him he talked about how great it was to be an aviator. He even visited Germany and brought back a portable record player, which was very rare in Japan at that time. My uncle said that if I joined the Navy I also could get things like that. So, quite naturally, I started to dream about becoming a Japanese Navy pilot. I joined the Navy on 1 June 1937 at Yokosuka as a student of the 40th class. I studied to be an observer, and on 19 November 1938 I was transferred to the Ōmura *Kōkūtai*. On 29 January 1940 I joined the 12th *Kōkūtai* and flew some combat missions in China. Later that same year I went on board the carrier *Kaga* on 1 November.

Flying the Type 97 & *Tenzan kankō*

The Type 97 *kankō* was very stable and easy to fly. On torpedo attack missions the aircraft was armed with an 800 kilogram torpedo, so it was very heavy. Unfortunately, the Type 97 was armed with only a flexible 7.7 mm machine gun in the rear part of the fuselage, so we were easy "prey" for enemy fighters. Hence, the only thing you really could do was to get down at low altitude, just above the water, and try to evade the enemy attacks. Of course, you didn't feel safe, but that's the reality of being a carrier attack plane pilot. Towards the end of the war I flew the *Tenzan kankō*. We had a lot of engine trouble because the Navy had only 87 octane fuel, which didn't have enough octane for it to run well. By 1945 a lot of the aviators were rookies and didn't survive very long while flying combat missions.

Pearl Harbor

Prior to attacking Pearl Harbor we felt that, since our nation had suffered so much from harsh economic sanctions, it was a "do or die" situation for Japan. We had two options: either do nothing and slowly die or put up a fight to try to change the situation. Therefore, I felt we really had no choice but to attack Pearl Harbor. Before our mission to Hawaii we trained without any holidays. We even lived on the airfield in tents and had our meals brought to us. After completing intense training and being aware of the bad situation Japan was in, there is no question in my mind that attacking Pearl Harbor was the right thing to do. Furthermore, during my training right before the attack I did my utmost to do a good job, so I would be prepared to carry out whatever duty our Navy required of me in the coming months. My flying partners for the Pearl Harbor attack were pilot PO2c Yoshiyuki Hirata and radioman/gunner Sea1c Yukio Okada.[136] Hirata-san never lost his cool, even while flying combat missions, so I thought he was a good pilot. As for Okada-san, he was younger than I, and sadly I don't remember him well.

Akamatsu-san and his crew flew in a Type 97 kankō, *which was armed with one torpedo and participated in the first wave of the Pearl Harbor attack. The overall commander of twelve Type 97s armed with torpedoes was Lieutenant Ichirō Kitajima.*

A young Yuji Akamatsu in his early days in the Navy. (Akamatsu Collection)

PO3c Akamatsu in flight gear. (Akamatsu Collection)

When I flew towards Oahu Island I was looking down through some openings in the clouds. As the shoreline appeared below I said, "Oh my god, it is Hawaii!" All of a sudden my face became flushed, and my mouth became so dry that I lost my voice. Prior to taking off our maintenance crew put a bottle of *saké* in our aircraft for good luck. I ended up drinking the entire bottle of *saké* on the way to Hawaii, but I didn't get drunk!

After this the order came to get into attack formation, and then I saw tons of smoke from the dive-bombing attacks of our Type 99 carrier bombers. At this time we were flying at low altitude, so I could see men using fire hoses and sailors going back to their ships. While I was flying in the third position of our *chūtai* I became numb, and my mind went blank. My orders were to attack a California-class battleship, and that is what I did.

During training we were taught to break left after dropping our torpedo. However, on this occasion there was a lot of anti-aircraft fire coming from the left (of my target ship), so I broke right. My comrade Yoshino-san also broke right. If we didn't do this we probably would have died. In fact, five out of twelve Type 97s were shot down during this mission. Since we were flying so low I was able to see our torpedo hit the enemy ship. Then I flew to a predetermined rendezvous spot and met up with an *Akagi* Type 97 carrier attack plane. We waited for some Type 0 *kansen* to arrive, and when they showed up our aircraft flew back to our carriers.

According to Hawai Sakusen, *the official Japanese records for the attack, the ship that Akamatsu's torpedo hit was the USS* West Virginia. *After participating in the Pearl Harbor attack, Akamatsu-san and the two members of his crew stayed on board the carrier* Kaga, *but they didn't fly together anymore. For example, Sea1c Yukio Okada participated in the 21 January air strike on Rabaul, but the other two aviators did not. However, Akamatsu-san participated in the 19 February raid on Port Darwin, Australia, with pilot PO2c Yoshiyuki Hirata, but with a different radioman/rear gunner. The pair also flew together one more time on the Tjilitjap strike on 5 March 1942, but never again with Sea1c Okada.*[137] *Unfortunately, due to our limited time together Yuji Akamatsu never talked with me about his recollections of these missions.*

The Battle of Midway

*During our second meeting together, the ex-*kankō *veteran and I talked briefly while touring the Saeki Peace Memorial Hall about his experiences during the Battle of Midway.*

An excellent southwestern view of Ford Island, which shows "Battleship Row" under attack by Japanese aircraft during the first wave. Note the water geyser above the battleship *Oklahoma*. (NHC via Wenger)

While I was eating my breakfast an alarm sounded, so I knew we were going to be attacked. Because I wanted to see what was happening I went up to the flight deck. I saw several enemy torpedo bombers trying to attack *Kaga*, but none were successful, and they were shot down by the Zero fighters. After this initial air attack we were attacked several times by torpedo bombers, but they didn't do any damage to our carrier. However, when the enemy dive-bombers swooped down on *Kaga* it was a different story. At that time I was on my way to the pilots' ready room. Then there was a big explosion, and it sounded like several bombs hit our carrier, but I lost consciousness and everything went black.

When I regained consciousness I went to the hangar deck. Because the iron became red hot the soles on my shoes started to melt; it was terrible. So I decided to try to escape and went up to the flight deck, but because it was so high above the water I was scared to jump. However, because of the thick smoke and fire, I had to act fast in order to survive. So I got some courage and ran across the flight deck, closed my eyes and jumped. A destroyer tried to rescue me while I was in the water, but it suddenly left the area when some American aircraft came to attack again. I'm not sure how many hours I spent in the water, but it was a long time before a destroyer rescued me, although I can't recall the ship's name. Later I transferred to the battleship *Kirishima*, and we went back to Japan. I couldn't believe that vehicles were waiting for us once we arrived in Kyūshū, so we would be escorted to the air base without talking to anyone about what happened during the battle.

Navy Days after Midway

Beginning in early July 1942 I became a flight instructor at an air base in Shizuoka Prefecture, and did this job for a little over one year. After this I was transferred to the escort carrier *Taiyō* on 20 December 1943. Shortly after, in February 1944, I went to Saeki

As Akamatsu mentions, five *Kaga* Type 97 *kankō*, which were armed with torpedoes, and fifteen men were lost during the Pearl Harbor attack. This is the one flown by Lieutenant Mimori Suzuki and his crew being recovered after the attack. (NA via Wenger)

Veteran Yuji Akamatsu in Tokyo, spring of 2000. (Werneth)

Air Base and transferred to the 931 *Kōkūtai*. In this assignment I flew patrol missions to escort ship convoys to the frontlines. For example, we went back and forth from the mainland of Japan to the Philippines. The escort carriers that were used in this role were the *Taiyō*, *Shinyō*, *Unyō*, and *Kaiyō*. My last assignment was with a *Kikusui* unit that was based at Kushira Air Base (in Kyūshū). My group was doing *tokkō* attacks with *Tenzan* carrier attack planes against targets, such as American ships off Okinawa. Fortunately, the war ended before I was sent to do a suicide mission. By mid-1945 the Navy had very few combat-worthy aircraft, so aviators had to use training aircraft to do their *tokkō* attacks and were shot down before they even came near a potential target. I was at Kushira Air Base when the war ended, and my last rank in the Navy was ensign. I was really lucky to survive, because if I was ordered to fly a *tokkō* mission I could not have refused, and would have died for nothing.

Postwar

After the war Akamatsu-san and his wife had one son and two daughters. He ran a traditional Japanese fish cake shop until his retirement, when one of his sons took over the family business. Throughout his later postwar years this aging veteran did his best to promote the message of peace, and was instrumental in the creation of the Saeki Peace Memorial Hall, which is located in Saeki City (Ōita Prefecture, Kyūshū). This facility, which opened in 1997, was built on a location that was part of Saeki Air Base during the war. It displays original World War II artifacts (including several items which were donated by Akamatsu-san) and models of the original air base, and the displays include testimonies from people who experienced the war over sixty years ago. One of the big themes presented in this facility is the importance of peace and the negative effects of war.

Even when Yuji Akamatsu was in his 80s, he still traveled to Hawaii to attend several symposiums and reconciliation events with his American counterparts who fought against him at Pearl Harbor. He also played a key role in a tree planting ceremony by several Japanese and American WWII veterans on the grounds of the Saeki Peace Memorial Hall. This historic event was held to promote peace and friendship between the United States and Japan, while at the same time to commemorate the special relationship that these aging veterans of both sides shared so many years after the war.

Reflections

Frankly speaking, I thought Japan could never win the war after our defeat in the Battle of Midway. During the wartime years we were educated to think that the ABCD countries were the most powerful nations in the world, and if we didn't fight for Japan, our country would be obliterated. Today I don't have any regrets for fighting in the war; I fought to protect my nation. I believe younger Japanese people don't want to hear about the war. They probably can't understand the feelings of the WWII veterans because they never experienced war, or are simply not interested. Last year I took some Japanese children to Hawaii with the hope that they could learn more about what we experienced during the war, so many years ago. It is important that Japan continues to have a good relationship with the United States.

When referring to the ABCD nations, the letter A stands for America, B stands for Britain, C stands for China, and D stands for the Dutch (or country of Holland). Yuji Akamatsu died on 9 January 2004, and his wife passed away shortly after due to a broken heart.

Lieutenant Takayoshi Morinaga

"I was calm, but I didn't think that I would survive."

While living in Japan for three years, I did an exhaustive search to locate experienced naval aviator veterans to interview for my book. One of my friends suggested that I speak with Takayoshi Morinaga, who lived in Ichikawa City, which is in the Chiba Prefecture, near Tokyo. My veteran friend said that Morinaga-san saw a lot of combat in the war and would be a good person to meet. He also participated in the Sino-Japanese War and the Pearl Harbor attack, and survived the sinking of two carriers. Throughout the war he flew as a reconnaissance man/navigator in several different types of aircraft. I met the ex-Navy pilot in the spring of 2003; he had big bushy eyebrows and looked very frail. Although his body was physically weak due to his age he was mentally very sharp. Prior to talking with me Morinaga-san began to chain smoke, but after the experienced veteran started to talk about his experiences he began to relax.

Morinaga's Early Days

I was born on 20 February 1918, in Saga Prefecture. There were eight children in my family. During World War I German pilots were very good because they were trained from a very young age. Since 1930 Japan had started a similar program called *Yokaren*, but this program was just basic training, and pilot training followed. About 150 out of 15,000 applicants from the entire nation were chosen to become part of the *Yokaren* program. I joined the Navy

A rare unpublished photo of a group of observers, which was taken at Usa Air Base in Ōita Prefecture, Kyūshū, in December 1940. Front row, from the left: Lieutenant Minoru Fukuda, PO2c Tokuichi Kimata, (instructor) WO Takayoshi Morinaga, WO Saku Akamatsu, and last three men are unknown. Back row, from the left: PO2c Tadao Tanzaki, PO2c Hiroshi Takada, and the rest are not known. (Morinaga Collection)

A young Takayoshi Morinaga is standing on the far left in this candid photo. However, the veteran never identified the other two men in the picture to the author. It was taken just after the Pearl Harbor attack. (Morinaga Collection)

on 1 May 1933, and did my basic training at Yokosuka. My basic training lasted for three years, and then I did an additional four months on a carrier. During my first three years in the Navy I mainly studied mathematics, physics, and English. After this, I did my flight training from September 1936 until 20 May 1937 at Kasumigaura and Yokosuka.

Combat in China

My first assignment after completing flight training was on the carrier *Kaga*. I was on board the carrier from November 1937 until December 1938. We went to China, and I flew 104 bombing missions from the ship. I flew on a Type 96 *kankō* as a radioman, but from August 1938 I started using the Type 97 carrier attack plane. My targets included railroad bridges, airfields, and enemy transportation vehicles. Fighters escorted me on my missions. I also was involved in the Canton attack operation and support missions for the Army. After this I transferred to *Akagi* in December 1938, and I went back to China and stayed two months there. On board the carrier I did nighttime torpedo training, because I never did that type of training before. Finally, I served as a flight instructor with the Usa *Kōkūtai*, and then transferred back to *Kaga* in September 1941.

Pearl Harbor

I went to Kagoshima Air Base and had intense training. Torpedo attack training and flying at low altitude were very important. The crew of each airplane was required to do this training exercise three times a day. During the training, each aircraft took off from the airfield and flew towards Kaimondake Mountain. Then we went south around the Ibusuki area, turned right, went through a valley between mountains, and went along the Kototsu River towards the ocean. When you looked at the beach on the island of Sakura Jima there was a lighted black mark that was the target point. You launched your dummy torpedo at this mark. At this time the Kototsu River was behind your back.

There was a village of prostitutes off the ocean, and their homes were located along the Kototsu River. There was an area where they dried their clothes. When you flew past this place your altitude was only about 50 meters (164 feet), and the ladies could see the faces of the pilots very well. One day a prostitute waved her red *koshimaki* at the pilots and the pilots waved back. The pilots did training every morning, afternoon, and night, so we were tired. However, the *koshimaki* waving encouraged us, and our skills improved a great deal.

In October 1941 we finished the specified amount of training, and everybody was given two full days of vacation. My classmate Shimizu-san and I decided to spend our time at the hot spring in Inomoto for relaxation. While we were drinking at dinner time a clerk said that there was a phone call from Kagoshima for me. I thought that this was odd, because nobody was supposed to know where I was. However, when I picked up the telephone the guy on the other end of the line was Warrant Officer Toyoshi Urata, who was two terms senior to me.[138] I asked him, "How did you find out where we are?" He said that his group was at the same hotel, but it was too noisy for them. So they decided to go for a drink in the next town, Kushikino, and were waiting at Inomoto Station. Urata-san said that I should come to the station quickly and join them. When I got there I saw him and other men in a parked car. Since there was a one hour wait for the train to arrive they decided to take a taxi. However, the taxi driver said that there was a festival going on, and the restaurants at Kushikino were full. He recommended a local restaurant in the area, and we got out of the taxi to check it out. We saw a country style restaurant called the Restaurant Takenoya. A young man greeted us and took us to a room. He said that one person could drink up to two bottles of beer and then he should drink *shōchū*. The waiter then asked us, "Which prison did you come from?" We said that we were in the Navy, and not prison wardens. His response was "You think we are just a bunch of dumb rednecks and you enjoy making fun of us. We actually know Navy people well. The other day warships came off Kushikino, and I saw a lot of Navy men. They were wearing feminine-like uniforms with sailor's caps, but your uniforms are different. In this emergency situation, you guys try to dress classy and say you're Navy people. This is outrageous; you are not citizens of Japan!"

After this outburst this waiter explained the situation to the owner of the restaurant; however, she went to Kagoshima as a *geisha* and knew a lot about the Japanese Navy. She then explained to him that sailors and officers had different style hats, and the guy over there with a dagger is an officer. The lady said, "These people are higher-ranking officers." So the waiter apologized to us and the atmosphere in the room changed dramatically. Beer was chilled, and after 2100 hours the other guests left the restaurant. The *geisha* and this young man started to sing and dance, which was a wonderful surprise, and this lasted until the next morning. This is an experience that I will never forget from my Navy days; it is a special story for me.

In the Navy, higher-ranking officers used to purchase their own uniforms, but lower-ranking men got their uniforms from the Navy. In November 1941 I was at Tomitaka Air Base in Miyazaki Prefecture; I was asked to bring both my summer and winter uniforms. Because of this I had a hunch that an attack on Pearl Harbor was imminent. I expressed my premonition to my group leader, Lieutenant Commander Takashi Hashiguchi, and he said, "Don't you ever say things like that again." After that incident I never talked about it again. When I learned that we would indeed attack Pearl Harbor, I wasn't surprised because I thought that this would happen anyway. We had a meeting while we were at Hitokkapu Bay, but we didn't know what our target would be. During the meeting they said that, prior to our actual attack, two reconnaissance planes would check out the situation and report to our ship. We received a report right before we took off and planned our mission accordingly.

According to Morinaga-san, the plan for his group of high altitude level Type 97 kankō *was to fly at an altitude of 3,000 meters (9,842 feet) and drop their 800 kilogram armor-piercing bombs simultaneously. Basically, there was a specially trained leading airplane, and the other planes in the group dropped their bombs on the command from this leading aircraft. He said, for example, if one plane out of five bombers hit the target their attack*

Although this is not a *Kaga* Type 97 *kankō* armed with an 800 kilogram bomb, it is a good photo that illustrates how the aircraft looked with this armament. In actuality, this is a Type 97 from *Hiryū*. (Makiel Collection via Wenger)

would be successful.[139] *With this type of bomb, they also had to drop their bombs at a high altitude so the bombs could penetrate the battleship's armor. Their target was the battleships, which were moored in two rows. The Type 97s (serving as level bombers) would target the inside ships, and the torpedo bombers would hit the outside ships.*

During the Pearl Harbor attack WO Takayoshi Morinaga was an observer, and his partners were pilot PO2c Masato Matsuyama, and PO2c Hajime Yonezawa was the radioman/rear gunner. PO2c Matsuyama survived the war, but PO2c Yonezawa died on 19 October 1944 off of Taiwan. Morinaga-san said that PO2c Yonezawa was his student prior to the Pearl Harbor attack, and that even though the mission was his first time in combat, he was very calm because he was flying with his former teacher.

Before the attack we received a rice ball and *miso shiru*. The soup was very delicious, and I heard that they put twice the amount of stock into it. Prior to taking off I wasn't nervous, but I didn't think that I would survive. I was the 43rd *Shōtaichō* for

Kaga's Type 97 *kankō* level-bombers making their way to the rendezvous point after making their attacks during the first wave. (NA via Wenger)

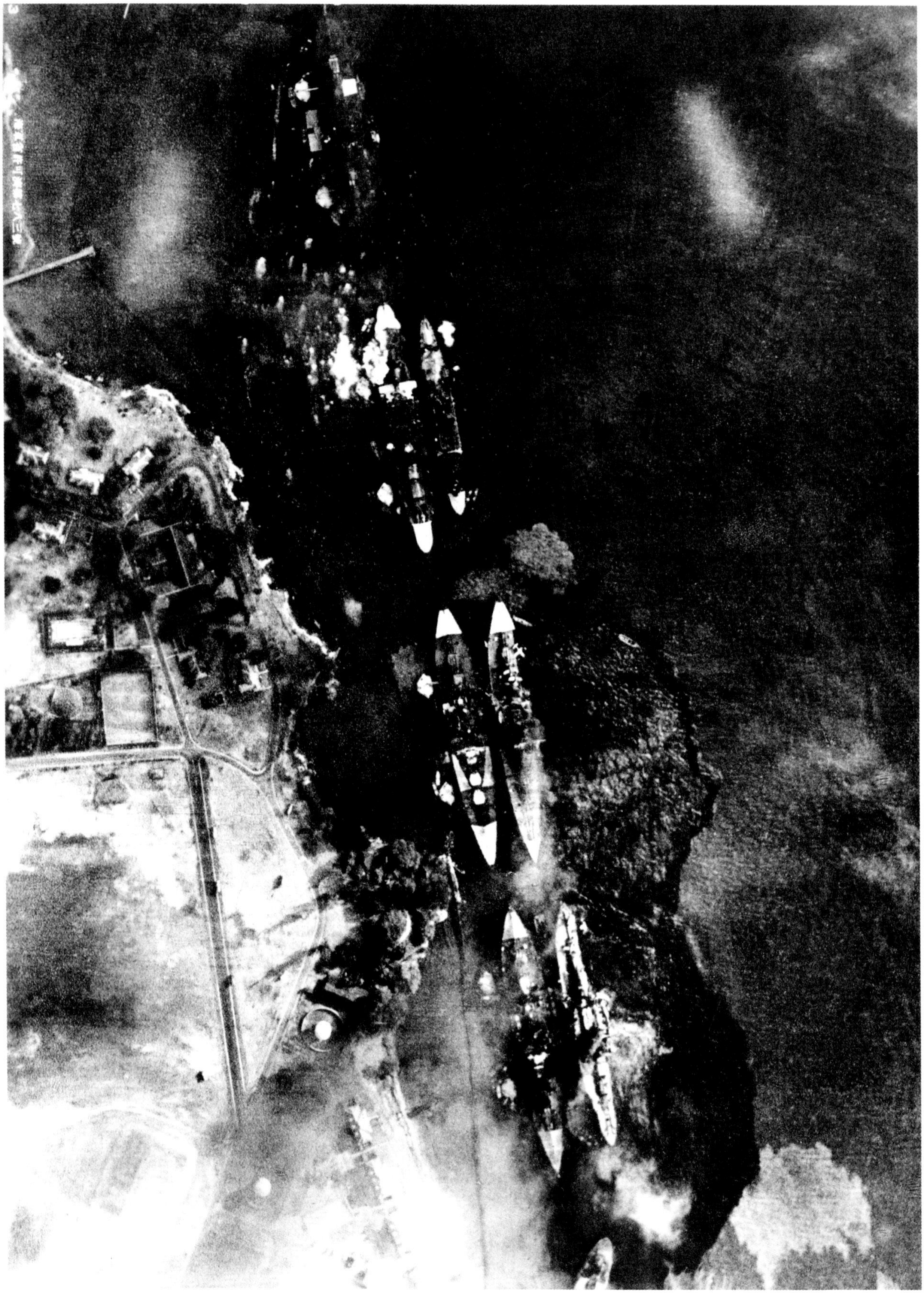

The view of Battleship Row that Morinaga-san and his fellow aviators would have seen while dropping their ordinance on the ships below. (Prange/Chihaya via Wenger)

the level-bombers in the first wave attack. When my plane was near Battleship Row, the ship right before the *Maryland* was on fire because bombs from another airplane had hit it. There was an extraordinary fire coming out of that ship because its turret blew up, and I never saw anything like this before.[140]

Our leader, Lieutenant Yoshitaka Mikami, was in the first airplane; however, during our "bomb run" his Type 97 switched positions with the second aircraft, which had the most experienced pilot and bombardier pair on board. *This second Type 97* kankō *was flown by pilot PO1c Nobuo Uemura, bombardier PO2c Junichi Fujii, and radioman/rear gunner Sea1c Saburō Oike.*[141] We all dropped our bombs following the lead of this crack team in the second aircraft. I believe my bomb successfully hit the *Maryland*, but I couldn't see where my bomb hit.[142] I think our group hit the *Maryland* successfully twice. There also was a lot of anti-aircraft fire during this time. The aircraft that attacked before my Type 97 didn't receive a lot of anti-aircraft fire, but my plane did. This is because our *kankō* was the last one to drop our bombs from our group. The enemy 10,000-ton cruiser (possibly the *Helena*) at the dock also tried to fire at me, but our aircraft was not damaged. At this time the sky turned black because of the intense anti-aircraft fire. On the way back to the carrier I went to Barbers Point, and met up with some fighters and helped them get back to our ship. After I landed, I felt that I had accomplished my mission.

Morinaga-san stayed on board Kaga *until the ill-fated Midway operation when his carrier sunk, and he spent several hours in the water before being rescued.*

The Battle of Midway

At that time everyone thought that the mission would be a simple task to accomplish; that's why I feel we didn't do enough planning before the Midway operation. However, in reality it was much different. On board *Kaga* I was waiting to fly the next attack mission. Suddenly American dive-bombers began to attack, and I saw the first three bombs drop near the ship. When the fourth bomb came I thought that it would hit us. So I closed my eyes, covered my ears, and ducked down. I was blown over because of a bomb blast, and there were about ten people in that area; but only three people, including myself, survived. After the bomb hit, I went to the section of the flight deck that had wires to stop the aircraft.

Next, I tried to help put out the fire in the hangar with water. We did a relay using a bucket of water, but the water evaporated quickly, and it was useless. I was ordered to jump into the water. At that time I only had underwear on, and I didn't know what would happen to me. Even though it was June the water was very cold. The last time I saw *Kaga* there was a huge chain reaction explosion due to a detonation of bombs and other ammunition. It was an extraordinary sight! The most impressive explosion occurred when the twenty-seven 800 kilogram (1,764 pound) bombs and twenty-one torpedoes blew up.

I didn't see much damage on the carrier itself, but I saw some fire. However, the *Kaga* didn't sink, and after it became dark a destroyer sank it with a torpedo. After going into the water I swam for six hours before getting rescued by the destroyer *Maikaze*. At night I had a difficult time breathing, and the next morning I vomited blood. On the destroyer I couldn't be treated, so I was transferred to the battleship *Kirishima*. On board the battleship I was x-rayed and told that I had to be hospitalized. I transferred to a hospital ship anchored near the island of Hashira Jima, which is located in the Inland Sea of Japan. Admiral Isoroku Yamamoto once came to visit me when I was in bed. He had a dark complexion and was statute. Admiral Yamamoto impressed me as being very kind and dignified. I was hospitalized for two weeks, but I was quarantined and not treated well. When I saw people leaving the hospital ship after suffering from lung disease I felt very strange. Because of this, I thought that if I stayed longer here I would get the same ailment. I requested permission to leave and was granted my wish.

The Battle of the Philippine Sea

After this, I went to Ohi *Kōkūtai* and worked as an instructor for a little longer than a year. Next I transferred to the carrier *Shōkaku*, and participated in the Battle of the Philippine Sea. In those days I felt that our naval aviators were not well trained, so many people didn't return from their missions. I was an observer aboard a Nakajima *Tenzan* carrier attack plane.[143] I flew a reconnaissance mission and covered an area above the ocean approximately 600 miles.[144] Before reaching the end of our search quadrant area I saw an enemy Grumman Avenger torpedo bomber. I thought that if I followed him, I would find the enemy fleet. However, the Avenger hid in the clouds and then reappeared. Our aircraft followed him for thirty minutes, but the pilot of my plane said that we should return. After this we turned and flew another sixty miles and came back. Luckily, we were able to find our carrier; and when we landed, the engine stopped.

Once I landed I wanted to smoke, but I couldn't find any tobacco in my uniform. Because of this I tried to get tobacco from my quarters, but many hatches were closed. I had to opened several hatches and had no luck. I finally gave up and went up to the flight deck and got some tobacco from my friends. I feel very fortunate, because a torpedo hit the area where my quarters were located. The carrier then started to sink from the front. Pilots were told to go to the front and give their life jackets to the wounded men. I jumped into the ocean, but a threatening storm made it most difficult. I was exhausted and cold.

The cruiser *Yahagi* later rescued me, but I couldn't even walk. At that time I suffered from severe pain in my buttocks from flying for such a long time. I think a lot of aviators suffered from this ailment due to sitting in the same position during long missions. The *Yahagi* took me back to Japan, and then I switched to the *Zuihō* and went to Ōita Harbor. I still was not able to walk, so Lieutenant Kitao carried me on his back and said, "You should relax for awhile," and brought me to a hot spring in Beppu, and I stayed there for one week.

Shōkaku *was torpedoed by the American navy submarine USS* Cavalla *and sank on 19 June 1944.*[145] *Just after Morinaga-san's and other patrols had landed she was hit at 1222 by three, possibly four torpedoes in the starboard side, forward, and amidships. Large fuel fires ignited in the hangar and the ship began to settle by the bow. Though damage control initially hoped to save her, the flooding forward and the fires intensified. As Morinaga-san describes, the blazing carrier steadily sank by the bow, and while the crew were gathering to abandon ship just before 1510 she suddenly rolled over to port, upended, and went to the bottom. Loss of life was very heavy: 58 officers and 830 petty officers and men, in addition to 376 members of 601* Kōkūtai *and eight civilians shared the fate of the vessel for a total of 1,272 dead. 570 survivors, including Captain Hiroshi Matsubara, were rescued by light cruiser* Yahagi *and destroyers* Urakaze, Wakatsuki, *and* Hatsuzuki.[146]

Morinaga's Last Days in the Navy

After this Lieutenant Takayoshi Morinaga was a member of K-262 from July-November 1944. Morinaga's final assignment was with K-501, and he was a member of that group until the end of the war.[147]

Postwar

In his postwar years Morinaga-san joined the Maritime Self-Defense Force and did work related to radio equipment; he was skilled in this field. After this he worked for Toshiba and then retired. Sadly, Morinaga-san died on 23 March 2004 at the age of eighty-six. I feel fortunate to have met him before he passed away.

2007 Postscript – a USS *Cavalla* Veteran Speaks

While researching the sinking of Shōkaku, *I was fortunate to locate and interview U.S. Navy veteran Captain Ernest J. Zellmer, who was the Communications Officer on board the* Cavalla *during the battle.*

My hometown is Milwaukee, Wisconsin. I lived through the depression years, and the idea that an appointment to a military academy would provide four years of college, and entry to a career was enticing. I contacted my state senator in 1938 and eventually got a Presidential appointment to the Naval Academy in 1940. By then Europe was at war, and even though I now had two years of college behind me, going to the Naval Academy was a good way to get into the military. I thought that the war would continue for a long time, and it would probably bring the United States into the conflict.

I graduated from the Naval Academy in June 1943 and was commissioned as an ensign in the U.S. Navy. My class did the course in three years, but retained our regular class number (i.e.'44). We then went to Florida for six weeks, to be indoctrinated in naval aviation at various naval air stations. The purpose was to give us an understanding of the capabilities of air power. Then, my group had thirty days leave before reporting for our first assignment. At the beginning of September I reported to Submarine School in New

Morinaga-san after our interview, during the spring of 2003. (Werneth)

U.S. Navy submarine veteran Ernest Zellmer in March 1944. This photo was taken while the USS *Cavalla* was preparing to head out to the Pacific Ocean for it's first patrol. (Zellmer Collection)

The *Cavalla*, the submarine which sunk the carrier *Shōkaku* during the Battle of the Philippine Sea in June 1944. This photo was taken on 31 March 1944 shortly before the submarine left New London, Connecticut, bound for the Pacific. (USN via Zellmer)

London, Connecticut. Once again it was a shortened course. After graduating from Submarine School I received orders to the USS *Cavalla* (SS-244) and reported on 1 January 1944. The *Cavalla* was assembling her crew and training while waiting completion. Construction was completed, and *Cavalla* was commissioned on 29 February 1944. Then I began an intensive training period, before departing for the Pacific in early April.

The *Cavalla* was my first ship. My job on board was Communications Officer. As head of the Communications Department, I was responsible for the radio, radar, and sonar equipment and personnel. My battle station was Plotting Officer in the conning tower. On the morning of 19 June 1944 *Cavalla* dove to avoid an airplane. With the periscope we were able to see several small planes circling. *Cavalla* headed in that direction, and sonar soon reported propeller noises on the same bearing. We then saw the tops of several ships directly under the small planes still circling. *Cavalla* came to a normal approach course and went to battle stations as the oncoming ships were tracked. Short periscope observations were made to get range, bearing, and angle on the bow, and to identify the target. There was a carrier, two cruisers, and a destroyer that could be seen as we approached. Sonar reported additional ships.

In just over an hour after *Cavalla* dove because of the enemy aircraft, she was in position to launch torpedoes at the carrier. We fired a spread of six torpedoes and heard three definite explosions that were timed properly for the projected torpedo runs. I learned a few years ago that the Japanese believed the carrier had been hit by four torpedoes. I didn't feel any remorse about possibly killing some Japanese Navy personnel because I had read about Japan's brutality in China and the bestiality they inflicted on our prisoners of war. The latter was reported by several of our POWs that had escaped from POW camps in the Philippines.

After launching our torpedoes, our submarine started to go deep to evade the Japanese destroyer that, on the last periscope observation, was seen heading directly toward us. Two minutes after we had fired our torpedoes that Japanese destroyer started dropping depth charges. The first two salvos of four charges each were quite close. *Cavalla* continued down toward her test depth.

However, she was heavy and unable to stop her descent until she was 100 feet below her test depth. The main induction was flooded! That added about fifteen tons of sea water and made the boat heavy. It was necessary to increase our speed and put an up angle on the boat to check the descent. Then *Cavalla* clawed back up to its test depth. In addition, we had water in the forward torpedo room bilge. This water came from an overflowing "water around torpedo" tank (WRT). A poppet valve had stuck open, and the WRT tank continued taking water from the open torpedo tube until it overflowed into the Forward Torpedo Room bilge. The valve was finally closed, but by then there were several inches of water in the bilge. With the up angle of the boat, that water surged to the after bulkhead and flooded the two motors that trained our two high frequency sonar heads. This flooding was probably not related to the depth charges, but caused by a sticky valve. The water in the forward torpedo room bilge not only made the boat heavy, but located forward made it difficult to hold the desired up angle on the boat. The trim and drain pumps were relatively noisy; their noise would aid the destroyers in tracking us. Instead of pumping the excess water back to sea, we would remain heavy and use a little extra speed to hold our depth. That was the quieter way.

For two and a half hours, three and then two destroyers remained in our area and tried to find and sink us. They dropped a total of 105 depth charges. Finally the depth charges got farther away from us, and we then returned to periscope depth to find the area clear. Almost three hours after our attack the low frequency sonar reported four very large explosions; they continued to rumble for many seconds. They came from the direction of our attack on the carrier. However, they were not depth charges! The sonar operator also heard "breaking up" noises. We were confident that the carrier had sunk.

We then started the pumps and brought *Cavalla* to a neutral trim, reloaded our torpedo tubes, and surfaced. It was time to report our action and to provide the location of the Japanese ships and their original course and speed. The *Shōkaku* was the first enemy ship that *Cavalla* sank. On our first patrol we had gotten a major prize and survived an extended counterattack!

After our fourth patrol, our Executive Officer was detached and the Engineering Officer moved up to take his position. I was then given the job of Engineering Officer, and my battle station changed to Diving Officer. After the fifth patrol I got orders in August 1945 to proceed to New London to put the USS *Cusk* (SS-348) in commission. My assignment was to be Engineering Officer of the *Cusk*. En route, I was authorized thirty days home leave and was in Milwaukee when the Japanese surrendered and World War II was finally over.

Lieutenant Commander Hirata Matsumura

"I joined the Navy to fight for our country."

When I met Hirata Matsumura in June 2002, he was one of the most senior Pearl Harbor attack pilots that was still alive. During the attack he was second in command of the torpedo bombers during the first wave. When I initially asked my veteran friends if he was still alive, they said that he died. Nevertheless, after doing some research I found out that he indeed was alive and willing to be interviewed.

During our afternoon together, Matsumura-san looked very frail and got tired very easily, due to his age. However, he was very sharp and clear while talking about his experiences. Even though it has been over sixty years since the Pearl Harbor attack, Matsumura-san was very proud of what he did, and got teary eyed when talking about his feelings about participating in the attack. Mounted on the wall in his living room was an antique Japanese gun, which was a family heirloom. In my personal book he signed his name very boldly in large kanji characters as a memory of my visit.

A rare unpublished photo of a group of Japanese Navy officer pilots; note the Naval Academy class numbers after their names. From left to right: Lieutenant (junior grade) Rokurō Kikuchi (64th Term), Lieutenant (junior grade) Hiroji Kadano (65th Term), Lieutenant Masaomi Tanaka (59th Term), and Lieutenant (junior grade) Hirata Matsumura (63rd Term). It was taken at Ōmura Air Base in November 1940. During the Battle of Midway Kadano participated in the air attack of Midway Atoll, but was severely wounded and later had one of his legs amputated. As for Kikuchi, he also participated in the Midway Atoll attack and had to ditch his damaged aircraft but survived. (Matsumura Collection)

A wartime picture of Hirata Matsumura in September 1941. (Matsumura Collection)

Matsumura in Hainan, China (September 1940). (Matsumura Collection)

Matsumura's Early Days

I was born on 9 June 1913, in the Togawa village, which is in Saga City, Kyūshū. I was the eleventh child of twelve children in my family. I liked the Navy because I thought that it was impressive, especially the Navy uniform and the ornate daggers that officers wore. I joined on 1 April 1933 as a 63rd Term student at the Navy Academy and graduated on 23 March 1937. After we graduated, I did my training cruise on board the *Yakumo* and visited many places, such as Seattle, San Francisco, Los Angeles, New York City, Cuba, Mexico City, etc. I was one of forty people who was chosen, out of 160 men, to be an aviator. I did my flight training and graduated on 30 June 1938.

My first assignment was with the Tateyama *Kōkūtai*, and I did additional flight training there. I initially used the Yokosuka B4Y1 Type 96 *kankō*, but later changed to the Nakajima B5N2 Type 97 carrier attack plane. The Type 97 was a modern monoplane, and it was extraordinary. The aircraft was completely different than other aircraft, especially the speed. In those days it was the newest airplane with retractable landing gear, and the only aircraft for us to use. I stayed in Tateyama for six months of training, and got some good experience as an aviator. Next, I became a flying instructor at Ōita *Kōkūtai* and started to teach. After this I joined the aircraft carrier *Hiryū* on 1 November 1939.

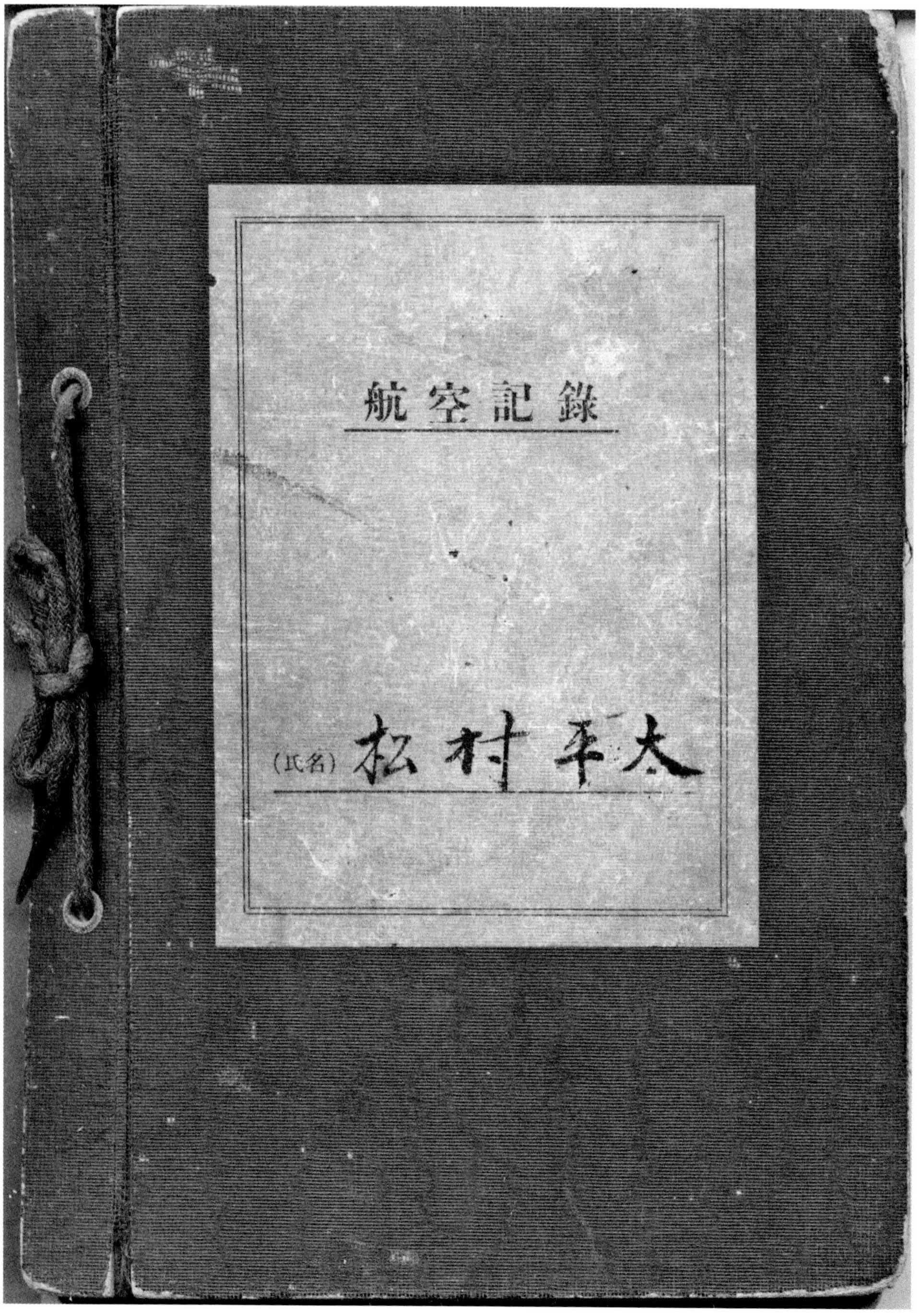

During my visit Matsumura-san showed me his wartime log book. Since he had all the records of his missions we were able to verify all of the veteran's accounts. (Werneth)

Pearl Harbor Training and Mission

I was the most experienced person on *Hiryū* and I organized the group. I considered myself to be very serious. The *Hiryū* and *Sōryū* Type 97 *kankō* pilots did their training in Izumi, in Kagoshima Prefecture, for the Pearl Harbor attack. We did both low-altitude training and high-altitude bombing training in formation, flying at 3,000 meters (9,842 feet). On our way back we practiced low-altitude training by hitting a rock off Akune.[148] My group didn't use real bombs or torpedoes. Instead, we used our imagination and did shadow training. We didn't use any armament on our aircraft because we had to practice numerous times. The target was usually a rock, but if there was a carrier available we used it as a target. However, we also used practice torpedoes a few times. In all, we did training at Izumi between early August to November 1941.

During the attack, Matsumura-san was a pilot of a Nakajima B5N2 Type 97 kankō, *which was armed with a single 800 kilogram (1,840 pounds) torpedo. He flew as a member of the 1st attack wave of 183 aircraft and took off from the carrier* Hiryū.

Basically, both of the members of my crew for the Pearl Harbor mission were hard working people.[149] My airplane was a leader's aircraft, so only competent people were chosen to fly on it. The observer on my plane was PO1c Takeo Shiro, and the radioman/rear gunner was PO1c Sadamu Murai. Unfortunately, Murai-san died later in the war.[150] Shiro-san is still alive, and after the war he became a leader in the education field for the Kagawa Prefecture. He has good character and is a great guy.

Shortly after my Pearl Harbor mission started, I felt that I would be shot down by enemy fighters or by anti-aircraft guns during the attack. In reality, however, the anti-aircraft guns did not hit my aircraft. In the beginning of my mission my Type 97 *kankō* was armed with a torpedo, and it added a lot of weight to my plane. Because of this my aircraft went down below the deck level after taking off. Therefore, I increased the speed, but I had to be careful so my Type 97 didn't stall. I then banked left and turned around before setting my course for Pearl Harbor.

I just followed on the right side of the leader, Lieutenant Commander Shigeharu Murata.[151] In total, it was a four and a half hour mission for me, from take off to my return on the carrier. I was the leader of the *Hiryū* and *Sōryū kankō*, and my assignment was to attack a carrier. The day before the attack we received reports that said there were no carriers in the harbor, but maybe this would change, so I was not sure if there would be any present during our attack. In the morning prior to our attack, a reconnaissance aircraft reported that several destroyers and other ships were there, but didn't say anything about the carriers.

My assignment was to find and attack a carrier in the harbor, so I tried very hard to locate one. But I could not find a carrier, so I hit a battleship. The Type 99 *kanbaku* were supposed to attack after the Type 97s (armed with torpedoes), but there was a miscommunication between the aircraft and the Type 99s attacked first.[152]

Matsumura participated in the Pearl Harbor attack while he was assigned to *Hiryū*, and his target during the mission was the battleship *West Virginia*. (NHC via Wenger)

I saw smoke coming from Ford Island but didn't go into it. Instead, I took a detour and flew in the airspace off Hickam Field, but I didn't plan to do this. During my initial attempt to drop my torpedo I was too close to another aircraft. Because of this, my Type 97 was rocked by this plane's "prop wash," so I had to turn around and come back again. You have to be 30 meters (98 feet) above the target to hit it, and Murata-san once said "you should be as low as you can be." So I tried to be 20 meters (66 feet) above the target, and then hit it with my torpedo and turned right. Actually, my torpedo hit the *West Virginia*, but this was not the ship I was supposed to hit.[153]

After dropping the torpedo I asked, "How was it?" to the observer, and he saw white bubbles coming up and said it was okay. I asked the observer PO1c Shiro to take a picture, but he misunderstood me and thought I said, "Shoot the enemy." Also, during this time the enemy was shooting at us. Hence, PO1c Shiro asked PO1c Murai to fire his gun, and he started to shoot at many targets. Because of this Murai-san accidentally shot the wire that transmitted our radio messages to the carrier, and could not send our message about our success. Then I said to him, "You are an idiot because we cannot send a message now." After my attack I ordered PO1c Murai to take some pictures.

Then I flew to Kaena Point, which was west of the harbor, and proceeded to fly north, back to the carrier. I had finished my mission and felt good because I was alive. I thought that I would die and was lucky enough to survive. When I landed, Lieutenant Commander Tatsuo Sakai, the *Hiryū's* Chief Gunnery Officer, saw me.[154] He was in an area of our carrier, above the deck. After the mission Sakai-san said that I looked very relieved and happy after I landed my aircraft. He teased me about this. As I look back, I thought I was very lucky and happy at that time. There was no damage to my Type 97, which was very strange, because other airplanes were attacked and had some damage. I also didn't do anything to avoid the enemy fire, but in general the anti-aircraft fire was heavy, especially from the left. However, I was flying low, and maybe they didn't try to shoot me because they thought they would hit other American ships.

After the mission I wondered what would happen next, because we were fighting against the United States and Britain. Also, I thought about how the war would end. It was only natural to fight for Japan because I joined the Navy to fight for our country. That's why I became a pilot. You cannot quit just because we started a war; you have to defend your country. After the Pearl Harbor attack I went to Kasumigaura to become a flight instructor. Usually people spent only one year on a carrier, because it was physically exhausting. Nevertheless, I spent four years on a carrier (1939-1942), which was too long, and I became weak. I was diagnosed with tuberculosis. Then, in 1943 I was at Rabaul, and my condition worsened.

This image was taken by Matsumura's crew after they completed their attacks over the harbor, circled around Hickam Field, and exited the target area. (Matsumura Collection)

Action in the Solomons

The Allied war machine was rolling through the Solomon Islands in the fall of 1943. After successfully securing Guadalcanal Island, the Russell Islands, and the New Georgia group of islands, the plan entered its final stage—the capture of the last major Japanese-held territory in the area, Bougainville Island. If Allied forces took over the island, the entire area would be firmly in their control, so it was very important to succeed in this mission. Furthermore, the capture of Bougainville would enable them to cut off Rabaul, Japan's large air and naval base, and finally neutralize it. D-day for the invasion was set for 1 November 1943, and the American 3rd Marine Division, along with the Army's 37th Division, landed at Cape Torokina on Bougainville.[155] *Although the troops secured a beachhead at Torokina, there still was much fighting to do on the island.*

Rabaul-based Japanese aircraft, on several occasions, tried to attack American landing forces and U.S. Navy ships, but suffered heavy losses. Matsumura-san and his comrades, who were flying from Rabaul, were involved in air attacks against these forces, as well. They also participated in attacks against the 1st Marine Division, which landed at Cape Gloucester, on New Britain Island, on 26 December 1943.[156] *The Marines' goal was to capture the Japanese airfield there, which occurred that same month. The Allied plan to cut off "Fortress Rabaul" by encircling it and pounding it through massive air assaults saved countless lives, and helped change the course of the war.*

On 1 November 1943 I became the *Zuikaku hikōtaichō*, and did this job until 31 January 1944. Our group was based at Rabaul (New Britain Island) from 12 December 1943 until 27 January 1944. During this time I flew twenty missions. I went to the island of Bougainville to attack, but the situation was really bad, and many airplanes were damaged. It was the kind of war that Japan couldn't possibly win. On some occasions, I heard that the enemy was at Cape Gloucester, on New Britain Island, and was told to attack them at night, because it was not possible to attack them in the daytime. Our group used the Nakajima Type 97 *kankō*, and we did both torpedo and level-bombing attacks. Our targets included enemy transports going to Bougainville, an airfield, and enemy

A wartime photo of Lieutenant Commander Matsumura in his flight gear. (Matsumura Collection)

troops trying to land.[157] In January 1944 my group went to Truk Island. We went there, but our forces received an enemy air raid from carrier-based planes and we were devastated. However, I departed from Truk Island on 10 February 1944, one week prior to the air raid, and returned to Japan. But I had no idea why I was called back to the homeland at that time.

Back to Japan

Usually in the Navy there were two annual physicals, which were done in March and November. In late March I had my physical, and the x-ray showed that I was not healthy. A senior officer that I knew, who also was very ill in the past, told me that I better try to get over my illness before it gets really bad. Then, at Kasumigaura several doctors evaluated my health and said that it was impossible for me to continue working. So I had a choice between staying in a hospital or going back to my house in Kyūshū. I chose the latter and went home to recuperate. Nevertheless, while trying to get better, I also went to Sasebo and worked there. I stayed at Sasebo until the end of the war.

Even before the official surrender I thought that Japan would lose, and this really came true. It was an unfortunate situation to lose the war, but I think that it was natural for our nation to lose. At that time I also thought about what would happen after this, but the United States was very good to Japan and the Japanese people. My final rank was lieutenant commander, and my flying hours were 2,257 hours.

Postwar

After the war I spent ten years trying to recuperate from my illness. Once I regained my health, I was able to work for a public housing corporation and remained there until retirement. I then started to work for an apartment complex service company. Next, I worked as CEO of Hayashi Construction Company and retired at the age of eighty years old. My wife and I have two sons and two daughters.

Reflections

In the world of today there are some wars going on, but if there were no wars, it would be better. However, human beings have a desire to do something. So even if President Bush makes a speech, not everyone will agree with him. War is unavoidable, because each country is thinking about its own best interests. Because of this, this problem is not easy to solve, and it's unfortunate. In conclusion, I feel the United States is really a good nation now because it is a leader in democracy. So I want the American people to continue to do this and watch over the world.

Unfortunately, Matsumura-san died about eight months after my visit on 26 February 2003 and his wife is deceased.

Matsumura-san was physically very frail but mentally very sharp when I met him. He also became very emotional when talking about his Pearl Harbor memories. (Werneth)

Ensign Taisuke Maruyama

"Since I was young, I never worried whether I would live or die."

Back in the summer of 2000, I first heard about veteran Taisuke Maruyama's background while preparing to attend the annual National Museum of the Pacific War symposium, which was held in September of that year. During this time I got to know him and several other Japanese Navy veterans very well. When Maruyama-san attended this event in Texas, I was his "tour guide" for a few days. After recovering from his long journey to Texas, he told me about his experiences during the war in great detail. Every time I tried to ask him about his personal feelings during the war he seemed very reluctant to say much; I felt that Maruyama-san was almost trying to "hide" deep feelings of pain. However, once he started talking about Pearl Harbor and his other missions, this war veteran became very teary-eyed and emotional.

Maruyama-san was incredibly lucky to survive several dangerous low-level missions with his Type 97 kankō *that was protected with only one 7.7 mm machine gun. He participated in a number of combat sorties, including the Pearl Harbor attack, the Battle of Midway, and Santa Cruz. These were all missions in which the Japanese Navy aviators were essentially "slaughtered," and very few survived to the end of the war. This lucky veteran was fortunate to survive, and because of this, he did his utmost to teach future generations about the horrors of war. He currently lives in Obu City (part of Nagoya City), Japan. Some of the material that follows was kindly provided by the National Museum of the Pacific War (Fredericksburg, Texas) because Maruyama-san wrote down a number of his World War II experiences in preparation for their annual symposium six years ago.*

Maruyama's Early Years

I was born on 11 November 1922. My grandfather volunteered to be in the Navy and fought in both the Russo-Japanese War and the Sino-Japanese War. My father graduated from Waseda University and studied English literature.[158] He was an English middle school teacher, but during the war my father was a supervisor of a POW camp. Because of his job, after the war, he was suspected of being a war criminal and was detained at Sugamo Prison.[159] However, he turned out to be innocent and was later released. I was the oldest son, and had four brothers and two sisters. At that time, the basic policy of the school system gave full support to the military. For example, I wore military style shoes to school. The main reason for this was the war in China. I think everyone was influenced by this. Also, during the same time all the children in my family were hoping to go to college.

Joining the Navy

During my fourth year of Tomita Middle School (in Mie Prefecture) I took a test to join the Navy. I passed this test and entered the Navy on 1 October 1938, at Yokosuka as a 3rd Term Student. I was surprised that I passed and accepted the challenge. There were 260 students in my class, but 85% of them died during the war. In addition, my third brother was a 75th Term Naval Academy student.

Just before the end of basic training we were separated into two groups, observers and pilots. This was determined by taking a one week course, which was actually a test. As a result, I was put into a training class for observers at Suzuka Air Base. This course lasted six months, and I studied such things as bombing technique, gunnery, and wireless radio operation. After this I took a three month class about the Type 97 *kankō* and completed my flight training on 25 March 1941. Then, after completing my flight training I transferred to the aircraft carrier *Hiryū*.

In July 1941 we participated in the Buin operation, and after that we went back to Japan. Between July and late November we had unified training as one fighting unit, rather than individual groups. We did this flying from land bases, except for take off and landing training, which was done from the carrier. As for myself, I did torpedo training every day. During training nobody thought that we would one day fight America. As a member of a group of eight airplanes which were selected from the carrier *Hiryū*, we did training over Nishikie Harbor, in Kagoshima Prefecture, and our land base was Izumi. Finally, we did nighttime torpedo training at Toyogo waterway (or canal) against a battleship fleet. At Kinko Bay the target always stayed in the same position, but in the Bungo Channel the target was always floating or moving at night.

A wartime picture of the dashing young Taisuke Maruyama in his flying gear. He is wearing a lightweight "summer" flight suit and a fur-lined flight helmet. (Maruyama Collection)

Pearl Harbor

I was in the first wave attack group, which had 183 airplanes, and out of that group there were forty Type 97 *kankō* armed with torpedoes.[160] Lieutenant Hirata Matsumura was the leader of my group of Type 97s. I was aboard a torpedo bomber from the carrier *Hiryū*. My partners for the Pearl Harbor attack were PO1c Hachirō Sugimoto (pilot) and Sea1c Masateru Fujiyama (radioman/rear gunner). Unfortunately, Sugimoto-san died during the Battle of Midway on 4 June 1942, during the second strike mission against the carrier *Yorktown*. Fujiyama-san died on 8 March 1945. I believe our airplane torpedoed the battleship *Oklahoma*.[161] During this mission I was a little nervous, but confident in my skills, which were sharpened in the intense training we did. Because of this I was able to accomplish my duty calmly. I felt that it was the enlisted man's purpose to accomplish his duty, so even if he died in the war, it was something honorable. Since I was young I never worried whether I would live or die.

At 0615 I took off from my carrier, and after my airplane joined the formation, circled over our fleet and headed towards Pearl Harbor. We were 230 miles, directly north of Oahu, and flew at an attack altitude of 3,000 meters (9,842 feet).[162] The weather was sunny, but there were some scattered clouds. Below the clouds I saw some whitecaps on the waves and confirmed the shape of the island of Oahu. My aircraft was above the north end of the island, Kahuku Point, which was located on the northern tip. We set our direction towards the west side of the island and received the overall commander's message "To. To. To.," which meant that every airplane should attack. Next we went to the south, gradually lowering our altitude, and headed toward the entrance of Pearl Harbor. At this time I could see a group of battleships moored alongside Ford Island.

Due to miscommunication between our pilots the attack sequence was in utter confusion. All of our aircraft were trying to attack at the same time. The other airplanes were supposed to wait for us to attack first, but they didn't. Because of a previous attack run by other Type 97s, I could see a lot of water columns going up near the battleships. The targets of our group of eight *Hiryū* Type 97 *kankō* were the battleships *West Virginia* and *Oklahoma*. At the entrance of the harbor there was a cruiser class ship anchored, and my aircraft passed over that ship at low altitude. On that ship American sailors were looking at us, dumbfounded. The row of battleships was approaching, and my altitude was 20 meters (66 feet). I aimed at the *Oklahoma* and then dropped the torpedo. Coming from my target ship was anti-aircraft fire, but my aircraft escaped and avoided the enemy fire. After this my torpedo hit the *Oklahoma*, which I later confirmed after seeing the water column (from above). Lastly, we went to the designated rendezvous spot and met up with several other aircraft. We congratulated each other on our successful mission by waving to our comrades in the other aircraft. Once I returned to the *Hiryū*, I felt relieved that I had accomplished the assignment given to me.

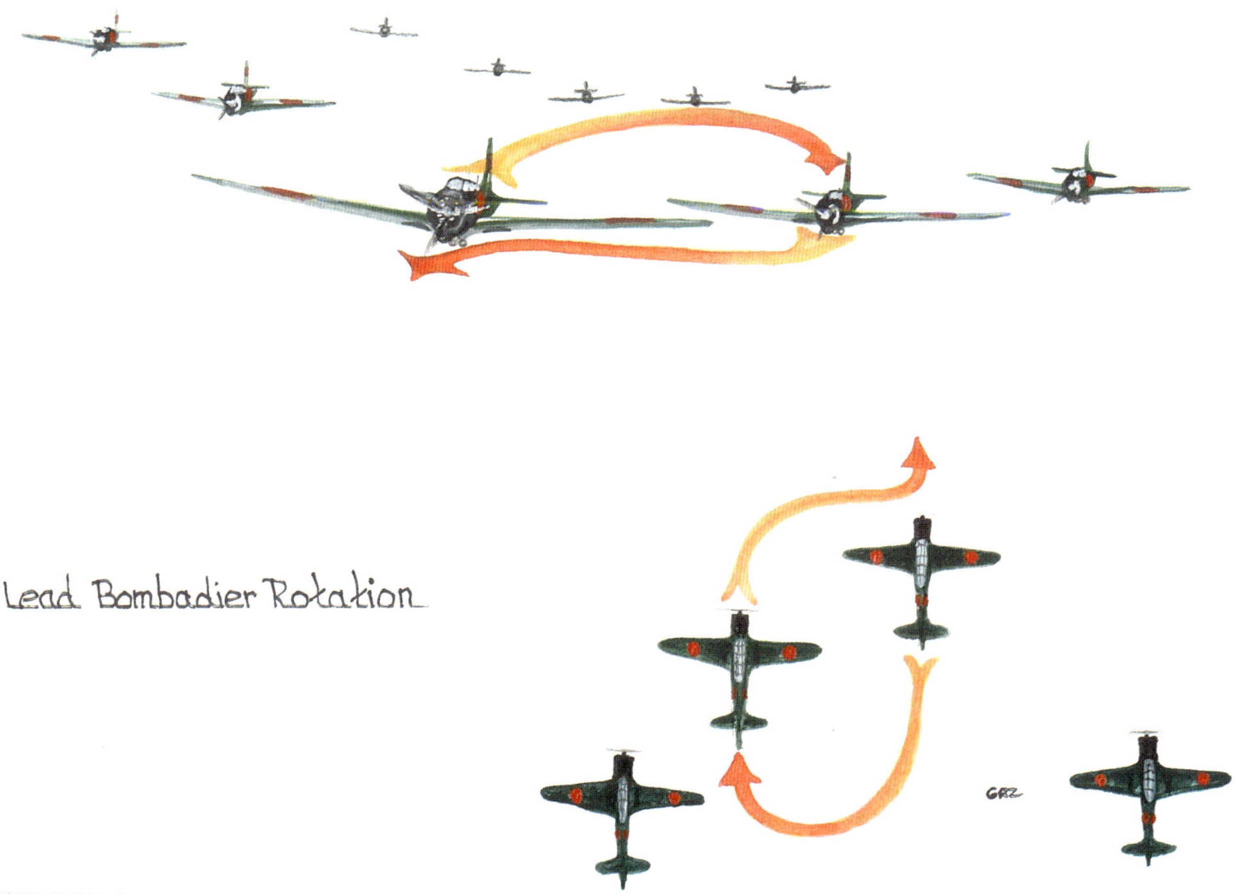

An illustration of the typical level-bombing technique utilized by *kankō* airmen during the war. (George Zielinski A.G.P.)

Port Darwin Attack

On 19 February 1942 a Japanese Task Force, comprised of the First and Second Carrier Divisions, attacked Port Darwin, Australia. The target was the harbor facilities. My Type 97 carrier attack plane was armed with an 800 kilogram land-based bomb. For this mission we did level-bombing. Anti-aircraft shells exploded near our formation, and it caused my airplane to swerve up and down, and also left to right. Still, our bombing was successful, and every airplane returned safely to our carrier.

Level-Bombing Technique

In the Japanese Navy Air Force, here is how level bombing was done. The aviators in the lead aircraft normally weren't the best skilled of our group; usually the pilot and bombardier in the second aircraft were the most proficient. While looking at the target with his bombsight, the bombardier would direct the pilot by using intricate change in tone, volume, and intonation to guide him. Doing this properly was vital to the success of the mission. For example, when a group of Type 97s did level bombing, the plane with the commanding officer aboard was not the aircraft with the best pilot and bombardier in the group. When the attack was being done, the leading aircraft (with the commanding officer) switched positions with the second aircraft (with the best pilot and bombardier from our group), and then we commenced our bomb run. On the Type 97 *kankō* that took control in the bomb run, the radioman raised a flag once the bombs were dropped. This occurred after the verbal signal of *Tei*, and then all of the aircraft in the group dropped their bombs. When all of this was flawlessly done, our bombs hit the target in an area that was a small inverted triangle.

The Battle of Midway

At 0430 my aircraft took off from the carrier *Hiryū*, armed with an 800 kilogram bomb. The target of our attack would be an anti-aircraft battery located on Sand Island, and was part of Midway Atoll. We did level bombing from an altitude of 3,000 meters (9,842 feet), and my aircraft was part of a group of eighteen Type 97 carrier attack planes. The commander of the Type 97s was Lieutenant Jōichi Tomonaga. We were escorted by nine Type 0 *kansen*, and the commander was Lieutenant Yasuhiro Shigematsu. In total, the first wave attack group consisted of thirty-six Type 99 *kanbaku* from *Akagi* and *Kaga*. There also were thirty-six Type 97s and thirty-six Zero fighters. I was in the latter group. In total there were 108 airplanes, and the overall commander was Lieutenant Jōichi Tomonaga.

Enemy Brewster Buffalo and Grumman F4F Wildcat fighters, which were flying from the Midway Atoll, attacked our group. During the attack I saw two *Hiryū* Type 97 *kankō* get shot down by the enemy fighters. Nevertheless, our Type 0 carrier fighters shot down several enemy airplanes. While we were dropping our bombs the anti-aircraft fire was accurate and intense. Anti-aircraft

A Brewster F2A-3 "Buffalo" fighter in flight. Midway Atoll's heroic Marine aviators suffered heavy losses flying this aircraft in combat against the nimble Mitsubishi A6M2 Zero fighter. (NA)

shells tore through our formation, and I could feel the wind blast from the explosions. I saw *shōtaichō* PO1c Sakamoto's aircraft blow up in the air, and another aircraft force-landed in the water.

Maruyama's group was engaged by aviators from Marine Fighting Squadron 221 (VMF-221), who flew eighteen of the infamous Brewster F2A-3 Buffalo and six Grumman F4F-3 Wildcat fighters at 0600.[163] *However, the F2A-3 fighter flown by Second Lieutenant Charles S. Hughes had engine problems, so he returned and didn't engage the enemy.*[164] *This initial group of twenty-three airplanes defending the island were later joined by two F4F-3 Wildcats flown by Captain Francis P. McCarthy and Second Lieutenant Roy A. Corry, who had just returned from their early morning patrol mission. They landed at 0615 and took off ten minutes later to join the other USMC aviators who were fighting against the incoming Japanese aerial armada.*[165]

The defenders met the group of enemy aircraft, which flew in tight "V" formations, but still maintained their original course throughout the American air attacks.[166] *They engaged the combat-seasoned Japanese Navy pilots at 14,000 feet, but after making their initial attacks, all of the divisions were separated and had to fight individually against the attackers.*[167] *Unfortunately, the brave men of VMF-221, flying mostly the outdated F2A-3 Buffalo fighters, simply couldn't handle the more nimble and faster Type 0 carrier fighters and suffered heavy losses.*

The 6 June 1942 VMF-221 After Action report paints a bleak picture of what occurred just two days earlier during the battle. Captain Phillip R. White stated this about his Buffalo fighter, "The F2A-3 is not a combat aeroplane. It is inferior to the planes we were fighting in every respect. The F2A-3 has about the same speed as an Aichi 99 dive-bomber. The Japanese Zero fighter can run circles around the F2A-3. It is my belief that any commander that orders pilots out for combat in a F2A-3 should consider the pilot as lost before leaving the ground." Several of the other survivors who contributed to this report also made similar statements about their negative feelings towards the F2A-3 Buffalo fighter, and felt that the aircraft was not suitable for combat duties.

Out of twenty-five USMC fighters that participated in combat over Midway Atoll, fifteen never came back. As for the heroic men of VMF-221, fourteen perished and four were wounded during this engagement.[168] *Japanese losses for this mission consisted of eleven aircraft lost and fourteen out of commission. Furthermore, an additional twenty-nine planes were damaged but still serviceable. In terms of personnel, there were twenty men lost and two other aviators wounded in action.*[169]

On our way back to the *Hiryū*, our reconnaissance airplane received a message that the enemy mobile fleet was spotted. In the meantime, B-17 bombers and other Midway based aircraft attacked our carrier. Between these attacks I landed on *Hiryū* and immediately started loading torpedoes. I was waiting in the pilot's ready room when *Akagi*, *Kaga*, and *Sōryū* were attacked by enemy aircraft. When I went up to the flight deck, I couldn't believe my eyes when I saw the terrible sight of our damaged ships. "Enemy airplanes in the air" was yelled out by someone on watch. Then I saw an enemy torpedo bomber, which was coming in close,

Aviators from VMF-221 on 14 July 1942 in Hawaii after the Battle of Midway. Front row (left to right): Second Lieutenant William V. Brooks, Second Lieutenant John C. Musselman, Captain Philip R. White, Captain William C. Humbred, Captain Kirk Armistead, Captain Herbert T. Merrill, Captain Marion E. Carl, and Second Lieutenant Clayton M. Canfield. Back row (left to right): Second Lieutenant Darrell D. Irwin, Second Lieutenant Hyde Phillips, Second Lieutenant Roy A. Corry, Jr., and Second Lieutenant Charles M. Kunz. (NA)

Maruyama's carrier *Hiryū* under attack by B-17 bombers, which occurred between 0800-0830 on 4 June 1942. The B-17s didn't score any hits on the carrier. (NHC via Parshall)

get shot down by a Zero fighter. On board the *Kaga* I could see airplanes exploding; soon it became an inferno. Also, in the middle of that, bombs exploded in a chain reaction. *Akagi* was in the same situation when two bombs hit the ship. Nevertheless, the engine itself was still running. However, *Akagi's* rudder was damaged, and it was circling at high speed.

At 1057 the Hiryū *launched eighteen Type 99* kanbaku *and six Type 0* kansen. *The overall commander of this strike was Lieutenant Michio Kobayashi, and the strike group attacked the carrier* Yorktown. *Unfortunately, only two Type 0s and five Type 99s returned to the carrier. An additional Type 0 carrier fighter, which was flown by PO1c Hitoshi Sasaki, ditched, but the pilot was rescued. A total of twenty-nine Japanese Navy aviators died during this mission, including the leader, Lieutenant Kobayashi.*[170] *Kobayashi-san was a well known and highly skilled dive-bomber pilot. He was shot down by fighters who were defending the carrier* Yorktown.

During the first attack wave on the Yorktown *by Type 99s and Zero fighters, the dive-bombers scored three hits on the carrier. Out of the three Type 99s that scored hits, two were shot down just*

A view from *Yorktown's* flight deck after the carrier was hit by three bombs from the dive-bombers' attack. (NA)

after releasing their bombs, while the other went out of control just as the bomb was released. The bomb, which was released from the later Type 99, made a hole in the flight deck ten feet by ten feet, but it was repaired in twenty-five minutes. Nevertheless, it also caused casualties, killing and wounding several men on the ship. The second bomb came from the port side, penetrated the flight deck, and then exploded in the stack. It caused serious damage to the Yorktown's *boilers, which caused the carrier to slow down to about six knots; then, about twenty minutes later, all of the engines stopped. The third bomb went through the starboard side of the No. 1 elevator and exploded on the fourth deck. This caused a fire in the rag stowage space, near the forward gasoline stowage and the magazines. Luckily, the gasoline in this area didn't ignite, because prior to the attack, the gasoline tank compartments were filled with* CO_2*. After repairs had been made to the boilers the engine room said that it would be possible to make 20 knots or better.*[171]

Maruyama-san participated in the second attack mission against the U.S. Navy aircraft carriers. The dashing Lieutenant Jōichi Tomonaga, who led this strike, took off well aware that his Type 97 kankō *had a leaking left wing fuel tank. This fuel tank was damaged when he flew in the morning strike against Midway Atoll, and couldn't be fixed properly prior to take off. Because of this problem Tomonaga-san and his crew, consisting of Ensign Saku Akamatsu (observer) and PO1c Sadamu Murai (radioman/rear gunner), probably wouldn't have enough fuel to make it back to the* Hiryū.[172]

On board my ship *Hiryū*, all of the pilots were lined up next to the bridge. Rear Admiral Tamon Yamaguchi and *Hiryū's* Captain Tomeo Kaku went down to the flight deck, and Yamaguchi-san spoke to us. He said, "There are three enemy carriers; you got that. The *kanbaku-tai* hit one of them, so there are two left. Try to hit a new carrier, which was not damaged, if you can, as a priority. If you do that, we can do a one to one fight." After he said this, he walked across the flight deck and shook hands with each pilot one by one. I could see three of our carriers in flames, and I thought that our group of pilots would surely avenge this. I personally was determined to do this before I took off.

At 1330 I took off with a feeling of desperation after hearing Admiral Yamaguchi's speech. The group of ten Type 97s was commanded by Lieutenant Jōichi Tomonaga and escorted by six Zero fighters. We only had this fighting power left. Tomonaga-san was a graduate of the 59th Term Naval Academy class and an experienced officer, who had combat experience in China. He was open-minded, a good leader, and took good care of his men. After about one hour had passed I saw the wakes of several ships between some scattered clouds and spotted a carrier.

Our leader, Lieutenant Tomonaga, sent a message, "*Zengun totsugeki seyo*!" and the two Type 97 *chūtais* split up and prepared to attack. Soon after this Grumman F4F Wildcat fighters started to attack us. Initially, our aircraft was attacked from the rear and above; then we turned around again. We were attacked again and attempted to escape, but our aircraft was very slow due to the 800 kilogram torpedo. During the third enemy attack our radioman, Sea1c Giichi Hamada, was wounded in the leg. Also, the tail of our aircraft looked like a honeycomb because it was full of holes, and the left fuel tank was leaking very badly. Nevertheless, I didn't

Another view of the *Yorktown* after it was attacked by the Type 99 *kanbaku*. (NA via Wenger)

Lieutenant Jōichi Tomonaga in his dress uniform. (NHC via Parshall)

want to die until I dropped my torpedo, and we continued to press on our attack. At this time we were gradually lowering our altitude and preparing to attack, but the anti-aircraft fire coming from the carrier was intense. We were in the middle of tons of enemy fire but managed not to get shot down. As we came closer to the ship we dropped our torpedo. In total, I believe two torpedoes from our planes hit the carrier *Yorktown*. Luckily the gas leak stopped, and we landed with only a little fuel remaining in our tanks. The *Yorktown* was doomed, and the Japanese submarine I-168 later finished it off.

Due to evasive maneuvering the Yorktown *was able to avoid at least two torpedoes. Nevertheless, Maruyama's group had two successful hits on the already damaged* Yorktown. *The first torpedo hit the port side at about 1443, and the second one shortly thereafter. This caused all power to be lost on the ship, and the rudder was jammed 15 degrees to the left, so the* Yorktown *was dead in the water. Because the* Yorktown's *list steadily increased to 26 degrees, there was a real danger of the carrier capsizing, so Captain Elliot Buckmaster gave the order to abandon ship. The survivors and the wounded personnel then transferred to the destroyers and cruisers nearby.*

The brave crew of the Yorktown *wasn't ready to give up yet, as the damaged carrier didn't sink. So on the morning of 6 June, Captain Buckmaster led a salvage party back to the ship and found the* Yorktown *in the same condition as they left it. The destroyer* Hammann *came along the starboard side of the* Yorktown *and provided water to help fight the fires on the burning carrier. Five additional destroyers (*Balch, Benham, Gwin, Anderson, *and* Monaghan*) also formed an anti-submarine and anti-aircraft screen around the* Yorktown *at a distance of about 2,000 yards, speed 14 knots.*

However, as Maruyama-san mentioned previously, the carrier was ultimately "doomed," as the submarine I-168, commanded by Lieutenant Commander Yahachi Tanabe, went after its wounded

Yorktown after being struck by a second torpedo launched from *Hiryū's* Type 97 *kankō*. (NA)

"prey." After sighting the Yorktown *and its screening ships, he fired four torpedoes at the group. Here is what happened, according to the* Yorktown's *After Action report, "The first torpedo hit* Hammann *approximately amidships and caused her to sink very rapidly. Two torpedoes hit* Yorktown *just below the turn of the bilge at the after end of the island structure. The fourth torpedo passed just astern of the* Yorktown. *Approximately a minute after* Hammann's *stern sank, a terrific explosion occurred, apparently from her depth charges. This explosion killed many* Hammann *and a few* Yorktown *personnel, who were in the water, and caused serious injuries to others from both ships, who were in the water and later rescued."*

The Yorktown *finally went under at 0501 on the morning of 7 June after the heroic efforts by the crew to save the carrier.*[173] *On board the carrier, fifty-seven enlisted men (no officers) died during the battle, and the ship's airmen losses consisted of sixteen officers and fourteen enlisted men (including Lieutenant Commander Donald A. Lovelace of VF-3, when he first came on board, near Pearl Harbor). The casualties for the destroyer* Hammann *were ten officers and seventy-four men.*[174]

After returning to *Hiryū* I was so exhausted. Because our Type 97 *kankō* was the last aircraft to return to the carrier, I told *hikōchō* Commander Susumu Kawaguchi about the attack. I also said that I took a picture and asked for it to be developed soon. The radioman of my plane, Sea1c Giichi Hamada, was bloody, but his injuries were not life threatening. However, it was painful to see him being carried to the sick bay. Out of the six Type 0s that escorted us, only three returned to our carrier. As for the Type 97s, five airplanes didn't come back from the mission, including the one piloted by Lieutenant Jōichi Tomonaga and his crew. This made me very depressed. At that time, the five remaining Type 99 *kanbaku* and ten Type 0 *kansen* were being prepared for a third wave attack. However, it seemed that we also would use the surviving Type 97s. There were only five useable Type 97 *kankō*, but my plane was not flyable.

While Maruyama-san was trying to recuperate from an exhausting day of combat, his carrier, the Hiryū, *came under attack by SBD Dauntless dive-bombers, which scored four direct hits with 1,000 pound bombs. Three of the bombs landed in a row on the forward third section of the flight deck, and the fourth one hit amidships near the bridge.*[175] *This last 1,000 pound bomb literally uplifted the front elevator, which caused it to stand up vertically, like a wall. In all, the* Hiryū, *just like the other three Japanese carriers (*Akagi, Kaga, *and* Sōryū*), was now doomed.*

I tried to relax in the pilot's ready room, and it looked like we were going to start fighting again, upon the completion of the maintenance work. Finally, at 1700 rice balls were served to the people who flew missions earlier in the day. Suddenly, at 1704 I heard a trumpet blast, which indicated that we should get ready for an enemy air attack because the aircraft were approaching (our

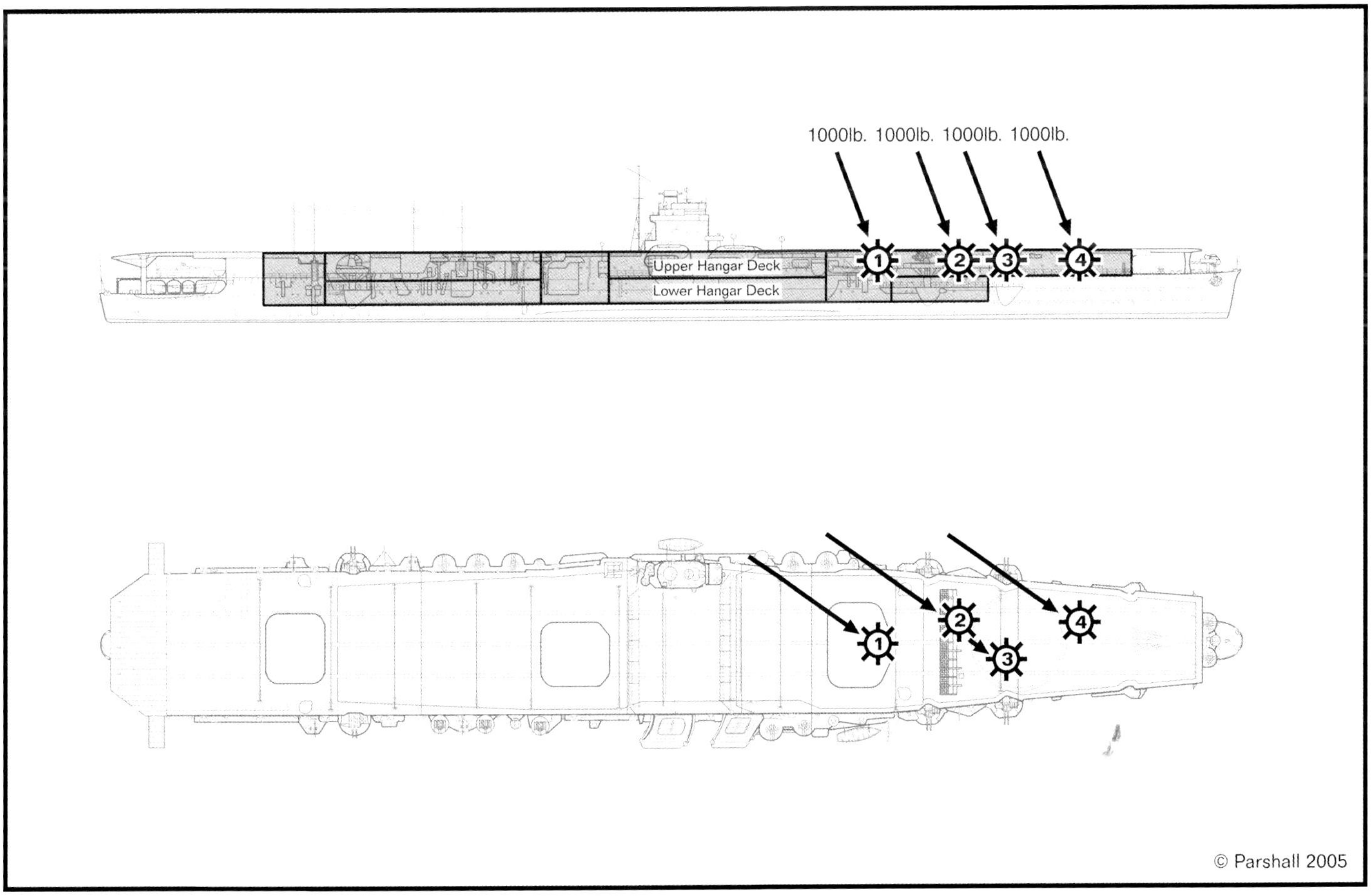

The hit locations on *Hiryū* during the Battle of Midway. (Jonathan Parshall)

ship). After this, the *Hiryū* swerved hard to avoid the enemy attack. However, at the same time I heard bombs smashing into our carrier and the lights went out. I was worried about the mechanics in the hangar. The ready room was next to the hangar, and smoke from the fire drifted into our room, so I had a difficult time breathing.

Meanwhile, the fire in the hangar became more and more intense. Then, our own bombs and torpedoes exploded in a chain reaction. There also were very strong vibrations, which sounded like the ship was split into two parts. Those intense vibrations continued on and on. The ready room was pitch black and I was groping my way out. Luckily, I was able to go out on the deck. At this time I saw the dividing wall of the rear hangar on fire. Water couldn't be used from the extinguishing pump because the water propulsion line was cut (during the attack). So several people tried to use seawater, but it vaporized immediately.

I was surprised to see a military doctor was doing surgeries without anesthetic on one corner of the rear deck. Some men who lost their hands or legs were carried to the rear deck, and there was nothing we could do to extinguish the fires. When I saw the sun through the smoke on the deck it looked red, which made me miserable. I felt it was like a castle being burned, once the battle was lost, back in the samurai days. There also were men still working in the engine room, which was under the hangar. They persevered in the heat and continued to work, even under such daunting conditions. In the end, however, contact was lost, and at 2300 the *Hiryū* was "dead" in the water with no power.

Our destroyers *Kazagumo* and *Furikaze* arrived, and because of their support the fires on the *Hiryū* started to subside. The next morning at 0230 all of us on board were ordered to gather on the flight deck. Half of the deck was completely burned away, and because the edges remained, it looked like a huge casket. Also, in the pockets along the flight deck there were charred bodies of the men who had manned the machine guns. They were hit by the blast from the bombs. All around me I could smell burned flesh. However, what surprised me most was a big wall that was standing upright in front of the bridge area. When I looked more carefully at it, I realized this wall was actually part of the front elevator.

After this, at 0250 Captain Tomeo Kaku and Rear Admiral Tamon Yamaguchi praised the men on board for fighting so bravely during the battle. Rear Admiral Yamaguchi said that we should make an effort to rebuild the Navy. Then, we paid our respects to the Imperial Palace and said "Emperor Bonzai" three times. After the order was given to abandon ship we were transferred to a destroyer. *Hiryū* was later scuttled by a torpedo from the destroyer *Makigumo*.[176] Sadly, Rear Admiral Yamaguchi and Captain Tomeo Kaku shared the same destiny as the ship. On board the destroyer

A well-known image of the burning *Hiryū* taken on the morning of 5 June 1942 by a *Hōshō* Type 96 carrier attack plane. (NHC via Parshall)

a trumpet played "*Kuni no Shizume*" (The Soothing of a Nation) while we clasped our hands together and said a final goodbye to our carrier. The Japanese Navy's losses were immense during the Battle of Midway, and it was the turning point of the Pacific War.

Action over Guadalcanal Island

After the Battle of Midway and the loss of his carrier Hiryū, *Maruyama-san transferred to the carrier* Hiyō *and participated in a disastrous attack on American shipping off Lunga (Guadalcanal Island) on 17 October 1942. He was very lucky to survive this mission, but many of his comrades weren't so fortunate. A comprehensive account of this mission can be found in Lieutenant (junior grade) Kaname Harada's story in this book. A few days after the 17 October mission fire broke out in the generator room, causing considerable damage to the condenser, and the carrier could only make 16 knots.*[177] *Because of this, the* Hiyō *went to Truk Island for repairs, while some of the pilots (including Maruyama-san) transferred to the carrier* Junyō.

The Battle of Santa Cruz

On 26 October 1942 we took off at 1306 from the carrier *Junyō*, and our group attacked the carrier *Hornet*. Our group consisted of seven Type 97 carrier attack planes and eight escorting Zero fighters (five *Junyō*, two *Zuikaku*, and one *Zuihō*).[178] The overall strike leader and commander of the Type 97s was Lieutenant Yoshiaki Irikiin, while the Zeros were led by Lieutenant Ayao Shirane (from the carrier *Zuikaku*). At the time of our attack, the *Hornet* had already been damaged by a previous group of Japanese airplanes, and it was being pulled by the cruiser *Northampton* at a speed of 10 knots. At that time there were no enemy fighters in the air. Before our torpedoes penetrated the ship the cruiser released the tow rope. In the middle of intense anti-aircraft fire we commenced our attack. The group of Type 97s from *Junyō* (including seven *kankō*, six of which carried torpedoes) were led by Lieutenant Irikiin, and carried out a devastating attack against the *Hornet* from the starboard side. Sadly, Irikiin's Type 97 was barraged by heavy anti-aircraft fire and fell into the sea nearby.

Out of my group of Type 97s, three torpedoes hit the *Hornet* and it later sunk.[179] I recall that some of our airplanes were shot down by anti-aircraft fire, but not by enemy fighters. The *Hornet* would later be scuttled by torpedoes from the Japanese destroyers *Akigumo* and *Makigumo*. The leader of the torpedo group, Lieutenant Yoshiaki Irikiin, and one additional Type 97 (flown by WO Takeo Yokoyama) were lost. Furthermore, two additional Zeros (piloted by PO1c Kiyonobu Suzuki and Sea2c Kiyoshi Nakamoto) didn't come back. Out of the surviving six Type 0 carrier fighters, three later had to ditch.[180]

Another view of *Hiryū* taken on 5 June that clearly shows some of the damage inflicted on Maruyama's carrier. (NHC via Parshall)

Navy Days from 1943 until 1945

I became a flight instructor of the Tainan *Kōkūtai* on 27 June 1943. I did this job until joining the 501 *Hikōtai* (K-501) on 23 October 1944. We flew the Yokosuka *Ginga* (Allied code-name "Frances") for combat missions. On 25 December 1944 we bombed Isley Field (where the B-29 bombers were based) on Saipan Island.

As Maruyama-san mentions, on the night of 25 December 1944 his group K-501, consisting of five Yokosuka P1Y "Ginga" (land-based bombers) and members of the 7th Sentai *(Imperial Japanese Army Air Group), which were flying Mitsubishi Ki-67 bombers, attacked Isley Field, Saipan.*[181] *In the fall of 1944 Isley Field was the home of the 73rd Bomb Wing and their Boeing B-29 Superfortress bombers, which would ultimately do bombing missions against targets on the Japanese mainland. During this time period K-501 was based at Katori, Japan, but for this mission they were using Iwo Jima as a forward air field.*[182] *The Japanese strike group destroyed one B-29 bomber, damaged three B-29s beyond repair, and caused minor damage to an additional eleven bombers.*[183]

Nevertheless, PO1c Hideyoshi Shimoyoshi and the leader of K-501, Lieutenant Commander Hideo Morimoto, failed to return. Morimoto's plane force-landed in the water 300 nautical miles, 150 degrees off Iwo Jima, and everyone on board perished. Morimoto-san had just become the leader of K-501 on 14 November 1944.[184]

In 1945 K-501 was based at Kanoya, then transferred to Miyazaki (both on the Japanese mainland). They operated from Miyazaki Air Base, while doing attack missions against American shipping off Okinawa. During this time the group also had a detachment at Miho, Japan. Then, in early July 1945 the group moved to Taisha, Japan, and was there until the end of the war.[185]

The Last Day of the War

I was at Taisha Air Base (in Shimane Prefecture) when the war ended. My final rank was ensign, and I flew about 3,500 hours in the Imperial Japanese Navy Air Force. When the fighting had finally stopped, I was overcome by the hollowness and fruitlessness of the war. I hope that someday there will be a world where people of all nations can understand each other and live together in peace.

Postwar

In his postwar years he managed a timber company and raised his family. Maruyama-san also participated in several World War II documentaries and attended several symposiums (as a veteran panelist) in the United States. The symposiums included one at the National Museum of Naval Aviation (Pensacola, Florida), and another at the National Museum of the Pacific War (Fredericksburg, Texas).

Maruyama-san (seated on the far right) with two of his buddies at a veterans' reunion in Japan. (Maruyama Collection)

Maintenance PO1c Kaname Shimoyama

"I kept thinking to myself, why are we doing this?"

I heard about Shimoyama-san through a veteran friend who subsequently introduced me. Initially, Shimoyama-san didn't respond to any of my letters until I asked my veteran friend to call him again. I was really excited to finally meet an aviation-related mechanic who served on board an aircraft carrier with the Imperial Japanese Navy. The ex-mechanic lives in Kashiwa, Chiba, which is about a one hour drive from central Tokyo. He is fit, has a dark complexion, and gray thinning hair, which is parted straight back. Shimoyama-san served on the carrier Akagi *from Pearl Harbor until it sank at Midway. He later became a flight engineer for the* Jinrai Butai, *the Thunder God Corps.*[186] *His group participated in* tokkō *missions using the Mitsubishi Type 1 "Betty" bomber mothership, which carried the* Ohka *suicide rocket planes.*[187]

Shimoyama's Early Days

I was born on 27 November 1920, in Mishima Village, which is part of Shizuoka Prefecture. In January 1941 I joined the Navy at Yokosuka to be an aircraft mechanic. The course lasted only three months; then I went to Hyakurigahara to do maintenance-related work on aircraft. Finally, I joined the carrier *Akagi* as a Type 97 *kankō* mechanic.

Pearl Harbor

I worked as a torpedo specialist on *Akagi*. Kagoshima Bay was similar to Pearl Harbor, so it was an ideal place to practice for an attack on Oahu. Pearl Harbor was very shallow in depth, so if we used the "old style" torpedo, it would simply stick into the bottom of the ocean. During training we did several things to overcome this potential problem. The pilots practiced dropping torpedoes at different angles. We also created a "new" torpedo with a plywood tail to allow for shallow depth during an actual mission. As a result of this training we were able to attack Pearl Harbor successfully. Furthermore, we practiced refueling our ships, which we needed to do for a journey to Hawaii.

A group photo of *Akagi's* aircraft mechanics. (Shimoyama Collection)

Veteran Kaname Shimoyama when he was a flight engineer on a Mitsubishi Type 1 *Rikkō* (Allied code name "Betty") bomber. (Shimoyama Collection)

Above: The carrier *Akagi* anchored in Hitokappu Bay. (*Maru* magazine via Wenger) Below: *Akagi's* aviators (foreground) and gun crews (right) on the flight deck while anchored in Hitokappu Bay. (*Maru* magazine via Wenger)

During all this training I kept thinking to myself, why are we doing this? After this *Akagi* went to Saeki Bay, and many high-ranking Navy officers came on board our carrier. Again, I was wondering, why are so many high-ranking officers coming aboard *Akagi*? I also was issued both cold and warm weather gear, which was strange. Finally, our crew loaded a large amount of supplies on our carrier, which again was puzzling.

Personally, I felt that this training seemed very different from my previous training, and kept asking myself, why are we doing all this? Normally, when you had training you knew the purpose for it. Our carrier arrived at Etorofu Island, in Hitokappu Bay, on 21 November at 0800. At that time we were told what our mission was all about, and that Japan was going to beat America.[188] I really felt tense after hearing this, because I thought that it was impossible to win a war against the United States.

By the end of 1941 Japan already had exhausted its resources in China, so why start another war against America? If a war with America would be successful, then it would've been okay, but we were really not sure if we could even beat the United States. Nevertheless, I still thought that it was a good chance to do something about the frustration that Japan had because our country was constantly being pressured by America to do things that we didn't want to do. Deep down I had mixed feelings about starting a war with the United States, but I thought that a very big event was going to happen. We were surprised that Japan was going to fight America.

During our trip the waves were terribly rough. I also heard that a Russian fishing boat was spotted, but we didn't want to sink it, because our chance of doing a surprise attack might be lost. There was a final refueling during the last leg of our trip before we turned ninety degrees towards Hawaii, and the wind finally became calm. I felt that our large formation of ships was state of the art and the most powerful fleet in the world.

The war began with the United States on 7 December 1941 and, before dawn, we prepared our aircraft for the attack. We lined up the aircraft three at a time; then they took off one by one. The flight deck was short, so we tried to get enough space for all the aircraft to take off. First we lined up the Zero fighters, which could still take off easily even with their belly tanks, then the Type 97 *kankō* (level-bombers), and lastly, the Type 97s armed with torpedoes. At that time I was assigned to remove the wheel chocks before the aircraft took off. Junior mechanics were usually assigned to do this job. When someone signaled to remove the wheel chucks, I grabbed them and escaped to the walkway along the flight deck. When aircraft took off I was hit by extraordinary blasts of wind, so I had to hold on to something. I was glad to do this job and tried my best.

Our pilots were well trained, so everything went according to plan. Every airplane on *Akagi* took off without problems, then went into a large formation and circled once over our carrier. When this happened we spontaneously clapped our hands and waved to them from the walkway along the side of the flight deck. During the first wave attack we didn't have any casualties, so our aviators were fortunate. However, during the second wave the enemy was waiting for us, so we suffered some casualties. After the Pearl Harbor attack, during landing, one of the Type 97s had a landing gear failure, so about twenty of us pushed that airplane overboard because other aircraft needed to land. I heard that the United States didn't expect our attack, but I still felt that Japan wanted to fight a fair war.

Action after Pearl Harbor

After returning from Hawaii our carrier docked at Yokosuka. Then we participated in operations in the Indian Ocean. I think we shouldn't have gone to the Indian Ocean. We should have attacked Hawaii again and finished off the American forces there. After the successful Pearl Harbor attack, we had the feeling that we could attack the enemy again very easily.

Daily Life on board *Akagi*

The carrier *Akagi* was not a new design, but it was remodeled from a battlecruiser hull. However, because of that the carrier had a lot of living quarters inside. Later carriers, such as the *Zuikaku*, had smaller living quarters, but other areas of the ship were larger in size. I personally felt that Vice-Admiral Chūichi Nagumo chose *Akagi* as his flagship because of the large living quarters. It also had three big guns on both sides, which I thought were useless. Our carrier also was slower than the *Sōryū* and *Hiryū*, which were designed as carriers and did 32 knots, whereas our carrier went only 27-28 knots. If you were in the stern section of our ship, the vibrations from the screws were extraordinary, and it was really hard to remain there. The vibration was really bad when our carrier was trying to escape in a "snake motion" at top speed during the Battle of Midway. It also was during these attacks that I clearly saw the faces of the American pilots. I felt they had guts and were very patriotic. As for my duties on *Akagi*, I initially did torpedo-related maintenance work before becoming the steward of Lieutenant (junior grade) Keizō Ōbuchi. I did things for him such as doing the laundry and serving food. Nevertheless, because I did this job I was able to get a lot of information from the officers.

The Battle of Midway

Prior to the Midway operation, when I was in Yokosuka, even Japanese civilians knew that we were going to attack; but it was supposed to be a secret. Because of the success that we had in Hawaii, Japan was not as careful as it should have been. We also were too confident. This was a sharp contrast to our Hawaii operation, when even people like me didn't know what was going to happen. In the beginning of the battle, I felt that our pilots were very confident because they were very skilled and had a lot of success in battle during the first six months of 1942.

After our air attack on Midway Atoll, Lieutenant Jōichi Tomonaga, the leader of the strike, sent a report stating that we needed to do a second wave attack. Because of this, on board *Akagi* we had to switch our torpedoes to bombs on the aircraft, which were used to attack land-based targets. However, at that time we were not sure if there was an enemy carrier in the area. Later, a report came in that there were several enemy carriers in the area, which made a big difference in the final outcome of the battle. The armament used to attack land-based targets was different

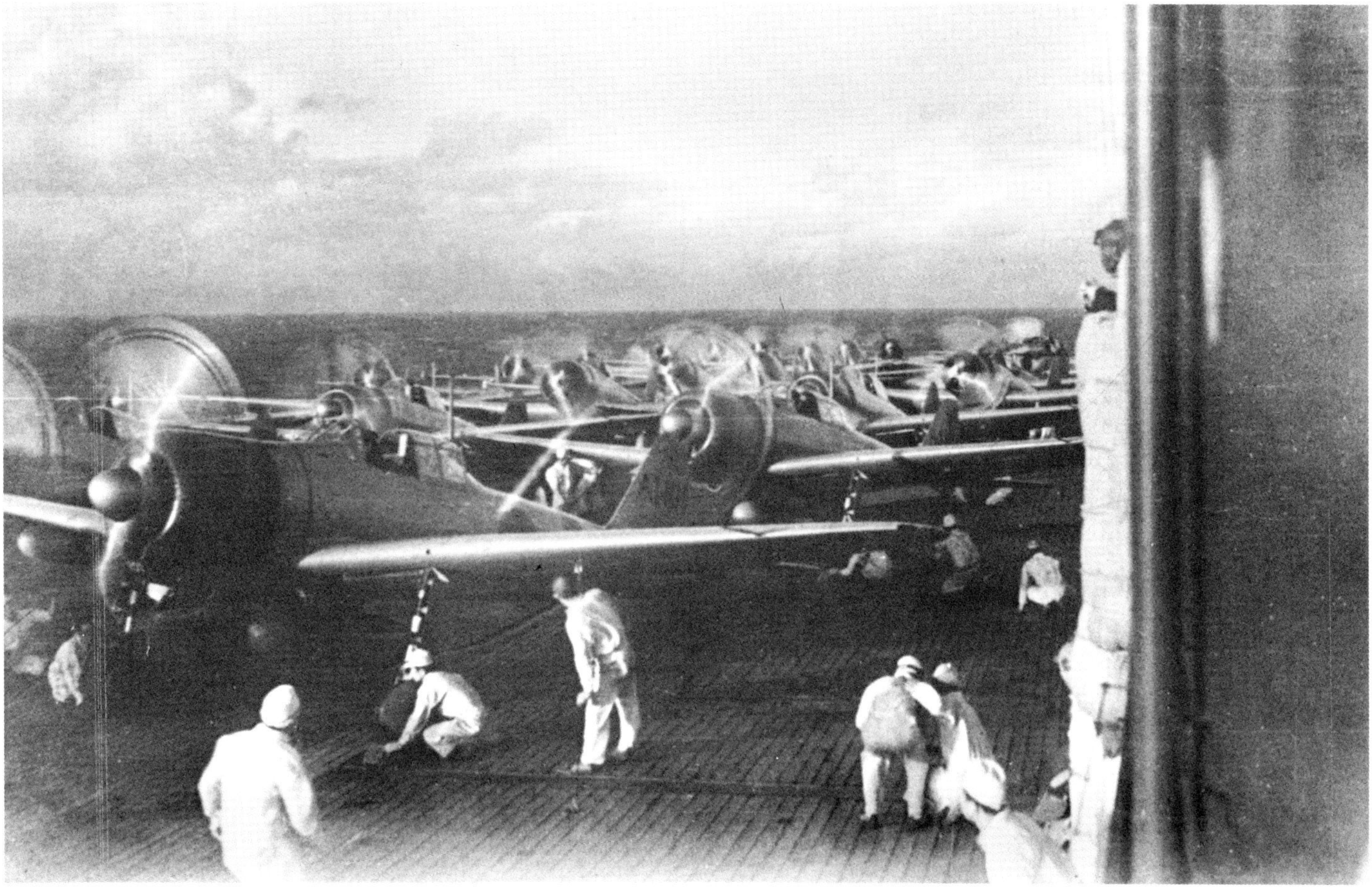

Above: *Akagi's* second wave strike aircraft just prior to take off. (Makiel Collection via Wenger) Below: The view that Shimoyama may have seen during the take off of the second wave on *Akagi*. Note the walkways, or "pockets," as the veterans call them, along the flight deck. (Makiel Collection via Wenger)

from those used to attack ships. Because of this, after the enemy carriers were found we had to change our aircraft armament once again back to torpedoes. There was utter confusion on *Akagi*; it would have been much easier to leave our aircraft as is. Inside our hangar there was very little room, and it was very hard to do this job. Our torpedoes also were very heavy and were manually loaded on our aircraft. In general, there were two groups of men; one group worked on the torpedoes, while the other group had the specific job of loading the torpedoes on the aircraft. When I looked at all this confusion, even though I was a low-ranking person, I thought, is it really wise to be doing this? In my opinion, prior to Midway Japanese leaders were overconfident and underestimated the difficulty of fighting a war against the United States.

In general, the winner of a carrier-based battle is the one who attacks first. I heard that the American dive-bombers attacked while we were trying to take off, which was very bad. They must have known when it was a good time to attack us. At that time I was in the torpedo adjusting room near the walkway (below the flight deck). I did see the enemy torpedo bombers trying to attack us, but not the dive-bombers. I was almost killed during the attack because the bomb penetrated the flight deck and I couldn't escape. Our bombs and torpedoes were exploding one after another in the hangar, so it was a very dangerous place. Inside the hangar, fueled and armed aircraft began to explode, one after another. It all happened so quickly. The hangar was very dark, but engulfed in a sea of fire. After hearing these explosions I thought that our carrier would sink at any moment. I saw some men who could not keep their composure and they lost all self control. They just went crazy and tried to escape. However, in my case I felt calm, because I knew that it was war, and I could die at any moment. Because of this, I was able to see everything in a very "level-headed" manner.

We were trapped in the torpedo adjusting room, which was pitch black. However, in the darkness my small group leader, Maintenance PO1c Jirō Hosokawa, kept on yelling "Porthole, Porthole, Porthole!" After hearing this I reached toward the porthole and desperately tried to turn the screw to open it. Even today, I can't forget the helpless feeling that I had during this moment. Once I opened the porthole, I put my face outside and fell down on the walkway as if I was pushed. The linoleum floor of the walkway was very hot, but I used it to go to the stern section. Luckily *Akagi* didn't sink quickly, but I still saw countless dead bodies in the stern section of our carrier.

I waited for other men to come out of the torpedo adjusting room, but I couldn't see anyone else and became worried. Suddenly, I saw a man that looked like a ghost, and his name was Muramatsu-san. His uniform was torn in many places, and both of his hands were dangling down. I put my hands on his arms and said, "You are saved." However when I did this, his skin peeled off his body like a rotten apple. When I asked him what happened to Maintenance PO1c Hosokawa, he said, "I was the last one to get out." Then there was a big explosion, and Muramatsu-san and I never saw each other again until after the war, at an *Akagi* veterans' meeting. I got burned around my neck when I squeezed through the porthole, but my wounds were not very bad. Fortunately, I was in one of the earliest groups of people to be rescued by a nearby destroyer.

After being rescued by the destroyer, I heard that *Akagi* would be scuttled by our torpedoes. At that time it was dark and our carrier was on fire. About two hours later it was hit by our own torpedoes, and a great column of fire shot up into the air; then *Akagi* went down. I remember the carrier going down in one piece and not breaking in half. It was painful seeing our ship sunk by our own

A group of 721 *Kōkūtai* pilots waiting to fly a mission. Note the Mitsubishi Type 1 bomber with the *Ohka* mounted underneath the aircraft. This unit was the first one that used the *Ohka*. (Shimoyama Collection)

Shimoyama-san as a member of the *Jinrai Butai* ("Thunder Gods"), a group that did suicide attacks using the *Ohka*, a rocket-powered glider, against Allied ships. The veteran was lucky to survive the war, because aviators used to fly the Mitsubishi Type 1 "Betty" bombers (which carried the *Ohka*) mounted on the bellies of the aircraft to the target suffered heavy losses because they were easy prey for Allied fighters. The back of this original picture had a Japanese poem written by Kaname Shimoyama, possibly because he didn't think he would survive the war. (Shimoyama Collection)

torpedoes. However, I felt relieved because I survived the battle. Since I hadn't eaten since the morning I felt confused mentally, but after seeing *Akagi* sink, I became very emotional. I was burned near my ears while escaping through the porthole, but it was not serious enough for hospitalization. After this I transferred to the battleship *Mutsu* and went back to Hashira Jima on the Japanese mainland.[189] When I arrived back in Japan, I was ordered to go to Kanoya Air Base for about one month, because the Navy didn't want the public to find out about our losses during the Battle of Midway.

Navy Days after Midway

After the Battle of Midway I worked as a Zero fighter mechanic at Tomitaka Air Base (in Miyazaki Prefecture). In March 1944 I took a three month mechanic training course, then took additional courses to be a flight engineer or flying mechanic.[190] Upon graduation I flew as a member of a transport unit at Kisarazu Air Base. My final assignment was with the *Jinrai Butai*, but the war ended before I could do my *tokkō* mission. I was a flight engineer on the Mitsubishi Type 1 bomber "mother" ship, which carried the *Ohka*, but never flew a combat mission doing this job.

The End of the War

When the war ended I was at Komatsu Air Base (in Ishikawa Prefecture). After Japan surrendered, I felt that we fought a stupid war, but I survived. I was one of those men who could have been ordered to do a *tokkō* mission. Nevertheless, those types of attacks were usually meaningless. For example, in March 1945 a large group of *tokkō* pilots were almost completely annihilated and had very little success. The *Ohka* was a very dumb weapon, and it didn't have much effect during the war. My final rank in the Imperial Japanese Navy was maintenance petty officer first class. In my postwar years I joined the Self-Defense Force as a mechanic, then worked for Japan Airlines. I retired last year, but now own a tea shop.

Reflections

As I look back on the Battle of Midway, my small group leader, Maintenance PO1c Jirō Hosokawa, saved my life when he said "Porthole, Porthole, Porthole!" I thought about this long after the war and will never forget it. My comrade Muramatsu-san and I would not be alive today if he didn't say that word. Maintenance PO1c Hosokawa also told me to go first, and later died in the torpedo

Kaname Shimoyama at the train station near his home in Kashiwa, Chiba, in Japan. (Werneth)

adjustment room. Right after I escaped through the porthole there was an explosion; however, I am not sure when he died because of the confusion. In 1955 I visited Hosokawa's home and grave; I wanted to do this for a long time. Long after the war ended, I also decided to create a stone marker as a memorial for future generations, and it is dedicated to Jirō Hosokawa to console his soul.[191] Muramatsu-san and I would not have survived the Battle of Midway without his help.

I feel there are many types of relationships between people. In some relationships, a person who is in a higher position may try to use his authority for his own benefit. Other relationships are based on love. Today we live in a world where sometimes one person tries to exploit others. It would be great if a story like this can help young people who don't know how to live their lives.

Ensign Hideo Honma

"I really wanted to sacrifice my life and make a contribution to my nation."

While I was doing research in Japan, I wanted to interview a Type 97 kankō *pilot that served on the carrier* Zuikaku *and participated in the Pearl Harbor attack. My veteran buddy, Haruo Yoshino, recommended his comrade Hideo Honma, who was in the same Navy training class. Remarkably, Honma-san was a "forgotten" veteran who was never interviewed, even by Japanese historians. After an introduction to Honma-san by our mutual friend Haruo Yoshino we decided upon an interview date. Honma's home was located in Iwaki City (Fukushima Prefecture), in a rural part of Japan. Iwaki City is about two hours from Tokyo, but well worth the visit.*

My first impression of the aging veteran was that he was very sharp and talkative. Honma-san also seemed very happy that a younger person was interested in learning more about the war. During our visit, the veteran Navy pilot was still getting over the recent passing of his wife and felt that he "would die soon," so it was important that we spoke to him that afternoon. Honma-san went out of his way to make sure my translator "Hammer" and I were comfortable in his home, and served us several different food dishes, snacks, and drinks.

Honma's Early Days

I was born on 27 January 1922, in Niigata Prefecture. We had a large family: I had five sisters and three younger brothers. Everyone is still alive, and we meet together once a year. Sadly, my mother died just when I entered the Navy, and my father passed away one year later. After my parents died, our family split up and moved in with other relatives, who lived in many different places in Japan. For example, one of my sisters went to Manchuria and became a teacher. After the war I had to find my brothers and sisters individually, but I was able to locate everyone.

Honma-san Joins the Navy

Since I was a young boy, I always wanted to become a pilot. When I was a middle school student, a Navy officer visited my school, so I thought by joining the Navy my dream could come true. Since none of my family members served in the Japanese military before I wanted to do something on behalf of my country. When I was sixteen years old I entered the Navy on 1 April 1938, and did my basic training at Yokosuka. After that I did my flight training at several air bases, including Tsukuba, Kasumigaura, and

PO2c Honma was assigned to carrier *Zuikaku* from June 1941 until the spring of 1942. (NHC via Wenger)

Tateyama. Next, I went to Ōmura Air Base and practiced basic flying techniques, such as doing formation flying.

1940 - Carrier Duty

On 21 October 1940 I transferred to the carrier *Ryūjō* but didn't fly any combat missions. During this time I did my best to practice all the skills necessary to become a better pilot. Then, on 15 June 1941 I was assigned to the carrier *Zuikaku*. Frankly speaking, I feel many of the aviators on the carriers *Zuikaku* and *Shōkaku* were really "green" and had very little flying experience. For example, only three pilots (including myself) had experience doing torpedo attacks using a Type 97 carrier attack plane. So compared to the aviators on our other carriers, most of our men were not that experienced as pilots. Hence, prior to Pearl Harbor, we did mostly basic flying maneuvers, such as take offs, landings, and a little bit of formation flying. We also did some level-bombing training with our Type 97s.

Pearl Harbor

Veteran Hideo Honma participated in the Pearl Harbor attack as a member of the second wave from the carrier Zuikaku. *He was a pilot of a Type 97* kankō *level-bomber and his target was Hickam Field. The young pilot was part of a group comprised of twenty-seven* Zuikaku *Type 97 carrier attack planes, which were led by Lieutenant Commander Shigekazu Shimazaki. They flew to the target an* Akagi *Type 0* kansen *unit that was supposed to control the airspace in the vicinity of Hickam Field. By the time Shimazaki's group arrived over Hickam Field, it was already attacked during the first wave by seventeen* Shōkaku *Type 99s, nine* Akagi *Type 0 carrier fighters, and several* Kaga *Zero fighters (but the exact number is not clear). The 18th Bombardment Wing was based at Hickam Field, and the group's aircraft were "sitting ducks" for the Japanese attackers because they were parked very close together, because of the fear that the local community of Japanese people may try to "sabotage" them.*

The only wartime picture that Honma-san had of himself was taken while he was a flight instructor at Yatabe Air Base towards the end of 1942. Honma is seated in the center of the group, and second from the left is Kaneo Matsuda. (Honma Collection)

During the fall of 1941, our *kankō* pilots did training at Usa Air Base, but three of the more experienced aviators (including myself) didn't do much training at this time. Instead, we had other duties to do, such as ferrying new aircraft from Kasumigaura to our air base. When we did this duty, we took a train to Kasumigaura and then flew back to our air base with the new aircraft. We did this assignment several times, so we didn't do much training prior to the Pearl Harbor attack. Since most of the men on our carrier were "rookie" pilots, we never dreamed that one day we would participate in an attack on Pearl Harbor. Before we left for the journey to Hawaii, we heard that our ship was participating in a big training exercise. We were told to leave most of our extra clothes and personal items at our base. This was done in order to save space for storing extra fuel on *Zuikaku* for the long journey.

I learned that we would attack Pearl Harbor after *Zuikaku* arrived at Hitokappu Bay. I was the pilot of our Type 97 *kankō*. The other two men on my crew were the observer PO2c Haranobu Idehara and the radioman/rear gunner, Sea1c Ryoichirō Morishita.[192] Keep in mind, I was a few years older than the other two airmen on my crew, and since they were only sixteen or seventeen years old, I felt they were still kids. We got along well, but our ranking was different, and I was the aircraft captain. However, since we flew on the same aircraft and could one day die together, I felt we had a strong, working relationship as a crew. I flew with these men for nine months until I became ill and had to be hospitalized. In 1942, when I was in a Kure hospital, Idehara's father and sister came to visit me.

The night before my "big" mission, I was ordered to take a bath. Normally when I took a bath, I was allowed to use just three buckets of salt water. However, on this occasion I could bathe with "pure" water and use as much as I wanted. I changed into a clean uniform and was ready for this important mission. I flew during the second wave attack on Pearl Harbor. I think the leader of our group, Lieutenant Commander Shigekazu Shimazaki, was well liked by most aviators from our group.[193] Before we took off, all of the *Zuikaku's* airmen gathered together on the flight deck. During this time, each crew of three men (from a Type 97 *kankō*) received one special cigarette which came directly from the Emperor's family. After the war, I thought that it was a really special "treat" to smoke, and I still do to this day, probably because of my experience on 7 December 1941! Our crew also got a small bottle of whiskey from a warrant officer from our group, but I am

Lieutenant Commander Shigekazu Shimazaki led *Zuikaku's* Type 97 *kankō* level-bombers during the second wave attack on Pearl Harbor. (Prange Collection via Wenger)

not sure why he gave it to us. Maybe this guy thought we wouldn't survive, or for good luck.

Normally, before I got on my aircraft, a mechanic would help me with the shoulder straps and help me in the cockpit. However, on this occasion the mechanic who was helping me suddenly left. Then he came back to my Type 97 *kankō* and put an *omamori* in the cockpit and wished me good luck. After I took off I joined the other aircraft and circled above the carrier; then our group flew in formation to Oahu Island. When we arrived over Hawaii, I could see lots of black smoke, which was probably coming from the burning battleships. I flew to my target, which was Hickam Field. Our group of level-bomber Type 97s wanted to drop our bombs on a large hangar, but it was attacked by another group of Japanese aircraft and exploded. So, we lost our original target and decided to turn around over the ocean and try again.

Hickam Field was Honma's target during his mission 7 December 1941. (NA via Wenger)

When I was flying at 3,000 meters there was a lot of ant-aircraft fire and black smoke in the air. I thought that I would surely get hit by some of this anti-aircraft fire and get shot down. I was able to see an enemy destroyer circling around the harbor and shooting at our formation. Even with all the enemy aircraft fire and action occurring during my mission, I still felt very calm. Since I was young and my parents were already deceased, I really didn't worry too much about dying during the attack. However, I wasn't a well-known pilot in the Navy, so if I died, my name probably would not have been in the newspaper. Because of this, I tried to fly close to Lieutenant Commander Shimazaki's aircraft. I figured if we both got hit and crashed at the same time, my name would at least get mentioned in the newspaper.

After turning around, I could see a car speeding down a road and thought that it might make a good target. I felt this way because my *kankō* had already come under heavy anti-aircraft fire, and we were at war. Nevertheless, prior to our mission we were told not to hit civilian targets, so I didn't drop my bombs on the car. When I arrived over Hickam Field again, since my original target (the hangar) was already destroyed, I dropped my bombs at random over the air base. During the "bomb run" the observer, PO2c Idehara, pulled a wire and then bombs were released. We then left the area and flew to the rendezvous point off the northern part of Oahu Island. Once we arrived there, we were told to wait for other "friendly" aircraft, then go back to *Zuikaku*. A little while after that, a Type 99 *kanbaku* flew behind our Type 97 carrier attack plane. After some time passed this particular Type 99, which may have been hit in the fuel tank, flew in front of my aircraft, just banked and then crashed into the sea. I believe this Type 99 crashed about 80-100 miles away from Hickam Field, but I am not sure.

After I landed on *Zuikaku*, I checked my Type 97 *kankō* for any damage and noticed several holes from anti-aircraft fire in my horizontal stabilizer, near one of the elevators. So I was lucky to make it back safely. I don't remember any of the other Type 97s having any damage, though; my aircraft seemed to be the only one that was hit. Fortunately, none of our aircraft were shot down during the second wave. We were acknowledged for our contributions during the mission and each given one pack of the Emperor's cigarettes. Since it was lunchtime after we got dismissed, all of the aviators were given "hearty" meals, which were delicious.

On the journey back to Japan I heard rumors that we might have to attack Midway Atoll, but that never materialized. After we got closer to the Japanese mainland, we were allowed to take off

A *Zuikaku* Type 97 *kankō* (EII-307) over Hickam Field during the second wave attack. (Matsumura Collection)

Above: A view looking southwest from the Hickam Parade Grounds shows some of the carnage on the ground after it was attacked. (Cleveland Collection via Wenger)
Below: The Hale Makai Barracks building was one of the targets for the Japanese attackers during the Pearl Harbor raid. (Celeveland Collection via Wenger)

and fly to our air base, so we came home one night earlier then our carrier. Once we arrived in Ōita, we had a crazy night of partying and had some fun with prostitutes in the local "red-light" district.

During the first wave, the mess hall of the Hale Makai Barracks building took a direct hit from a 250 kilogram bomb, killing thirty-five men.[194] *Other targets during this initial attack were the Hawaiian Air Depot's engineering building and hangar area, which were filled with aircraft that required thorough, heavy-duty maintenance work.*

As for the second wave attack, Honma-san and his comrades struck Hickam Field once again. Besides hitting the Hawaiian Air Depot and Hale Makai Barracks building, they also dropped their bombs on a baseball field because Japanese maps erroneously indicated it was the location of an underground fuel storage dump. Due to a change in plans the fuel tanks were located elsewhere.[195] *During the raid, the Japanese attackers also hit the base theater (which also served as a chapel), post exchange, enlisted men's beer garden, fire station, and the guardhouse.*[196] *Casualties at Hickam Field were 182 United States Army Air Force men, three members of the Honolulu Fire Department, and two people who worked for the federal government.*[197] *Out of the fifty-nine aircraft at Hickam Field during the Japanese attack, eighteen were destroyed, twenty-one put out of commission, and nineteen airplanes survived intact.*[198]

Combat after Pearl Harbor

The next mission for PO2c Honma occurred on 21 January 1942 when Zuikaku's *aircraft attacked Lae Aerodrome, which was located on the northern coast of Papua New Guinea and used by Allied forces. The strike group consisted of eighteen Type 97* kankō *level-bombers under the command of Lieutenant Commander Shigekazu Shimazaki, nine Type 99* kanbaku *led by Lieutenant Akira Sakamoto, and Lieutenant Masatoshi Makino's nine Type 0 carrier fighter escorts. Honma-*san *was once again a pilot of a*

Hickam Field's Hangar 11 took a direct hit during the attack. At the right of the picture is the tail of Brigadier General Jacob Rudolph's wrecked Douglas B-18. (NA via Wenger)

Type 97 carrier attack plane (in Shimazaki's group). Take off time was at 1000, and the strike group hit their target about two hours later. None of Zuikaku's *aircraft were shot down, and just one of the attackers was hit by anti-aircraft fire. The strike group returned to the carrier at 1340.*[199]

We bombed a small airfield at Lae. There was no anti-aircraft fire from the ground and only one enemy aircraft tried to engage us, but it was promptly shot down. So it felt like a training mission to me. I think only a few of our bombs actually hit the airfield, but after the mission, our commander said that we had a 100% hit ratio. Since Japan was doing so well in the war thus far, I really felt we were doing a good job.

Back to Japan

As I briefly mentioned earlier, I became ill with a gall bladder problem, so I was sent to the Navy hospital in Kure. After I recovered I became a flight instructor at Yatabe Air Base. I did this job from 1 June 1942 until 7 June 1944, but really hated it. I abhorred working as a flight instructor because my students were officers who recently graduated from the Naval Academy. I thought that this situation was ridiculous, because even though I technically had more time in the Navy than these young officers, they still outranked me. So I asked for a transfer and was sent to an air base at Toyohashi, in Aichi Prefecture.

Flying the *Ginga*

From Honma's early days in the Navy until the summer of 1944, he primarily flew just the Type 97 carrier attack plane and training aircraft, but never any other types. However, since he was "eager" to quit his job as a flight instructor, PO1c Hideo Honma was allowed to fly the advanced, twin-engine Yokosuka P1Y Ginga *(Allied code name "Frances"). This aircraft was designed to do both low altitude torpedo and dive-bombing attacks, but really didn't perform well until mid-1945, mostly because of ongoing maintenance issues with the aircraft's troublesome engines. Nevertheless, Honma-san thought that it was an "excellent" plane from his Navy days.*

A pilots briefing on the carrier *Zuikaku* sometime in early 1942. (Matsumura Collection)

A wartime photo of a Yokosuka P1Y2 *Ginga* bomber, which was the type of aircraft Honma-san flew while he was stationed at Toyohashi Air Base. (Lansdale Collection)

After I arrived at Toyohashi I was told to fly the *Ginga*, but I never flew a two-engine aircraft before. However, since I had been flying in the Navy for a number of years, my superiors allowed me to fly this new aircraft without any special training. The *Ginga* had great performance and could even do loops! It was manned by a crew of three aviators: a pilot, observer, and radioman/rear gunner. The nose section was separated from the cockpit, and the observer in front could not go into the cockpit area. I heard that this position was very scary for the aviator, especially during landing.

We were getting ready to do an attack mission off Taiwan, and the night prior to leaving Toyohashi we were given a delicious "send off" dinner of fresh seafood to eat (such as *sushi*). Since we could eat as much as we wanted, and the food was so good, I ate too much and got very sick. Because of this I had to spend a few days in the hospital. In the meantime, the rest of my group did torpedo attacks off Taiwan and were annihilated. So because of the crazy twist of fate I survived, while my comrades died in combat.

The End of War

Next, I transferred to Okazaki Air Base and became a flight instructor again. Since fuel was scarce, it was difficult to do any training flights in the summer of 1945. Because Okazaki was targeted by enemy aircraft, I was sent to Kyoto to continue training my students. Around this time I pleaded with some of the higher-ranking people at the base to be allowed to fly a *tokkō* mission. I really wanted to sacrifice my life and make a contribution to my nation. I really wasn't depressed about dying in a *tokkō* mission because I thought that I would die sooner or later anyway. Initially, I was turned down because my parents were deceased, and I had a lot of brothers and sisters in my family to support. However, when I pleaded with my superiors over and over, they agreed to let me go. To show how passionate I was to die for my nation, I took out my razor and cut my finger, then signed my name in blood, which was very painful.

I finally was allowed to do my *tokkō* mission, and was sent to Ōhi Air Base to get fuel and armament for my aircraft. My target was supposed to be some American ships in Tokyo Bay. After I landed I had a strange feeling, because there were no mechanics on the airfield to greet me. So I went to the officers' quarters, and when I opened the door there was a guy relaxing on a sofa. When I asked what was wrong, he said that the war was over. I was discharged from the Navy, and my final rank was ensign.

Postwar

My wife and I had five sons, but two died when they were babies. Since my wife passed away, I live with one of my sons and his

Veteran Hideo Honma in the spring of 2002 after our interview. (Werneth)

wife. After the war I joined the Japanese Self-Defense Force, and continued to fly a number of different aircraft, such as the C-46, and flew over 8,000 hours during my days as a military aviator. I retired as a lieutenant colonel in 1971, and then took a position with Japan Air Lines as a manager of a company dormitory. I retired from my second career on 31 March 1984. These days, I try to stay active and attend various veteran functions all across Japan. I also enjoy walking and gardening in my spare time.

Reflections

I am proud to have fought for Japan during World War II, but really didn't do anything unusual. It is your duty as a human being to contribute to your nation in time of need. I also feel that I was really "lucky" to survive. After the war, I feel Japan was really fortunate that our country was occupied by the United States, instead of Russia (the former USSR); I feel really thankful for this. If Russia would have occupied Japan everything would have been much different. I believe the United States taught Japan how to govern our nation properly and the true meaning of a democratic government. Furthermore, after the war they gave us food and really helped the Japanese people. So I believe the United States helped Japan become the prosperous nation that it is today.

Sadly, this outgoing and kind ex-Navy pilot passed away on 12 May 2003. I feel very honored to be the only person ever to have interviewed him about his wartime experiences.

Part 3

Fighter aircraft (*kansen*) veterans' accounts

The third section of this book covers Japanese Navy fighter pilot veterans. They flew the *kansen*, or carrier fighter (in English). The full Japanese name is *kanjō sentōki*. To help make my text user-friendly and still utilize some original Japanese terminology, in the case of the Zero fighter, I chose to use either *kansen* or Type 0 carrier fighter, or simply Zero fighter. Because various models of Type 0 carrier fighter were the most prevalent aircraft used by Japanese Navy pilots during the war, many people who I have met over the years seem to think this is the only Japanese WWII fighter. However, Japanese Naval aviators also flew other superb fighters, such as the Kawanishi *Shiden* and *Shiden-kai* (Allied code name "George"), Mitsubishi *Raiden* (Allied code name "Jack"), and the twin engine Nakajima *Gekkō* (Allied code name "Irving"). In this section, I won't talk about either the *Raiden* or *Gekkō* because the fighter pilots in this book really didn't fly those aircraft in combat.

The Mitsubishi A5M Type 96 *kansen* (Allied code "Claude") was the Japanese Navy's first modern monoplane, and saw combat in China beginning in the early fall of 1937. All of the models of this aircraft that saw action in the Sino-Japanese War were armed with two 7.7 mm Type 89 machine guns, which were mounted in the upper fuselage decking. It also could carry two 30 kilogram (66 pound) bombs. The first version of this fighter to see combat was the A5M1, which was powered by one Nakajima Kotobuki 2 KAI 1 nine-cylinder, air-cooled radial engine, rated at 580 horsepower for take off. The next model, the A5M2, had about thirty more horsepower at take off, and had a Nakajima engine (2 KAI 3A) as well. Later variants of this *kansen* were equipped with one Nakajima Kotobuki 41 or 41 KAI nine-cylinder, air-cooled radial engine that had one-hundred more horsepower than previous powerplants.

The Japanese Navy also experimented with an enclosed cockpit version of this aircraft, designated A5M2b, Model 2-2, but pilots disliked the enclosed cockpit, and they preferred the original version better. A5M2s had a lot of success against the Polikarpov 1-16 fighters, which were flown by Chinese and Russian pilots. The Type 96 *kansen* also was known for being very durable, even though it had a lightweight airframe. The A5M4 was manufactured in the largest numbers out of all the models of this fighter. In 1938 this aircraft was delivered to front-line units in China and was very successful against enemy fighters.

Undoubtedly, out of the Japanese Navy fighters to participate in the Sino-Japanese War and World War II, the aircraft that is most well known is the Mitsubishi A6M Type 0 *kansen*. During the wartime years, Mitsubishi and Nakajima manufactured approximately 10,449 Zero fighters, which was more than any other Japanese-built military aircraft. The first operational model, the A6M2, was powered by a Nakajima NK1C Sakae 12, fourteen cylinder, air-cooled radial engine that had 940 horsepower at take off. Later models (A6M3-A6M5) were equipped with one Nakajima NK1F Sakae 21, fourteen cylinder, air-cooled radial engine, which had 1,130 horsepower for take off. The typical complement of armament consisted of two 7.7 mm Type 97 machine guns mounted in the front fuselage and two wing-mounted 20 mm Type 99 cannons. Some A6M5s, which were used as night fighters, had the same armament as the other models, and were fitted with one additional oblique firing 20 mm Type 99 cannon mounted in the fuselage.

Throughout the war, the Zero fighter was known for having excellent range, maneuverability, and speed. However, the trade off to gain such performance was the lack of pilot armor and self-sealing fuel tanks. Because of this, the Type 0 *kansen* could get shot down easily by an Allied pilot who understood the weak points of his adversary's aircraft and opted not to dog-fight with him. One American WWII USMC fighter pilot once told me the Zero fighter was built like a "paper kite" compared to Allied fighters, such as the sturdy Grumman F6F Hellcat and the Vought F4U Corsair, which were able to take a lot of "punishment" and still survive the engagement.

The first combat mission for this Japanese Navy fighter occurred on 13 September 1940, when thirteen A6M2 Type 0s engaged twenty-seven Chinese fighters. This well-known aerial melee was a one-side affair, with sixteen to twenty of the enemy fighters being shot down without any losses on the Japanese side. During World War II, the Type 0 carrier fighter flew in just about every major operation from Pearl Harbor until the last days when the once proud *kansen* was being used for *tokkō* attacks.

As Allied fighter design became more advanced and began to dominate the Zero fighter in combat with newer aircraft, such as Grumman's F6F Hellcat, the Japanese Navy needed a new front-line fighter. This resulted in the development of the magnificent Kawanishi *Shiden* and *Shiden-kai*. Early models of the *Shiden* were plagued with engine and landing gear problems, but they still performed excellently in aerial combat when flown by seasoned pilots, such as Lieutenant Commander Iyozō Fujita, whose story is featured in this section.

The operational versions of both the *Shiden* and *Shiden-kai* were powered by a Nakajima NK9H Homare 21, eight-cylinder, air-cooled radial engine that had 1,990 horsepower at take off. Early models of the *Shiden* were armed with two fuselage mounted 7.7 mm Type 97 machine guns, two wing-mounted 20 mm Type 99, model 2 cannons, and two additional 20 mm cannons in wing gondolas. Later models of this *kansen* had four wing-mounted 20 mm Type 99 cannons.

Due to the *Shiden's* mid-wing body design, it had poor visibility and undercarriage problems. Hence it was redesigned as the *Shiden-kai* ("Improved *Shiden*") with a long-wing design, which made it better for mass production. When flown by experienced pilots such as the men in the elite 343 *Kōkūtai*, Japan's "Squadron of Aces," the Kawanishi *Shiden-kai* performed very well, even when they were outnumbered by their Allied counterparts. Please see Lieutenant Commander Yoshio Shiga's story for more information on flying this high-performance Japanese Navy fighter.[200]

Lieutenant (junior grade) Kaname Harada

"I feel very bad about shooting down pilots."

As I gazed out of the sleek bullet train, my eyes were filled with the sights of the countryside, complete with rolling mountains and fields. We had arrived at our destination, the city of Nagano, which was also home to the 1998 Olympics. I traveled to Nagano to meet eighty-six year old former Zero pilot Kaname Harada, who participated in many aerial encounters in the Pacific War. Even though this was our first meeting, Harada-san put me at ease with a friendly smile and warm greeting at the train station. Initially, during our conversation, the Navy fighter ace told me that he would have turned down my request for an interview, if a mutual friend had not introduced us. This is not because of dislike of Americans; instead, even to this day, talking about the war is a painful experience for this man. Even now he is still haunted by the painful memory of seeing his fellow Navy pilots die on Guadalcanal Island in October 1942; he would like to see their remains recovered in order to bring closure to their families.

Upon arriving at his farm, my translator and I were welcomed by the warm melodies of singing birds, which filled the air around us. Harada's house had numerous elaborate wood carvings and old mementos of his war years, including his flying helmet, Navy dagger, and other items. While researching this book, I was fortunate to get to know Harada-san quite well, and we frequently

Flight training days for Harada-san and his comrades. He is sitting in the center of this picture. (Harada Collection)

A wartime photo of Kaname Harada in his flight gear. (Harada Collection)

The young Kaname Harada as a Navy trainee. (Harada Collection)

exchanged letters. In his letters, he often spoke about his love for his family and children. Remarkably, even though Harada-san and his wife are in their upper eighties, they still run their kindergarten and work with young children on a daily basis. Lastly, during his postwar years, the well known Zero fighter pilot traveled to both England and the United States to make his peace with his former adversaries, and to try to teach the younger generation of the harsh realities of war.

Harada's Early Days

I was born in the Nagano Prefecture on 11 August 1916. During the Taishō Era (1912-1926), and especially after the great 1923 earthquake, Japan was in a period of depression. My parents were farmers and life was difficult. Furthermore, I disliked studying, so I wanted to join the Navy and see more of the world on a board a ship.

Harada at Saeki Air Base in 1937. (Harada Collection)

As for my reasons for becoming a pilot, when I was four or five years old, I saw a primitive biplane—a Tachikawa Type 93, called a "Red Dragonfly"—and got interested in airplanes.[201] So after I joined the Navy, I heard about a pilot training class and applied for it. Japan wanted more naval aviators, but they had to be trained really well. Our country realized that it cost a lot of money to train good pilots, so quite naturally it was difficult to be selected. Since that was Japan's policy, it was very difficult to graduate from a flight training class and many people dropped out.

Our training was very strict. We weren't physically abused, but there were a lot of minute warnings. For example, my flight instructor, Tomosaburō Iijima, was calm and easygoing on the ground, but once he was in the air, he became verbally abusive. I was reprimanded so many times that I decided to quit the Navy! When I said this to Iijima-san, his reply was, "I scold you because you are very talented and I want you to be the best aviator you can be." So after I heard this, I felt that being scolded meant being encouraged! I subsequently became the pilot that I always dreamed of being, and graduated at the top of my class. To me, this was a miracle.

Harada-san Goes to China

Upon completion of my flight training course I graduated in February 1937. After graduation I was assigned to the Saeki *Kōkūtai*. Next, I transferred on 1 October to the 12th *Kōkūtai*, which was based at Kunda, near Shanghai in China. The 13th *Kōkūtai* had the Mitsubishi Type 96 *kansen*, and we had the Nakajima Type 95 carrier fighter, which was an older model. The Type 96 was able to fly as far as Nansho, and it was involved in missions in that area. Our group just supported the Army, so there were no spectacular air battles. My first airbase was located in Kunda; then I moved to Jyoshu, and finally, Nanking.

There is a harbor named Koshu, near Shanghai, and in that year the Army landed in the middle of enemy-held territory. We used the Kunda University grounds as a landing strip for our aircraft. On 12 December 1937 I flew my first combat mission using the Type 95. At that time there were many small ships retreating upstream on the Yangtze River, so I was ordered to attack them. Among the ships there was a larger vessel that looked out of place with all the other small ships, and later we learned that its name was the USS *Panay*. It was bombed by mistake, and I heard that Japan paid a lot of reparations to take responsibility for this action, which could have started a war. I believe some of my comrades, who were involved in the sinking of the *Panay*, were told to go back to Japan.

As Japanese forces approached the city of Nanking, China, the gunboat USS Panay *was one of the vessels used to evacuate American officials and civilians from the besieged city. Ambassador Grew notified the Japanese government on 1 December of this plan, and the USS* Panay *and three Standard Oil barges departed ten days later. This little convoy was joined by two British gunboats and a few other British boats that hoped to escape. Unfortunately, war-hungry Japanese Army troops still fired on the group, and then notified their Navy counterparts that "Chinese troops" were trying to escape the area.*

On 12 December 1937, when the gunboat and the three barges were anchored at Hoshien, which was upstream from Nanking, they were attacked by three Japanese Navy aircraft. The attack occurred at 1330, and just about forty-five minutes later, Captain Hughes ordered to abandon ship. It subsequently sank, and two of the three tankers also were destroyed.[202] *Of the United States Navy personnel on board the gunboat, two men died, and another eleven officers and men were seriously wounded. As for the civilian passengers on the* Panay, *an Italian journalist Sandro Sandri was killed, and a Colliers magazine correspondent James Marshall had serious injuries.*[203]

The sinking of the USS Panay *could have started a war with Japan. However, a prompt apology from the Japanese government and their offer to make reparations for the loss of the gunboat and casualties prevented a major conflict to happen between the two countries.*

Back to Japan

In China I had very few opportunities to be in combat, and I returned to Japan in January 1938. I then served as a flight instructor with the Saeki, Tsukuba, Hyakurigahara, and Ōita *Kōkūtais*. Also, my wife and I got married on 1 January 1941. We had one daughter and three sons.

Pearl Harbor

I transferred to the carrier *Sōryū* in September 1941. I asked to be a member of the Zero pilots who participated in the attack mission on Pearl Harbor but was refused, and was instead assigned to do combat air patrols over the fleet. I also was the first pilot who took off from *Sōryū*, and actually followed the fighters who were going to attack Pearl Harbor for a while because I was a bit jealous.

This is how the patrols were done. There were five shifts on that day, and I participated in the first and third shifts. I did CAP (Combat Air Patrol) 3,000 to 4,000 meters (9,842-13,123 feet) above the ships after the airplanes took off, and my shift lasted two hours.[204] I was the *shōtai* leader of the three aircraft formations from the *Sōryū*. The *shōtai* leader was responsible for assuring the safety of the carrier. Normally, the three planes flew in a tight formation to watch for incoming enemy aircraft.

During the second shift, while I was resting, a group led by PO1c Yukio Kubota was flying.[205] We had a radio communication system, but it was primitive, so we didn't use it much. Japan had limited technology, and we were told to use the Morse signal. If the enemy came the signal was like to-to-to, but this signaling was difficult to do sometimes, so we often used hand or facial signals. You could do these types of signals within a small group, but if we tried to communicate with another small group it was very difficult. Hence, each small group made decisions with the guidance of their leader, in accordance with the situation. Basically, there was no specific distance to cover, and we depended on our eyesight. So if we saw an enemy aircraft we engaged them. We usually just covered the airspace over our own carrier; it was always in sight.

In retrospect, I believe many people view the Pearl Harbor attack just like the 11 September terrorist attacks. This is because

Sea1c Kaname Harada with a Type 95 carrier fighter. (Harada Collection)

Harada-san wearing all his flight gear including life-vest and parachute harness. (Harada Collection)

Pearl Harbor was a "sneak attack," and our country attacked without any warning beforehand. It is very hard for me to be considered a terrorist. I think these types of decisions should be done notifying the enemy beforehand. At that time I heard that Japan notified the United States before the attack, but in reality a mistake occurred and this was not the case. When I attended a symposium in the United States, I said that although I wasn't involved directly in the raid, I was in a main supporting role. I actually didn't engage or kill any Americans at that time, but my comrades did, so I still feel some responsibility.

Wake Island Attack

*After the attack in Hawaii, Carrier Division 2 (*Sōryū, Hiryū*), Cruiser Division 8 (*Tone, Chikuma*), and two destroyers (*Tanikaze *and* Urakaze*) left the other ships that participated in the raid so they could support the invasion of Wake Island.*[206] *During the first attack on the island on 21 December 1941, the fighter group (including a Zero fighter flown by Harada-san) came back without encountering any Grumman F4F Wildcat fighters. The* Sōryū *group consisted of fourteen Type 99* kanbaku *that were led by Lieutenant Commander Takashige Egusa and nine Type 0* kansen *commanded by Lieutenant Masaji Suganami. The* Hiryū *also launched fifteen Type 99s under Lieutenant Michio Kobayashi, nine Zero fighters led by Lieutenant Sumio Nōno, and two Type 97s that served as "guides" to the target.*[207] *The Japanese attackers bombed and strafed Battery D's position, but didn't really cause much damage.*[208]

The second attack on 22 December was a different story. Six Zeros were assigned to protect thirty-three Type 97 kankō *that were the horizontal bombing unit. The Zeros and the Type 97s took off from the* Sōryū *at 1100, and* Hiryū *launched its aircraft eight minutes later.*[209] *The person that Harada-san is referring to is Zero ace Lieutenant Commander Iyozō Fujita (at that time a lieutenant, junior grade), who led the three Zero fighters from the* Sōryū. *Harada-san didn't participate in the mission on 22 December, but he talked about it during our interview.*

My comrades were assigned to escort a group of *Sōryū* type 97 carrier attack planes that were going to bomb Wake Island. The Grumman F4F Wildcats were waiting for them (in the air) and attacked our airplanes. It was a difficult mission, and they tried to shoot them down. The lead Type 97 was engulfed in flames immediately, and our fighter pilots couldn't respond fast enough. Our group of Type 97s received damage, and the Japanese Navy lost some of our best pilots: PO1c Noboru Kanai (plane commander), WO Haruo Satō (pilot), and PO2c Yoshiichi Hanada (radioman). Fujita-san thought that this was his responsibility and regretted this. Kanai-san lived in Nagano, and I visited his grave to pay my respects.[210]

Remarkably only two Wildcats were flyable, due to limited resources when the island was under siege, and they battled the much larger group of attackers. The Wildcat fighters were flown by Second Lieutenant Carl R. Davidson and Captain Herb Freuler. Even with the odds against the American defenders, Freuler managed to draw first blood and shoot down two Type 97s, one of which had the well known veteran Kanai-san on board. However, after this Freuler was wounded in his back and shoulder by an attack by Hiryū *Zero pilot PO3c Isao Tahara. His F4F Wildcat fighter also had extensive damage, but he managed to survive by putting his aircraft in a steep dive, so the Zero pilot didn't follow him. Unfortunately Davidson, on the other hand, was not so lucky, and was shot down by Tahara. With the loss of both its last two fighters and pilots Wake Island's fate was sealed, and its defenders surrendered to Japanese forces on 23 December 1941.*[211]

Indian Ocean Operations

After this mission and a brief rest at Usa Air Base in Japan, Harada-san and his comrades returned to Sōryū *on 11 January 1942.*[212] *They then participated in the attack on Port Darwin, Australia, on 19 February, but had no air battles with the enemy. Next, the airmen rested at Kendari (in Indonesia) before departing on 26 March for their next major operation in the Indian Ocean, and their purpose was to destroy the British presence in that region.*[213] *Flushed with success, the Japan war machine was ready to take on the British forces based at Ceylon (now renamed Sri Lanka), in the Indian Ocean, and attacked the island base on 5 April, Easter Sunday. Beforehand the British had been expecting the Japanese attack, so they tried to scatter as many ships as possible from Colombo harbor to minimize their losses.*[214]

At 0600, from a distance of 120 miles out to sea, the carriers Akagi, Sōryū, Hiryū, Shōkaku, *and* Zuikaku *launched their airplanes, which consisted of fifty-three Type 97 carrier planes and thirty-eight Type 99 carrier bombers escorted by thirty-six Zero fighters. The Type 97s served as horizontal bombers and were led by Commander Mitsuo Fuchida (an observer aboard Lieutenant Mitsuo Matsuzaki's airplane), while the Type 99s were commanded by Lieutenant Commander Kakuichi Takahashi. Finally, the fighters were in the overall command of Lieutenant Shigeru Itaya from* Akagi, *and he also was the leader for nine fighters from his ship. The other groups of nine fighters apiece were commanded by Lieutenant Masatoshi Makino (*Zuikaku*), Lieutenant Sumio Nōno (*Hiryū*), and Lieutenant Iyozō Fujita (*Sōryū*).*[215]

The Zero fighter pilots from my group were once again ordered to escort our Type 99 *kanbaku* and Type 97 *kankō* to bomb the British-held Colombo airfield, on Ceylon Island. The air battle occurred near an airfield in Colombo, and happened just before our aircraft dropped their bombs. At that time five Type 99s and one Type 0 carrier fighter were attacked. The enemy aircraft didn't fly in formation, and neither did our group.

I don't know the exact number, but they probably had about one hundred airplanes, and so did our side. Each airplane chased their opponents individually. The Hurricane fighters didn't want to engage us because our Zero fighters were faster, so we had to go after them. They also wanted us to fight in their airspace. Initially I used my 7.7 mm machine guns, and the enemy tried to escape using a snake-like flying motion. Then I came closer to my opponent and opened up with my 20 mm cannons to shoot him down.

I fought against five airplanes and shot down three, which were later confirmed. One of the airplanes was flown by Commander

John Sykes. I also chased another Fairey Fulmar which made a forced landing, but it was not confirmed. The fifth aircraft was smoking, but it also couldn't be confirmed.

I was told not to pursue the enemy aircraft too long, but I got carried away. Hence, I was late for the predetermined rendezvous time to meet with the other Japanese aircraft and fly together back to our carriers. I was not confident about going back to the carrier by myself, so I was thinking about committing suicide by crashing my Zero fighter into an enemy target. Just as I was contemplating what to do, a young Japanese pilot flew alongside my aircraft. I didn't want him to die with me. Therefore, I had a "nothing to lose attitude" and did my best to go back to the carrier. We were lucky to return from this mission.

During the attack, twenty-one Hawker Hurricanes from 30 Squadron, fourteen Hawker Hurricanes from 258 Squadron, and six Fairey Fulmars (three apiece from 803 and 806 Squadrons) attempted to take to the air to engage the Japanese attackers. These airplanes were based at Ratmalana and Racecourse airfields on Colombo, but the latter was not attacked.[216] *The British losses for the attack were two Consolidated PBY Catalinas, fifteen Hawker Hurricanes, four Fairey Fulmars, and five Fairey Swordfish.*[217] *The Japanese losses consisted of five Type 97s damaged and six Type 99s lost, with seven more damaged, and one Type 0 carrier fighter lost with three others receiving damage.*[218]

On 6 August 2001 an unusual meeting occurred in the United Kingdom. Harada-san traveled there to meet one of the men he shot down during the battle, Commander John Sykes. This was their first meeting since that fateful battle in 1942, and it occurred because of the research conducted by historian Christopher Shores and photo journalist Marcus Perkins. During this particular battle Sykes was a pilot of a Fairey Fulmar and a member of the 806 Naval Air Squadron. Earlier in the war he also served with the 64 Squadron during the Battle of Britain. After this Sykes served with the 807 Squadron, a fleet fighter unit; then he was posted to the 805 Squadron in Egypt before transferring to the 806 Squadron, which was based on Ceylon.[219]

Commander John Sykes was one of Harada's opponents on 5 April 1942 over Ceylon. He was shot down by Harada-san that day, but six decades later they met and became friends. (Marcus Perkins)

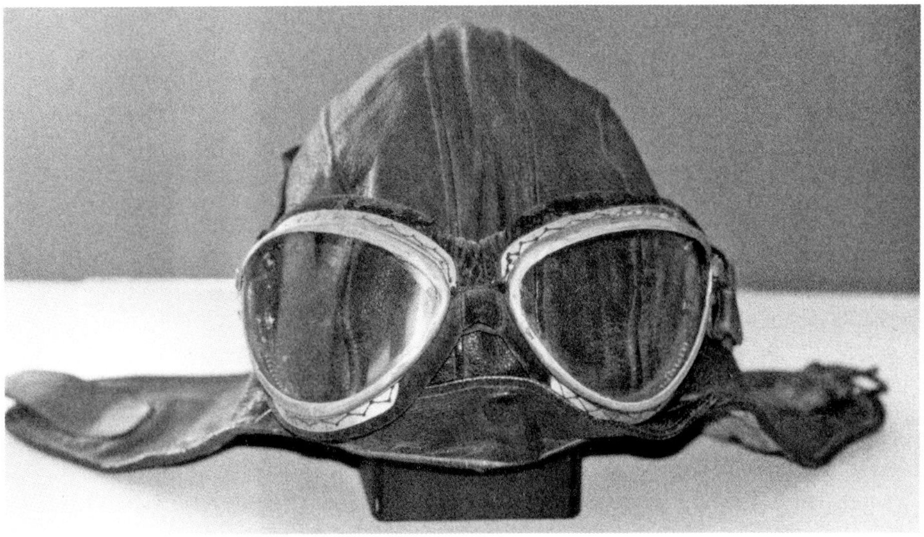

Harada's treasured war mementoes: his flying goggles and flight helmet. He gave the goggles to Commander Sykes but kept his flight helmet, which the Zero ace donated to the National Museum of the Pacific War in late 2007. (Harada Collection)

On 5 April 1942, at Ceylon, he was having breakfast as the Japanese planes came to the airfield to attack, so the British pilots scrambled to meet them. Sykes took off after his comrade did, and while he was a making a left turn Harada-san commenced his attack. The Zero pilot managed to shoot some bullets through the side of the fuselage of Syke's aircraft, which subsequently damaged the control mechanisms of his aircraft, and he lost control of his Fulmar. Just as the young British aviator began to say his prayers out loud he pulled back his control stick, and the aircraft landed in a paddy field. Sykes was unhurt, but a few Japanese airplanes came back and strafed him on the ground.

During their meeting, Harada-san said that he thought Sykes did a fine job of evading his attack from the rear by moving side-to-side. However, in reality the British veteran stated that his plane was actually out of control, so it went sideways because of this. Nevertheless, the meeting of the two former enemies was a special event for them, and they made peace with the past. Sykes presented the Zero pilot with his wings and a photo, and in exchange Harada-san gave him his treasured wartime flying goggles.[220]

Harada's Feelings for the Zero Fighter

As for my feelings regarding our aircraft in those days, I thought the Zero was simply the best fighter in the world, and I trusted it. The fighter also looked very sleek, and the maneuverability was superb. Furthermore, the engine was reliable, and it was able to fly for long periods of time. The Type 0 *kansen* was very strong in terms of attacking ability, so I thought that it was the best fighter at that time. However, when compared to American airplanes such as the Grumman F4F Wildcat, it gave poor protection for the pilot, because the Zero had no armor or self-sealing fuel tanks. The only American fighter that I fought against was the Grumman F4F Wildcat, and the performance was probably the same as the Zero fighter. Nevertheless, I was impressed with the American pilots' attacking spirit and skills.

Differences between Enlisted Men and Officers

Regarding the differences between enlisted men and officers, it was not as bad as the Army, but some elite people in the Navy were a bit arrogant. Sometimes they behaved like they were superior to other men. When I read the book written by Zero pilot Lieutenant (junior grade) Saburō Sakai, I also felt we were inferior.[221] In general, however, pilots were well treated and had better salaries, but people who were lower than petty officers were treated very badly. Nevertheless, after they became officers everyone was treated very well.

The Battle of Midway

During the battle of Midway I also served as a combat air patrol pilot. At 0430 on 4 June I took off from *Sōryū* with two other Zero fighters, which were flown by PO1c Takashi Okamoto and PO3c Genzō Nagasawa, but we didn't encounter enemy aircraft. We returned to our carrier three hours later, and were having breakfast when an air raid siren rang. I remember taking off and battling nine enemy torpedo bombers during this part of the battle. I recall shooting down two torpedo bombers, but my wingman, Nagasawa-san, perished.[222] My comrade's death was very painful for me.

After my bullets ran out I landed back on *Sōryū*, but quickly took off again to battle the next wave of American attackers. I recall fighting some twenty enemy aircraft and shooting down two of them. Then, after running out of bullets, I saw a third aircraft that crashed into the water because the enemy pilot seemed to be shocked when I flew near him. During this phase of the battle my favorite Zero fighter was badly damaged. My carrier *Sōryū*, along with *Akagi* and *Kaga*, were on fire, so I had to land on *Hiryū*.[223]

After landing on *Hiryū*, my Type 0 carrier fighter was dumped into the ocean because of battle damage, so I assisted other personnel near the bridge with signaling duties for aircraft. Then, a useable Zero fighter was found in the hangar and I was ordered to take off. However, soon after I took off, the *Hiryū* was also attacked. I wanted to fulfill my duty, so I continued to fight against the enemy aircraft until my Type 0 *kansen* was damaged and the fuel had run out. I was forced to land in the ocean, and after my plane landed in the water I scrambled out quickly. After some time had passed the destroyer *Makigumo* came to rescue me, but it came under attack by a group of B-17 bombers, so it promptly fled the area. Once the ship left I thought that I would surely die; it was pitch black. Four hours passed before the destroyer reappeared and rescued me. The deck of the ship was filled with survivors from the battle, and it looked like a scene from hell.

The Hiryū *was not salvageable, and the evacuation of survivors was completed by 0430 on 5 June, so it was scuttled by a torpedo at 0510.* [224] *Harada-san remembers seeing the ship beginning to go down but didn't see it actually happen. The* Makigumo *sped off because the crew thought that it would surely sink. However, in reality the* Hiryū *didn't sink. Later, at 0630 a plane from the light carrier* Hōshō *spotted the burned out wreck of the carrier, and it still had some survivors on board. The destroyer* Tanikaze *was dispatched to pick up any survivors, but it came under attack by American dive-bombers. The once mighty carrier finally sank into the depths of the ocean, but some survivors were later picked up by the American seaplane tender* Ballard *on 18 June.*[225]

Reflections on the Battle of Midway

During the Battle of Midway Japan lost four carriers, and a lot of good men died in the engagement. I think this is one of the reasons why Japan eventually lost the war. I also heard this from a lot of historians. Furthermore, our lack of luck could have made the difference between winning and losing this battle. If there would be any way to recreate what happened in this engagement, I would want to see it. Before Midway, I thought that the main job of a fighter pilot was to attack, but during this battle I realized how important combat air patrols were. I also thought that our leader, Vice Admiral Chūichi Nagumo, lacked good judgment, and even low-ranking personnel like myself felt this way.

A big mistake was not having an experienced person on board our carrier to lead the combat air patrols. So once the pilots left our ships they were on their own, and the patrols were poorly coordinated. If our patrols were coordinated between someone on the carrier and a designated leader of our CAP fighters, we would have been able to look up and see the dive-bombers from above. However there was no coordination, and we were preoccupied with the low flying torpedo planes. If anybody told us to look above for dive-bombers we would have done so. Generally, our pilots thought that it was spectacular to do attack missions, but participation in patrol missions was not highly regarded. In retrospect, I now feel that doing combat air patrols was more important than attacking.

Back then we used to think torpedoes were the most destructive and scariest things. We always overestimated the power of torpedoes. In fact, I heard later that American torpedo bombers were not that effective in this battle, and bombs from the dive-bombers actually sunk our carriers. I also feel everything was so disorganized for us during this battle. The Battle of Midway was a loss for Japan, but our country didn't want to disclose this to the Japanese people, so the survivors of the battle were kept at Kasonohara Air Base in Kagoshima, Kyūshū. We stayed there for one month and were not allowed to have contact with outsiders, in order to keep the loss of the battle a secret.

Gunfight over Guadalcanal

On 31 July 1942 Harada-san was ordered to become a member of the carrier Hiyō. *During this period of the war Japan was focusing all of her resources to reclaim Guadalcanal Island. The young aviator served as escort pilot for a 17 October mission to attack American transport ships off Lunga (Guadalcanal Island). This would be his last combat mission of the war. Aircraft from both the* Hiyō *and* Junyō *participated in this mission, and launched their planes at 0515 from a distance of 180 miles north of Lunga. The carriers sent eighteen Type 97* kankō *along with eighteen Type 0* kansen *to escort them; however, one Type 97 developed engine trouble and returned back to the* Junyō.[226]

The target of our mission was a group of American ships off Lunga Point. Our aircraft flew in two groups. First came eight *Junyō* Type 97s, but there should have been nine of them. One Type 97 (flown by WO Tatsuyasu Ōtawa) returned back to the carrier because of engine trouble. My group of nine Zero fighters from *Hiyō* were assigned to escort them, and flew above the formation of Type 97 *kankō*. Then came the second group of nine *Hiyō* Type 97s, along with nine *Junyō* Type 0 carrier fighters.

I heard that the *Junyō* Type 97 carrier attack plane leader (Lieutenant Tadao Itō) was more experienced than the *Hiyō* leader (Lieutenant Yoshiaki Irikiin).[227] Regarding the Zero fighter leaders, I also heard the *Hiyō* fighter leader (Lieutenant Tadashi Kaneko) was more experienced than the *Junyō* fighter leader (Lieutenant Yoshio Shiga). That's why it was such a strange formation, with *Hiyō* Zeros escorting the *Junyō* Type 97s and *Junyō* Zeros escorting the *Hiyō* Type 97s. So I believe the more experienced pilots were chosen to lead the attack. I was escorting the *Junyō* Type 97 group, which was commanded by Lieutenant Itō, but they were going the wrong way.[228] Nevertheless, the second group, which was commanded by Lieutenant Irikiin, hit the target successfully.

My group of escorting Zero fighters flew 400-500 meters (1,312-1,640 feet) above the formation of Type 97s. The Zeros flew in three groups of three, with the fighter in the top center being the leader, and the second airplane on the left, and the third one on the right. The escorting Zero fighters were faster than the bomb-laden Type 97s, so if we continued to fly normally it would have been too fast. However, we couldn't just stop, so we did snake movements to slow down. Sometimes though we got separated at a greater distance, and the Grumman F4F Wildcat fighters were waiting for this moment to attack our Type 97s. The enemy fighters were not trying to attack our Zero fighters; instead, they went after the vulnerable Type 97 *kankō*, because it was wiser to attack them. It was difficult to defend our Type 97s against the Wildcat fighters.

During this mission I saw a series of clouds that could only be found on a clear day. With this particular type of cloud, an enemy fighter pilot could hide his aircraft and still see the sky below very well. These clouds were 700-800 meters (2,297-2,625 feet) above, and to the right of us. We never expected to see Wildcat fighters coming from behind these clouds, and I thought that these clouds

Above: Henderson Field, on Guadalcanal Island, was a vital airfield as Allied forces went on the offensive for the first time in the Pacific Theatre. The Guadalcanal Campaign, which lasted from August 1942 until February 1943, was one of the most important operations in the war. (NA) Below: During his last combat mission of the war on 17 October 1942, Harada-san fought against a Grumman F4F Wildcat fighter similar to the one pictured here. The rugged F4F was well armed, and could put up a good fight against the Mitsubishi Zero fighter in combat. This photo was taken at Henderson Field in early 1943. (NA)

were an ominous sign. In reality, the enemy fighters were waiting to attack us. As I mentioned earlier, our group made a directional error, and while we were changing our course we were attacked. During this attack we were annihilated. Right in front of my eyes six Type 97s were on fire, and two of these crash-landed. After the *kankō* were attacked, our nine Zero fighters tried to chase the Wildcats while they were trying to escape. However, one Grumman F4F Wildcat fighter turned around and came back to fight us.

However, when I made a sudden directional change to get into position to fight him I became lightheaded because of the g-forces. At this time I released my throttle, and because of this my position was lower than the Wildcat fighter. So when I came to my senses I was in a disadvantageous position, and the enemy was above me. I thought that if I tried to escape I would be shot down for sure, so I decided to fight him, even in an unfavorable position. It was one airplane against another. The battle was one short head-on encounter, and I must have hit his airplane numerous times.

In my case, I had to return to my carrier, which was far away, so I wasn't able to get back. My left arm was badly wounded, and I wasn't able to control my Zero fighter. So I decided to ditch on Guadalcanal Island, and crash-landed about forty kilometers (twenty-five miles) from Cape Esperance, a bit off the coast near a river. On normal occasions a landing in the ocean would have been better, but since my left arm was injured I decided to land in the jungle. The area where I crashed was located between Cape Esperance and Henderson Field, but probably closer to Cape Esperance. I believe that Henderson Field was about thirty kilometers (nineteen miles) from my crash site.

The engine of my Zero fighter was damaged, and so were the fuel tanks. During this time gasoline had spread around the area of my seat, and I was worried about a possible fire. So I switched off the engine and had to land as soon as possible. From above the area where I was going to land looked flat, but actually there was a palm tree about fifty meters (164 feet) tall. First, the left wing hit the palm tree and was severed from the fuselage; then the airplane flipped over and landed on the ground. Luckily for me, since I shut off the engine there was no fire. The palm tree actually served as a cushion, because if I had landed directly on the ground the friction might have caused a fire.

I passed out when the airplane hit the palm tree, and I don't know how long it took for me to regain consciousness. I awoke after a cool shower of gasoline poured down on me from my crashed aircraft. I was in an upside position in the cockpit, and it was like a sealed room. The gasoline became vaporized, and it was choking me, so I had to get some air quickly! My left arm was badly injured, so I used my right hand to dig a little bit, which gave me some air to breathe; then I dug some more. Fortunately it was soft, leaf-decayed soil, so I was able to dig and crawl out. I dug so much that my nails were almost completely worn away. I also used my legs and pushed against the butts of the machine guns, which helped me crawl out. Once my face was out it became very easy to get out, but before that it was difficult. I was really desperate, so I dug like a crazy man, and don't remember exactly how long it took to get out. During my struggle to escape I used up every ounce of my energy; I collapsed after getting out of my plane. At that time I was very thirsty, and the only source of water was a mosquito egg infested puddle. In spite of that I had to drink, and after I did I calmed down a little bit.

After I slept for a while I gained some energy, and started to walk through the jungle. Suddenly, I saw an aviator with a bloody face about 500 meters (1,640 feet) away; it was WO Hisao Satō, who was one of the two aviators who survived the crash of a Type

Second Lieutenant William B. Freeman (left) with legendary USMC fighter pilot Joe Foss. Freeman was the pilot who shot Kaname Harada down on 17 October 1942. Foss met the Zero pilot at a postwar reunion and the ace thought he shot down Harada. However, Freeman is the only American pilot credited with a Zero fighter for that day of combat. The author also located and interviewed William B. Freeman, who verified that he shot down Harada, and their stories match up. (James Lansdale Collection)

97 carrier attack plane. Six airplanes were damaged during the mission, and Sato-san was one of the aviators whom I escorted. Satō's aircraft normally was flown by a crew of three men. Unfortunately, the pilot of his Type 97, Lieutenant (junior grade) Setsuo Kuno, was shot in the head and died in the aircraft. However, the reconnaissance man, PO1c Tadao Maruyama, was still alive, and he was trapped in the wrecked aircraft. PO1c Maruyama was moaning in pain as well. Satō-san and I tried to save him, but my left arm was injured, so it was difficult to get him out. We were not able to rescue him because he was trapped very firmly inside the wrecked aircraft. Sadly we had to give up, and he died. However, before Maruyama-san died he asked us to bring some of his hair and nail clippings back to Japan for his family.

Satō-san and I spent the night with the dead aviators and had a wake for them, because they couldn't have a proper burial. We made offerings of flowers and palms to them. Unfortunately, the two other aviators are still on the island because their remains were never recovered. After the war I asked the people who worked at the hotel near the crash site to locate it, so the families could recover their loved ones; but the crash spot is difficult to locate after so many years. The next day we started to walk from 0800 in the morning along the beach eastward towards Henderson Field. I think we walked for about ten kilometers (six miles), and it took two days before we met an advance party of fifteen or sixteen engineers who came to the island to begin construction of a mini-submarine base at Kamimbo Bay (Tambea). Later, I learned that the base was never constructed.[229]

Out of the original eighteen Japanese Type 97 attack planes, only eight returned to their carriers, including the aircraft flown by WO Ōtawa, which aborted the mission. Seven Type 97s (six Junyō, *one* Hiyō*) were shot down, and three others (two* Junyō, *one* Hiyō*) crash-landed. Harada-san and his comrades were intercepted at 0732 by Major Davis' eight VMF-121 Wildcats. After the battle, American pilots made claims for eight "dive-bombers" and two Zeros. Second Lieutenant "Big Bill" Freeman put in the claims for the two Zeros, so it is possible that he wounded Harada, as he was the only VMF-121 pilot to claim any Zeros for that mission.*

The only other known living Japanese veteran who survived this mission is Ensign Taisuke Maruyama (who is not related to the late Tadao Maruyama, who died during the 17 October 1942

Harada and USMC fighter pilot ace Joe Foss at a postwar reunion. (Harada Collection)

mission). Maruyama-san flew as an observer on one of the Hiyō *Type 97s. He recalled seeing thick anti-aircraft fire from the ships and the American air attack of their group, "Each of the stricken Type 97s went spinning downward, emitting a bright light which could be seen when the aircraft was burning up; they looked like leaves that were fluttering down." Finally, the* Hiyō *Type 97 carrier attack plane group attacked the U.S. Navy destroyers* Aaron Ward *and* Lardner, *which were shelling the supply dumps near Kokumbona, but scored no hits.*[230]

The End of the War

After meeting up with the Japanese engineers (who were working on the submarine base), Harada-san and WO Hisao Satō were sent to a Navy hospital on Truk Island. Once the men were treated they returned to Japan. When Harada-san recovered from his battle wounds, he became a flight instructor at Kasumigaura. While serving as a flight instructor he met up with Satō-san again. Sadly, according to Harada-san, Satō-san died soon after, on a suicide mission off the cost of Taiwan. In late March 1945 Lieutenant (junior grade) Kaname Harada was sent to Chitose, in Hokkaido, to train pilots, because there were too many enemy planes in the vicinity of Kasumigaura, the usual training location. He stayed at Chitose until the end of the war.

On the day that the war ended, I was told that there would be an important announcement by the Emperor on the radio, but the signal was not clear. Due to the poor radio reception I wasn't able

Lieutenant (junior grade) Harada (left) with WO Hisao Satō after they recovered from their wounds sustained during the 17 October 1942 mission. Satō later died in the war doing a tokkō attack mission. (Harada Collection)

Harada in his Navy dress uniform with dagger at the Tsukuba Shrine. (Harada Collection)

to hear the message well, but I still understood that Japan had lost. I felt relieved because the war ended, but I was worried about how Japanese people would be treated, because we had lost.

When Harada-san was discharged from the Navy his final rank was lieutenant (junior grade), and by his own estimation, he flew about 5,000 hours during the war. He is officially credited with shooting down nine enemy planes.[231]

Postwar

After the war the American occupation forces were generous enough to let veterans work, like everyone else; but we were not allowed to have public service jobs. So in this case we were not treated fairly. Many people around here knew that I was a veteran, but didn't know what I did. I also was worried about being "blacklisted" because of killing so many people in the war. I feel that all of the aviators were "blacklisted." For example, I was told to write my resume in both English and Japanese for the occupation forces. I also was told that if I were to leave for more than two days from my house, I had to report what I was going to do.

As I mentioned before, I was banned from working for public service, but it was permissible to work for private companies. But most of the private companies didn't want veterans to work for them. Nobody hired me, so I became a farmer.

In 1965 I was told to become a community leader when new apartment complexes were built in this area, because I had lived here for a long time. I also was asked to take care of the children in this area, so I decided to build a small facility for them. At first it was a daycare center, but it later became a kindergarten, which we still run today.

17 October 1942 Mission – Postscript 2006

During the course of researching this mission over the past five years several remarkable things occurred. First, I was able to track down Second Lieutenant William "Big Bill" Freeman. After almost six months of searching through various veteran contacts and organizations I was able to track down Freeman, who was living in Bonham, Texas. When I got his mailing address, I quickly wrote a letter to him, not knowing what would happen next, or even if he was still alive after all these years. Remarkably, after several weeks passed the veteran called me. During our conversation Freeman confirmed that he did indeed do a head-on air battle with a Zero fighter sometime in mid-October 1942, near Guadalcanal Island, and recalled seeing bullets smashing through the cockpit. He was pleased to hear that his opponent did indeed survive his attack and the war. Freeman said "Please tell Mr. Harada I was aiming for his aircraft, not him. I am happy to hear that he is well." Later, Harada-san sent his best wishes to Freeman via a letter, and was very pleased to hear from him after all these years.

As a side note, in his postwar years, the ex-Zero pilot met one of his former American opponents, legendary U.S. Marine Corps fighter ace Joe Foss. They met at a stateside symposium and compared notes. The veterans both thought that they fought against each other on 17 October 1942, until I researched this event more thoroughly with the help of historians John Lundstrom and Henry Sakaida. After checking official American records, which showed Second Lieutenant William B. Freeman as the only American pilot to make claims for a "Zero fighter" on 17 October 1942, we determined he was Harada's actual opponent. Secondly, in late 2005 I discussed the above story with historian and founder of the pacificwrecks.com website, Justin Taylan. He wanted to help Harada-san locate the remains of his long-lost comrades and their aircraft. Prior to embarking on his trip to Guadalcanal Island, Taylan was able to get a map with possible locations for Harada's aircraft and the Type 97 carrier attack plane. He also researched a number of possible crash sites and known aircraft wrecks on the islands. After traveling to the island, Taylan conducted an exhaustive search with his friends and other contacts there. Unfortunately, they couldn't find these long lost airplanes during this trip, but the search will be continued in the future.

As for Harada-san, he learned that the late Maruyama-san attended the same junior high school that he attended in Nagano. He searched for surviving members of Maruyama's family to talk about his last mission during the war. Unfortunately, Harada-san couldn't locate anyone from Maruyama's family. However, he was able to meet members of the Satō family in Fukushima Prefecture, and they prayed together to console the soul of Hisao Satō.

Reflections

The initial feeling after shooting down someone was relief, because it was not me who was shot down. My next thought was that I was a better pilot, so I felt superior to the enemy aviator who was shot down. These feelings lasted only for a short time. When we shot at each other, we were at very close range, and during this time I could see my opponent's face very well. When I saw the enemy's face, it looked terrible because he was going down. Soon after this I felt very bad, because I could imagine that my opponent had a family of his own, and I killed him. Therefore, to this day I feel very bad about shooting down pilots during the war. In general, I have a bad feeling about being involved in the war, and I feel guilty about killing other people in combat. I also feel that the war should not have happened in the first place. This is because the governments of countries around the world don't make an effort to resolve their differences. Instead, they order their armed forces to kill each other. I believe World War II veterans know this best, because we were used as "pawns" by our government to fight a war.

Unfortunately I was involved in the war, and I'm lucky to be alive now. Nevertheless, I still feel guilty, so I have to redeem myself by telling the younger generation that today we are lucky to have peace, and we should try to stop any future wars from happening. I feel the responsibility to say this now, so I teach young kids how important life is, and if people think that their lives are precious, they will treat others very well. Sometimes I try to teach children how precious life is, but they are too young to understand. So I try to teach them that things like birds or tree branches shouldn't be destroyed because they have their own roles to play as well. If we, the veterans, don't try to tell younger people about what happened, soon those stories will be gone. I think that it is our responsibility to say what really happened.

Above: Cape Esperance, Guadalcanal Island, in 2005. Harada believes he crashed his Zero fighter about twenty-five miles off this cape during his crash landing on 17 October 1942. (Justin Taylan) Below: Kamimbo Bay (Tambea), Guadalcanal Island, in 2005. During the war this was the site of a Japanese mini-submarine collection point, but never a fully-equipped base. Harada and Satō walked to this area on the beach when they were wounded and were rescued by Japanese personnel there. (Justin Taylan)

A picture of Harada-san and his wife taken a few years ago. He is a family man, and cares deeply about his wife and his children. Harada also loves kids and working with them, which keeps him a "young" ninety years old. (Harada Collection)

I believe that during Japan's wartime years we were "brainwashed." Since I was young, I was taught that Japan was a great nation, and everything that it did was the right thing to do. I grew up in this type of environment. I personally didn't think of invading other nations. I was told before the war that Japan was forced into a difficult situation because of the ABCD nations, and that war was inevitable. Consequently, I felt I had to do my utmost to protect Japan.

I think the world today is a strange and crazy place. One reason is because of the terrorist attack on America and the Middle East situation with Palestine and Israel. As far as Japan goes, there are politicians who are dishonest, and there is still a controversy about the visitation of the Yasukuni Shrine. I think that it's only natural to pay respects to the people who died in the war, and we do have the freedom of religion.

It's a strange and absurd concept that Japan might start a war just because we are paying respects to the people who died. I believe, that in reality, it is quite the opposite. There are some positive and encouraging things happening today; even if the world itself is in total chaos. Some people recognize that war is dangerous. Everyone has to learn from the mistakes of the past and try not to repeat them in the future. This is the best way to prevent future wars, and I believe a lot of younger people think this way.

Lieutenant Commander Iyozō Fujita

"I want to be remembered as a survivor."

During my first trip to Japan in the spring of 1999 I was able to meet some experienced naval aviators, who regrettably either have since died, or don't grant interview requests anymore, due to their advancing age. Legendary Zero pilot Iyozō Fujita is one of these men, and after our initial interview he frequently corresponded with me and sent me his detailed war diaries. When I met him he looked physically fit and was very mentally alert. He reminded me of a retired professor who had a lot of knowledge and awareness of the world around him. Fujita's personality was easy-going yet proper. During our interview he was very animated, and used hand gestures to describe his flying exploits. Fujita-san was very fortunate to survive several close calls with death during Pearl Harbor, Midway, Iwo Jima, and other battles.

Life Before Joining the Navy

My father's name was Gorō Fujita. After getting a medical license at age eighteen, he went to Tianjin, China, and founded the Tenshin Hospital. While working at the hospital he developed very close relationships with many prominent Chinese people. He also became friends with the commander of the Japanese Army in Manchuria, who lived in Tianjin. My father also strived to promote a friendly relationship between China and Japan. I think he belonged to the "*Genyo-sha*," a political organization led by Mitsuru Toyama. I also recall him often examining Chinese people who were suffering from illness, and they often collapsed at the gate of his hospital.

In 1938 he went back to his hometown in Ōita, Japan, to recuperate from illness. This was the same time the China Incident happened and the war started. The shock of all of this made him sick; it was simply too much for him to bear, and he passed away in April (of the same year). A flag draped in black was sent to his funeral from Chiang Kai-shek.[232] I heard the locals whispering to each other, "A flag was sent from the leader of our enemy." My mother was born in the Izu region, and she was the daughter of a farmer. She was a licensed nurse, and made her way to Tianjin by herself.[233] My step-mom started working at my father's hospital after his first wife passed away.

I was born on 2 November 1917, in the Shantuag Province, China, and was the eldest son in our family. At age five, after being vaccinated for smallpox, I developed a fever above forty degrees Celsius and lost consciousness. I was unconscious for three days. Both of my parents, judging from their medical point of view, seemed to have given up on me. Fortunately, all of a sudden my fever went down on the fourth day, and I regained consciousness. Prior to being sick I talked a lot. However, after recovering from this illness, perhaps because of high fever damaging the speech control centers of the brain, I didn't speak much. I also stuttered badly when I spoke. I entered elementary school while suffering from this speech impediment. Although my grades were the lowest in the class, I was spared from becoming a repeater and moved up to the fourth grade, thanks to my father, who also was the school's doctor.

Our teacher had an idea to have us elect a president and a vice-president of the class. I was elected to be vice-president, which must have been because of my athletic ability. I felt very lucky that athletic skills weren't damaged by my childhood illness. I was the fastest runner in the class and a great baseball catcher. Also, I was a home-run slugger on our baseball team. It may have been because I was elected class vice-president that I became interested in books and began to read. I read any books that I could put my hands on, and even learned to speed-read. Because of this my grades in school really improved. By the time I was in fifth grade I was the second highest academically in my class.

After graduating from elementary school I had to go to Japan in order to take an entrance exam at a junior high school in the Ōita Prefecture. When I was worried about traveling alone my mom yelled at me, "A man can go anywhere as long as he has ears, eyes, and a mouth!" Although I was just eleven years old, I had to travel alone from Tianjin (in China) to Hiji, Ōita Prefecture. At my father's suggestion I took an entrance exam and was admitted to Kitsuki Junior High School in Ōita. My uncle, who practiced medicine in the area, let me stay at his house, and I commuted to school for five years. As the fastest runner in the junior high school class, I also joined the track and field club.

A never before published photo of Fujita in his Navy dress uniform. (Fujita Collection)

An alumnus, who was my senior by two grades, had entered the Naval Academy and came home during the summer. I had a chance to talk with him, and he let me borrow two reference books (algebra, geometry). He used these books to study for the entrance exam to the academy. The books were interesting, and I began to read them. Unlike other summers before, I did not go back to my parents' place in Tianjin. Instead, I stayed at my uncle's house studying the two books. I woke up at 0300 and read the books thoroughly while it was still quiet until about 0600. I was able to finish them in one month during summer vacation. Perhaps, because of my extra effort, I passed the entrance exam to the Naval Academy the following year.

Naval Academy Days

I entered the Naval Academy in April 1935, as a member of the 66th class. Being beaten was part of daily life, and I was hit more than 100 times before the summer vacation in August. However, I think the beatings filled us with Navy spirit. Due to the war in China our graduation was moved up to September 1938. After graduation I went on board the training ship *Yakumo*. Together with its sister ship, the *Iwate*, it was part of a training group that went on long distance cruises. Everybody who graduated from the Naval Academy had to sail aboard a fleet-ship for about six months, to learn how the fleet worked. After six months you would be given your assignment. The ships included destroyers, cruisers, and battleships, but not submarines or aircraft carriers. After the cruise everyone had to take an exam to see if he was suited to be an aviator. At the end of the cruise in February 1939 I took a flying aptitude test at the Tsukuba Air Base, which showed that I had the skills to become a pilot.

Early Flying Days in the Navy

In late February I was assigned to the fleet and placed on the battleship *Kongō*, which gave me experience at sea. In November 1939 I became an air cadet and joined the Tsukuba *Kōkūtai*. I received flight training as one of thirty-three air cadets. My training began with a Nakajima Type 3 carrier fighter as my primary training aircraft; then I practiced in a Tachikawa K5Y-1 Type 93 intermediate trainer. When I flew solo for the first time, I raised my hands and screamed "*banzai*!"

After finishing my basic flight training I was transferred to Ōita *Kōkūtai* on 29 June 1940. During this time I did flight training that focused on all the aspects of flying a fighter aircraft. I had intense training in various air maneuvers, formation flying, gunnery, and navigation. Next, I joined the Mihoro *Kōkūtai* on 10 April 1941 and went to Shanghai, China. Our air group went to Shanghai because of the China Incident. In China I flew patrol missions from Shanghai to Hankow in an open-cockpit Mitsubishi Type 96 carrier fighter, but never had any air battles with enemy aircraft.

Pearl Harbor

On 1 September 1941 I was assigned to the carrier *Sōryū* and went to Saeki Air Base, where they trained fighter units. I was placed in Lieutenant Fusata Iida's group and trained in the Zero fighter. We were trained in gunnery, aerial combat maneuvers, and navigation. The fighter groups did not do any specialized training for Pearl Harbor, but we did practice flying in formation. The torpedo bombers, however, did special training in Kagoshima Bay, which looked similar to Pearl Harbor. The commanding officer of the *Sōryū* fighter unit was Lieutenant Masaji Suganami, who used to be one of my instructors at Tsukuba *Kōkūtai*.[234]

Fujita was on board the carrier *Sōryū* from September 1941 until it was sunk in June 1942 during the Battle of Midway. (*Sekai-No-Kansen* magazine via Wenger)

In October 1941 Commander Minoru Genda flew to Saeki Air Base and gathered the officers together.[235] He then announced that Pearl Harbor would be the target of our attack. When I heard about the attack I didn't know when it would happen, but that I would probably die during this future mission. I thought this because I heard that the American pilots, along with their planes, were very good. Furthermore, since we would be fighting over American soil, I felt that I wouldn't survive.

One month later, in November, the *Kidō Butai* departed from Japan for Hitokappu Bay, off Etorofu Island in the Kurile Islands. We stayed there and awaited further developments. Our group of ships left Hitokappu Bay on the twenty-sixth of that month. While sailing for Hawaii we attended several meetings to study enemy aircraft, or to discuss various combat scenarios. On one of the last occasions we were questioned, "What should you do if you were hit in the fuel tank (by enemy fire) and couldn't return to your carrier?" After we gave our opinions, the *buntaichō*, Lieutenant Fusata Iida, said at the end of the conversation, "If it happens to me, I will find a good target on the ground and crash into it." All of us were very moved by his statement. In fact, he did exactly that at Pearl Harbor, right in front of my eyes. During the war we all believed that becoming a prisoner of war was such a dishonor; it was worse than death.

Lieutenant Fusata Iida was a *buntaichō* when I was being trained as an air cadet, and a member of the Tsukuba *Kōkūtai*. He had a very easygoing personality, but there was a time when he got angry and admonished us for poor conduct. Iida-san said, "Some of you will be in my air group in the future, and be aware that I'll thoroughly retrain you then." Later, when I became a member of Lieutenant Iida's group on the carrier *Sōryū*, I told him that I wanted to be retrained. Instead, he took me out for dinner and drinks that night. I was happy to hear his stories about combat in China.

Afterwards I thought about my family; I was the eldest son among six brothers and sisters. Although my father and mother died in April and June 1938 respectively, I didn't have to worry so much about my younger siblings. They were all taken care of by relatives. I, however, felt that this war was like a strong-willed child challenging a strong adult to fight, and I would probably die during the Pearl Harbor attack. Therefore, I couldn't fall asleep the night before the attack. Since I usually slept well after drinking alcohol I drank before going to bed, but it didn't help me on this

A Japanese view of Kaneohe Naval Air Station between the first and second waves of the attack. (Makiel Collection via Wenger)

Lieutenant Fusata Iida was one of the Japanese aviators lost during the Pearl Harbor attack. (Prange Collection via Wenger)

occasion. Perhaps, because of my youth, I never felt tired for the entire day.

On 7 December 1941 a lower-ranking sailor came for a wake up call, and I went up to the bridge. Lieutenant Masaji Suganami told me to immediately calculate the course and the time it would take to return from Kahuku Point on Oahu Island, and to then notify all the other aviators in our group. I asked the helmsman what the expected location was of the fleet in five hours, and the meteorological observers about the direction and velocity of the wind at an altitude of 34 meters (112 feet). I quickly drew a map, calculated the course and the time required for the mission, then informed all the pilots in both divisions and made them take notes.

I was ordered to direct the take off, and helped line up the first wave attack unit in this order: first, the Type 0 *kansen*, then, the Type 97s (armed with bombs), and lastly, the Type 97 *kankō* (with torpedoes). After this, each plane of the second wave attack unit was put on the carrier's elevator, one after another, and the crewmen pushed them out to their positions on the flight deck. In the meantime, the pilots were making their last minute arrangements, given an admonitory speech, and got ready to go. The crew finished preparations, and we got in our own airplanes. After this we were ordered to take off, and flew together towards Oahu Island.

When we began to recognize the island through an opening in the clouds we heard the order of "charge." With no sign of the enemy, we followed the leader to Kaneohe Naval Air Station and began to strafe. The ground fire was extremely heavy. By the time we were about to do our third strafing attack we lost the target, due to the thick billowing smoke caused by the attack of our Type 97 *kankō* (horizontal bombing unit). The leader shifted the target to Bellows Field nearby and attacked it.[236] Lieutenant Iida waggled the wings of his Zero fighter, signaling us to go into formation. During this time I saw that both Iida's and PO1c Takashi Atsumi's fighters were leaking fuel. It seemed that their fuel tanks must have been damaged.

The unit moved back above Kaneohe. It was not long before Lieutenant Iida signaled me by hand, "I have no more fuel, so I'll crash into the target." He waved at me, banked his aircraft, and dove towards Kaneohe Naval Air Station. Right in front of my eyes Iida-san did exactly what he told us to do (prior to the mission). I kept watching until the sight of his plane disappeared into the murky smoke. During the war, we all felt that becoming a prisoner of war was really worse than death. Then, leading the remaining aircraft, I headed towards Kahuku Point, the rendezvous point. Suddenly I heard cracking sounds. I looked back and saw enemy fighters attacking in a four-plane formation. An air battle started instantly. During most of my missions I never really thought so much. It was almost instinctive; you were doing your duty. There were eight of our fighters against nine American fighters of an older design. We were in a mixed dogfight, and suddenly one American fighter attacked me head on—I thought that I would now die! At first I was going to ram him, but the enemy fighter broke off and started climbing. Suddenly, as he pulled upward, exposing his fighter's belly, I shot at it with all my might. I shot one hundred rounds or so into his aircraft and thought that I shot him down.

After the dogfight was over my engine, which was hit during the fight, began to run very rough. It stopped running, then immediately started up again. Nevertheless, I still felt that my Zero fighter could make it back to the carrier, and the air battle also seemed to be over. I signaled to form up (with my aircraft), and only two other Zero fighters from my original group joined me. We reluctantly decided to go back with only three of us. On the way home, I also flew back with three Type 99 *kanbaku*. My first thought was that since the dive-bombers had navigators aboard, I could follow them and find my way home. Before I left for my

Fujita and the other *Sōryū* Zero fighters engaged four Curtiss P-36A fighters like the one pictured here during the second wave of the Pearl Harbor attack. (NA via Wenger)

mission against Pearl Harbor, I went to the bridge on the carrier and asked the helmsman where our ships would be five hours after my departure time. After speaking to him, I made calculations and explained to everybody the return course to the carrier.

As we were trying to make our way back to the carriers, I realized that the Type 99s were ten degrees off course to the left. At the same time I was wondering what to do, because they had navigators aboard their airplanes and I was all by myself. If worse came to worse, it would be my responsibility if the wrong course was chosen, so I veered off in the correct direction. I quickly corrected the course according to my own previous calculations. When it came to the estimated time that I thought our fleet would appear, I took a hard look and saw our ships thirty degrees to the right. Eventually, I found my carrier, *Sōryū*; if I had gone with the Type 99 carrier bombers I may have never come back from the mission. Once I had my carrier in sight I attempted an emergency landing. Since my engine was running roughly and my fuel level was very low, I disregarded the proper traffic pattern and did a "straight in" approach. Gears down, flaps down, hook down, and when I looked at my instrument panel, the oil pressure gauge read zero. I then said to myself, "Oh my goodness, the engine could stop at any moment." Just at that very second I touched down on the carrier, and my number one engine cylinder fell off! That was a close call.

The aerial melee that Fujita-san described happened when the surviving Sōryū *Zero fighters engaged four Curtiss P-36A fighters, which were flown by pilots of the 46th Pursuit Squadron. This particular squadron was based at Wheeler Field on Oahu Island. The air battle took place at 0945, and during the engagement Second Lieutenant Gordon H. Sterling, Jr., was shot down, probably by Fujita-san.*[237] *Out of the original group of nine Zero fighters led by Lieutenant Iida, three didn't return from their sortie: Iida-san himself, PO1c Takashi Atsumi, and PO2c Saburō Ishii.*[238]

In December 1999 a remarkable meeting took place in Hawaii between Elfreida Tsukayama and Kikuyo Iida, the wife of Lieutenant Iida's cousin. Tsukayama was the daughter of Sam

Second Lieutenant Gordon H. Sterling, Jr., was probably shot down by Fujita on 7 December 1941. His body was never recovered, but there is a memorial stone dedicated to him at Arlington National Cemetery (Arlington, Virginia). (NA via Wenger)

Chun, the man who pulled Iida's body out of his crashed Zero fighter. Chun decided to take the flying helmet from the deceased enemy pilot with the hope of returning it back to his family some day. Unfortunately, he died in 1967, but his daughter was finally able to return the battle-scarred flying helmet to Kikuyo Iida. Mrs. Iida brought the flying helmet back to Japan, where it was put in a museum that her husband built in Yamaguchi Prefecture, to honor his late cousin.[239]

Combat Operations after Pearl Harbor

After finishing the Oahu attack, our carriers *Sōryū* and *Hiryū* were transferred to support the attack on Wake Island. Between 21-23 December we provided aerial support, and annihilated the remaining enemy fighters to allow landing shortly afterwards. During the 21 December air raid, initially we didn't see any enemy aircraft and began to strafe the ground. Then we came back and found that one of our Type 97 *kankō* (piloted by WO Noboro Kanai) in our horizontal bombing unit was shot down by an enemy fighter. We continued strafing the ground and left, but it was really a shame to have our aviators lost from the excellent horizontal bombing unit. Our group completed our Wake Island assignment on 23 December, and we returned home to Japan.

The Sōryū *returned home to Kure Naval Base on 25 December. Fujita and his men left the carrier to go to Usa Air Base for some rest and relaxation. They later returned to their carrier on 11 January 1942, and the* Sōryū *departed for the Pacific the following day.*[240] *Fujita's unit then participated in the 19 February attack on Port Darwin, Australia, but encountered very little enemy opposition. The group later went to an airfield near Kendari (on the island of Celebes, now Sulawesi) for some rest and training, but later left for its next assignment, the Indian Ocean Operation, on 26 March. Fujita's fighter unit also participated in the 5 April attack on the*

United States Army Air Force fighter pilots who fought in aerial combat during the Pearl Harbor raid are decorated on 1 July 1942. Left to right: 2ndLt. Harry W. Brown (Silver Star), Philip M. Rasmussen (Silver Star), 1stLt. Lewis M. Sanders (Silver Star), 2ndLt. Kenneth M. Taylor (Purple Heart), and John J. Webster (Silver Star, Purple Heart). (Sanders Collection via Wenger)

A frontal view of the smooth lines of an A6M2 Zero fighter in flight. (NHC via Wenger)

British base at Ceylon (now called Sri Lanka) and in the 9 April raid on Trincomalee.[241]

I was on the 5 April attack mission to Ceylon, and on this mission I had a dog-fight with a twin-seat fighter and shot it down.[242] I saw the pilot bail out. I also intercepted some enemy planes coming to attack our carriers, but I never got a shot at the enemy because all of the other pilots shot them down.[243]

With the Indian Operations complete, the Sōryū *began its voyage home for Japan. On the way back the ship tried to locate the American task force that bombed Tokyo, but they were unsuccessful. The* Sōryū *later returned to port on the 22 April.*[244]

Fujita's Views on the Zero fighter

The carrier *Sōryū* had such excellent aviation mechanics that maintenance problems were quite rare with the Zero fighters. The Type 0 was a superb fighter; I felt as if I was soaring and the aircraft was a part of me. The trim during level flight could be adjusted exactly to the point that I could fly level, without touching the controls. I even fell asleep on the way back from missions, which made the second and the third planes (in my group) worry about me! This fighter was designed to have excellent maneuverability by being as lightweight as possible. However, due to the lightweight construction, Japanese Navy pilots had very little protection during air combat. The enemies' bullets went right through our aircraft with no problem, and many of our aviators perished because of the fighter's light construction. The two wing-mounted twenty-millimeter cannons were quite powerful. However, they held only sixty bullets, and novice pilots would run out by firing them just twice. Skilled aviators could spread the ammunition to last for five to six firings.

The Battle of Midway

After the Indian Ocean Operation, we received new equipment and were trained at the Kasanohara base. On Navy Day 1942 our *Kidō Butai*, minus the aircraft carriers *Shōkaku* and *Zuikaku*, sailed for Midway.[245] On 4 June I took off from the carrier earlier than other attacking aircraft in order to patrol over the fleet. I tried to intercept the B-17 bombers that were trying to approach our fleet since the previous night; however, their flying altitude was much too high for me. I realized that they were bombing our fleet, but fortunately, their bombs did not hit us.

Soon after the Midway attack aircraft took off I received a message that additional enemy aircraft were approaching, so I flew towards their reported position. I then saw several B-26 bombers coming at low altitude, but I couldn't catch up with them in time. At that very moment, I also received information that other enemy aircraft were coming toward our ships, so I let my comrades handle the B-26 bombers while I went after this new group of aircraft. This new group of enemy aircraft consisted of twenty planes, which were flying in formations of five aircraft apiece in a four-step echelon. I had never seen this type of formation before.

At that time I was all alone, so I tried to think of the best way to shoot down as many enemy aircraft as possible. I gazed at the formation and decided against an attack from above and behind because the rear gunners would definitely shoot me down. Suddenly, an idea flashed in my mind; why not try to attack them with a diagonal frontal attack? My attack plan was successful, because when I looked back, I saw two aircraft engulfed in smoke and falling. After attacking them several times using this technique, probably half of them were shot down. Another Zero fighter then joined me and attacked the enemy aircraft, as well. Because of our attacks there were just three enemy aircraft left, and I raced after them to block their maneuvers. Following their attacks, I chased the surviving aircraft and shot them down. Next I received information that yet another group of aircraft were coming to attack. This time I found about twenty torpedo bombers flying at a low altitude, and they were flying in the same formation (as the previous group). I attacked them in the same way as I did before. After some other Zero fighters helped me attack them, we shot down about half of this group. The three surviving aircraft attacked our ships with torpedoes, but luckily none of them scored hits.

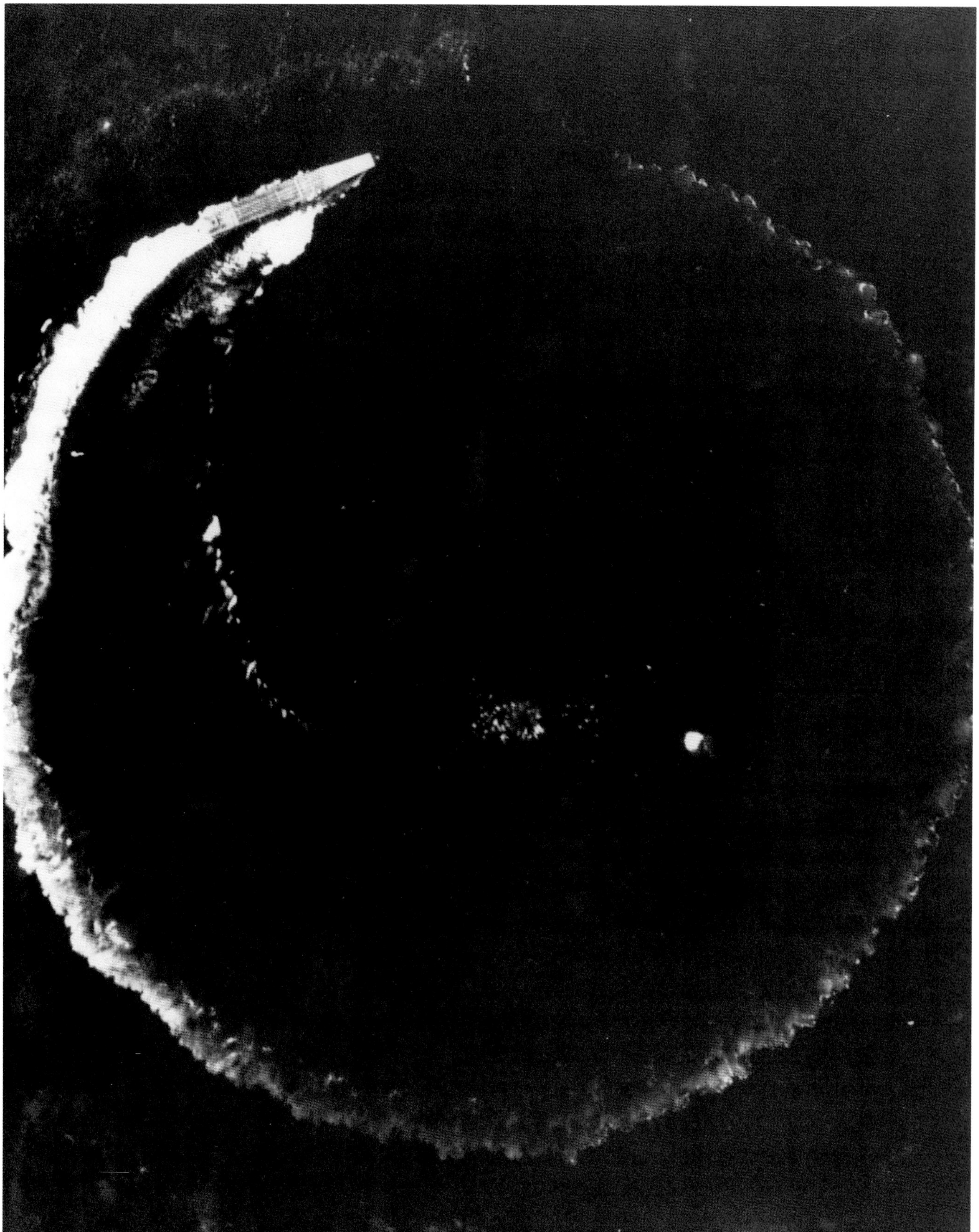

The carrier *Sōryū* under attack by B-17 bombers. (NHC via Parshall)

After these aerial melees I returned to the *Sōryū*. I then finished my report on the bridge and was waiting for my food, some rice balls. At that very moment I received a message that still another group of aircraft were coming to attack. My two comrades and I jumped into three Type 0 *kansen* which were being prepared to fly. While waiting to take off, I was finally given some rice balls to eat. However, just as I was taking a bite of one of them I received a signal to take off and had to reluctantly throw my food away.

Our group of Zero fighters then flew to the reported position and saw a formation of torpedo bombers. This group of aircraft attacked the same way as before and came very near our aircraft carrier. However, there were only four torpedo bombers, but numerous *kansen* were trying to attack them at the same time. Because I was worried about colliding with some of our own aircraft, I just made one attacking pass and decided to return to the *Sōryū*.

Suddenly, the belly tank of my fighter was hit by anti-aircraft fire from our ships. I then heard a big bang at my feet, and white smoke and fire spread through the cockpit.

In order to protect my face I pulled my goggles down over my eyes and wrapped my muffler around my neck. While I was looking for a good spot to do an emergency landing fire spread into the magazine of 7.7 mm bullets, and they started to crack off, so I knew I had to bail out in a hurry. After gaining some altitude I slid back my canopy. However, as I stuck my head out, I couldn't move because of the powerful g-forces. I don't know why, but suddenly I recalled a story that one of my teachers, Lieutenant Masao Satō, told me when I was doing my flight training. This particular instructor had a similar experience while doing his flight training. During one of his training missions another plane came close to his aircraft and severed the tail. While he was trying to bail out the same thing happened, and the pilot was stuck. He decided to put his feet up on the windshield and roll over. Suddenly, this memory flashed back to me, and I did the same thing. As I bailed out my altimeter read just 200 meters (656 feet). I was told that below 200 meters the parachute would not work, so I was yanking on my parachute rip cord, saying "Come on, open, open....." and at that same moment I splashed down. This all happened in about half a second. Luckily, my parachute opened just before I hit the water.

Although I was afraid of being attacked by sharks, I was exhausted, due to flying constant combat missions all day and a lack of food. While floating in the sea I could see three columns of smoke. I said to myself, "Wow, three ships were hit." I was on the high point of the wave and estimated the distance to the ships to be about twenty miles. I once had an experience of swimming ten miles, and it took me about twelve hours. I was hungry and exhausted, so there was no way that I could swim twenty miles. I simply said to myself, "Whatever happens will happen," and flopped down in the sea.

I must have been floating in the water for seven or eight hours before being woken up by some noise around me. When I looked around I saw *Akagi* burning not far from me. I then swam towards the destroyer *Nowaki*, which was helping with rescue operations. Since I was in the sun so long my face was red and my hair was messed up, and they thought that I could be an American pilot! They had their guns pointed at me, so I did a Japanese flag signal movement, to show that I was a Japanese officer. After this they retracted their guns and dropped a ladder. Two of my naval academy classmates, Aoki-san and Kanai-san, happened to be on board the ship, and thus I received good treatment. I often think about how lucky I was to survive the Battle of Midway; to this day, I really can't believe it.

Midway historian Mark E. Horan, who specializes in the aviation aspect of the battle, kindly explained which American groups Fujita-san fought against while doing CAP (Combat Air Patrol). "Fujita-san was the leader of the shōtai *forming* Sōryū's *third CAP flight of the day. He took off at 0710 during the height of the Midway based torpedo attack. Fujita-san engaged SBD Dauntless dive-bombers of VMSB-241.*[246] *He then landed at 0930, rearmed on deck, and took off again with the same wingmen at 0945 during the initial phases of VT-6's attack on* Kaga. *Fujita-san engaged the 2nd division of VT-6, then took off after the attacking aircraft from the carrier* Yorktown, *engaging Lieutenant Commander John S. 'Jimmy' Thach (flying a Grumman F4F-4 Wildcat) briefly and then chasing VT-3, probably being the group that chased them towards the carrier* Hiryū.*"*[247]

The Sōryū *was one of four Japanese aircraft carriers sunk during the Battle of Midway. On 4 June 1942 at 1025 the* Sōryū *was struck by three direct bomb hits which caused immense*

A Douglas TBD-1 Devastator, possibly from *Yorktown's* VT-3, armed with a Mk. XIII torpedo going to attack to the Japanese carriers during the Battle of Midway. (NA)

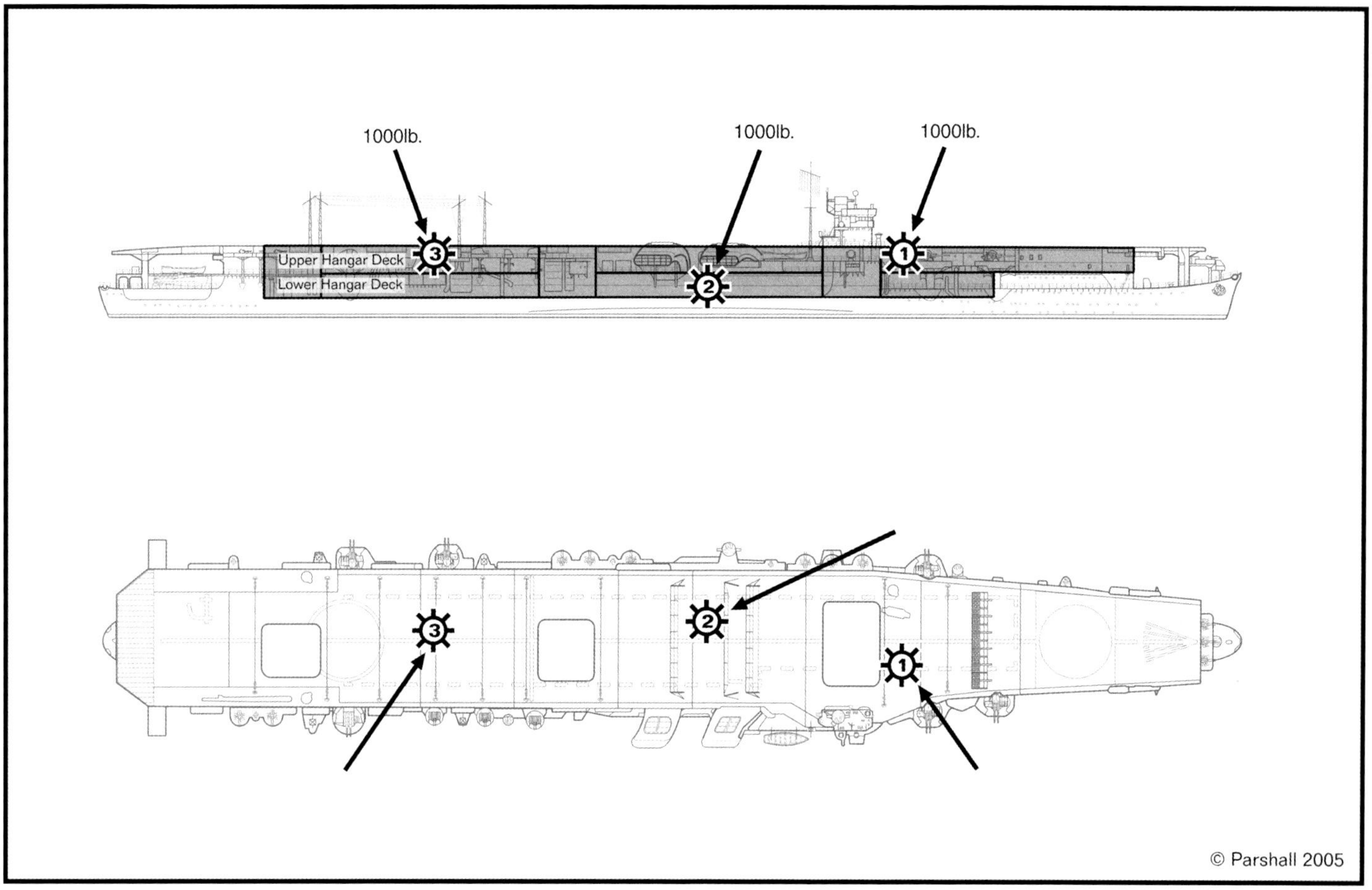

The hit locations on the *Sōryū* during the Battle of Midway. (Jonathan Parshall)

damage, and it was engulfed in flames.[248] *After the doomed carrier stopped dead in the water fifteen minutes after the air attack, the order was given to abandon ship. Later, the* Sōryū *was scuttled by the destroyer* Isokaze *with three torpedoes and 711 men perished, including Captain Ryūsaku Yanagimoto, who decided to go down with his ship.*[249]

Combat over Guadalcanal Island

After the battle of Midway, Fujita-san was assigned in July 1942 as the buntaichō *on the carrier* Hiyō. *It was during this time that the Imperial Japanese Navy was trying to reclaim the island of Guadalcanal. The* Hiyō *left Japan on 4 October and arrived just north of Guadalcanal on 17 October.*[250] *Unfortunately, the ship began to have engine troubles, so it was sent back to Truk.*[251] *As for the aviators on board the ship, some of them transferred to* Junyō, *and the remainder of the men, including Fujita-san, transferred to the heavily fortified Japanese base at Rabaul, New Britain Island. While stationed at Rabaul and later Buin (on Bougainville Island), he participated in the daily air melees over the skies of Guadalcanal Island. During our meeting, the ex-Zero pilot told me about one mission that really stood out in his mind from when he flew combat missions on a daily basis.*

All of the Japanese pilots like myself were very skilled. We would look at the American pilots as being equal to us, but not superior. On one occasion, either the enemy pilot was inexperienced, or what I did surprised him. I flew to attack Guadalcanal Island and began fighting a group of Grumman F4F Wildcat fighters. It was a mixed fight, and I climbed above the combat zone to see what was going on. Suddenly, I was attacked by an enemy fighter from the side. He got hits on my aircraft, and there was a big hole in the front section of my fuselage. My engine was failing, so I activated the manual hand pump and tried to restart it. The engine would not start, and by the time it restarted, I was only 1000 meters (3,281 feet) above the water.

I adjusted the throttle, but my fighter was barely flying. The Wildcat then came back and tried to get on my tail. Since my engine was failing, I knew that my fighter could not dog-fight. Still, I waited until the Wildcat was right in back of me—about 100 meters (328 feet)—and then I yanked back the stick, along with kicking my foot petal, which put my plane in a quick roll. Apparently the enemy pilot could not deal with this maneuver, and he just flew straight. When I finished my roll the American fighter was right in front of me, except I was out of 20 mm ammunition. I had 7.7 mm ammunition left, but they were inadequate against the

Wildcats. The enemy just dove away and broke off. On the way home to my base the engine stopped several times, and each time I had to restart it. I barely got back to Rabaul (New Britain Island).

We had several bases between Rabaul and Guadalcanal. Also there were islands in the vicinity that were occupied by the Japanese Army. These islands were marked on our maps with a red circle. If you were able to crash-land nearby any of these islands, you would at least be safe for the moment. Unfortunately, there was no guarantee that you could get back to your home base from there. I am sure that there were people that did not come back, but nobody knows what happened to them, so I cannot give concrete examples.

Combat over Iwo Jima

After serving as a buntaichō *of the fighter unit on the* Hiyō *until June 1943, Fujita transferred to the Tsuiki* Kōkūtai. *While serving with this unit, however, he did not participate in any combat missions. In November 1943 he became* hikōtaichō *of the brand new 301* Kōkūtai. *The commanding officer of the unit was Commander Katsutoshi Yagi.*[252] *On 4 March the unit was split into two groups, the 316 Fighter* Hikōtai *and 601 Fighter* Hikōtai.[253] *Fujita led the 601 Fighter* Hikōtai, *while Lieutenant Tadashi Minobe commanded the other group.*[254]

In June 1944, when I was a member the 301 *Kōkūtai*, we focused on training our pilots to fly the Mitsubishi *Raiden* fighter. During the same time we received an order to advance to Saipan Island. Our route was to fly via Iwo Jima Island, but the foul weather, caused by the heavy seasonal rain, forced us to return to Tateyama Air Base three times. Our *Raiden* fighters also had limited flying range, which made the flight difficult. Eventually headquarters became impatient, and ordered us to exchange our *Raiden* fighters for Zero fighters, then fly to Saipan Island. After we gave our *Raiden* fighters to a *kōkūtai* at Atsugi Air Base, our men spent one week gathering up the Type 0s to use for our unit. Unfortunately, we actually had a mix of older type A6M2 (Model 21) Zero fighters and newer type A6M5 (Model 52). We couldn't do any training prior to leaving.

I ended up assigning the older Zero fighters (Model 21) to the younger pilots, while the more experienced aviators were given the newer type (Model 52). After we advanced to Iwo Jima Island, our *kōkūtai* ended up staying there. During this time American forces had already began their invasion of Saipan Island. On 4 July our radar detected the enemy's mobile forces, and all of our aircraft took off to attack them. However, we never did locate any enemy aircraft, and maybe they did something to our radar (so it didn't get the proper location of their aircraft).

Shortly after we all landed the lookout reported, "There are a lot of incoming enemy aircraft flying at low altitude." We immediately took off, but by the time we gained some altitude there were air battles underway below us. In this mission (and others), you really didn't have time to think much about what you were doing, because all your thoughts were focused on what had to be done. Suddenly, I looked up and spotted an enemy F4U Corsair fighter. He started to fire at my aircraft, and I tried to out-maneuver him, but it was too late. The enemy pilot scored hits on my Zero fighter in the area between the engine and the cockpit. Fluids began to spray out of my damaged fighter and nearly blocked my view. I then took a shot at the Corsair before doing a crash-landing in my Type 0 *kansen*.

The following day our remaining planes intercepted the enemy, but the Model 52 Zero fighter was simply aggravating to fly. The aircraft's nose did not rise quickly enough, so it was hard to aim my machine-guns well. Because of this, I felt that I lost a lot of opportunities to get hits on enemy aircraft. Most of the land forces stationed on Iwo Jima dug caves and stayed inside them, where it was extremely hot, due to geothermal heat. I felt badly for them, because they must have experienced hell until they were killed, when American forces started to land on the island.

Fujita's unit suffered heavy losses and retreated to Japan via transport. The unit was disbanded on 10 July after returning to Japan.[255]

Action in the Philippines

In July 1944 Fujita became hikōtaichō *for the 402* Hikōtai, *which was consolidated into the 341* Kōkūtai.[256] *They flew the Kawanishi* Shiden *fighter in air melees over Taiwan and the Philippines. The air group was in charge of protecting the Philippines and suffered heavy casualties. During the fall of 1944 the first* tokkō *attacks were made against the Allied ships.*

The Kawanishi *Shiden* fighter was not that bad of an aircraft, and it flew very well—when everything worked correctly. The flaps worked well, and the armament was very powerful. However, I never flew any combat sorties with the *Shiden*. On one occasion, Japanese Army fighters attacked our formation and my wingman was shot down. We knew that their fighters were Japanese, but they did not recognize us.

The real problem with the *Shiden* fighter was the mechanical failures. What really made this problem worse was the lack of spare parts. It was hard to get extra parts, since all of our ships were being sunk and the transport aircraft were being shot down. Out of thirty-six airplanes in our unit, only about eight fighters were flyable. Therefore, I decided to take the 20 mm cannons from the non-flyable aircraft and put them into mounts. The cannons were used as anti-aircraft guns and manned by pilots. Commanding officers gave firing instructions to the pilots, who would follow their orders. Remarkably, they shot down about five enemy planes this way! Unfortunately, the next day the Americans came back with a large group of dive-bombers and devastated our air base.

In the Philippines I was asked to select twelve people from my *kōkūtai* to be pilots for a *tokkō* mission. I immediately went to the command post and asked, "Why do you want my men to do *tokkō* missions?" I also asked how many aviators were scheduled to make suicide missions. They responded that maybe one hundred men were scheduled to go, but many pilots couldn't fly because of illness. I said to them, "If you were on death row and made to wait for several days, of course you would get sick." Afterwards I

A wartime picture of Lieutenant Commander Iyozō Fujita, fighter pilot ace and officer in the Imperial Japanese Navy. (Fujita Collection)

exploded, and strongly disagreed with my superior officers. Then they seemed to look down on me.

After this incident happened I spoke with some other high-ranking officers in my *kōkūtai* and told them the story. Their response to me was that if the high command says to do this, we have to select the pilots. I said to them, "I refuse to do this. If you want to do it, I have nothing to do with this decision; you select the pilots." I then returned to my quarters and laid down on my bed. In the end, my superior officers selected the pilots for the *tokkō* mission. When the pilots were getting ready to take off I went to see them off. After they took off I could not stop crying.

I also want to emphasize the fact that I was not totally against doing the *tokkō* attacks. If a *tokkō* mission could achieve meaningful results, it was acceptable. But it was not always this way. For example, I had to escape from Clark Field in the Philippines because there were about four hundred American landing crafts in the Lingayen Gulf. I rode on a truck from the airbase and we were attacked by guerillas. Luckily, we found a transport aircraft and flew out of the Philippines to Taiwan.

When we arrived, there were four Type 0 *kansen* at the base. A high-ranking officer noticed that our pilots had escaped from the Philippines and said to the men, "We have four Zero fighters; go and do *tokkō* attacks against the landing craft in Lingayen Gulf." I told him, "What would a single *tokkō* attack do against 400 enemy ships?" Probably three out of the four Type 0s would have been shot down before even making their suicide attacks. At this time in the war I believe that the high command was going crazy. In the end the group of fighters still went on their mission, and nothing was ever heard from them again.

The Last Day of the War

On the last day of the war I heard the Emperor's radio broadcast at Fukuchiyama base and felt dejected, realizing that the war was finally over. I also felt sad, wondering if those who had fought the war, including me, would be put to death as war criminals.

Some sources state that Fujita had forty-two victories, while other sources claim eleven victories, but the number of recognized destroyed were seven.[257] *His final rank in the Imperial Japanese Navy was lieutenant commander.*

A postwar picture of Fujita-san with a model of his beloved Zero fighter. (Fujita Collection)

Postwar

After the war, he once again returned to the air and flew as a pilot for Japan Air Lines before retiring in 1977. Fujita-san flew an amazing 18,030 flight hours (both in the military and commercial airlines). He participated in several symposiums, such as the Battle of Midway Symposium at NAS Pensacola, and once served as the president for the Zero Fighter Pilots Association.

Reflections

When the war began, I knew that Japan would never win against the United States. I always wondered if any other country would have intervened and stopped the war. I always hoped that this would have happened. I really don't know how I want to be remembered—perhaps as a survivor. I want to be remembered as a survivor who was fortunate to survive from the start of the war at Pearl Harbor until getting shot down at Midway. It was a miracle that I survived; I often wonder how it was possible. It is just one of those things that is beyond human comprehension.

Sadly, Iyozō Fujita died on 1 December 2006, and couldn't see his story in this book. Coincidentally, his funeral was held on 8 December, which was the 65th anniversary of the Pearl Harbor attack (Japanese time). Blue skies Fujita-san, thank you for all your help.

Lieutenant Commander Yoshio Shiga

"I saw someone pedaling a bicycle as if this was a normal Sunday morning."

During my first research trip to Japan in the spring of 1999, I was fortunate to meet several very experienced WWII Japanese naval aviators; Lieutenant Commander Yoshio Shiga was one of those men. Shiga-san saw a lot of air combat in the war, and flew missions in China prior to participating in the Pearl Harbor attack. After war broke out with the United States, he took part in aerial actions over Rabaul, Dutch Harbor, and Guadalcanal Island. Then he became a test pilot, and his last assignment in the Navy was serving as the Executive Officer for the famed 343 Kōkūtai, *Japan's squadron of aces.*

During my visits to his Tokyo home he kindly showed me his large photo albums filled with photos from his days in the Navy.

Shiga's Early Days

I was born on 28 March 1914, and my surname was Yotsumoto before I got married. My family was originally from Kyūshū, but I was born in Tokyo. The Yotsumoto family came from the former samurai class, so I was raised very strictly. Even though the class system was abolished in Japan after the Edo period, class consciousness was still evident in our country when I was a young man.

My father, Kensuke Yotsumoto, graduated from the Naval Academy at Eta Jima in December 1893. While serving on board the cruiser *Matsushima*, he saw combat during the Russo-Japanese War in the Battle of the Yellow Sea. During the battle he was wounded in his leg by some shell fragments. I remember as a child when my father showed me the tattered trousers he wore during the battle and talked about his war stories. Furthermore, he was the head instructor at the Naval Academy when such important people as Admiral Isoroku Yamamoto, Admiral Teijirō Toyoda, and Vice Admiral Jisaburō Ozawa were students. My father retired as a rear admiral and died in 1927.

Shiga's Interest in Flying Blossoms

In April 1931 I entered the Naval Academy as a member of the 62nd Class. The Naval Academy was strict about giving all students equal opportunity, and being the son of a former instructor did not benefit me in any way. I won a medal in a speech contest while I was a student there. I also feel the academy provided me with a good education, and helped produce broad-minded people who would one day become the backbone of our nation.

I became interested in being a pilot during my senior year at the Naval Academy after seeing a demonstration by a group of three fighter biplanes called "Genda's Circus."[258] This flight demonstration team was formed in the pre-war days to promote the value of military aircraft. On this particular occasion, the three biplane fighters swooped down in formation right above us. We were impressed by their gutsy acrobatic demonstration and the roar of their fighters' radial engines. After holding hands with my good buddy Tadao Takahashi, we pledged together that we would one day become fighter pilots; it was as simple as that!

After graduation in November 1934 I served on board the battleship *Fuso*. On 1 April 1936 I transferred to the light cruiser *Jintsū*. While on this ship I went to Shanghai, China, and helped the emergency Navy brigade there. Finally, towards the end of the same year in December, I joined the Kasumigaura *Kōkūtai* and attended flight school. I completed my primary flight training in September 1937, and then my fighter aircraft training at Saeki *Kōkūtai*.

First Combat in China

After finishing my fighter aircraft training, I was simply thrilled to be assigned to the 13th *Kōkūtai* on 30 January 1938. My spirits were high when I did some additional training with the Type 96 *kansen* at Ōmura Air Base. Before leaving Japan, I dropped by a restaurant in Beppu to pay off the money that I owed to the madam. She began to weep and said "Yo-chan, are you going to die?"[259] Why on such a joyous occasion did she cry? I pressed her for an answer, but she wouldn't respond. Later, I found out that two other Navy pilots that she knew had already died in combat.[260]

Sea1c Hiromitsu Takahara and I arrived at the 13th *Kōkūtai* air base in Nanking, China, on 18 February. We flew to the base guided by a Type 94 *kanbaku*. However, on the same day Lieutenant Takashi Kaneko (a former flight instructor of mine) didn't return from an attack mission to Hankow. My first combat mission was 25 February, with PO3c Hirokazu Kashimura and another pilot

Yoshio Shiga when he was a young aviator in the Navy. (Shiga Collection)

An excellent photo of a Type 96 carrier fighter in flight. Shiga-san flew this type of aircraft when he was in China. This Type 96 was based on the carrier *Akagi*. (Matsumura Collection)

as my wingmen.[261] I also scored my first victory on this mission. Next, I transferred to the 12th *Kōkūtai* on 22 March 1938, and was a member of this group until August of that year. In August I went back to Japan and served as a flight instructor at Yokosuka *Kōkūtai*. I subsequently served on the carrier *Akagi* from 15 December 1938 until November of the following year, when I became *buntaichō* for the Ōita *Kōkūtai*.

Shiga-san the "Stunt" Pilot

On one particular occasion, when I was a member of the Ōita *Kōkūtai*, there was a small flying demonstration. Back then, when private corporations sponsored the cost of manufacturing a Mitsubishi Type 96 *kansen*, an acrobatic team was temporarily formed by the local *kōkūtai* in that region, and they performed a flying demonstration using the sponsored aircraft. As a rule bombers flew in a level formation, while fighters flew in a formation of three aircraft and did aerobatics.

For this particular demonstration, Lieutenant Commander Katsutoshi Yagi selected me to be the leader.[262] The second and third Type 96s were flown by PO2c Isao Hiraishi and PO3c Yukiharu Ozeki.[263] After looping in formation we dove down as if we were attacking the spectators on the ground. I remember well getting reprimanded by Yagi-san after our demonstration because I dove too low and made some school girls cry!

Both men flying with me were excellent pilots. Unfortunately, they both didn't survive the war. I will talk later about Hiraishi's death. In the fall of 1944, Ozeki-san was a member of the 203 *Kōkūtai* and flew combat missions in the Philippines. Sadly, he participated in a mission on 24 October 1944 but never returned. I often pray for my comrades who died in the war.

Shiga's Family

My wife and I got married in September 1940. Since her parents had no sons, I took their family name when we got married. So my last name changed from Yotsumoto to Shiga. After we settled down, my wife and I had five daughters.

Pearl Harbor

In the spring of 1941 I was on the carrier *Kaga* as a *buntaichō*, but then was temporarily assigned to the carrier *Hiryū* for combat operations in mid-1941, which were in the South China Sea. When war (with America) began, I was back on *Kaga* as *buntaichō* and participated in the Pearl Harbor mission as a member of the first wave attack group. Pearl Harbor was truly revolutionary, in that six aircraft carriers and their aircraft fought together as one unit. Our Type 0 fighters were based at Kōnoike Air Base (Kagoshima, Japan) in July 1941, and we began doing intense training. In September 1940 our Zero fighters moved to Saeki Air Base. Then, in October of that year, the commanders of the fighter units (including myself) had a meeting at Saeki Air Base. Commander Minoru Genda flew in on a Type 0 *kansen* and asked all lower-ranking men present to leave our meeting.

We gathered together in a small concrete room, and Genda-san told us about the plan to attack Pearl Harbor. I asked, "Why do a surprise attack? Why not intercept the fleet of the United States Navy in the middle of the Pacific Ocean as we always planned?" Genda-san told me that he was actually thinking that we would have to do a one-way attack in the beginning. I realized what he meant, that the U.S. fleet was a very formidable enemy, and the Imperial Japanese Navy was not sure if we could beat them with orthodox tactics. I worried very much whether I could keep this a secret for the next month or so until the attack.

I remember my Naval Academy classmate, Lieutenant Fusata Iida, well, because we were very good friends. He visited my home before the Pearl Harbor attack. This was just after my daughter was born. I told him to get a wife and settle down. He then pointed to my baby daughter and said, "I'll take her when the war is over." I said "Come on, are you going to wait for twenty years?" Iida-san said that he sure would, but unfortunately he died during the Pearl Harbor attack. Ironically, my daughter never did get married, and I sometimes think that maybe it happened because he is still waiting for her.

On 7 December, while on board the carrier *Kaga*, I saw Nakajima Type 97 *kankō* planes armed with live torpedoes for the first time. My only hope was that the American carriers would be at Pearl Harbor (when we attacked). During my mission there was a blue flare fired in the air, which signified a total surprise attack, but an additional flare was shot off. This really confused us; was our attack really a surprise or not?

Unfortunately, I saw no enemy aircraft carriers in the harbor, and observed our Type 97s near the west side of the island at low altitude, getting ready to attack. I looked for our Type 99 *kanbaku*, but they weren't around. Suddenly, I spotted them as they were making their dive-bombing attacks. However, they were supposed to go after the Type 97s finished their runs. "Idiots," I thought to myself.

The aviators who flew the dive-bombers were well seasoned and did not miss. I saw a bomb hit smack in the middle of a hangar. Luckily, the smoke (from their bomb hits) did not interfere with the torpedo bomber attacks because of the direction of the wind. I thought, "Shouldn't we be attacking the dock facilities and repair shops instead, so they can't fix their damaged ships?" I saw a yellow civilian biplane flying in the air. I thought nobody would attack this plane; but anything could happen in combat. I hoped that the biplane would get out of the air as soon as possible before it got into trouble. However, PO1c Akira Yamamoto (from our carrier) shot it down.[264] I also saw Lieutenant Shōichi Ogawa's Type 99s attacking a large B-17 bomber as it was landing.[265] I thought "Come on, you'll never down him with your puny 7.7 mm machine guns."

During the Japanese attack, around 0810 twelve B-17 bombers from the 38th Reconnaissance Squadron and 88th Reconnaissance Squadron were trying to land on Oahu Island. The unarmed bombers were flying from Hamilton Field, California, with "skeleton" crews. Furthermore, in the heat of the battle, the B-17s were targets for friends and foes alike. Out of the twelve

In the foreground of this photo is a B-17E bomber that landed safely at Hickam Field. It may have been piloted by First Lieutenant Karl T. Barthelmess. Note the smoke from the burning ships in the background. (NA via Wenger)

Captain Raymond Swenson's burnt out B-17C bomber at Hickam Field. (NA via Wenger)

B-17 bombers, one ground-looped at Bellows Field, two landed at Haleiwa Field, one landed on a small strip near a golf course, and eight of the bombers landed at Hickam Field. However, one of the B-17s which landed at Hickam Field, piloted by Captain Raymond T. Swenson, was destroyed while landing when it was attacked by a group of Type 0 fighters led by Akagi's *Lieutenant Commander Shigeru Itaya.*[266]

I saw no enemy fighters in the air, and our Zero fighters started to hit the deck and strafe the enemy airfields. At 0805 I personally led my unit down to strafe Hickam Field. As I strafed, I could see 20 mm shells bursting on the runway. I also could see the shells hitting the aircraft on the ground and exploding. I then switched targets and followed a paved road to Ewa Marine Air Corps Station. I saw someone pedaling a bicycle as if this was a normal Sunday morning. I also could see some single-engine aircraft that looked like fighters, and I destroyed three of them on the ground. Lastly, I flew to a predetermined rendezvous point and came home following a Nakajima Type 97 *kankō*.

During the Pearl Harbor attack, two Type 0 fighter pilots were lost from the carrier Kaga: *PO2c Seinoshin Sano and PO2c Toru Haneda.*[267]

The Loss of a Good Buddy

I lost my wingman, PO2c Isao Hiraishi, over Rabaul on 23 January 1942. Prior to joining my group, Hiraishi-san had a problem with his superior officer and was demoted. However, I thought that he was an exceptional pilot and requested him. I then succeeded in restoring Hiraishi's status. During this particular mission enemy opposition was expected to be very light. Prior to taking off Hiraishi-san brought me a parachute, but I said it wouldn't be necessary, because there were going to be no enemy fighters over Rabaul.

As I predicted we saw no enemy fighters over Rabaul, and ground targets also were scarce. I went low for a single strafing run and Hiraishi-san followed me down. After pulling out I saw him speeding towards (my aircraft) to join formation. I was alarmed to see fire shooting out of his exhaust stacks. Hiraishi-san pointed to his mouth, which was a gesture for not having enough fuel and that he couldn't return to the carrier. He then banked sharply, and I saw that his Zero fighter was shot in the belly by ground fire. Sadly, Hiraishi-san went into a split-S and crashed into the sea. I still blame myself for his loss because I told him not to wear a parachute.

I was then assigned to Tateyama *Kōkūtai* on 15 April 1942. I pleaded to be transferred to a frontline unit, because if I went back to Japan for a while my readiness to engage the enemy pilots would wear off. Then I probably would die when I flew combat missions again. After my request was granted, I immediately transferred to the carrier *Junyō* on 3 May, where I served as *hikōtaichō*.

While on board the carrier Junyō *Shiga-san participated in the Dutch Harbor attack, which was part of the Midway operation in the Aleutian Islands. Both Shiga-san and Lieutenant Commander Zenji Abe, whose account was in the first section of this book, were on the carrier* Junyō *during this operation. Lieutenant Commander Shiga was the leader of the escorting Type 0* kansen, *and Abe-san commanded the Type 99* kanbaku. *After the Type 99 carrier bombers completed their attacks on Dutch Harbor, they were engaged by eight Curtiss P-40 fighters flown by members of the 11th Fighter Squadron. Unfortunately, four of Abe's Type 99s were lost during the mission, and even sixty-five years later, Abe-san wonders what happened to Shiga's group of Type 0 carrier fighters that were supposed to protect his men. Nevertheless, Shiga's group of Zero fighters shot down two Curtiss P-40 fighters and lost none of their aircraft during the mission. Lastly, as a side note, one of the pilots who flew with Shiga-san for this mission was his buddy Yukiharu Ozeki (now a PO1c), whose story was mentioned earlier.*

Shiga-san also was one of the leaders for the disastrous 17 October 1942 mission to attack American shipping off Lunga (Guadalcanal Island). Zero fighters and Type 97 kankō *from both the* Junyō *and* Hiyō *took part in the mission and suffered heavy losses. This is the same mission that was mentioned in Lieutenant (junior grade) Kaname Harada's account in this book.*

Working as a Test Pilot

Shiga's next assignment was serving as a test pilot. In this role, he flew a number of advanced Japanese Navy fighter aircraft, including the Kawanishi N1K1-J Shiden, *N1K2-J* Shiden-kai, *and the Mitsubishi A7M* Reppu. *He was based at Oppama Airfield at Yokosuka base.*

On 16 January 1943 I transferred to the *Hikō Jikkenbu* (Flight Test division), which was part of the *Kōkū Gijutsushō* (Air Technical Arsenal). I became the leader of the Kawanishi N1K1-J *Shiden* fighter and N1K2-J *Shiden-kai* fighter development team. When I was transferred to this unit, I was not happy to be removed from the front lines at all. Furthermore, I was told that the Navy would not pay me any extra yen to do this dangerous job, but I could not refuse this assignment.

The Kawanishi N1K1-J *Shiden* fighter was a good airplane. It was heavily armed and structurally strong, which made it excellent for combat. So, I felt it was better than the Zero fighter, in that respect. I think the *Shiden* fighter was not bad overall, but I felt the N1K2-J *Shiden-kai* was better. The *Shiden* could be compared to a lively downtown girl. Our fuel octane level was down to just eight-five octane because the gas was mixed with oil extracted from pine tree roots (which was a volatile oil). Thus, the power from the Homare radial engine was much lower than its factory rating. However, even under such conditions, fighter aces such as Lieutenant Takashi Oshibuchi and Lieutenant Naoshi Kanno said that the *Shiden-kai* was very good up to around 9,144 meters (30,000 feet), and excellent to use for combat missions.[268] In my opinion, the *Shiden-kai* could deal with Grumman F6F Hellcats, but had a hard time against P-51 Mustang fighters.

Lieutenant Takashi Oshibuchi, who had six victories in the war. He died in action on 24 July 1945 while fighting VF-49's Hellcat fighters over the Bungo Straits. (Sakaida Collection)

Lieutenant Naoshi Kanno, who was credited with forty-eight victories during the war. He perished in combat on 1 August 1945 while engaging B-24 bombers over Yaku Shima. However, he wasn't hit by an enemy aircraft. One of his 20 mm cannons blew up in his wing and he never returned from the mission. (Sakaida Collection)

The Mitsubishi A7M *Reppu* fighter was a beautiful design, with large wings for low wing loading. However, the idea to design such a fighter with low wing loading for maneuverability was an idea that derived from peace time dog-fight training. In real combat, you don't want to get yourself even involved in a dog-fight. I compare the *Reppu* to a high society girl sheltered from the facts of the real world.

I was very ill in the summer of 1944. I recovered just as 343 *Kōkūtai* was being formed, and I was assigned to be the group's *hikōchō* on 25 December 1944.

343 *Kōkūtai* Days

Shiga's last assignment in the Navy was with the famed 343 Kōkūtai, *"The Squadron of Aces." They were an elite group of fighter pilots led by the legendary Captain Minoru Genda. This* kōkūtai *flew one of the best Japanese fighters of the war, the Kawanishi N1K2-J* Shiden-kai *against much larger groups of American aircraft, which were involved in combat missions over Japan. A number of well known aces flew with the group, such as Lieutenant Takashi Oshibuchi, Lieutenant Naoshi Kanno, and Ensign Shōichi Sugita.*[269] *Unfortunately, all of these aces and a number of other aviators from this group did not survive the war. As for Shiga-san, he ended the war with this* kōkūtai *and retired from the Navy at the rank of lieutenant commander.*

Postwar

In his postwar years, Shiga-san was the president of Nobel Industry Co., Ltd. The Tokyo-based firm was very successful, and produced fluorescent lamps for many companies and businesses throughout Japan. They also produced a successful line of products for the police, including the Nobel Lamp, Nobel Lantern, and an elastic nightstick. He served as president of the Zero Fighter Pilots Association from 1992 until 1997.

Reflections

During the war and today I abhorred the Japanese Army. When I was in the Navy, I remember one time when a two-seat Army aircraft landed at Saeki Air Base, and the pilot pleaded for some gas. I happened to be there at the moment and asked him, "How much fuel does your aircraft consume?" His answer was, "I'm not sure." Next, I asked another question, this time about lubricant consumption, and got the same dumbfounded answer. After his

The lethal Grumman F6F Hellcat was one of the toughest enemy aircraft that Japanese Navy pilots faced during the war. It had excellent armament, maneuverability, and armor. The one pictured here is from VF-17. (NMNA via Sakaida)

aircraft was refueled I told him, "Your airplane doesn't fly on your words alone; never come back here!"

I also didn't like the Army because it started a needless war in China and dragged the Navy into it. Our Navy lost a lot of good pilots and planes which were meant to be reserved for fighting the United States Navy in the Pacific Theatre. Recently, there are some historians that criticize Admiral Isoroku Yamamoto as being a mediocre leader. I feel this is very wrong. Admiral Isoroku Yamamoto promoted some notable projects during the war, including the licensing of the Oerlikon 20 mm cannon and the adoption of the strong Extra Super Duralumin (ESD) used for the construction of the Zero fighter.

Yoshio Shiga died at age 92 on 25 November 2005. He is survived by his wife and five daughters.

CPO Shoichi Sugita was one of the top aces in the 343 *Kōkūtai* with 120+ victories. He was killed on 15 April 1945 Kanoya Air Base. (*Maru* magazine via Sakaida)

Above: A group photo of the 301st *Hikōtai* of the 343 *Kōkūtai*, which was taken at Matsuyama Air Base in January 1945. Front row, left to right: second is Lieutenant Naoshi Kanno; fourth is naval aviation pioneer Captain Minoru Genda, commander of the group; and to the right of him is Lieutenant Commander Yoshio Shiga. CPO Sugita is third from the right in the second row. (Shiga Collection via Sakaida) Below: Shiga, doing his preflight checks prior to take off of a *Shiden-kai* fighter with "stars and bars" and no armament. (Shiga Collection)

During my interviews with Shiga-san, he spoke very well of his American veteran friend, Lieutenant Willard Pedrick, who was a Marine intelligence officer in the war. They are seen together in this photo when Lieutenant Commander Shiga was involved in the surrender of three *Shiden kai* fighters to occupation forces for evaluation purposes. The men became friends and stayed in contact after the war was over. (Shiga Collection)

Veteran Yoshio Shiga at his Tokyo home after our meeting in 2001. (Werneth)

Postscript

While living in Japan I worked as an English teacher and lived in Saitama Prefecture, which is very close to Tokyo. During my three year stay in Japan I was able to learn a lot about the country, culture, and people. The only aspect of the war that many of the Japanese people (who I encountered) seemed to know about is the atomic bomb and all the suffering their ancestors had because of World War II. Every time I heard this, I said to myself, "What about Pearl Harbor?"

Many Japanese people who I know (including my wife) said that one of the main reasons why they don't know much about the war is because very little time is spent covering modern history in school. For one thing, current history curriculum in Japanese schools is too long. Whether at a middle or high school level, students learn both world and Japanese history beginning with ancient times. They need to make time (in their school year) to study about recent history, and ideally this could be spent covering some of the 20th century conflicts, such as World War II. One would think that more time would be spent on this war so that the Japanese people could get a better understanding of what happened sixty years ago, and how Japan rose from the ashes of WWII to become the nation it is today. I feel another reason may be is that the war is simply a dark and painful period in Japanese history, so instead of remembering the conflict, it is much easier to put everything in a "dark corner" and try to forget it. Sadly, because of the above factors and because Japan lost the war, the people who fought and sacrificed so much are largely forgotten or misunderstood. I heard those sentiments from my WWII Japanese veteran buddies on countless occasions.

After the end of WWII, it was the veterans who helped rebuild the country. They became the businessmen, doctors, and educators, and worked in other professions that ultimately helped Japan become one of the richest countries in the world. Regrettably, I think only a few of the Japanese WWII veterans made their own personal peace with the war, such as Kaname Harada, who traveled to the United Kingdom to meet Commander John Sykes, the man he shot down during the war, and they became friends. Remarkably, even though Harada-san is now ninety years old, he continues to work at his family-run kindergarten and teach children about the importance of appreciating the world around them. Other veterans, however, still seem to feel a lot of sadness and bitterness because their sacrifices are largely forgotten today in Japan. It is my hope that these men will one day be remembered and appreciated for what they did for Japan over half a century ago.

I am happy to say that recently there seems to be a renewed interest in Japan about the war. For example, last year there was a successful movie produced, which portrayed the daily lives of the men who served on the battleship *Yamato*. There also is another recent film, *Letters from Iwo Jima*, which was directed by Clint Eastwood, and it tells the story of the Japanese men during the Battle of Iwo Jima. I believe that accurate and thoughtfully crafted works in modern Japanese media will help future generations understand what really happened over sixty years ago, and people will remember the men who sacrificed so much on behalf of their country.

During the three year period that I lived in Japan, I became good friends with many of the Japanese Navy veterans featured in this book. I am indebted to them for trusting me with preserving their stories for future generations. One unplanned "bonus" of my stay in Japan was meeting my wife Kaori. It was an honor for our family to have several of these distinguished gentlemen at our wedding in Tokyo four years ago. We will never forget these veterans and what they did for our family.

On a personal note, because of my research in Japan and passion for aviation history, I began to collect all the artifacts (such as flying gear, insignia, uniforms, etc.) related to WWII Japanese Navy aviators. Regrettably, when these men pass away, their families frequently don't know what to do with their WWII-related items, and sometimes the artifacts are even thrown away. Because of this I tried to save as much as I could of these special mementoes with the hope of preserving them for future generations. So if you're a reader of this book who may have some of the items mentioned above, please feel free to contact me via my website at www.beyondpearlharbor.com, or by regular postal mail at Ron Werneth, P.O. Box 564343, Chicago, IL, 60656. My website also will have additional articles, related links, etc. that will undoubtedly be of interest to people who enjoyed this book.

When you look on television at all the wars and death in this day and age, you have to ask yourself, Do people today really understand the horrors of war? I think if we did, there wouldn't be any more wars. Wouldn't that be a great way to remember all the people (of all nations) who died fighting in past conflicts? Global peace.

Color Gallery

WW II Japanese fighter pilot Kaname Harada traveled to the United Kingdom to make his peace with John Sykes, the RAF pilot he shot down on 5 April 1942 over Ceylon (now named Sri Lanka). This special event occurred as the result of the research by well known UK-based historian Christopher Shores and photographer Marcus Perkins. It was a very moving event for both veterans, and as a gesture of friendship Mr. Harada gave his wartime goggles to Mr. Sykes. (Marcus Perkins)

Distinguished dive-bomber pilot Kiyoto Furuta with a painting of his Pearl Harbor aircraft, a Type 99 *kanbaku*, which was painted by George Zielinski and given to him as a gift. (Furuta Collection)

A special reunion of probably the last surviving wartime Type 99 crew, pilot Kiyoto Furuta and observer Keiichi Arima. They met together with the author in Tokyo, February 2006. The men were lucky survivors of heavy combat in 1942 that claimed the lives of many of their comrades. (Werneth)

Pearl Harbor veteran (battleship USS *West Virginia*) Richard Fiske (left) and Japanese Pearl Harbor torpedo pilot Takeshi Maeda (who attacked his battleship) make their peace over half a century after the attack at a reunion in Hawaii. They were good friends until Fiske's passing in April 2004. (John DiVirgilio)

Veteran Takeshi Maeda with his wife, daughter-in-law, and granddaughter. (Maeda Collection)

Haruo Yoshino in his home with a painting of his Type 97 *kankō*, which was painted by George Zielinski as a gift to him. (Yoshino Collection)

The author with veteran Haruo Yoshino, his two daughters, and granddaughter during a visit to Yoshino's beautiful one-hundred year old family home in rural Mobara, Chiba (fall 2003). (Werneth)

Akagi veteran Hiroshi Suzuki and the author's longtime interpreter, Keigo "Hammer" Nakahama. "Hammer" was the person responsible for translating the majority of the interviews and diaries used in this work. In the upper left corner of the picture is one of Mr. Suzuki's prized rose bouquets, which is his passion to this day. (Werneth)

The late Yuji Akamatsu pictured with a stone marker that commemorates the planting of some trees by both American and Japanese World War II veterans in the name of peace and friendship in Saeki City, Japan. ((John DiVirgilio)

The author with *Shōkaku* and 601 *Kōkūtai* aircraft mechanic Hachirō Miyashita. This warm-hearted veteran introduced the author to several important Japanese Navy airmen featured in this book and assisted him with his research in Japan. (Werneth)

Wedding day for the author and his wife Kaori in Tokyo (5 October 2003). They were honored to have several WWII Japanese veteran friends attend the ceremony. (Left to right): Minoru Toyonaga (302 *Kōkūtai Gekkō* pilot), Takeshi Maeda (*Kaga* veteran), Mrs. Iwashita, Kunio Iwashita (the last president of the Zero Fighter Pilots Association), Tomokazu Kasai (343 *Kōkūtai* ace), Jirō Yoshida (Public Relations Director of *Unabarakai* (Association of World War Two Japanese Naval Aviators), and Haruo Yoshino (*Kaga* veteran). (Andrew Weiss)

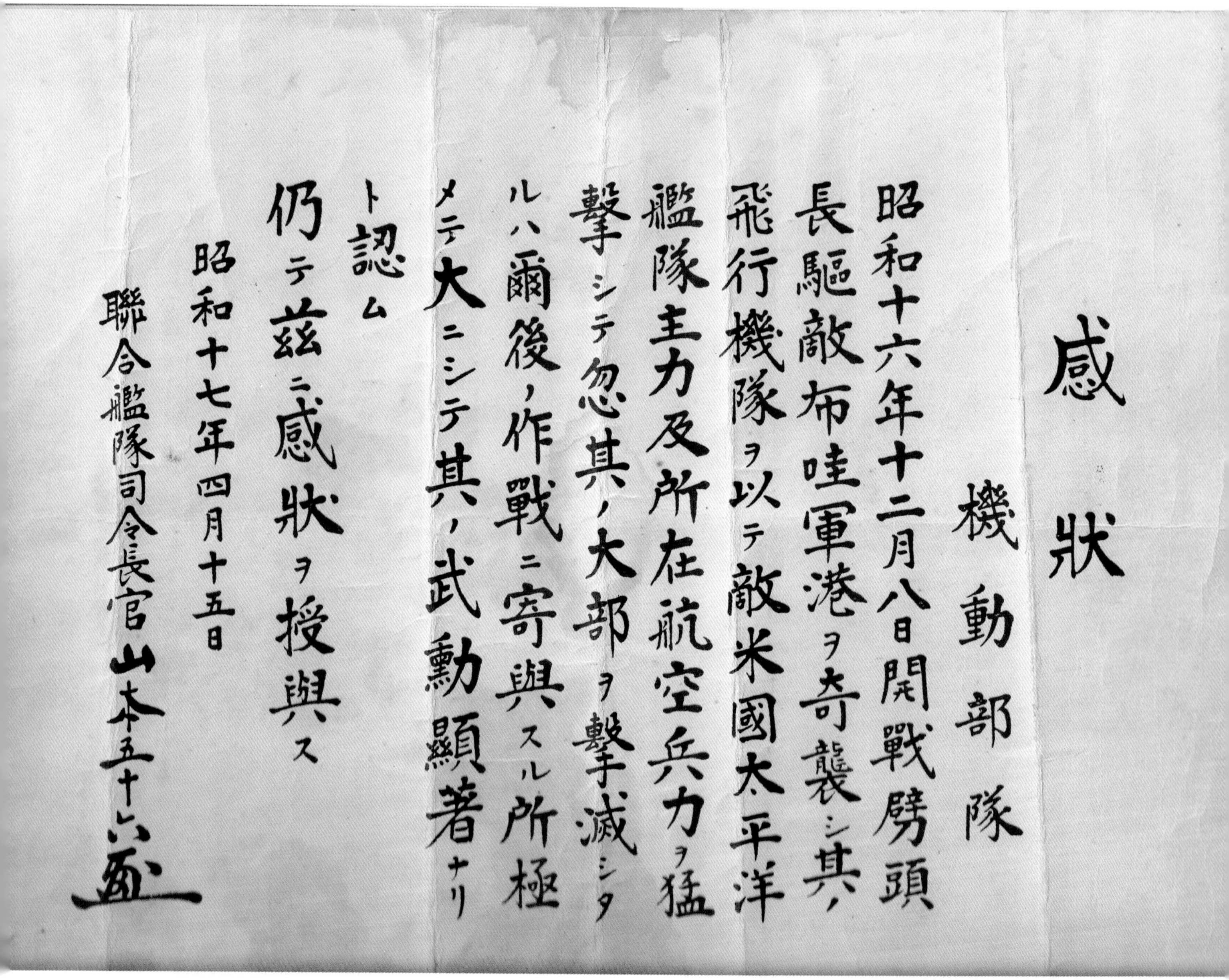

感狀

機動部隊

昭和十六年十二月八日開戰劈頭
長驅敵布哇軍港ヲ奇襲シ其ノ
飛行機隊ヲ以テ敵米國太平洋
艦隊主力及所在航空兵力ヲ猛
擊シテ忽其ノ大部ヲ擊滅シタ
ルハ爾後ノ作戰ニ寄與スル所極
メテ大ニシテ其ノ武勳顯著ナリ
ト認ム

仍テ茲ニ感狀ヲ授與ス

昭和十七年四月十五日

聯合艦隊司令長官 山本五十六

The citation given to PO2c Hideo Honma, a Type 97 *kankō* pilot from the carrier *Zuikaku*, for attacking Pearl Harbor. It was written by Admiral Isoroku Yamamoto, Commander in Chief of the Combined Fleet. According to my research, this citation was given to every man (not only pilots) who participated in the Pearl Harbor Operation. Nevertheless, out of all the Pearl Harbor veterans whom I met, Honma-san was the only person who still had this award. To my knowledge, there were no other awards or commendations given for participating in this mission, only this citation. (Hideo Honma Collection)

Here is the translation:
"Citation is made for outstanding services rendered by the aforementioned unit in connection with a strike on the enemy naval harbor at Hawaii by carrying out a long voyage at the very beginning of the war on 8 December 1941, when the unit did a surprise attack and destroyed the main force of the U.S. Pacific Fleet as well as most of the enemy air strength existing there by fierce assaults by the unit's aircraft group. It is recognized that its action greatly contributed to our operations to be developed thenceforth."

Signed, Isoroku Yamamoto, Commander in Chief of the Combined Fleet

Kaga Kitajima-tai on 6 December 1941, the day before Pearl Harbor (left to right, on the photo): first row, fourth position: PO3c Yuji Akamatsu; second row, third position: Lieutenant Ichirō Kitajima; fourth position: Lieutenant Minoru Fukuda; fifth position: WO Takayoshi Morinaga; and fourth row, sixth position: PO2c Takeshi Maeda. (Yoshino Collection)

Aichi D3A1 Type 99 *kanbaku* (Allied code name "Val")
This profile depicts Type 99 (tail # EII-238), armed with one 250 kilogram "land" bomb for attacking land targets, from the carrier *Zuikaku* on 7 December 1941. It flew during the first wave and attacked Wheeler Field. The crew consisted of pilot PO2c Kenji Hori and observer/radioman Lieutenant Reijiro Ōtsuka. Hori is still alive today, but Lieutenant Ōtsuka died on 26 October 1942 during the Battle of Santa Cruz. (Profile by George Zielinski, A.G.P.)

Aichi D3A1 Type 99 *kanbaku* (Allied code name "Val")
This profile depicts Type 99 (tail #AI-251) armed with one 250 kilogram "ordinary" bomb for attacking ships. It flew during the second wave and attacked the fleet oiler *Neosho*. The crew consisted of pilot PO1c Kiyoto Furuta and observer/radioman Lieutenant Takehiko Chihaya. Furuta is still healthy today, but Lieutenant Chihaya died on 11 June 1944 in the Marianas; he was promoted posthumously two ranks to captain after his death. (Profile by George Zielinski, A.G.P.)

Yokosuka D4Y4 *Suisei* Type 43 *kanbaku* (Allied code name "Judy")
This profile depicts D4Y4 (tail# 601 35) armed with one 800 kilogram bomb, which was semi-recessed beneath the fuselage. This *Suisei* flew with the 601 *Kōkūtai*, and was based at Hyakurigahara Air Base (in Ibaraki Prefecture) during the summer of 1945. It was designed to be flown as a single seat aircraft with no radioman/gunner for *tokkō* attack missions. (Profile by George Zielinski, A.G.P.)

Nakajima B5N2 Type 97 *kankō* (Allied code name "Kate")
This profile depicts Type 97 (tail # AII-305) armed with one 800 kilogram torpedo from the carrier *Kaga* on 7 December 1941. It flew during the first wave and attacked the battleship USS *Oklahoma*. The crew consisted of pilot PO2c Ichiji Nakagawa, observer PO2c Haruo Yoshino, and radioman/rear gunner Sea1c Mitsuo Kawasaki. Only Yoshino survived the war, and helped with the research for this book. Remarkably, the veteran and author discovered the original tail number of his Pearl Harbor aircraft written on the back of a sixty-five year old crew photo of Yoshino and his comrades. (Profile by George Zielinski, A.G.P.)

Nakajima B5N2 Type 97 *kankō* (Allied code name "Kate")
This profile depicts Type 97 (tail # AII-312) armed with one 800 kilogram torpedo from the carrier *Kaga* on 7 December 1941. It flew during the first wave and attacked the battleship USS *Virginia*. The crew consisted of pilot PO3c Yōshirō Yoshikawa, observer PO2c Koji Ohjino, and radioman/rear gunner PO2c Takeshi Maeda. Maeda is the only member of this crew that is still alive. One controversial topic is whether or not Type 97 *kankō* (during the Pearl Harbor strike) were painted with a brown vertical tail. According to all my own research and comprehensive interviews with several *Kaga* veterans, there was no simply no reason why the tails of their aircraft would be brown. Furthermore, there are no period photos that depict *Kaga's* Type 97s with brown tails. (Profile by George Zielinski, A.G.P.)

Nakajima B6N2 *Tenzan kankō* (Allied code name "Jill")
This profile depicts *Tenzan* (tail# 12-382) armed with one "practice" torpedo with a red warhead for training purposes. It flew with the 312 *Hikōtai*, 601 *Kōkūtai*. The time period is just prior to the Battle of the Philippine Sea (June 1944). (Profile by George Zielinski, A.G.P.)

Nakajima C6N1 *Sauin* carrier reconnaissance airplane (Allied code name "Myrt").
This profile depicts a *Sauin* that flew with the 102 *Hikōtai*, 752 *Kōkūtai*, and was based at Kisarazu Air Base. On 30 October 1945 it was one of two C6N1s that were surrendered to American occupational forces at Oihama (part of Yokosuka) Air Base. Please note the lack of armament, and it is not known if this particular *Sauin* had any special tail markings. (Profile by George Zielinski, A.G.P.)

Mitsubishi A6M2 (model 21) *kansen* (Allied code name "Zero" or "Zeke")
This profile depicts an A6M2 Zero fighter (tail # BI-151) that flew from the carrier *Sōryū* during the second wave of the Pearl Harbor attack. The pilot was Lieutenant Fusata Iida, and his aircraft was damaged while strafing Kaneohe Naval Air Station. Because Iida knew that it was impossible to return to his carrier and he didn't want to become a POW (prisoner of war), the young pilot decided to crash his damaged A6M2 into an area near Kaneohe Naval Air Station. (Profile by George Zielinski, A.G.P.)

The last meeting of some of the WW II Japanese Navy veterans, friends, and family who participated in the *Beyond Pearl Harbor* book project. This photo was taken at the Navy Club in Tokyo on 29 November 2007. This club is on the grounds of the Tōgō Shrine (dedicated to Navy hero Admiral Heihachirō Tōgō) and a popular meeting spot for Japanese Navy veterans. The author was very moved and emotional at this special meeting of so many fine people and long-time friends. Front row (Left to Right): Saburō Abe (Zero pilot), Hiroshi Masui (historian), Kaname Harada, Hiroshi Suzuki, Keiichi Arima, Mrs. Harada, Angie Ralph, and Hachirō Miyashita. Back row: Kaori Werneth, Ron Werneth, Takeshi Maeda, Jiro Yoshida, Roger Paykert, and Yoshie Okabe. (Yoji Kutsuzawa Photography)

Appendix 1: WWII Japanese Navy Air and Seaplane Base Map

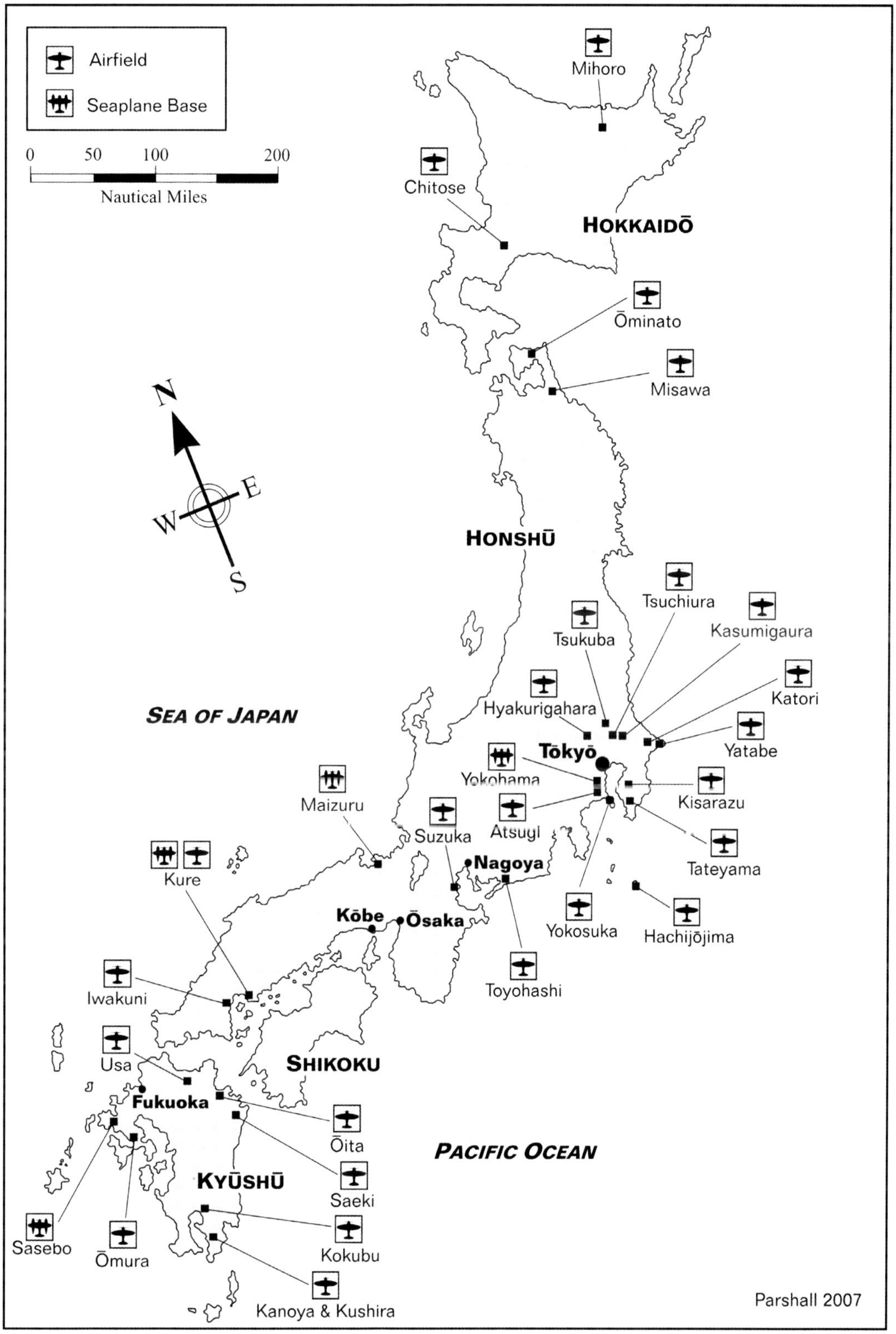

A locator map of some of the airfields and seaplane bases in Japan during the war. Note this map doesn't include every single base or small airstrip in the country. It focuses on several of the air bases mentioned in the veterans' accounts to help the reader get an idea where the stories took place. (Created by Jonathan Parshall with the help of historian Osamu Tagaya)

Appendix 2: Routes flown by the Pearl Harbor strike aircraft

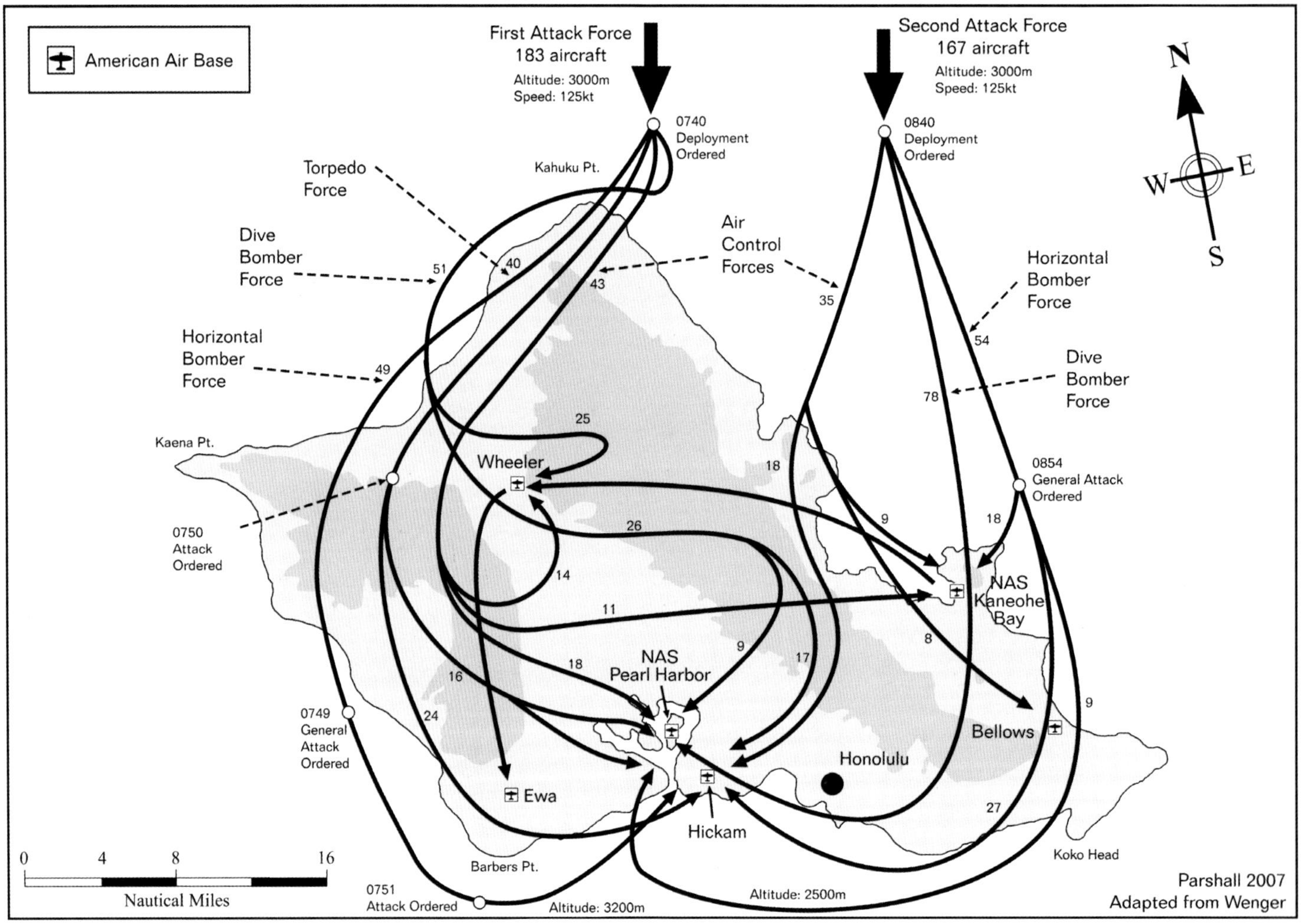

The routes taken by both the first and second wave attacking Japanese Navy aircraft are clearly shown in this illustration. (Created by Jonathan Parshall with the help of historian J. Michael Wenger)

Glossary of Japanese Terms

Buntai – A group or division; a *Hikō Buntai* – Flying group
Buntaichō – Division officer
Buntaishi - A leader of a section in a *buntai* but still under the command of the group's *buntaichō*
Chūkō – A casual unofficial term (see *rikkō*), being short for *Chūgata kōgekiki* (i.e. medium-size attack aircraft). It was used by Japanese Navy personnel as a casual-reference generic term to refer to twin-engine, medium-sized bombers such as the Mitsubishi Type 1 "Betty" to distinguish them from larger aircraft in the same category.
Chūtai – A unit of six to nine aircraft
Chūtaichō – Commander of a *chūtai*
Go - A traditional two-player Japanese board game which is based on strategy
Giman-shi – This word literally means "radar cheating paper" which was similar to "chaff" that was used by Allied pilots to confuse radar controlled guns
Ginmeshi – This literally means silver rice (pure rice) which wasn't mixed with barley. Only officers in the Imperial Japanese Navy (both commissioned and warrant) had the privilege of eating *ginmeshi*
Hikōchō – Air Officer
Hikōkitai – Literally, it means "aircraft unit," but in vernacular English it signifies the flight echelon or aircraft echelon of the carrier (as opposed to other elements of the ship, such as the machinists in the boiler room, or the sailors manning the flight deck). This term was used for both carrier-based and land-based aircraft units
Hikōtai - Flight echelons of land-based units or carrier-based units
Hikōtaichō – Leader of a flight echelon
Hinomaru - The red disc that represented Japan which was painted on the aircraft's wings and fuselage. It also could be found on a number of other items such as Japanese flags, insignia, etc.
Hanchō – Leader of a small group
Jima – an island, for example, *Hachijō Jima* can be called Hachijō Island
Kanbaku – The abbreviation used for a carrier bomber (dive-bomber), *Kanjō bakugekiki*
Kanbaku-tai – carrier bomber (dive-bomber) unit
Kankō – The abbreviation used for carrier (torpedo) attack plane, *Kanjō kōgekiki*
Kankō-tai – carrier attack plane unit
Kansen – The abbreviation used for carrier fighter, *Kanjō sentōki*
Kidō Butai – It literally means mobile force. The official designation for the Japanese carrier attack force
Kikusui – This is an ancient Japanese symbol dating to medieval times. Tradition ascribes it to Kusunoki Masashige, a warrior whose legendary loyalty to the emperor led him to die willingly in battle against overwhelming odds. It literally means "chrysanthemum and water" or "floating chrysanthemum," and was the overall name given to the series of *tokkō* sorties during the Okinawa campaign
Kōkūtai – A land-based Japanese Navy Air Group
Koshimaki - A slip type undergarment, which was worn with kimonos by women. During Japan's wartime years, they didn't wear panties while wearing kimonos, only *koshimakis*
Miso shiru - Soybean paste soup
Mochi - Rice cake
Mugimeshi – A mixture of rice and barley which was served to enlisted and petty officer ranks in the Imperial Japanese Navy
Norimaki – Rice that is wrapped in dried seaweed and the inside can be filled with such things as sour plums or fish
Omamori – A Japanese good luck charm which is usually an amulet covered in cloth and inside there is a piece of paper or wood that has a prayer that is supposed to bring good luck to the person
Raigeki-tai – torpedo bomber unit
Rikkō – A more official term than *chūkō* used to describe land-based attack aircraft such as a Mitsubishi Type 1 "Betty" bomber. It is an abbreviation of *Rikujō kōgekki*, the proper designation for this category of aircraft
Saké – An alcoholic drink brewed mainly from rice
Shōchū - An alcoholic drink made from sweet potatoes
Shōtai – A unit of two to four planes (usually three)
Shōtaichō – Commander of a *shōtai*
Shuho – The Japanese version of a P/X on the carrier where the crew could buy alcohol, tobacco and other personal items
Taichō – This term literally means "leader"
Tatami – Traditional Japanese flooring mats made of woven straw
Tei – Term used after a Japanese aviator says "*yōi*" during his attack, literally means to "launch" or "fire" the torpedo or bomb
Tokkō – a suicide attack mission using a variety of methods such as crashing into a target by airplane or a boat, which most westerners refer to as kamikaze but Japanese people normally use this term instead; *Tokkō-tai* – a Japanese military unit that did suicide attack missions
Yōi – Term used when a Japanese aviator is preparing to drop his armament such as torpedo, literally means "ready"
Yokaren - Flight Reserve Enlisted Trainee Class System; *Otsu-yokaren* – Pilot trainees from the second grade of advanced primary school or middle school (fifteen years old or older); *Kō-yokaren* - Pilot trainees from the fourth grade of middle school (seventeen years old or older)
"Zengun totsugeki seyo!" - "All forces attack!"

Endnotes

1 Source of this chart: Ikuhiko Hata and Yasuho Izawa, *Japanese Naval Aces and Fighter Units in World War II*, xii.

Part 1 - Overview
2 Some of the technical details such as horsepower and armament were derived from: René J. Francillon, *Japanese Aircraft of the Pacific War*, 268-276 and 454-461. Hereafter *Japanese Aircraft of the Pacific War*. Osamu Tagaya also was instrumental in putting this overview together.

"Everyone thought about how to beat the enemy."
3 Commander Takashige Egusa was a well-known pilot in the Imperial Japanese Navy. He died on 15 June 1944.
4 Henry Sakaida, *Imperial Japanese Navy Aces 1937-45*, 6-7. Hereafter *Imperial Japanese Navy Aces 1937-45*.
5 Egusa's partner for the Pearl Harbor attack was WO Tatsuki Ishii. Ishii-san later died in action on 17 June 1944 in the Marianas.
6 According to 356-357 *Hawaii Sakusen* and map supplement, Furuta's target was the fleet oiler *Neosho*.
7 *Mizumi-kai* is the name of a veteran's group that is comprised of Japanese Navy veterans, both aviators and mechanics, who served on board carriers during the war. Several of the people in this book, including Furuta-san, Hachirō Miyashita, Keiichi Arima and Hiroshi Suzuki, are members of this group. They held an annual meeting at the Yasukuni Shrine in Tokyo until 2005. However, this was the last year for the meeting as many members are too old or have died.
8 The background of the results of the Japanese attack were taken from: Jonathan Parshall and Anthony Tully, *Shattered Sword: The Untold Story of the Battle of Midway*, 203. Hereafter *Shattered Sword: The Untold Story of the Battle of Midway*.
9 www.combinedfleet.com
10 Ibid.
11 Lieutenant Commander Mamoru Seki was the overall commander of the attack force which consisted of twenty-seven Type 99s and ten Zero escort fighters.
12 John Lundstrom, *The First Team and the Guadalcanal Campaign*, 136-138. Hereafter *The First Team and the Guadalcanal Campaign*.
13 War Damage Report No. 59, "USS *Enterprise* (CV6) War History", Bureau of Ships, Navy Department., hereafter War Damage Report No.59.
14 *The First Team and the Guadalcanal Campaign*, chart, 147.
15 War Damage Report No. 59
16 USS *Enterprise* Action Report for 26 October 1942.
17 *The First Team and the Guadalcanal Campaign*, chart, 418.

3 "I don't understand why we had to go to war with the United States."
18 Seki's background was kindly provided by researcher Jean-Francois Masson using original Japanese records.
19 The 1st Air Fleet consisted of the 1st Carrier Division (*Akagi*, *Kaga*) and 2nd Carrier Division (*Sōryū*, *Hiryū*) under the command of Vice Admiral Chūchi Nagumo.
20 The *Suisei* carrier bomber and Type 0 fighter were very close in top speed. For example, a *Suisei*, D4Y2 (Model 12) had a top speed of 313 kt at 5,250m (360 mph at 17,225 ft) while an A6M5 (Model 52) Type 0 fighter had a top speed of 305 kt at 6,000m (351 mph at 19,685 ft). *Japanese Aircraft of the Pacific War*, 377, 461.
21 According to Yokosuka *Kōkūtai*, "Lessons (air operations) of the Sea Battle off Hawaii," I, 37, (typescript in Prange Collection, via Michael Wenger), Abe's actual target was the *Raleigh*.
22 According to Michael Wenger, records indicate Abe-san hit the *Cornwall* rather then the *Dorsetshire*. The *Akagi* unit split its attacks with Abe's lead division going after the *Cornwall* and the second division going after the *Dorsetshire*. *Akagi Kōdōchōsho*, 5 April 1942
23 Many of the "hits" were most likely very near-misses, which ultimately were responsible for the loss of the underwater integrity of both cruisers. Wenger analysis/opinion using the After Action Reports for the *Dorsetshire* and *Cornwall*.
24 *Maru Nishi* translated into English is "Zero West." The American name for this landmark was Ship Rock. It was a large rock formation which was located in the waters off Umnak Island.
John Haile Cole, *The Aleutian Warriors, A History of the 11th Air Force & Fleet Air Wing 4*, 126. Hereafter *The Aleutian Warriors, A History of the 11th Air Force & Fleet Air Wing 4*.
25 According to Abe, his classmate Lieutenant Yasushi Nikaido died in a mid-air collision. This occurred on 8 May 1942 off of Izu.
26 Abe-san is correct about this, he is talking about the airbase at Otter Point on Umnak Island. The Japanese Navy didn't know about this airbase prior to their attack. After the battle, it was renamed Cape Field, in honor of Second Lieutenant John Cape who died in air combat on 4 June 1942. *The Aleutian Warriors, A History of the 11th Air Force & Fleet Air Wing 4*, 127.
27 All of the information regarding the American side of the air battle came from the official 11th Fighter Squadron History.
28 According to the official 11th Fighter Squadron History, Cape was posthumously awarded the Distinguished Flying Cross for his actions on 4 June 1942. It says that while Cape was in the process of shooting down a Zero fighter in order to protect another friendly aircraft, a second Zero fighter shot him down.
29 Remarkably, McIntyre's P-40E fighter's remains were recovered in September 1998 by the US Army and Coast Guard. It is now on display at the Alaskan Aviation Heritage Museum (Anchorage, Alaska) awaiting restoration.
30 *The Campaigns of the Pacific War*, United States Strategic Bombing Survey (Pacific) Naval analysis Division, 1946.
31 The objective of the pilot was to make a three point landing, a perfect landing, within this circle.
32 Unfortunately, Kaneko died just three days later on 14 November 1942 in action off Guadalcanal Island.
Ikuhiko Hata and Yasuho Izawa, *Japanese Naval Aces and Fighter Units in WW II*, 381. Hereafter
Japanese Naval Aces and Fighter Units in WW II.
33 *The First Team and the Guadalcanal Campaign*, 472-473.
34 Admiral Yamamoto was killed on 18 April 1943 when his Mitsubishi G4M1 , Model 11, "Betty" bomber was intercepted and shot down by P-38 fighters flown by members of the 339th Fighter Squadron.
35 Zenji Abe and Michael Wenger, *The Emperor's Sea Eagle*, 160. Hereafter *The Emperor's Sea Eagle*.
36 According historian Michael Wenger, Abe-san commanded only the naval portion of the garrison. The overall garrison commander was Major Shigeo Imagawa.
37 *The Emperor's Sea Eagle*, 161.
38 LST stands for Landing Ship, Tank. During the war, these amphibious vessels carried troops, supplies and tanks. (The USS LST Ship Memorial website)

4 "I thought we did something extraordinary."
39 Kenji Hori was in the same class as Takeshi Maeda whose story is also in this book.

40 There should have been twenty-seven Type 99s in Hori's group but on this mission the group was short two aircraft, possibly due to mechanical problems.
41 Two second wave *Kaga* Type 0 carrier fighters (out of a total of nine) were shot down during the second wave so it is hard to determine if all nine actually hit Wheeler Field. However, several sources state that eight *Kaga* Zeros struck this target.
42 VII Fighter Command History: 1 November 1940-7 December 1941, AFHSO, Bolling AFB, Reel 8576, File 744.01, p.8 (provided by Michael Wenger)
43 Report from Brigadier General Howard C. Davidson, Commanding General, VII Interceptor Cmd. To Commanding General, HAF, 18 December 1941. (provided by Michael Wenger)
44 Please see Haruo Yoshino's account of the 20 January 1942 Rabaul attack for more background information.
45 Please see Kaname Harada's story for more background information about this mission.
46 Japanese sources quote 1126-1140 as their attacking time, but action report of the of the USS *Neosho*, 25 May 1942, states the time was between 1201-1218 when their vessel was attacked by twenty-four enemy planes. However, the After Action Report of the USS *Sims*, 18 May 1942, states 1155 as the time that the enemy aircraft began engaging the USS *Neosho*.
47 After Action Report of the USS *Neosho*, 25 May 1942
48 Ibid.
49 Official USN Combat Casualty List (kindly provided by James Sawruk)
50 All of the background information on the attack of the *Sims* was gathered from the After Action Report of the USS *Sims*, 18 May 1942.
51 After Action Report of the USS *Neosho*, 25 May 1942
52 Official USN Combat Casualty List (via James Sawruk)
53 John B. Lundstrom, *The First Team: Pacific Naval Air Combat from Pearl Harbor to Midway*, 270-271. Hereafter *The First Team: Pacific Naval Air Combat from Pearl Harbor to Midway*.
54 Ibid.., 224.
55 Official USN Combat Casualty List (via James Sawruk)
56 Ibid.
57 Please see Hachirō's Miyashita's story in this book for a vivid description of the attack on *Shōkaku*.
58 *Kōdōchōshos*, *Shōkaku* and *Zuikaku*, 26 October 1942 (provided by Michael Wenger).
59 Richard B. Frank, *Guadalcanal*, 397. Hereafter *Guadalcanal*.
60 *The First Team and the Guadalcanal Campaign*, 448
61 Negishi-san later died on 29 March 1944 off Okinawa.
62 *Guadalcanal*, 397
63 *The First Team and the Guadalcanal Campaign*, 448.
64 Ibid., 450.
65 *Guadalcanal*, 400.
66 Lieutenant Yukio Seki led the first successful Kamikaze mission on 25 October 1944. During this mission he commanded five Type 0 carrier fighters and was escorted by four additional Zero fighters. Seki's group was responsible for sinking the *USS St. Lo* and seriously damaging the *USS Kalinin Bay*. They also had a near miss on the *USS White Plains* when anti-aircraft fire shot down the fighter, and it crashed near the ship (in the water). Lastly, the *USS Kitkun Bay* was struck by one of the Kamikaze attackers, and the Zero fighter crashed into the port catwalk, which killed one man and wounded sixteen others. (http://www.bosamar.com/)

5 "We trained very hard so I was ready to attack."
67 Kanto is the name which refers to the region in Japan where Tokyo is located. It includes seven prefectures including Tokyo, Gunma, Tochigi, Ibaraki, Saitama, Chiba and Kanagawa. An 8.3 magnitude earthquake hit this region on 1 September 1923, and devastated Tokyo, Yokohama and the nearby area. In all, about 100,000 people died with another 40,000 missing.
68 This place is located in Tokyo, near Tokyo Bay.
69 Shibayama-san was a 35th Term Naval Academy graduate (according to Miyashita-san).
70 Takahashi-san was a 29th Term Naval Academy graduate (according to Miyashita-san).
71 The city of Beppu is a popular vacation spot for Japanese people. It is located on the northeast coast of Kyūshū Island and famous for its hot springs.
72 Hiroyuki Agawa, *The Reluctant Admiral, Yamamoto and the Imperial Navy*, 95. Hereafter *The Reluctant Admiral, Yamamoto and the Imperial Navy*.
73 Ono-san was a 39th Term Naval Academy graduate (according to Miyashita-san).
74 This ceremony was held to celebrate the 2,600th anniversary of the Emperor Jimmu, the nation's first emperor. It was held in a plaza before the Nijubashi entrance to the Imperial Palace (where the emperor resided in Tokyo). *The Reluctant Admiral, Yamamoto and the Imperial Navy*, 201.
75 Jōjima-san is a 40th Term Naval Academy graduate (According to Miyashita-san).
76 Takahashi was the overall dive bomber commander for the 1st wave during the Pearl Harbor attack. He is a well-known Japanese naval aviator. Takahashi later died on 8 May 1942, during the Battle of Coral Sea.
77 According to Miyashita-san, Noda survived the war but died a few years ago.
78 Jirō Kimata, *Nihon kūbo senshi*, 233-34. (kindly provided by historian Anthony Tully) Hereafter *Nihon kūbo senshi*.
79 Arima-san was a 40th Term Naval Academy graduate (according to Miyashita-san).
80 *Nihon kūbo senshi* (kindly provided by historian Anthony Tully)
81 http://www.cv6.org/default.htm (USS *Enterprise* Association website).
82 Bernard Millot, *Divine Thunder: The Life &Death of the Kamikazes*, 110-111.
83 Official USN Combat Casualty List (via James Sawruk).
84 Ibid.
85 The information for the background information about the *Saratoga* was derived from the website: http://www.uss-saratoga.com/ (the *Saratoga's* Association's official website)
86 Captain Rikihei Inoguchi, Commander Tadashi Nakajima and Roger Pineau, *The Divine Wind*, 123.
87 Official USN Combat Casualty List (via James Sawruk).
88 *Japanese Naval Aces and Fighter Units in WW II*, 75.

6 "I felt no hatred towards the enemy."
89 http://www.combinedfleet.com/Zuikak.htm
90 http://www.combinedfleet.com/unryut.htm
91 http://www.combinedfleet.com/Shinano.htm

Part 2 – Overview
92 Some of the technical details such as horsepower and armament were derived from: *Japanese Aircraft of the Pacific War*, 411-416, 429-434 and 288-291. Osamu Tagaya also was instrumental in putting this overview together.

7 "Japan lost the war, but we were still lucky."
93 Lieutenant Akira Sakamoto died on 15 August 1942 due to an "operational cause." This could have been a landing accident or a similar incident. (Sakamoto's *keireki* or service record via Michael Wenger)
94 Please see Kenji Hori's Coral Sea account in this book for more information about Seijirō Kishida.
95 He participated in the Pearl Harbor attack as a member of the first wave *Kaga* Type 97 *kankō* level-bombing unit and his leader was Lieutenant Hideo Maki. The "target" ships of that group were the *Arizona* and *Vestal*.
96 "*Amanohashidate*, roughly meaning "bridge in the heaven," is a 3.6

kilometer long, pine tree covered sand bar, spanning across Miyazu Bay on the Tango Peninsula, northern Kyoto Prefecture. It is ranked as one of Japan's three most scenic views. " (taken from: http://www.japan-guide.com/e/e3990.html)
97 This translates to literally a "group" led by Lieutenant Commander Takashi Hashiguchi.
98 An interesting side-note is that a department store with the same name currently exists today in Ginza, an up-scale shopping area in Tokyo.
99 Japanese room sizes for homes, apartments, etc. are done according to the size of the *tatami*. In this case, 4.5 *tatami* is equal to about 6.89 square meters or about 23 feet in size.
100 http://www.nps.gov/archive/usar/phcas.html
101 The information about the damage on the *West Virginia* came from, Stan Cohen, *East Wind Rain*, 51, 126
102 Please see veteran Haruo Yoshino's Pearl Harbor account for more information about what happened on this aircraft when the rear gunner/radioman PO2c Yasuji Inoue was severely wounded.
103 *Hawai Sakusen*, 600, 604, 612-614
104 *Akagi*, *Kaga*, *Shōkaku* and *Zuikaku Kōdōchōshos*, 20 January 1942 (provided by Michael Wenger)
105 Carroll V. Glines, *The Doolittle Raid*, 69.
106 The majority of the background of this mission was derived from the informative official Doolittle raider website, http://www.doolittletokyoraiders.com/doolittle_raid.htm. It was written by official Doolittle historian Carroll V. Glines.
107 Ibid.
108 Commander Amagai also was *hikōchō* in his previous carrier, the *Hiryū*.
109 Author's correspondence with Midway historian Jonathan Parshall.
110 http://www.cv6.org/1942/midway/midway_3.htm
111 *Shattered Sword: The Untold Story of the Battle of Midway*, 478.
112 *Kaga* ground to a halt around 1300.
113 *Shattered Sword: The Untold Story of the Battle of Midway*, 250.
114 http://www.combinedfleet.com/kaga.htm
115 Hachijō Jima is located about 200 miles south of Tokyo.
116 PO2c Yuzo Watanabe participated in the Pearl Harbor attack as a member of the Type 97 torpedo unit. He was a radioman/rear gunner.
117 The mission is described in great detail in Kaname Harada's story in this book.
118 *Koku Gijutsu no Zenbo* (Vol. 2), 217 (research provided by Osamu Tagaya).

8 "We thought that they were the enemy and nothing else."
119 Yoshino-san was the plane captain of his plane used during the attack on Pearl Harbor, and the crew remained together until May 1942, when they were separated for other assignments.
120 Yoshino-san and the author found his tail number written on the back of his crew for mission during an interview sixty years after the event.
121 Fifteen high-level Type 97s from the carrier *Kaga* were scheduled to attack Pearl Harbor but there was one mechanical abort. The "level bombing" Type 97s were commanded by Lieutenant Commander Takahashi Hashiguchi. The twelve Type 97 carrier attack planes armed with torpedoes were led by Lieutenant Kazuyoshi Kitajima.
122 Yoshino's target was verified by the *Hawai Sakusen*, 355, map supplement.
123 The radioman Yoshino-san is talking about is PO2c Yasuji Inoue. His chin was smashed due to American gunfire. After the Pearl Harbor attack, he was discharged from the navy and underwent plastic surgery operations at Kure and Sasebo navy hospitals. Fellow *Kaga* comrade Takeshi Maeda met him out of the blue in 1960 near Misaki Pennisula at a hospital. Inoue-san was a fisherman and died in late 1960.
124 This island is the northwestern-most Hawaiian Island beyond Kauai.
125 USS *Oklahoma*; Report of Damage Sustained during Action at Pearl Harbor, 20 December 1941. (via Michael Wenger)
126 http://www.nps.gov/archive/usar/phcas.html
127 http://www.history.navy.mil/photos/sh-usn/usnsh-o/bb37.htm
128 All of Yoshino's information regarding this mission concur with the original Japanese records.
129 *Zuihō* was hit at 0830 by two bombs aft. Damage was lift but it couldn't do any flight operations after being bombed. So, it returned to Truk Island escorted by the destroyers *Hatsukaze* and *Maikaze*. (source:www.combinedfleet.com)
130 Toyohashi City is located near Nagoya and is in the southeastern edge of Aichi Prefecture. The city borders the Shizuoka Prefecture and Yumihari mountains.
131 Tateyama is located at the southern tip of the Boso Pennisula in Chiba, Japan.
132 Matsushima is located thirty minutes from Sendai City, the largest city in the Tohoku Region (which literally stands for "North East" region of Honshu Island.
133 *Iwo* means sulfur in Japanese while *Jima* is an island.
134 The background information of the sinking of *Zuikaku* was derived from:
http://www.combinedfleet.com/Zuikak.htm
135 http://www.nasm.si.edu/research/aero/aircraft/nakamyrt.htm

9 "There is no question in my mind, that attacking Pearl Harbor was the right thing to do."
136 PO2c Yoshiyuki Hirata died on 14 October 1944, off Taiwan and Sea1c Yukio Okada died 8 December 1942, but it is not known how and where he died. (Research by Michael Wenger)
137 Information provided by Michael Wenger using official Japanese wartime records.

10 "I was calm but I didn't think that I would survive."
138 WO Urata died on 19 June 1944 during the Battle of the Philippine Sea. He was a Type 97 "level-bomber" pilot during the Pearl Harbor attack. (Research provided by Michael Wenger).
139 However, during the actual Pearl Harbor attack only four out of the five Type 97 level bombers from Morinaga's group actually participated in the mission because one aircraft had engine trouble.
(Research kindly provided by Michael Wenger using official Japanese records).
140 Morinaga-san is probably talking about the explosion of the battleship *Arizona's* forward ammunition magazines.
141 *Hawai Sakusen*, 597 (via Michael Wenger)
142 During the Pearl Harbor attack, the battleship *Maryland* was hit by two Japanese bombs during the second wave by Type 99 carrier bombers but the damage was minimal. There were no hits on the battleship during the first wave. According to the *Hawai Sakusen*, 355, map supplement, Morinaga's target was actually the *West Virginia*.
143 The tail code for Morinaga's aircraft was "363". This was provided by historian Jim Sawruk using official Japanese records.
144 *Shōkaku* launched eleven search planes at 0530 local time on 19 June. Together with two reconnaissance planes from the cruiser *Mogami*, they were assigned to fly out some 560 miles on the sector covering from 20 to 105 degrees True – that is, roughly the northeast and eastern sectors. By 0920 they had reached the outermost point of the search, and started the return flight. Morinaga-san returned to *Shōkaku* just before she was torpedoed at 1222. (This information was provided by historian Tony Tully.) *Nihon kūbo senshi*, 638-639.
145 The *USS Cavalla* was commissioned on 29 February 1944 and sunk *Shōkaku* during her maiden patrol. The submarine was later awarded a Presidential Unit Citation for this action. She is currently a memorial to the lost submarine *USS Seawolf* and on display in Sea Wolf Park, Galveston, Texas. Information provided by the Cavalla Historical Foundation
146 *Nihon kūbo senshi*, 638-639. and Yusuke Edo, *Mariana oki no shichimenchouchi*, 252-261.
147 "K" equals *Kōgeki* (in Japanese) or "attack group" so K-262 denotes Attack Group 262.

11 "I joined the navy to fight for our country."

148 This area is located in the southwestern part of Kyūshū.
149 There is an interesting episode about Matsumura-san which happened on board his carrier *Hiryū* during the journey to Pearl Harbor. During the entire trip he wore a gauze mask that covered his mouth and nose. This type of mask is still worn today by Japanese people when they want to protect themselves from germs. At that time, he didn't even take the mask off to eat; instead he just pushed the food in his mouth without taking it off! The young pilot said that he did this because he didn't want to get sick before this important mission. Just prior to attack, he took off his mask and to the delight of his men he was sporting a new mustache. Matsumura's daughter told me this story in one of her letters to me.
150 PO1c Sadamu Murai died on 4 June 1942 during the Battle of Midway while serving as the radioman for legendary pilot Lieutenant Jōichi Tomonaga when their aircraft was shot down while attacking the *Yorktown*.
Shattered Sword: The Untold Story of the Battle of Midway, 522.
151 Matsumura-san is referring to ace torpedo pilot, Lieutenant Commander Shigeharu Murata. During the attack on Pearl Harbor, he led the *Akagi* Type 97 carrier attack planes (which were armed with torpedoes) during the first wave. This pilot later died during the Battle of Santa Cruz on 26 October 1942, when he was shot down by Lieutenant Stanley W. "Swede" Vejtasa. Thomas G. Miller, Jr., *The Cactus Air Force*, 164-165.
152 In regards to the miscommunication between planes, this occurred at 0740 during the flight to Hawaii. The overall attack leader, Commander Mitsuo Fuchida, fired a single flare into the air, which meant that the attacking airplanes should fly a "Surprise sequence." During this sequence, the escort Zero fighters would take control of the air while the low-flying, vulnerable torpedo bombers made their attacks, followed by the dive-bombers and high-level bombers. Nevertheless at this time, according to Fuchida, the Zeros didn't see the first flare, so Fuchida fired a second flare. However, the leader of the dive-bombers, Lieutenant Commander Kakuichi Takahashi, saw both flares and thought that surprise was lost. In that situation, the dive-bombers and high-level bombers were supposed to attack first, followed by the torpedo bombers. Because of Takahashi's error, the dive-bombers actually struck first.
153 His target was confirmed with the *Hawai Sakusen*, 355, map supplement. Michael Wenger kindly provided this information.
154 Lieutenant Commander Tatsuo Sakai was born on 10 February 1907. He entered the Naval Academy at Etajima on 1 April 1925 and graduated 99th out of 111 graduates on 16 March 1928. After the regular postings for junior officers, Sakai-san specialized in gunnery, graduating from the Advance gunnery course from the Naval Gunnery School. He was Chief Gunnery Officer and Division Officer of the aircraft carrier *Hiryu* from 20 August 1941 to 27July 1942. This information was kindly provided by Jean-Francois Masson using the *Gen-eki kaigun shikan Meibo* [Register of Naval officers in active duty].
155 Jack Murphy, *History of the US Marines*, 99.
156 Ibid., 100.
157 The airfield at Torokina became operational on 10 December 1943 after forty days of work by the Seabees. The first group to land there was VMF-216 with seventeen Corsair fighters and a handful SBD Dauntless dive-bombers. RNZAF squadrons also began operating out of Torokina after 1 January 1944.
Source: *www.pacificwrecks.com*

12 "Since I was young, I never worried whether I would live or die."

158 Waseda University is located in Shinjuku, Tokyo and regarded as one of the most prestigious schools in Japan.
159 Sugamo Prison was built in the 1920s and located in Ikebukuro, Tokyo. After the war, it was used to house Japanese war criminals including Prime Minister Hideki Tojo (who was later executed in 1948). In 1971, it was demolished and the sixty-story "Sunshine 60" building is located on the site. However, there is a memorial rock which reads "Pray for Eternal Peace." Source: Wikipedia Online Encyclopedia.
160 Out of the forty Type 97 carrier attack planes armed with torpedoes, twelve came from *Akagi*, another twelve from *Kaga*, eight from *Sōryū* and lastly, another eight aircraft came from *Hiryū*.
161 Maruyama's target was confirmed as the battleship *Oklahoma* in the *Hawai Sakusen*, 355, map supplement by the research of Michael Wenger.
162 According to the exhaustive research done by Michael Wenger, due to various factors, the launch points were considerably east of north. This is much farther than other historians have supposed.
163 *The First Team: Pacific Naval Air Combat from Pearl Harbor to Midway*, 337.
164 After Action Report, VMF-221, 6 June 1942
165 Robert J. Cressman and Steve Ewing, *A Glorious Page in Our History: The Battle of Midway 4-6 June 1942*, 62. Hereafter *A Glorious Page in Our History: The Battle of Midway 4-6 June 1942*.
166 After Action Report, VMF-221, 6 June 1942.
167 Ibid.
168 *A Glorious Page in Our History: The Battle of Midway 4-6 June 1942*, 66.
169 *Shattered Sword: The Untold Story of the Battle of Midway*, 513-19.
170 Ibid., 520-21.
171 This background paragraph is a summary of the damage reported in the After Action Report, USS *Yorktown*, 18 June 1942.
172 *Shattered Sword: The Untold Story of the Battle of Midway*, 290, 522.
173 The three background paragraphs about the fates of the *Yorktown* and *Hammann* was taken from the After Action Report, USS *Yorktown*, 18 June 1942.
174 Official USN Combat Casualty List (via James Sawruk)
175 www.combinedfleet.com
176 The *Hiryū* actually didn't sink after being hit by the *Makigumo's* torpedo. Please see Kaname Harada's story for more details on this.
177 www.combinedfleet.com
178 *The First Team and the Guadalcanal Campaign*, 446.
179 Irikiin's torpedo struck the aft section of the carrier *Hornet* but the other five *Junyō* torpedo planes failed to get any additional hits on the doomed carrier. *The First Team and the Guadalcanal Campaign*, 447
180 All of the data (on the names of the pilots who were lost) and information regarding the loss of the Zero fighters was found in, this source: Ibid.
181 Yasuho Izawa, *Rikkō &Ginga, Fighting Story of Japanese Navy Twin-engine Bombers*, 242. Hereafter *Rikkō &Ginga, Fighting Story of Japanese Navy Twin-engine Bombers*. This is a privately published book by Izawa, in English.
182 Ibid., Appendix 1, 15.
183 Hist. Air War POA, III,48;TC-FN-25-9,XXI BC to CG, 20th AF, 25 December 1944.
184 *Rikkō &Ginga, Fighting Story of Japanese Navy Twin-engine Bombers*, 242.
185 Ibid., Appendix 1, 16.

13 "I kept thinking to myself, why are we doing this?"

186 The *Jinrai Butai* is the name given to the 721 *Kōkūtai* whose primary mission was to do suicide attacks using the Ohka (see the next endnote).
187 The *Ohka* was a very simple designed rocket powered aircraft which had a 1,200 kilogram (2,645 pound) warhead in the nose. The aircraft was flown to a target area mounted under the belly of a Mitsubishi "Betty" bomber. Once over the target area a pilot climbed into the *Ohka* and the aircraft was released. The pilot then fired the gunpowder-fired rockets on the aircraft and attempted to slam it into his target ship.
188 Most of the men (on board the ships) did not learn that Pearl Hawaii would be their objective until arriving at Hitokappu Bay
189 According to the "Wikepedia" encyclopedia website, this battleship later sank on 8 June 1943, possibly because of the mishandling of ammunition during a familiarization tour. Over 1100 men died during the sinking.
190 According to historian Osamu Tagaya, during the latter part of war, a shortage of flight-rated engineering personnel forced the Imperial

Selected Bibliography

Books

Abe, Lieutenant Commander Zenji. *The Emperor's Sea Eagle: A Memoir of the Attack on Pearl Harbor and the War in the Pacific.* Edited by Michael Wenger and translated by Naomi Shin. Hawaii: Arizona Memorial Museum Association, 2006.

Agawa Hiroyuki. *The Reluctant Admiral: Yamamoto and the Imperial Navy*. Translated by John Bester. Tokyo: Kōdansha International, 1979.

Attack Force Pearl Harbor. Tokyo: Model Art Co. Ltd., 2000.

Ballard, Robert. *Return to Midway*. Toronto, Ontario: Madison Press Books, 1999.

Bishop, Chris and Chris McNab. *Campaigns of World War II, Day by Day*. London, UK: Amber Books, Ltd., 2003.

Boatman, Alec C. *The Pacific Appointment*. Santa Barbara, CA: Fithian Press, 1996.

Cloe, John. *East Wind Rain, A Pictorial History of the Pearl Harbor Attack*. Missoula, MT: Pictorial Histories Publishing Co., 1981.

Cloe, John. *The Aleutian Warriors, A History of the 11th Air Force & Fleet Wing 4*. Missoula, MT: Pictorial Histories Publishing Co., 1991.

Cressman, Robert, Steve Ewing, Barrett Tillman, Mark Horan, Clark Reynolds, and Stan Cohen. *A Glorious Page in our History: The Battle of Midway*. Missoula, MT: Pictorial Histories Publishing Company, 1990.

Cressman, Robert. *A Magnificent Fight: The Battle for Wake Island*. Annapolis, MD: Naval Institute Press, 1995.

Francillon, René. *Japanese Aircraft of the Pacific War*. Annapolis, MD: Naval Institute Press, 1987.

Frank, Richard. *Guadalcanal*. New York: Penguin Books, 1990.

Fuchida, Mitsuo and Masatake Okumiya. *Midway: The Battle that Doomed Japan*. Annapolis, MD: Naval Institute Press, 1955.

Glines, Carroll V. *Attack on Yamamoto*. Atglen, PA: Schiffer Publishing, Ltd., 1993.

Glines, Carroll V. *The Doolittle Raid*. Atglen, PA: Schiffer Publishing, Ltd., 1991.

Goldstein, Donald M., Katherine V. Dillon, and J. Michael Wenger. *The Way It Was: Pearl Harbor, the Original Photographs*. Dulles, VA: Brassey's, Inc., 1991.

Hata, Ikuhiko and Yasuho Izawa. *Japanese Naval Aces and Fighter Units in World War II*. Translated by Gorham. Annapolis, MD: Naval Institute Press, 1989.

Inoguchi, Captain Rikihei, Commander Tadashi Nakajima with Roger Pineau. *The Divine Wind*. New York: Bantam Books, Inc., 1958.

Izawa, Yasuho. Rikko & Ginga, *Fighting Story of Japanese Navy Twin-engine Bombers* (privately published English book by the author).

Kimata, Jirō. *Nihon Kōkū Senshi* (Japanese Carrier Battle History). Tokyo: Kokusho, 1977.

Lord, Walter. *Incredible Victory*. New York: Harper Collins, 1967.

Lord, Walter. *Day of Infamy*. New York: Henry Holt and Company, Inc., 1957.

Lundstrom, John. *The First Team: Pacific Naval Air Combat from Pearl Harbor to Midway*. Annapolis, MD: Naval Institute Press, 1984.

Lundstrom, John. *The First Team and the Guadalcanal Champaign: Naval Fighter Combat from August to November 1942*. Annapolis, MD: Naval Institute Press, 1994.

Miller, Jr., Thomas G. *The Cactus Air Force*. New York: Harper & Row, Publishers, Incorporated, 1969.

Millot, Bernard. *Divine Thunder: The Life & Death of the Kamikazes*. Translated by Lowell Blair. New York: The McCall P ublishing Company, 1971.

Murphy, Jack. *History of the U.S. Marines*. North Dighton, MA: World Publications Group, Inc., 2002.

Naito, Hatsuho. *Thunder Gods: The Kamikaze Pilots Tell Their Story*. Translated by Mayumi Ichikawa. Tokyo: Kōdansha International, 1989.

Morison, Samuel Eliot. *History of the United States Naval Operations in World War II, Vol. IV*. Boston: Little, Brown and Company, 1988.

Morison, Samuel Eliot. *History of the United States Naval Operations in World War II, Vol. V*. Boston: Little, Brown and Company, 1989.

Nila, Gary. *Japanese Naval Aviation Uniforms and Equipment 1937-45*. Osprey Elite Series, No. 86. Oxford, UK: Osprey Publishing Ltd., 2002.

Parshall, Jonathan and Anthony Tully. *Shattered Sword: The Untold Story of the Battle of Midway*. Dulles, Virginia: Potomac Books, Inc., 2005.

Prange, Gordon W., in collaboration with Donald M. Goldstein and Katherine V. Dillon. *At Dawn We Slept*. New York: McGraw-Hill Book Company, 1981.

Prange, Gordon W., with Donald M. Goldstein and Katherine V. Dillon. *Miracle at Midway*. New York: McGraw-Hill Book Company, 1982.

Rouke, Norman Edward. *War Comes to Alaska: The Dutch Harbor Attack*, June 3-4, 1942. Shippensburg, PA: Burd Street Press, 1997.

Sakaida, Henry. *The Siege of Rabaul*. St. Paul, MN: Phalanx Publishing Co., Ltd., 1996.

Sakaida, Henry. *Imperial Japanese Naval Aces 1937-45*. Osprey Aircraft of the Aces, No. 22. Oxford, UK: Osprey Publishing Ltd., 1998.

Sakaida, Henry and Koji Takaki. *Genda's Blade: Japan's Squadron of Aces, 343 Kōkūtai*. Surrey, UK: Ian Allan Publishing Ltd., 2003.

Sheftall, M.G. *Blossoms in the Wind: Human Legacies of the Kamikaze*. New York: NAL Caliber, 2005.

Shores, Christopher, Brian Cull with Yasuho Izawa. *Bloody Shambles Vol. 1: The Drift to War to the Fall of Singapore*. London, UK: Grub Street, 1992.

Shores, Christopher, Brian Cull with Yasuho Izawa. *Bloody Shambles Vol. 2: The Complete Account of the Air War in the Far East, from the Defence of Sumatra to the Fall of Burma, 1942*. London, UK: Grub Street, 2002.

Smith, Carl. *Pearl Harbor 1941: The Day of Infamy*. Osprey Campaign Series, No. 62. Oxford, UK: Osprey Publishing Ltd., 1999.

Tagaya, Osamu. *Mitsubishi Type 1 Rikko "Betty" Units of World War 2*. Osprey Combat Aircraft Series, No. 22. Oxford, UK: Osprey Publishing Ltd., 2001.

Tagaya, Osamu. *Imperial Japanese Naval Aviator 1937-45*. Osprey Warrior Series, No.55. Oxford, UK: Osprey Publishing Ltd., 2003.

Tillman, Barrett. *Carrier Battle in the Philippine Sea: The Marinas Turkey Shoot June 19-20, 1944*. St. Paul, MN: Phalanx Publishing Co., Ltd., 1994.

Umeda, Atsushi. *Japan: A Bilingual Atlas*. Tokyo: Kōdansha International, 1991.

Index